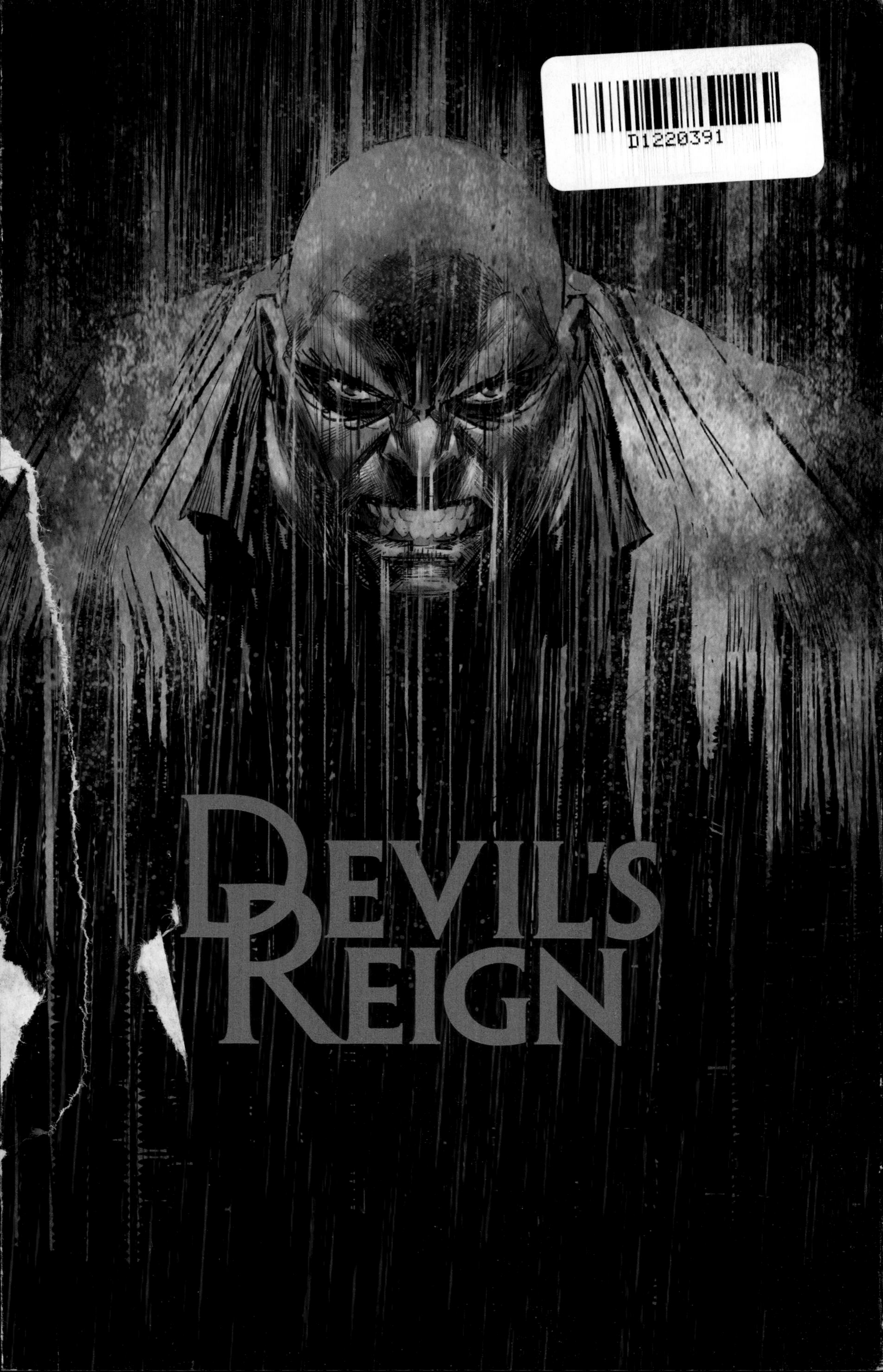
DEVIL'S
REIGN

Years ago, teenager **MATT MURDOCK** was blinded after being exposed to radioactive waste. He lost his sight, but his remaining senses began to function with superhuman acuity and gifted him with an ability similar to echolocation. Dubbed his 'radar sense,' it grants him a unique perspective on the world as he tries to better it as the costumed vigilante called **DAREDEVIL.**

No foe has stood in the way of Murdock's pursuit of justice more than **WILSON FISK** — formerly the **KINGPIN** of a vast criminal empire that touched every corner of New York (and beyond), now the duly elected mayor of New York. Despite his best efforts, Fisk has failed to truly grow into his office and wash his hands of his old life — and the bloodshed it bore.

Now, after wedding **TYPHOID MARY** and retreating to upstate New York for their honeymoon, Fisk has discovered a secret that has made his blood boil…

DEVIL'S REIGN

WRITER **CHIP ZDARSKY** | ARTIST **MARCO CHECCHETTO**

COLOR ARTIST **MARCIO MENYZ** | LETTERER VC's **CLAYTON COWLES**

DEVIL'S REIGN: OMEGA

"FALL AND RISE"
WRITER **CHIP ZDARSKY**
ARTIST **RAFAEL DE LATORRE**
COLOR ARTIST **FEDERICO BLEE**
LETTERER VC's **CLAYTON COWLES**
ASSOCIATE EDITOR **TOM GRONEMAN**
EDITOR **DEVIS LEWIN**

"MAYOR FOR HIRE"
WRITER **RODNEY BARNES**
ARTIST **GUILLERMO SANNA**
COLOR ARTIST **DIJJO LIMA**
LETTERER VC's **CLAYTON COWLES**
ASSOCIATE EDITOR **TOM GRONEMAN**
EDITOR **DEVIN LEWIS**

"CLEANING HOUSE"
WRITER **JIM ZUB**
ARTIST **LUCIANO VECCHIO**
COLOR ARTISTS **CARLOS LOPEZ**
& **JAVA TARTAGLIA**
LETTERER VC's **CLAYTON COWLES**
ASSOCIATE EDITOR **ANNALISE BISSA**
EDITOR **TOM BREVOORT**

COVER ART **INHYUK LEE**

LOGO DESIGN **JAY BOWEN** WITH **CHIP ZDARSKY**

ASSISTANT EDITORS **DANNY KHAZEM** & **TOM GRONEMAN**

EDITOR **DEVIN LEWIS**

COLLECTION EDITOR **JENNIFER GRÜNWALD**
ASSISTANT EDITOR **DANIEL KIRCHHOFFER**
ASSISTANT MANAGING EDITOR **MAIA LOY**
ASSOCIATE MANAGER, TALENT RELATIONS
LISA MONTALBANO

VP PRODUCTION & SPECIAL PROJECTS
JEFF YOUNGQUIST
BOOK DESIGNER **JAY BOWEN**
SVP PRINT, SALES & MARKETING **DAVID GABRIEL**
EDITOR IN CHIEF **C.B. CEBULSKI**

DEVIL'S REIGN. Contains material originally published in magazine form as DEVIL'S REIGN (2021) #1-6 and DEVIL'S REIGN: OMEGA (2022) #1. First printing 2022. ISBN 978-1-302-93284-8. Published by MARVEL WORLDWIDE, INC., a subsidiary of MARVEL ENTERTAINMENT, LLC. OFFICE OF PUBLICATION: 1290 Avenue of the Americas, New York, NY 10104. © 2022 MARVEL No similarity between any of the names, characters, persons, and/or institutions in this book with those of any living or dead person or institution is intended, and any such similarity which may exist is purely coincidental. **Printed in Canada.** KEVIN FEIGE, Chief Creative Officer; DAN BUCKLEY, President, Marvel Entertainment; JOE QUESADA, EVP & Creative Director; DAVID BOGART, Associate Publisher & SVP of Talent Affairs; TOM BREVOORT, VP, Executive Editor; NICK LOWE, Executive Editor, VP of Content, Digital Publishing; DAVID GABRIEL, VP of Print & Digital Publishing; SVEN LARSEN, VP of Licensed Publishing; MARK ANNUNZIATO, VP of Planning & Forecasting; JEFF YOUNGQUIST, VP of Production & Special Projects; ALEX MORALES, Director of Publishing Operations; DAN EDINGTON, Director of Editorial Operations; RICKEY PURDIN, Director of Talent Relations; JENNIFER GRUNWALD, Director of Production & Special Projects; SUSAN CRESPI, Production Manager; STAN LEE, Chairman Emeritus. For information regarding advertising in Marvel Comics or on Marvel.com, please contact Vit DeBellis, Custom Solutions & Integrated Advertising Manager, at vdebellis@marvel.com. For Marvel subscription inquiries, please call 888-511-5480. **Manufactured between 6/10/2022 and 7/12/2022 by SOLISCO PRINTERS, SCOTT, QC, CANADA.**

10 9 8 7 6 5 4 3 2 1

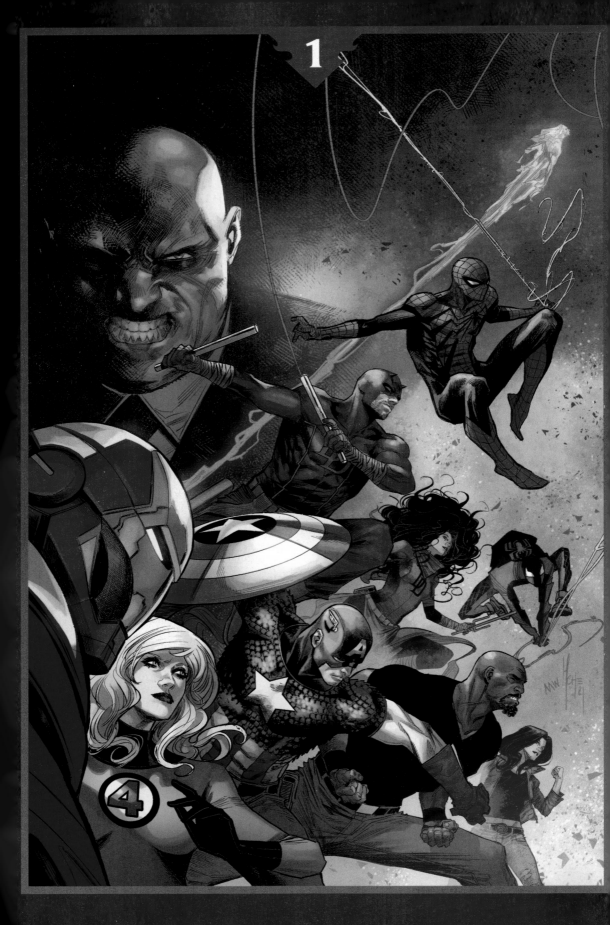

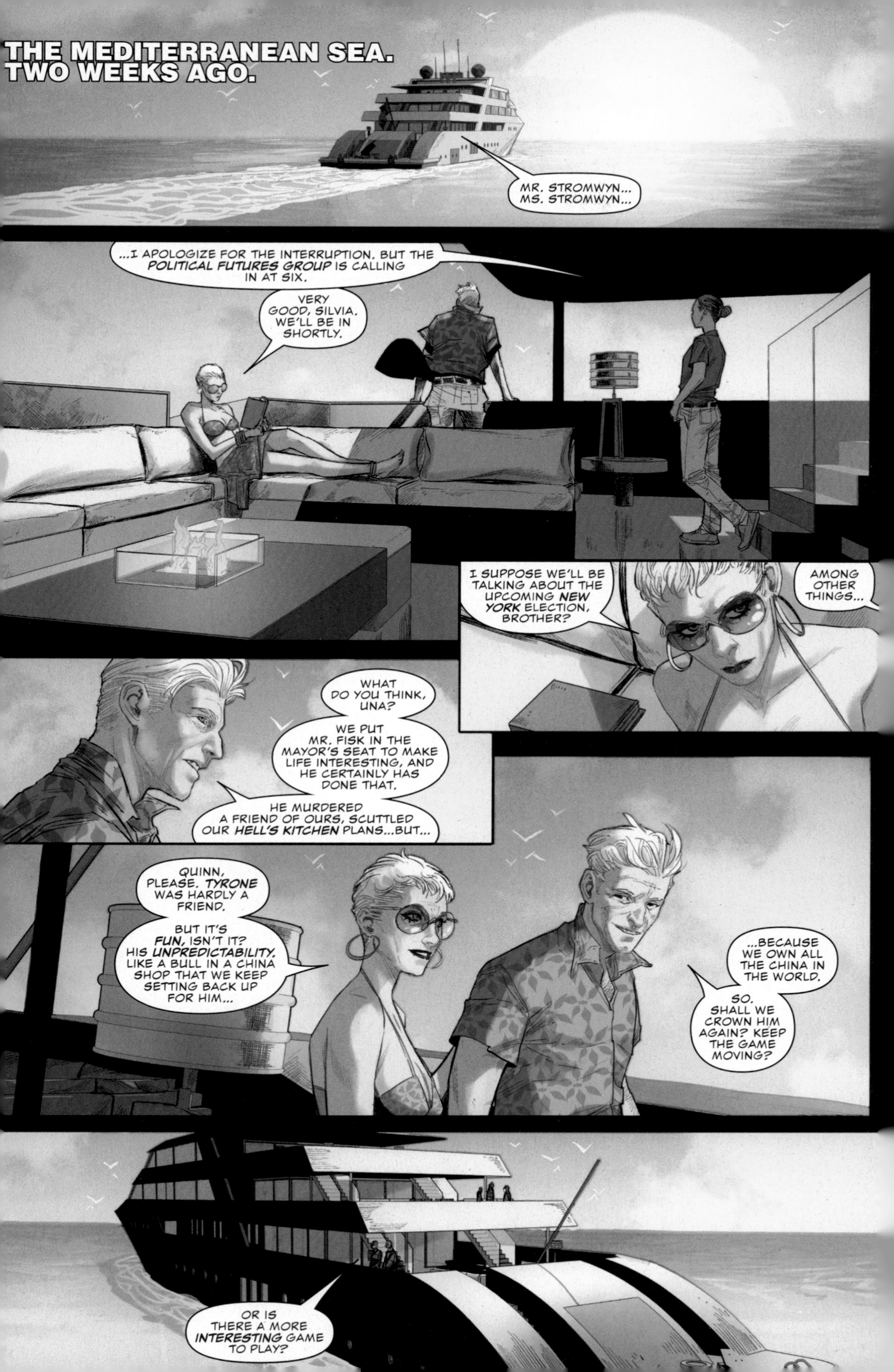
THE MEDITERRANEAN SEA. TWO WEEKS AGO.
MR. STROMWYN... MS. STROMWYN...
...I APOLOGIZE FOR THE INTERRUPTION. BUT THE POLITICAL FUTURES GROUP IS CALLING IN AT SIX.
VERY GOOD, SILVIA. WE'LL BE IN SHORTLY.
I SUPPOSE WE'LL BE TALKING ABOUT THE UPCOMING NEW YORK ELECTION, BROTHER?
AMONG OTHER THINGS...
WHAT DO YOU THINK, UNA?
WE PUT MR. FISK IN THE MAYOR'S SEAT TO MAKE LIFE INTERESTING, AND HE CERTAINLY HAS DONE THAT.
HE MURDERED A FRIEND OF OURS, SCUTTLED OUR HELL'S KITCHEN PLANS...BUT...
QUINN, PLEASE. TYRONE WAS HARDLY A FRIEND.
BUT IT'S FUN, ISN'T IT? HIS UNPREDICTABILITY. LIKE A BULL IN A CHINA SHOP THAT WE KEEP SETTING BACK UP FOR HIM...
...BECAUSE WE OWN ALL THE CHINA IN THE WORLD.
SO. SHALL WE CROWN HIM AGAIN? KEEP THE GAME MOVING?
OR IS THERE A MORE INTERESTING GAME TO PLAY?

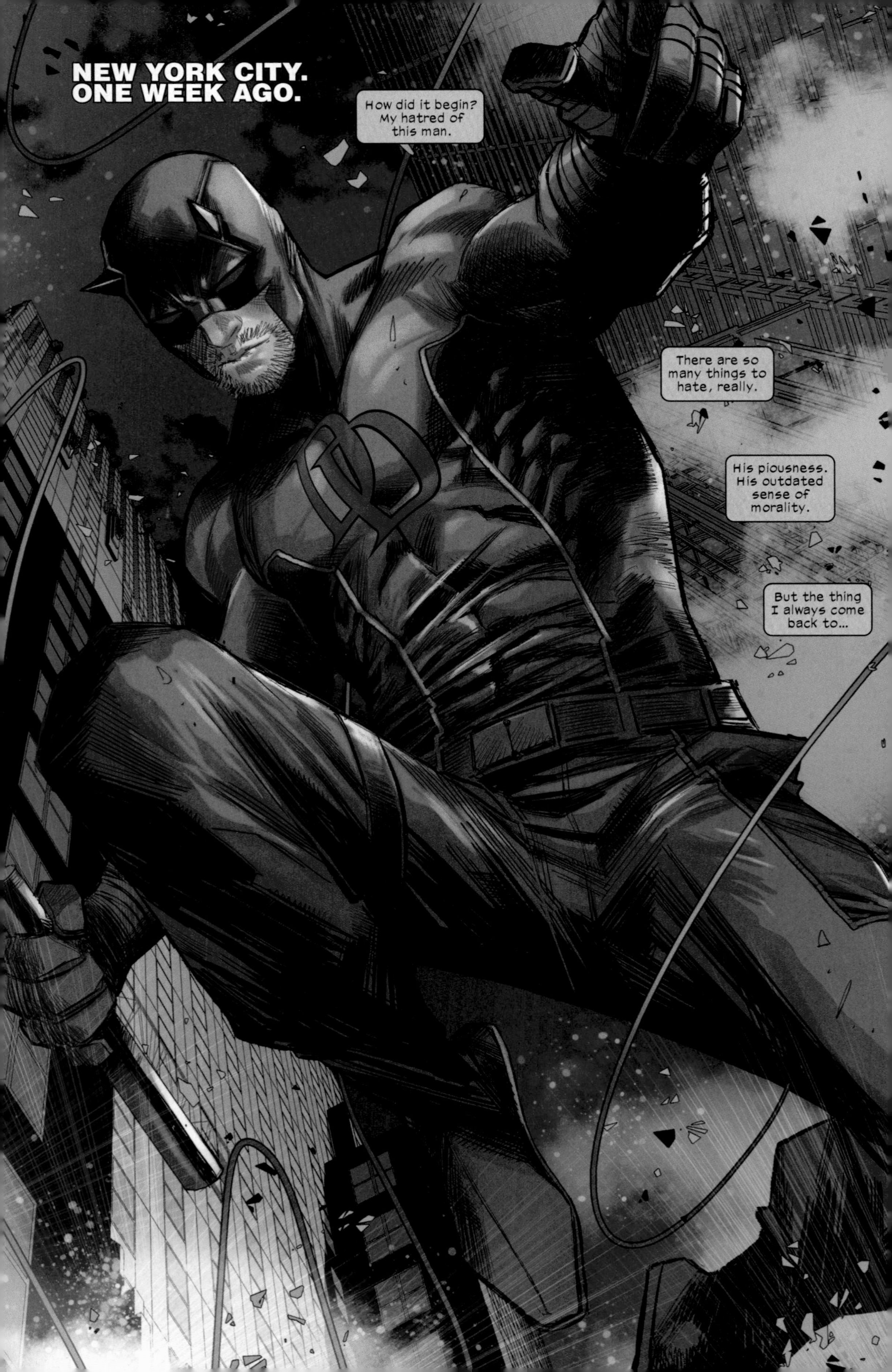
NEW YORK CITY. ONE WEEK AGO.
How did it begin? My hatred of this man.
There are so many things to hate, really.
His piousness. His outdated sense of morality.
But the thing I always come back to...

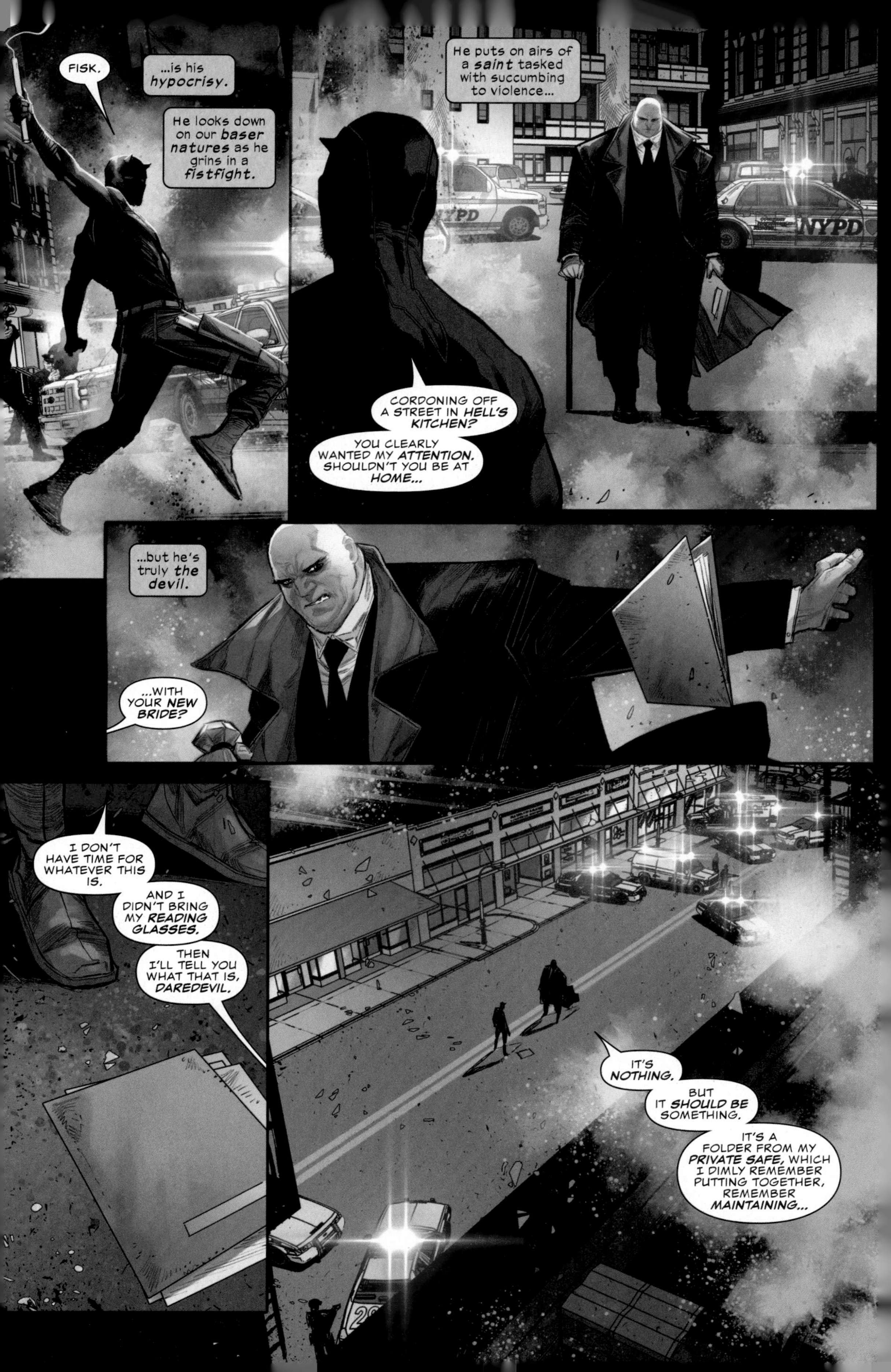
FISK.
...is his hypocrisy.
He looks down on our baser natures as he grins in a fistfight.
He puts on airs of a saint tasked with succumbing to violence...
CORDONING OFF A STREET IN HELL'S KITCHEN?
YOU CLEARLY WANTED MY ATTENTION. SHOULDN'T YOU BE AT HOME...
NYPD
NYPD
...but he's truly the devil.
...WITH YOUR NEW BRIDE?
I DON'T HAVE TIME FOR WHATEVER THIS IS.
AND I DIDN'T BRING MY READING GLASSES.
THEN I'LL TELL YOU WHAT THAT IS, DAREDEVIL.
IT'S NOTHING.
BUT IT SHOULD BE SOMETHING.
IT'S A FOLDER FROM MY PRIVATE SAFE, WHICH I DIMLY REMEMBER PUTTING TOGETHER, REMEMBER MAINTAINING...

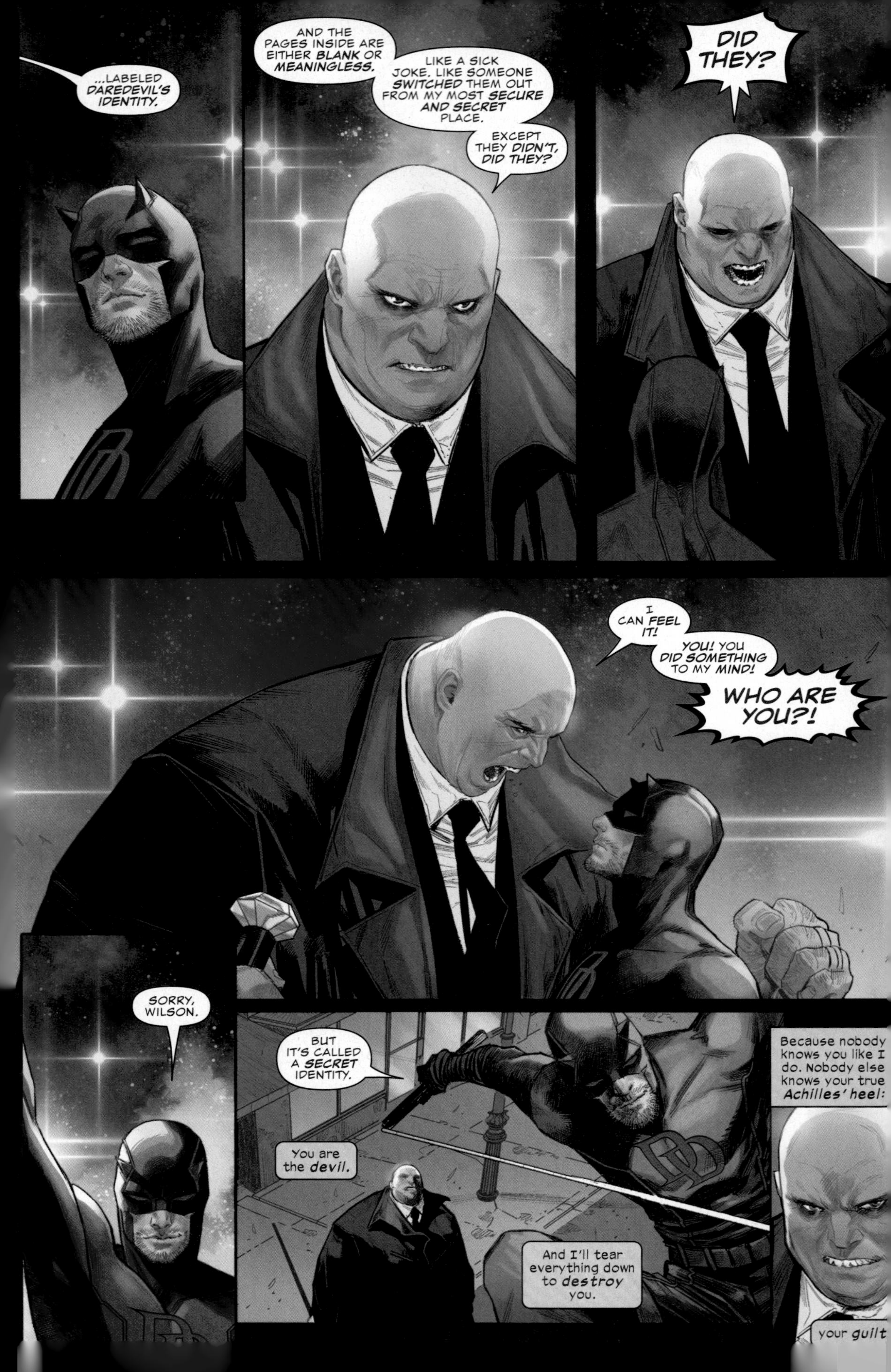

...LABELED DAREDEVIL'S IDENTITY.
AND THE PAGES INSIDE ARE EITHER BLANK OR MEANINGLESS.
LIKE A SICK JOKE. LIKE SOMEONE SWITCHED THEM OUT FROM MY MOST SECURE AND SECRET PLACE.
EXCEPT THEY DIDN'T, DID THEY?
DID THEY?
I CAN FEEL IT!
YOU! YOU DID SOMETHING TO MY MIND!
WHO ARE YOU?!
SORRY, WILSON.
BUT IT'S CALLED A SECRET IDENTITY.
You are the devil.
And I'll tear everything down to destroy you.
Because nobody knows you like I do. Nobody else knows your true Achilles' heel:
your guilt

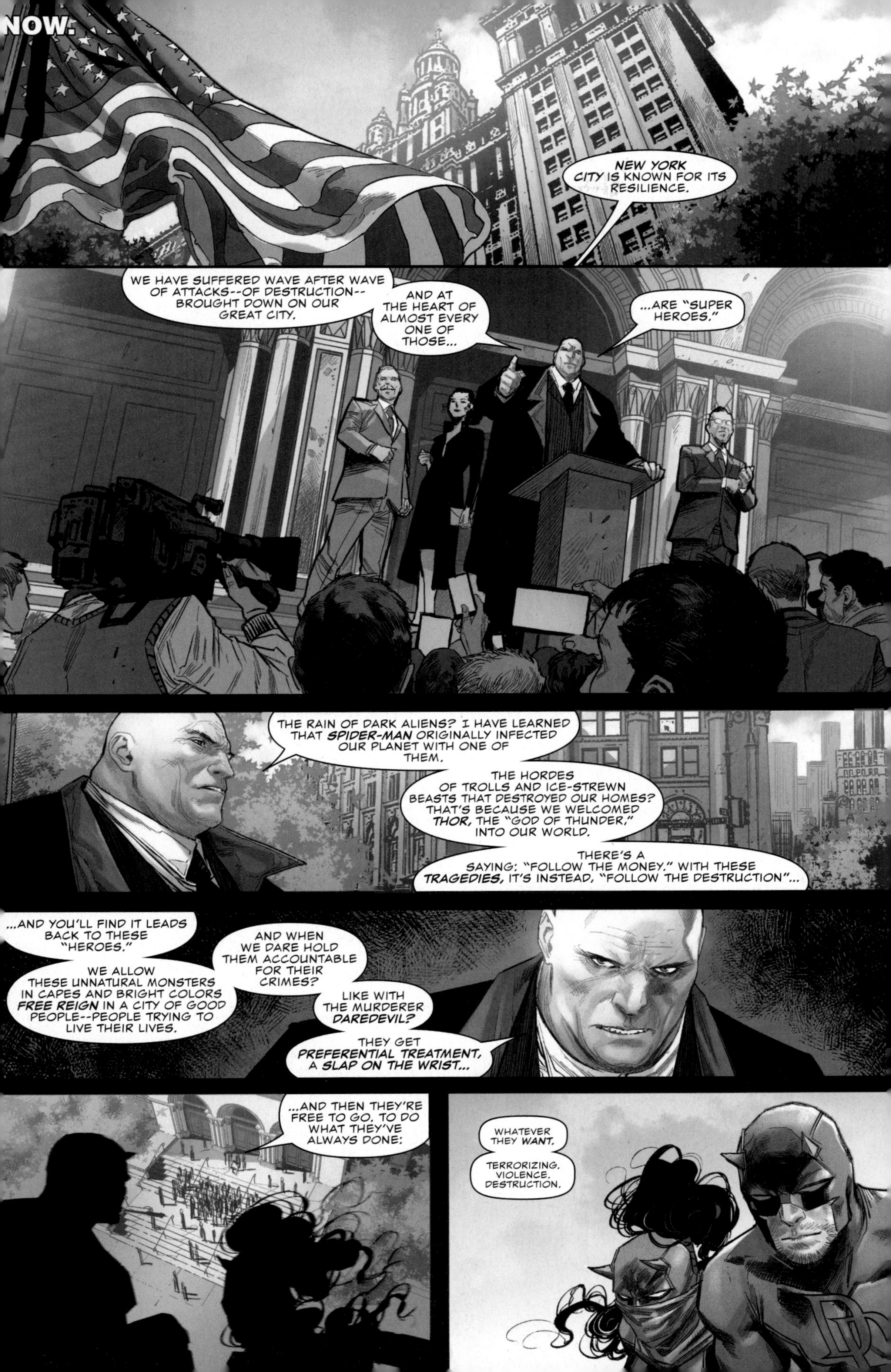
NOW.
NEW YORK CITY IS KNOWN FOR ITS RESILIENCE.
WE HAVE SUFFERED WAVE AFTER WAVE OF ATTACKS--OF DESTRUCTION--BROUGHT DOWN ON OUR GREAT CITY.
AND AT THE HEART OF ALMOST EVERY ONE OF THOSE...
...ARE "SUPER HEROES."
THE RAIN OF DARK ALIENS? I HAVE LEARNED THAT SPIDER-MAN ORIGINALLY INFECTED OUR PLANET WITH ONE OF THEM.
THE HORDES OF TROLLS AND ICE-STREWN BEASTS THAT DESTROYED OUR HOMES? THAT'S BECAUSE WE WELCOMED THOR, THE "GOD OF THUNDER," INTO OUR WORLD.
THERE'S A SAYING: "FOLLOW THE MONEY." WITH THESE TRAGEDIES, IT'S INSTEAD, "FOLLOW THE DESTRUCTION"...
...AND YOU'LL FIND IT LEADS BACK TO THESE "HEROES."
WE ALLOW THESE UNNATURAL MONSTERS IN CAPES AND BRIGHT COLORS FREE REIGN IN A CITY OF GOOD PEOPLE--PEOPLE TRYING TO LIVE THEIR LIVES.
AND WHEN WE DARE HOLD THEM ACCOUNTABLE FOR THEIR CRIMES?
LIKE WITH THE MURDERER DAREDEVIL?
THEY GET PREFERENTIAL TREATMENT, A SLAP ON THE WRIST...
...AND THEN THEY'RE FREE TO GO. TO DO WHAT THEY'VE ALWAYS DONE:
WHATEVER THEY WANT.
TERRORIZING. VIOLENCE. DESTRUCTION.

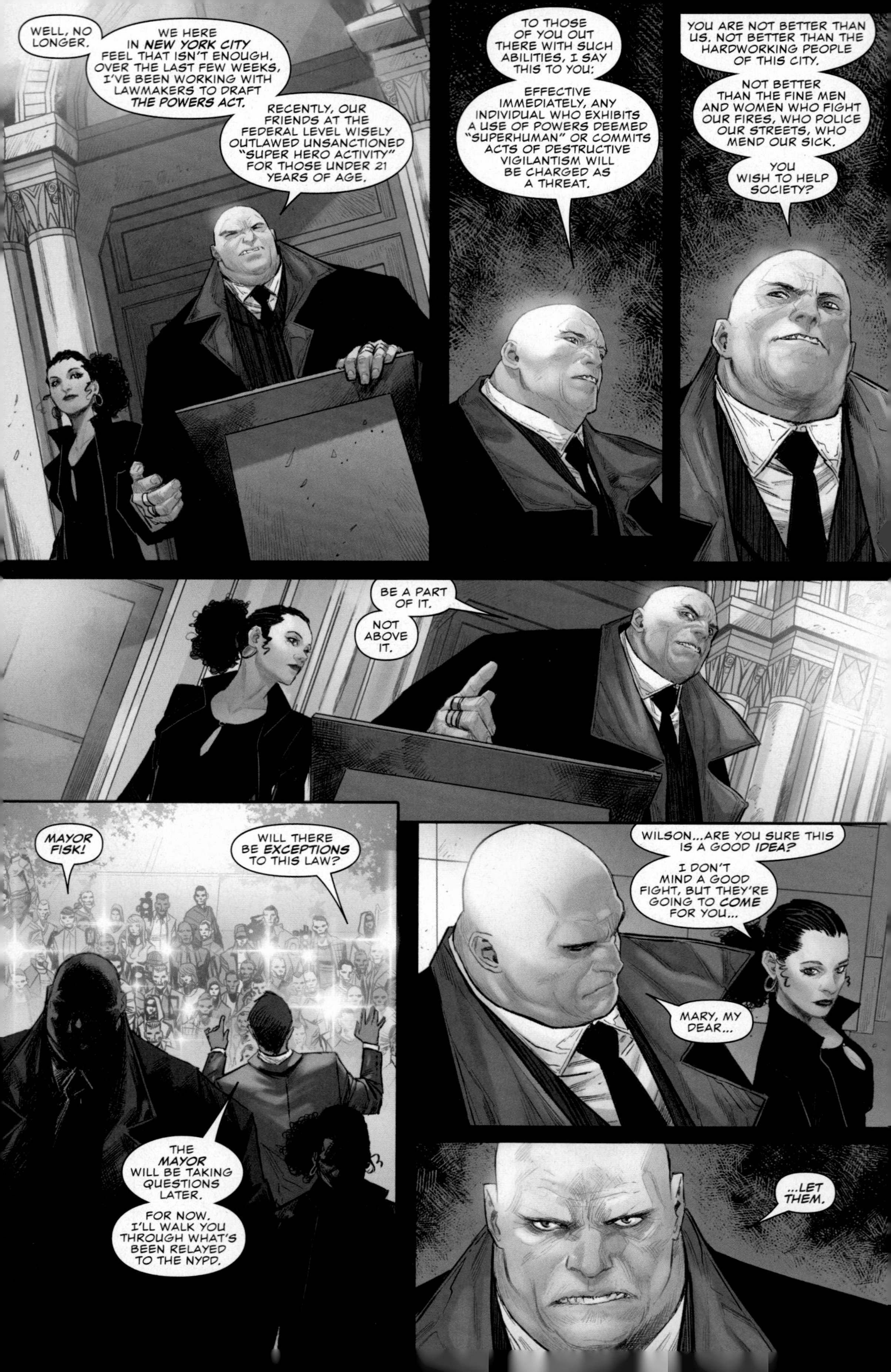
WELL, NO LONGER.
WE HERE IN NEW YORK CITY FEEL THAT ISN'T ENOUGH. OVER THE LAST FEW WEEKS, I'VE BEEN WORKING WITH LAWMAKERS TO DRAFT THE POWERS ACT.
RECENTLY, OUR FRIENDS AT THE FEDERAL LEVEL WISELY OUTLAWED UNSANCTIONED "SUPER HERO ACTIVITY" FOR THOSE UNDER 21 YEARS OF AGE.
TO THOSE OF YOU OUT THERE WITH SUCH ABILITIES, I SAY THIS TO YOU:
EFFECTIVE IMMEDIATELY, ANY INDIVIDUAL WHO EXHIBITS A USE OF POWERS DEEMED "SUPERHUMAN" OR COMMITS ACTS OF DESTRUCTIVE VIGILANTISM WILL BE CHARGED AS A THREAT.
YOU ARE NOT BETTER THAN US. NOT BETTER THAN THE HARDWORKING PEOPLE OF THIS CITY.
NOT BETTER THAN THE FINE MEN AND WOMEN WHO FIGHT OUR FIRES, WHO POLICE OUR STREETS, WHO MEND OUR SICK.
YOU WISH TO HELP SOCIETY?
BE A PART OF IT.
NOT ABOVE IT.
MAYOR FISK!
WILL THERE BE EXCEPTIONS TO THIS LAW?
THE MAYOR WILL BE TAKING QUESTIONS LATER.
FOR NOW, I'LL WALK YOU THROUGH WHAT'S BEEN RELAYED TO THE NYPD.
WILSON...ARE YOU SURE THIS IS A GOOD IDEA?
I DON'T MIND A GOOD FIGHT, BUT THEY'RE GOING TO COME FOR YOU...
MARY, MY DEAR...
...LET THEM.

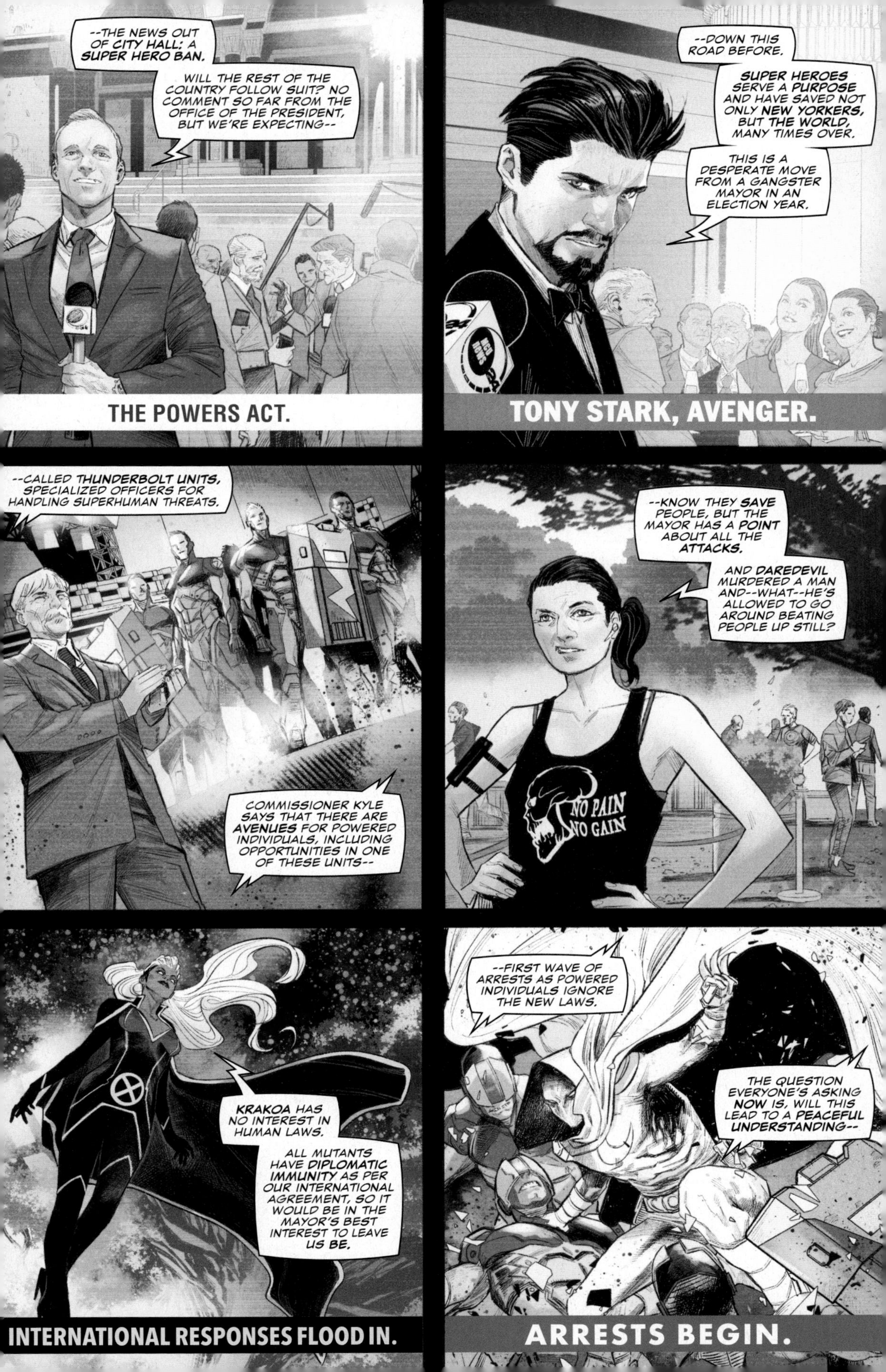
--THE NEWS OUT OF CITY HALL: A SUPER HERO BAN.
WILL THE REST OF THE COUNTRY FOLLOW SUIT? NO COMMENT SO FAR FROM THE OFFICE OF THE PRESIDENT, BUT WE'RE EXPECTING--
THE POWERS ACT.
--DOWN THIS ROAD BEFORE.
SUPER HEROES SERVE A PURPOSE AND HAVE SAVED NOT ONLY NEW YORKERS, BUT THE WORLD, MANY TIMES OVER.
THIS IS A DESPERATE MOVE FROM A GANGSTER MAYOR IN AN ELECTION YEAR.
TONY STARK, AVENGER.
--CALLED THUNDERBOLT UNITS, SPECIALIZED OFFICERS FOR HANDLING SUPERHUMAN THREATS.
COMMISSIONER KYLE SAYS THAT THERE ARE AVENUES FOR POWERED INDIVIDUALS, INCLUDING OPPORTUNITIES IN ONE OF THESE UNITS--
--KNOW THEY SAVE PEOPLE, BUT THE MAYOR HAS A POINT ABOUT ALL THE ATTACKS.
AND DAREDEVIL MURDERED A MAN AND--WHAT--HE'S ALLOWED TO GO AROUND BEATING PEOPLE UP STILL?
NO PAIN NO GAIN
KRAKOA HAS NO INTEREST IN HUMAN LAWS.
ALL MUTANTS HAVE DIPLOMATIC IMMUNITY AS PER OUR INTERNATIONAL AGREEMENT, SO IT WOULD BE IN THE MAYOR'S BEST INTEREST TO LEAVE US BE.
INTERNATIONAL RESPONSES FLOOD IN.
--FIRST WAVE OF ARRESTS AS POWERED INDIVIDUALS IGNORE THE NEW LAWS.
THE QUESTION EVERYONE'S ASKING NOW IS, WILL THIS LEAD TO A PEACEFUL UNDERSTANDING--
ARRESTS BEGIN.

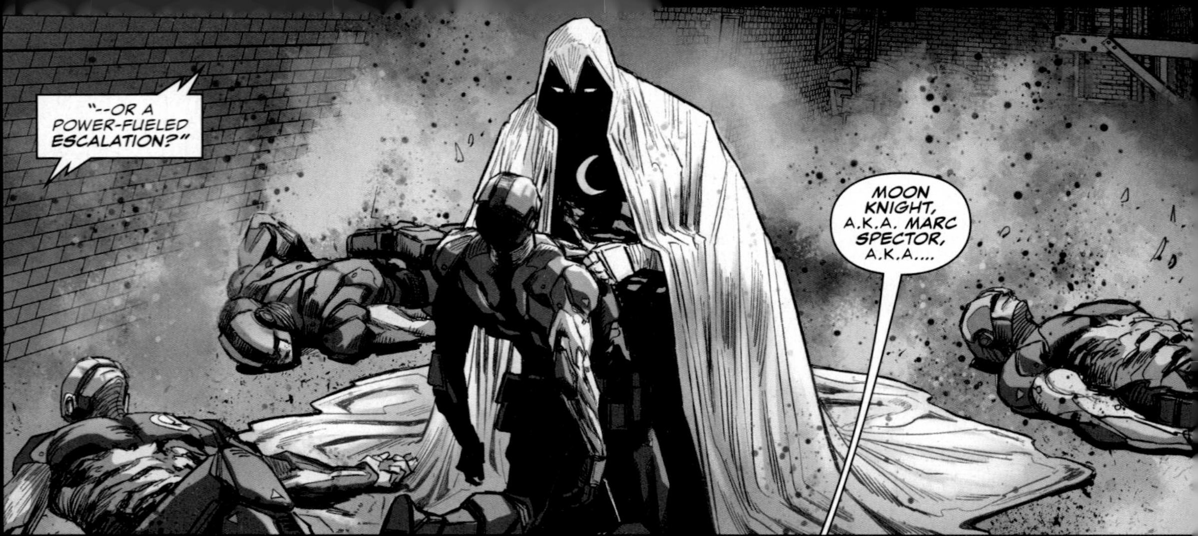
"--OR A POWER-FUELED ESCALATION?"
MOON KNIGHT, A.K.A. MARC SPECTOR, A.K.A....

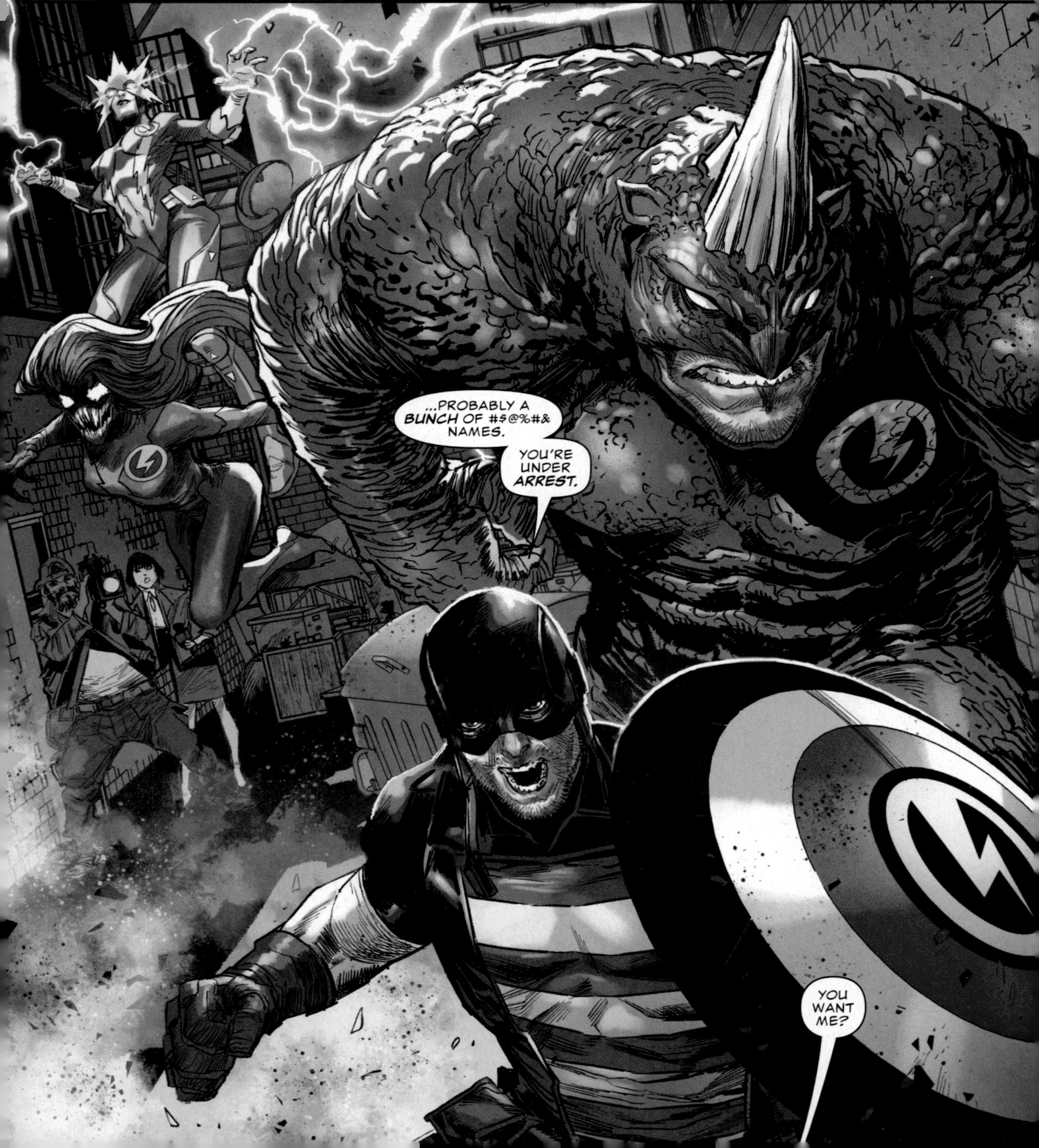
...PROBABLY A BUNCH OF #$@%#& NAMES.
YOU'RE UNDER ARREST.
YOU WANT ME?

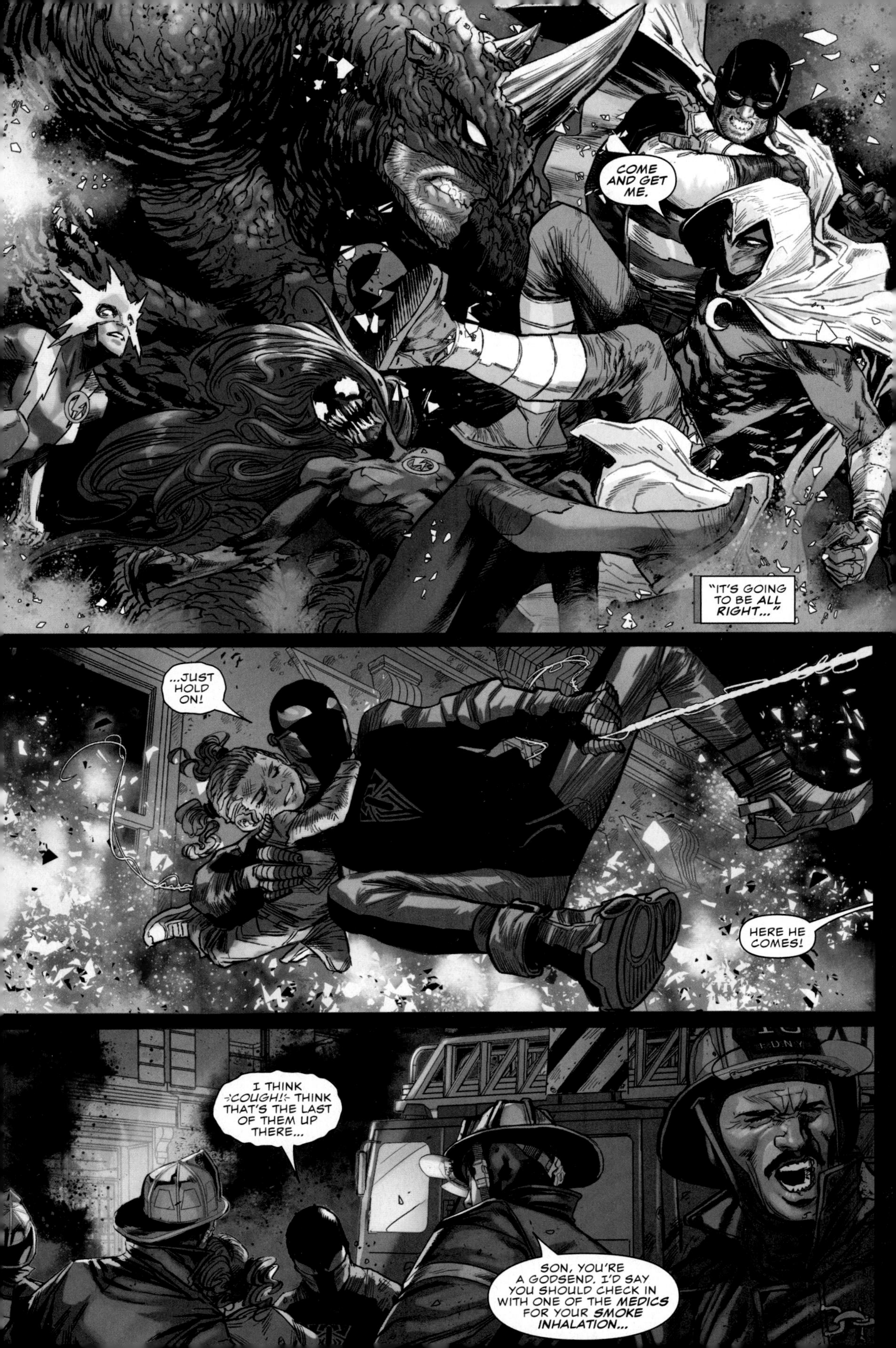
COME AND GET ME.
"IT'S GOING TO BE ALL RIGHT..."
...JUST HOLD ON!
HERE HE COMES!
I THINK -COUGH!- THINK THAT'S THE LAST OF THEM UP THERE...
SON, YOU'RE A GODSEND. I'D SAY YOU SHOULD CHECK IN WITH ONE OF THE MEDICS FOR YOUR SMOKE INHALATION...

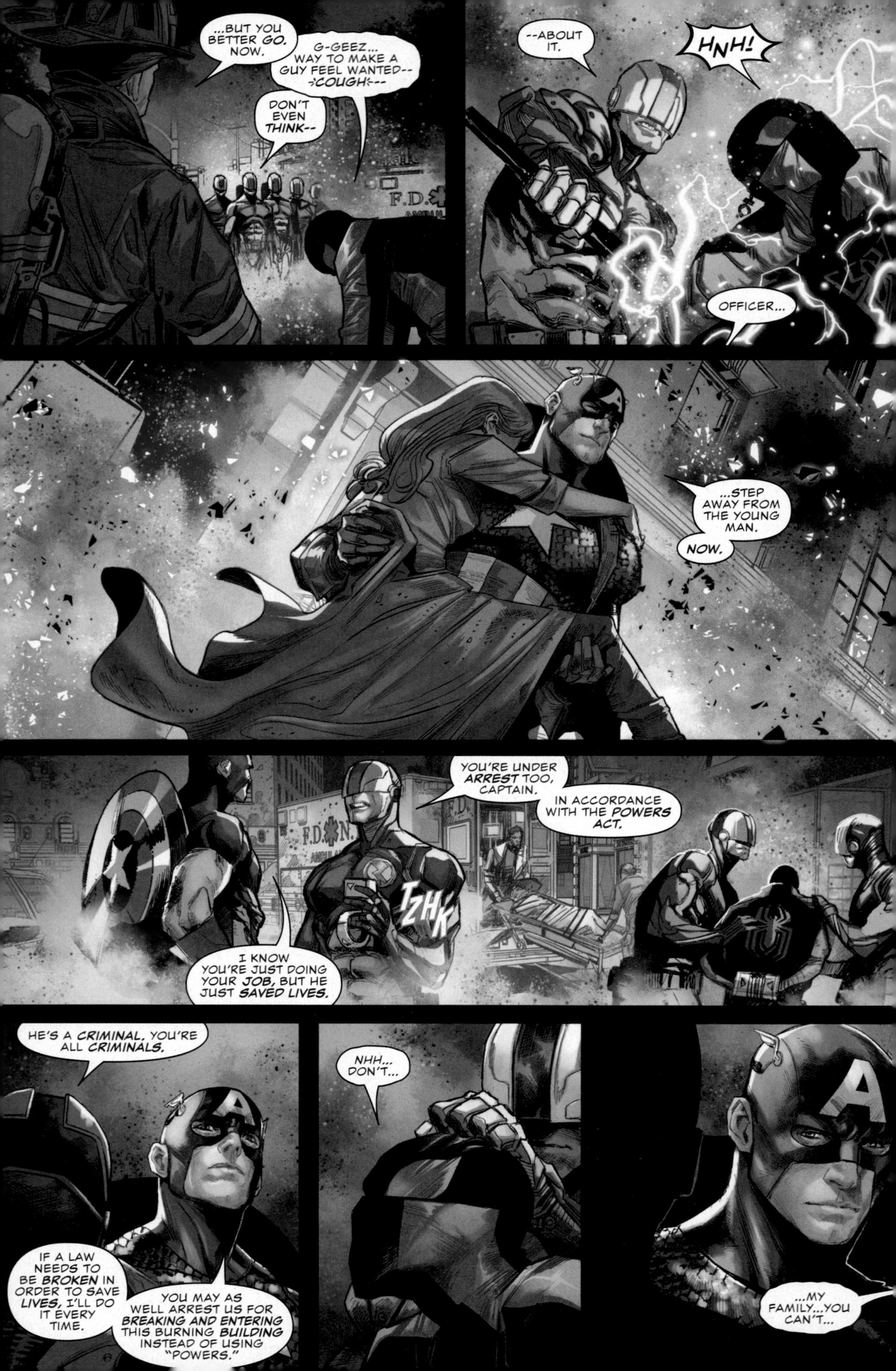

...BUT YOU BETTER GO. NOW.
G-GEEZ... WAY TO MAKE A GUY FEEL WANTED-- *COUGH*--
DON'T EVEN THINK--
--ABOUT IT.
HNH!
OFFICER...
...STEP AWAY FROM THE YOUNG MAN.
NOW.
YOU'RE UNDER ARREST TOO, CAPTAIN.
IN ACCORDANCE WITH THE POWERS ACT.
TZHK
I KNOW YOU'RE JUST DOING YOUR JOB, BUT HE JUST SAVED LIVES.
HE'S A CRIMINAL. YOU'RE ALL CRIMINALS.
IF A LAW NEEDS TO BE BROKEN IN ORDER TO SAVE LIVES, I'LL DO IT EVERY TIME.
YOU MAY AS WELL ARREST US FOR BREAKING AND ENTERING THIS BURNING BUILDING INSTEAD OF USING "POWERS."
NHH... DON'T...
...MY FAMILY...YOU CAN'T...

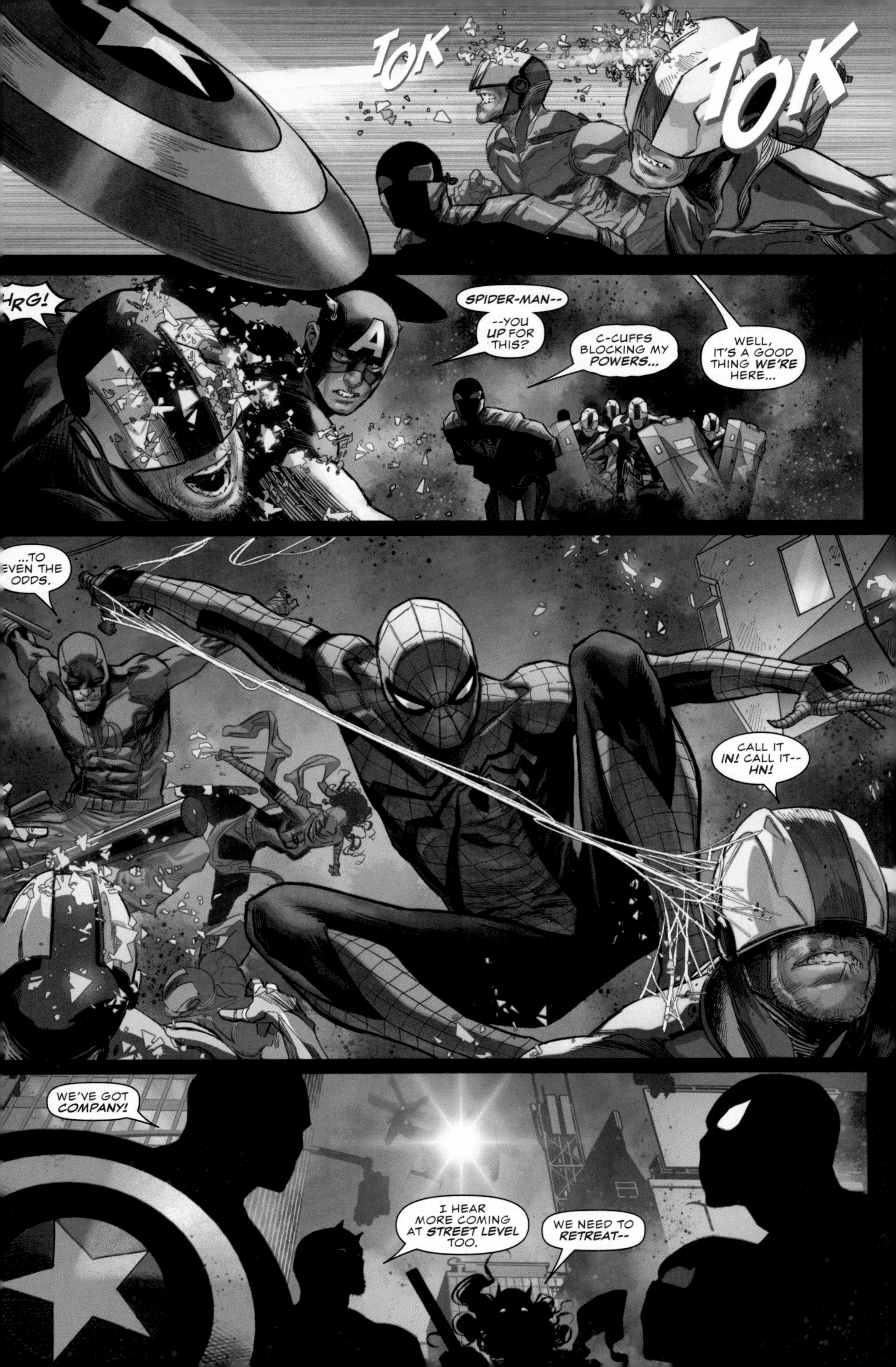
TOK
TOK
HRG!
SPIDER-MAN--
--YOU UP FOR THIS?
C-CUFFS BLOCKING MY POWERS...
WELL, IT'S A GOOD THING WE'RE HERE...
...TO EVEN THE ODDS.
CALL IT IN! CALL IT-- HN!
WE'VE GOT COMPANY!
I HEAR MORE COMING AT STREET LEVEL TOO.
WE NEED TO RETREAT--

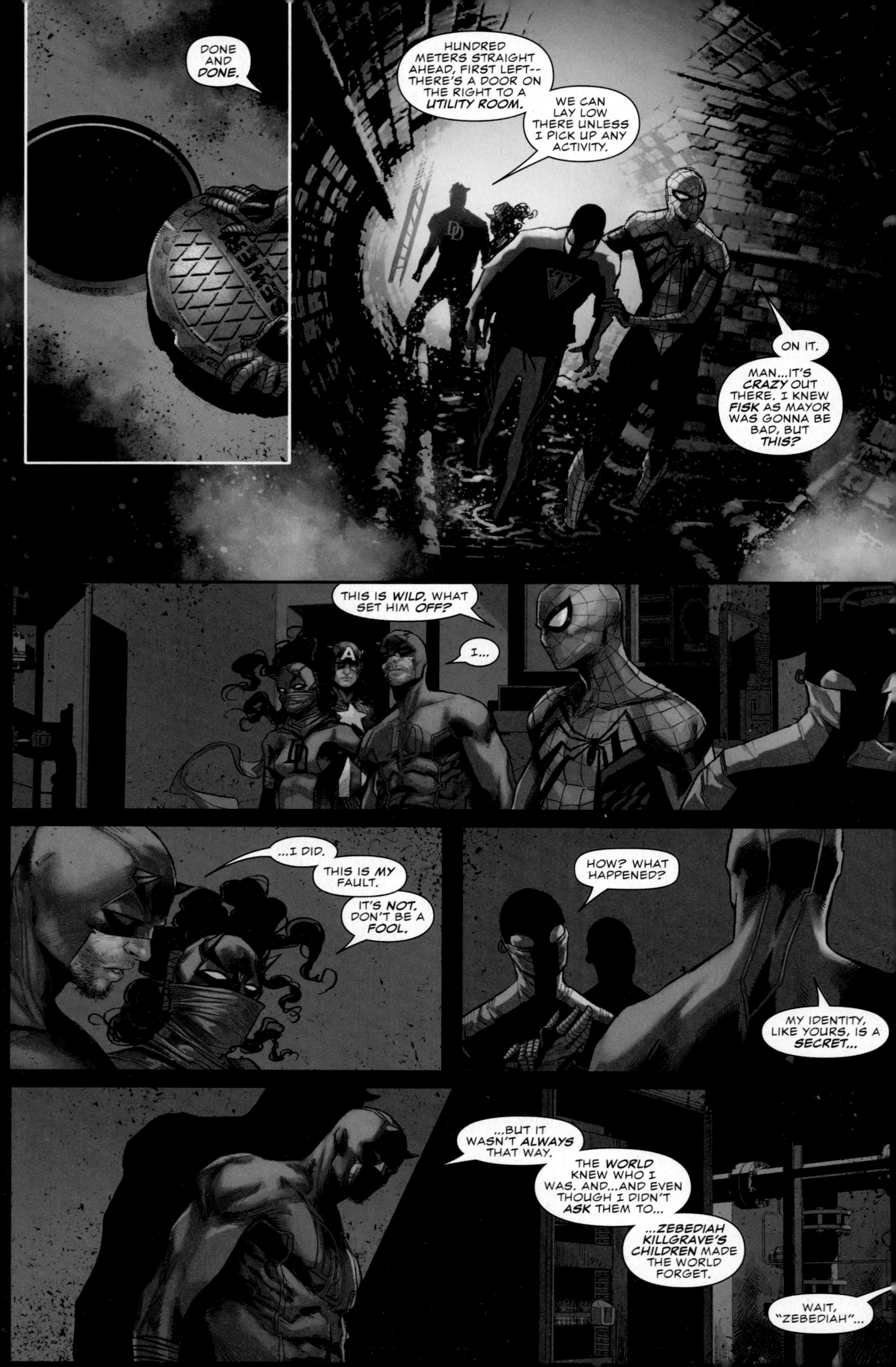

DONE AND DONE.
HUNDRED METERS STRAIGHT AHEAD, FIRST LEFT-- THERE'S A DOOR ON THE RIGHT TO A UTILITY ROOM.
WE CAN LAY LOW THERE UNLESS I PICK UP ANY ACTIVITY.
ON IT.
MAN...IT'S CRAZY OUT THERE. I KNEW FISK AS MAYOR WAS GONNA BE BAD, BUT THIS?
THIS IS WILD. WHAT SET HIM OFF?
I...
...I DID.
THIS IS MY FAULT.
IT'S NOT. DON'T BE A FOOL.
HOW? WHAT HAPPENED?
MY IDENTITY, LIKE YOURS, IS A SECRET...
...BUT IT WASN'T ALWAYS THAT WAY.
THE WORLD KNEW WHO I WAS. AND...AND EVEN THOUGH I DIDN'T ASK THEM TO...
...ZEBEDIAH KILLGRAVE'S CHILDREN MADE THE WORLD FORGET.
WAIT, "ZEBEDIAH"...

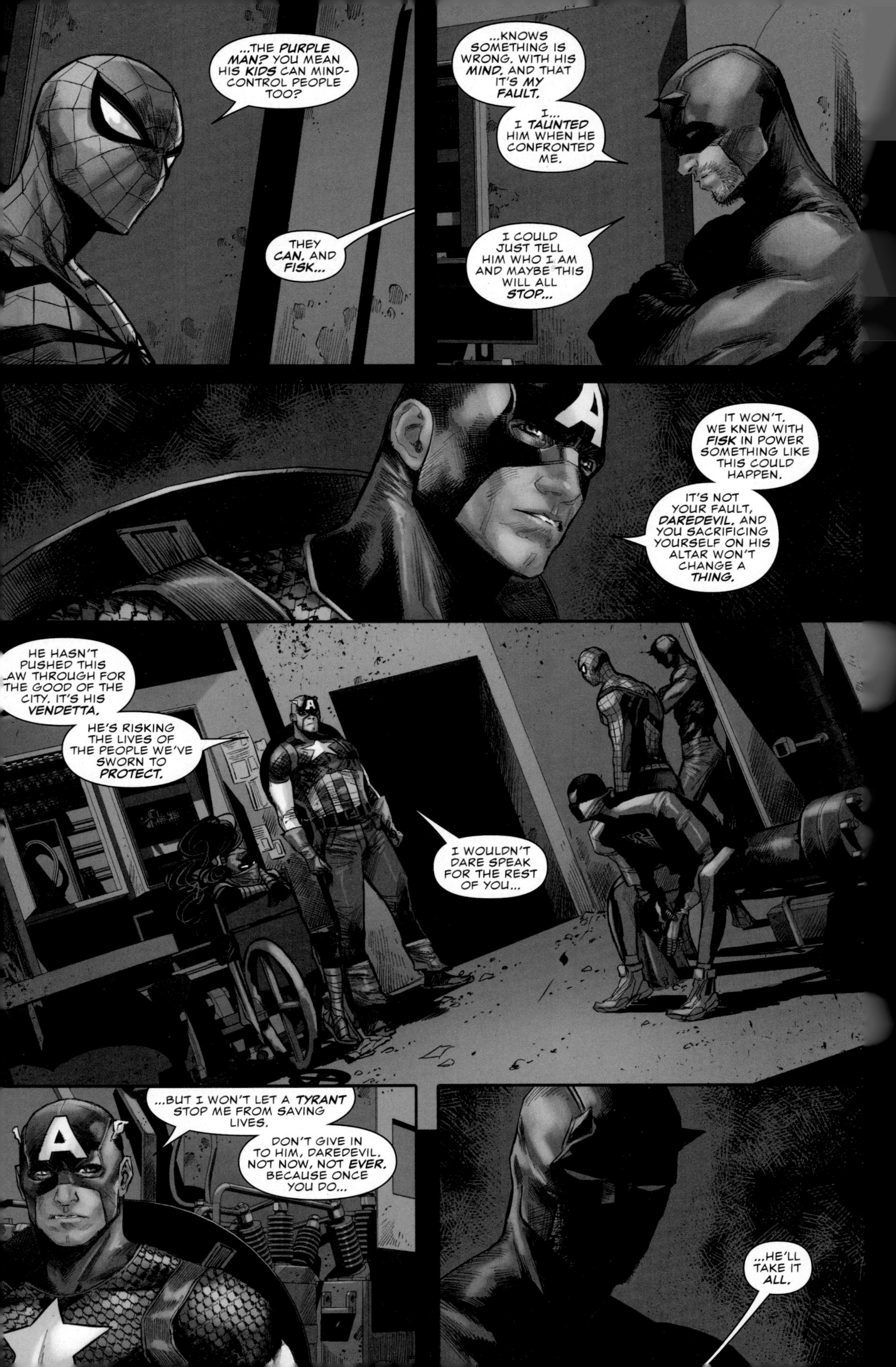
...THE PURPLE MAN? YOU MEAN HIS KIDS CAN MIND-CONTROL PEOPLE TOO?
THEY CAN. AND FISK...
...KNOWS SOMETHING IS WRONG. WITH HIS MIND. AND THAT IT'S MY FAULT.
I... I TAUNTED HIM WHEN HE CONFRONTED ME.
I COULD JUST TELL HIM WHO I AM AND MAYBE THIS WILL ALL STOP...
IT WON'T. WE KNEW WITH FISK IN POWER SOMETHING LIKE THIS COULD HAPPEN.
IT'S NOT YOUR FAULT, DAREDEVIL. AND YOU SACRIFICING YOURSELF ON HIS ALTAR WON'T CHANGE A THING.
HE HASN'T PUSHED THIS LAW THROUGH FOR THE GOOD OF THE CITY. IT'S HIS VENDETTA.
HE'S RISKING THE LIVES OF THE PEOPLE WE'VE SWORN TO PROTECT.
I WOULDN'T DARE SPEAK FOR THE REST OF YOU...
...BUT I WON'T LET A TYRANT STOP ME FROM SAVING LIVES.
DON'T GIVE IN TO HIM, DAREDEVIL. NOT NOW, NOT EVER. BECAUSE ONCE YOU DO...
...HE'LL TAKE IT ALL.

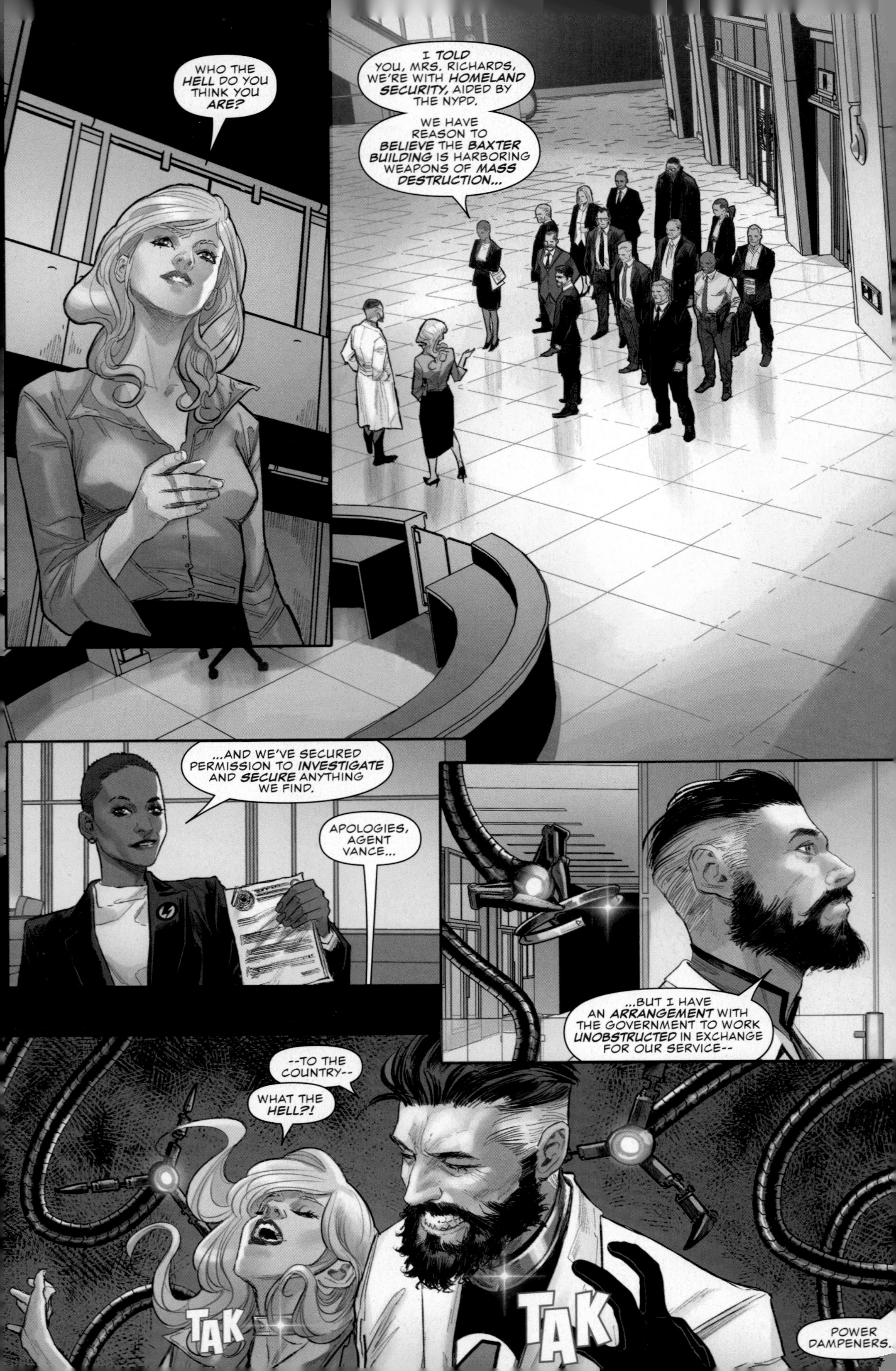
WHO THE HELL DO YOU THINK YOU ARE?
I TOLD YOU, MRS. RICHARDS, WE'RE WITH HOMELAND SECURITY, AIDED BY THE NYPD.
WE HAVE REASON TO BELIEVE THE BAXTER BUILDING IS HARBORING WEAPONS OF MASS DESTRUCTION...
...AND WE'VE SECURED PERMISSION TO INVESTIGATE AND SECURE ANYTHING WE FIND.
APOLOGIES, AGENT VANCE...
...BUT I HAVE AN ARRANGEMENT WITH THE GOVERNMENT TO WORK UNOBSTRUCTED IN EXCHANGE FOR OUR SERVICE--
--TO THE COUNTRY--
WHAT THE HELL?!
TAK
TAK
POWER DAMPENERS.

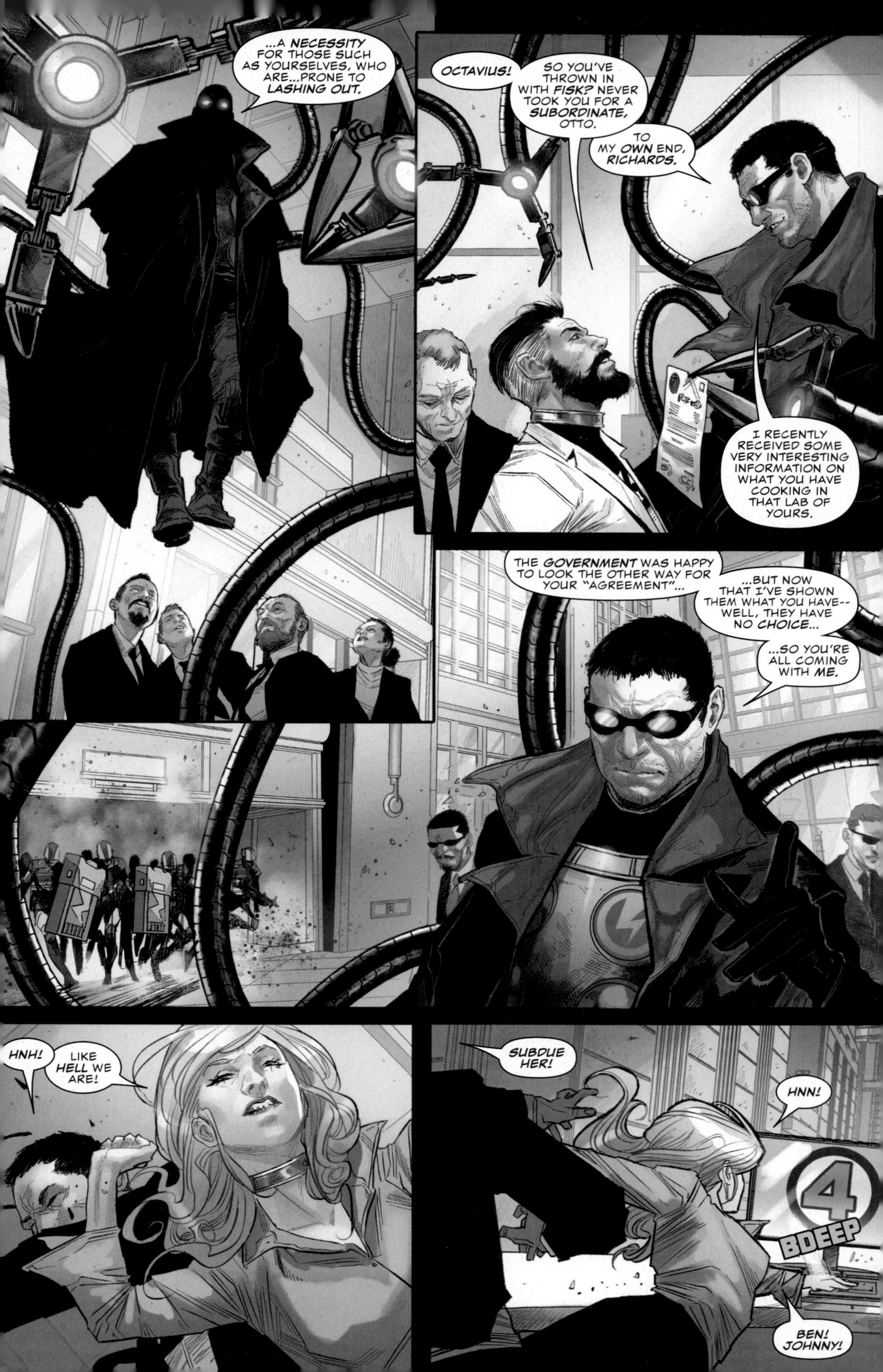
...A NECESSITY FOR THOSE SUCH AS YOURSELVES, WHO ARE...PRONE TO LASHING OUT.
OCTAVIUS!
SO YOU'VE THROWN IN WITH FISK? NEVER TOOK YOU FOR A SUBORDINATE, OTTO.
TO MY OWN END, RICHARDS.
I RECENTLY RECEIVED SOME VERY INTERESTING INFORMATION ON WHAT YOU HAVE COOKING IN THAT LAB OF YOURS.
THE GOVERNMENT WAS HAPPY TO LOOK THE OTHER WAY FOR YOUR "AGREEMENT"...
...BUT NOW THAT I'VE SHOWN THEM WHAT YOU HAVE-- WELL, THEY HAVE NO CHOICE...
...SO YOU'RE ALL COMING WITH ME.
HNH!
LIKE HELL WE ARE!
SUBDUE HER!
HNN!
BDEEP
BEN! JOHNNY!

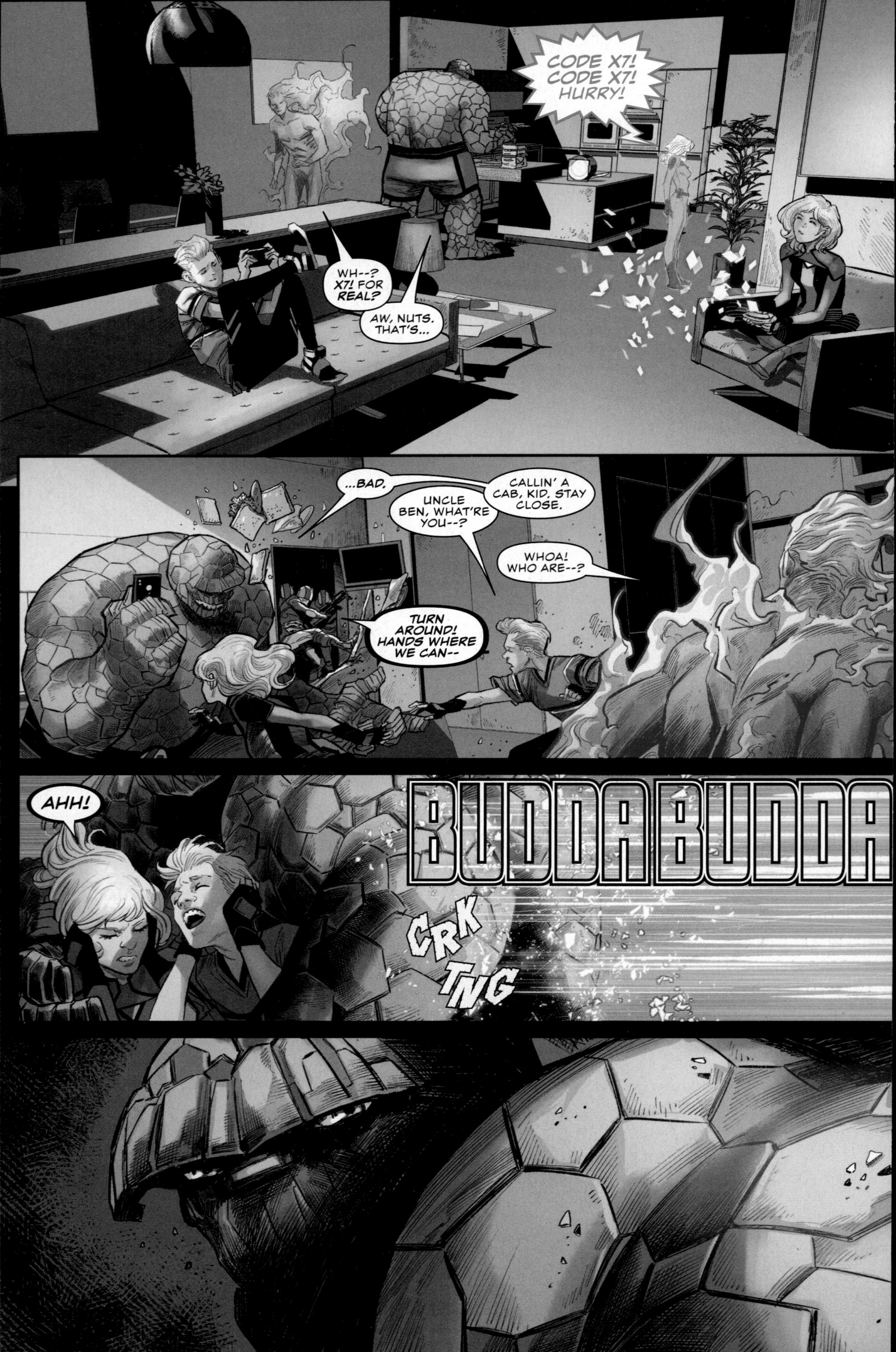
CODE X7! CODE X7! HURRY!
WH--? X7! FOR REAL?
AW, NUTS. THAT'S...
...BAD.
UNCLE BEN, WHAT'RE YOU--?
CALLIN' A CAB, KID. STAY CLOSE.
WHOA! WHO ARE--?
TURN AROUND! HANDS WHERE WE CAN--
AHH!
BUDDA BUDDA
CRK
TNG

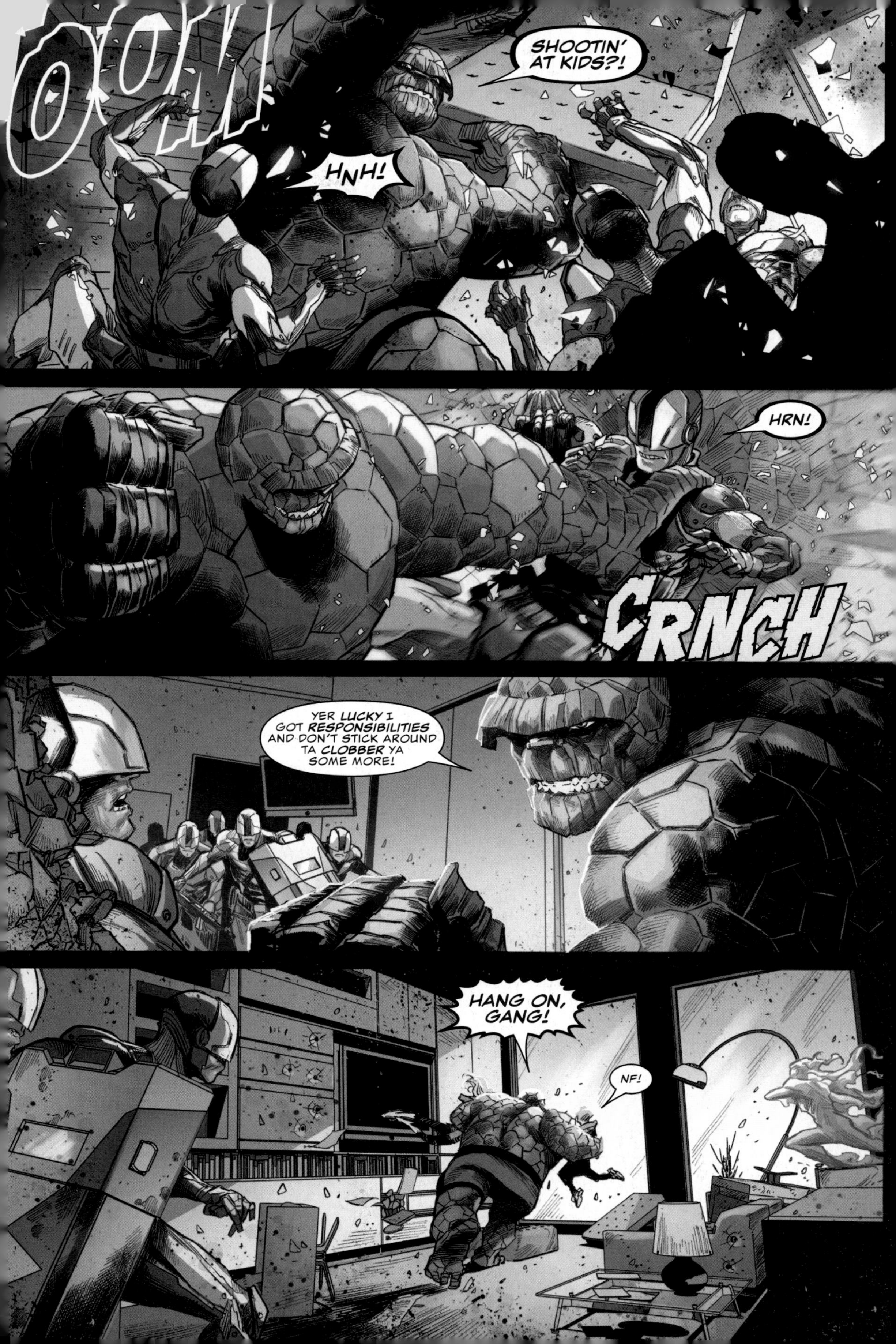
OOM
SHOOTIN' AT KIDS?!
HNH!
HRN!
CRNCH
YER LUCKY I GOT RESPONSIBILITIES AND DON'T STICK AROUND TA CLOBBER YA SOME MORE!
HANG ON, GANG!
NF!

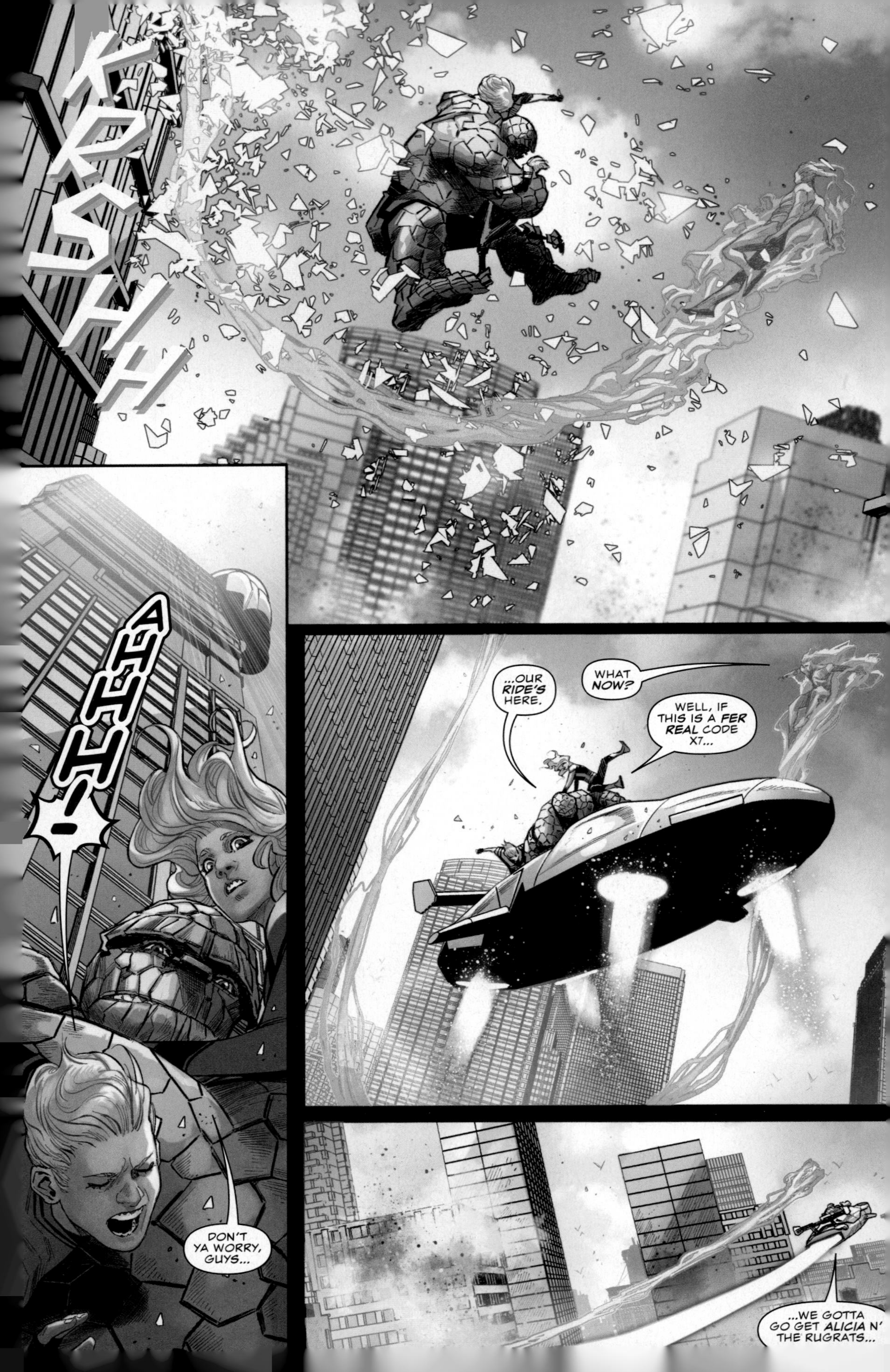
KRSHHH
AHHHH--!
DON'T YA WORRY, GUYS...
WHAT NOW?
...OUR RIDE'S HERE.
WELL, IF THIS IS A FER REAL CODE X7...
...WE GOTTA GO GET ALICIA N' THE RUGRATS...

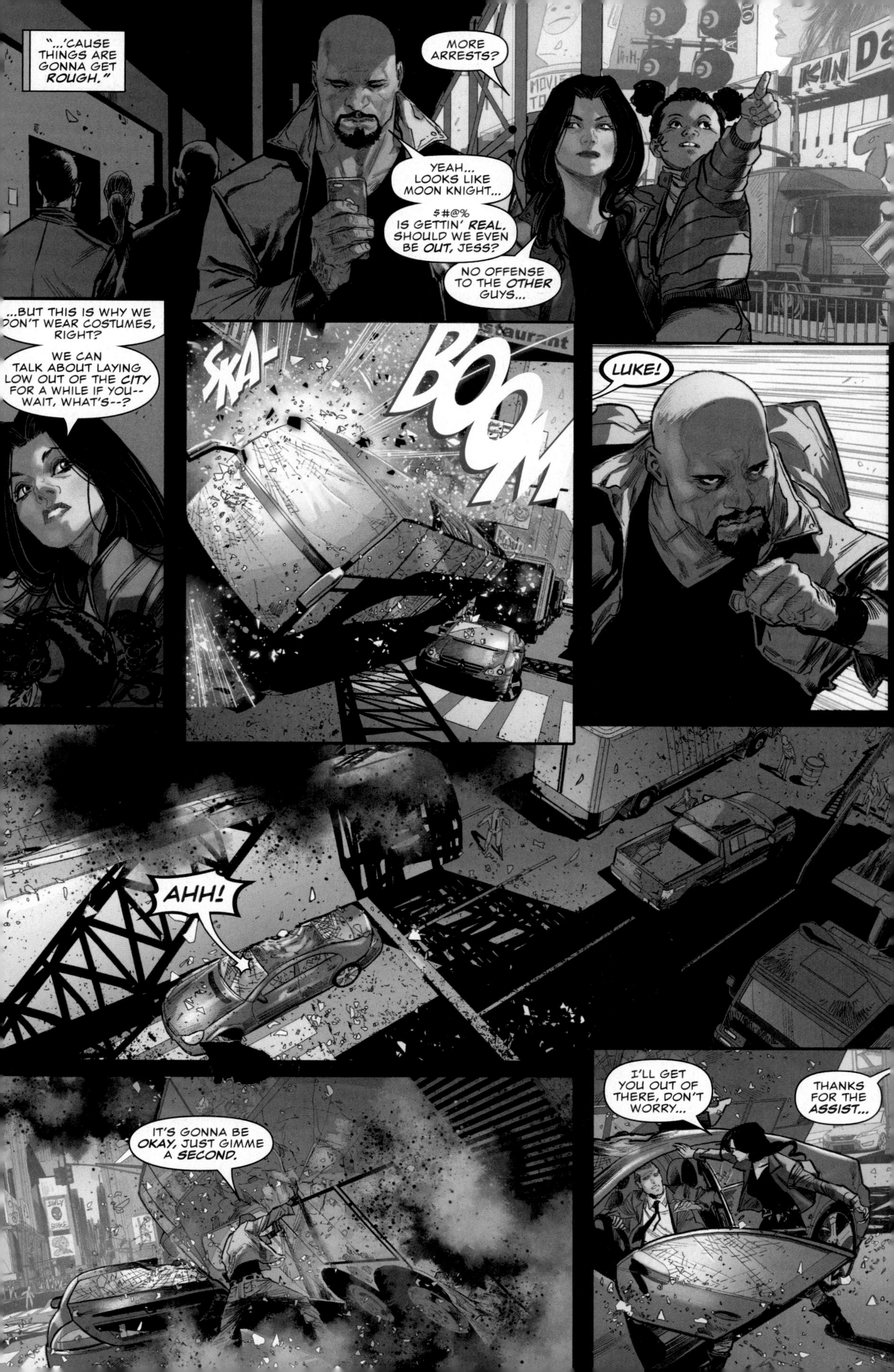
"...'CAUSE THINGS ARE GONNA GET ROUGH."
MORE ARRESTS?
YEAH... LOOKS LIKE MOON KNIGHT...
$#@% IS GETTIN' REAL. SHOULD WE EVEN BE OUT, JESS?
NO OFFENSE TO THE OTHER GUYS...
...BUT THIS IS WHY WE DON'T WEAR COSTUMES, RIGHT?
WE CAN TALK ABOUT LAYING LOW OUT OF THE CITY FOR A WHILE IF YOU-- WAIT, WHAT'S--?
SKA-
BOOM
LUKE!
AHH!
IT'S GONNA BE OKAY, JUST GIMME A SECOND.
I'LL GET YOU OUT OF THERE, DON'T WORRY...
THANKS FOR THE ASSIST...

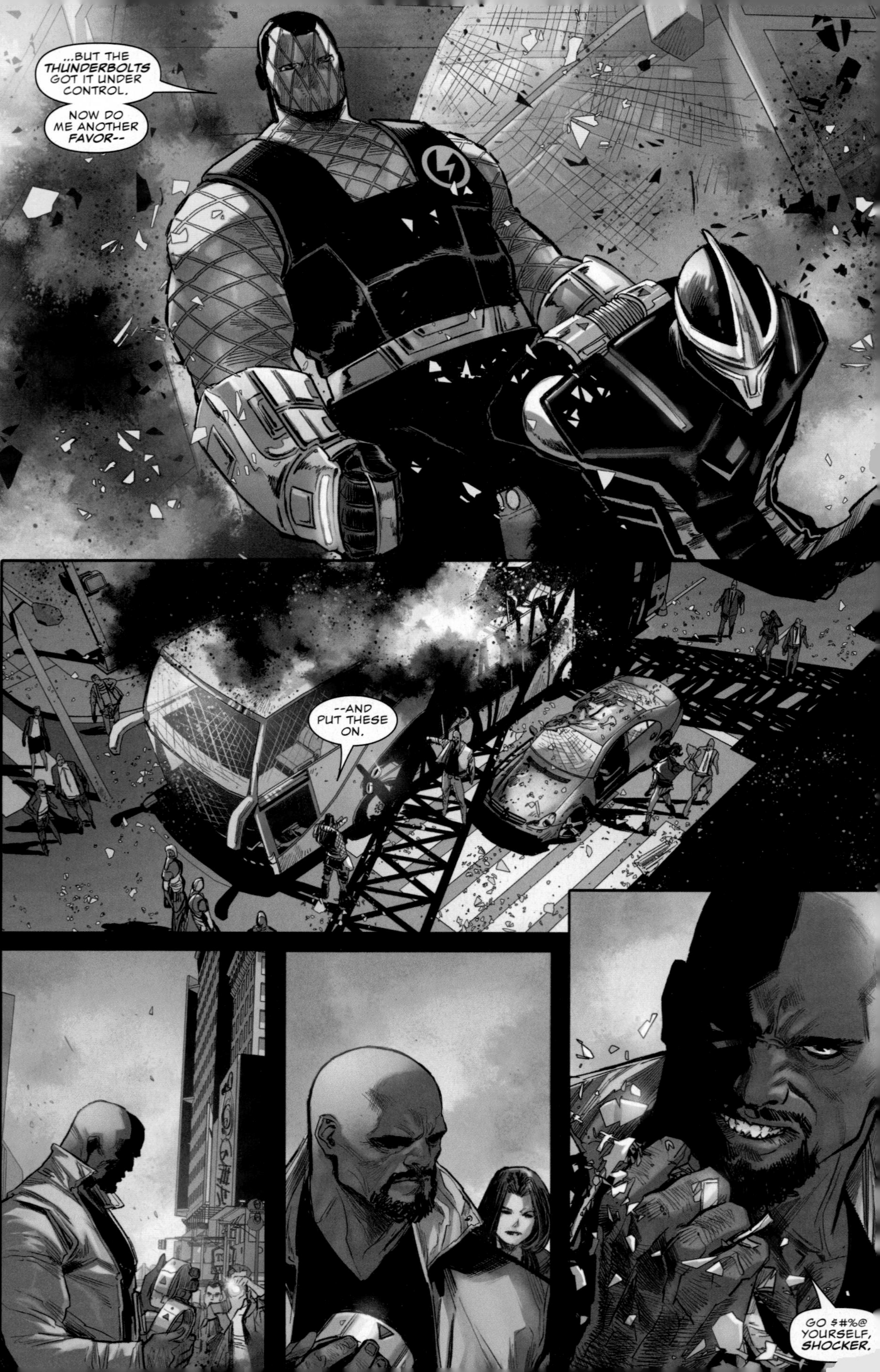
...BUT THE THUNDERBOLTS GOT IT UNDER CONTROL.
NOW DO ME ANOTHER FAVOR--
--AND PUT THESE ON.
GO $#%@ YOURSELF, SHOCKER.

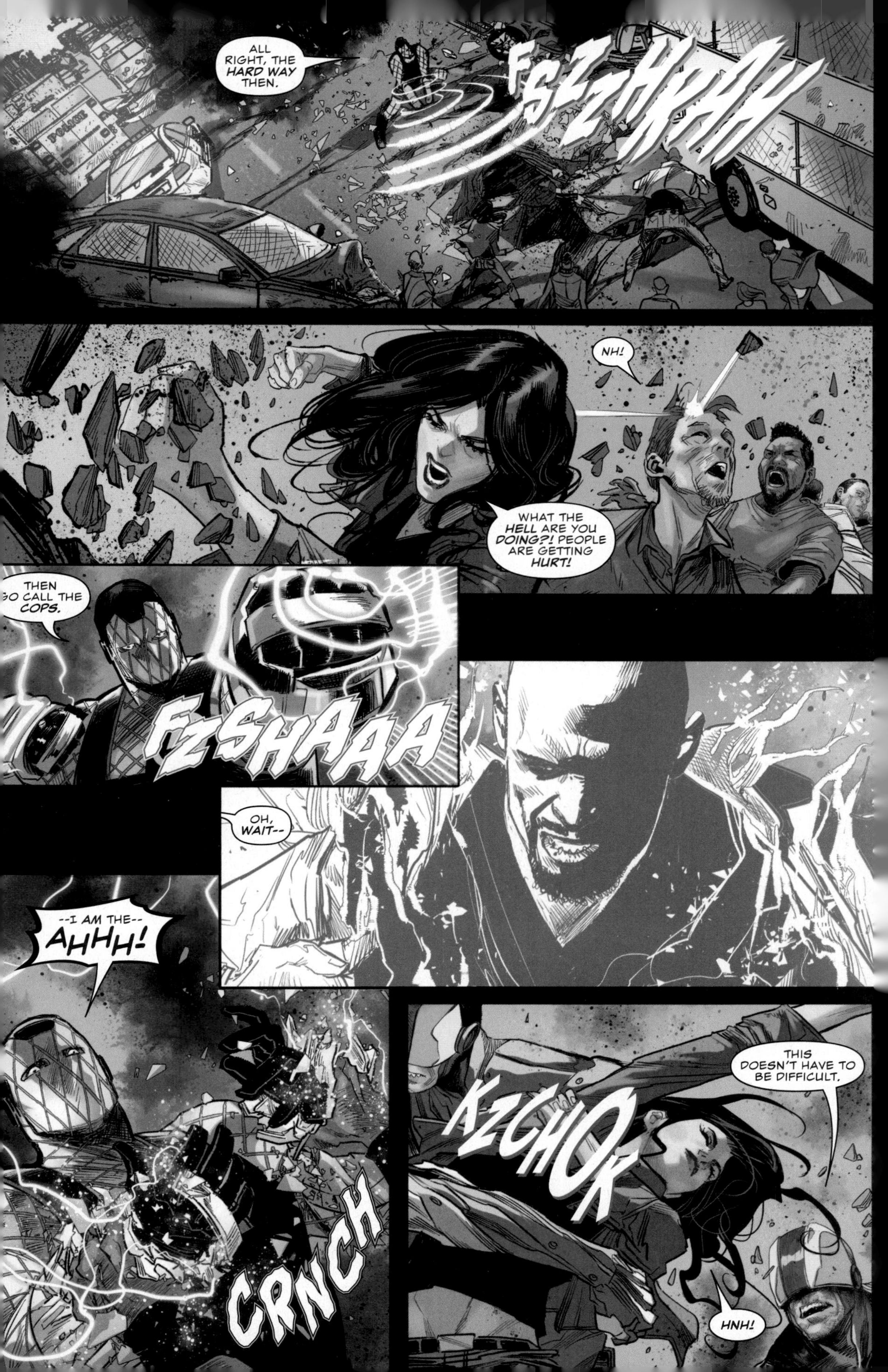

ALL RIGHT, THE HARD WAY THEN.
FSSZHHHH
NH!
WHAT THE HELL ARE YOU DOING?! PEOPLE ARE GETTING HURT!
THEN GO CALL THE COPS.
FZSHAAA
OH, WAIT--
--I AM THE-- AHHH!
CRNCH
THIS DOESN'T HAVE TO BE DIFFICULT.
KZCHOK
HNH!

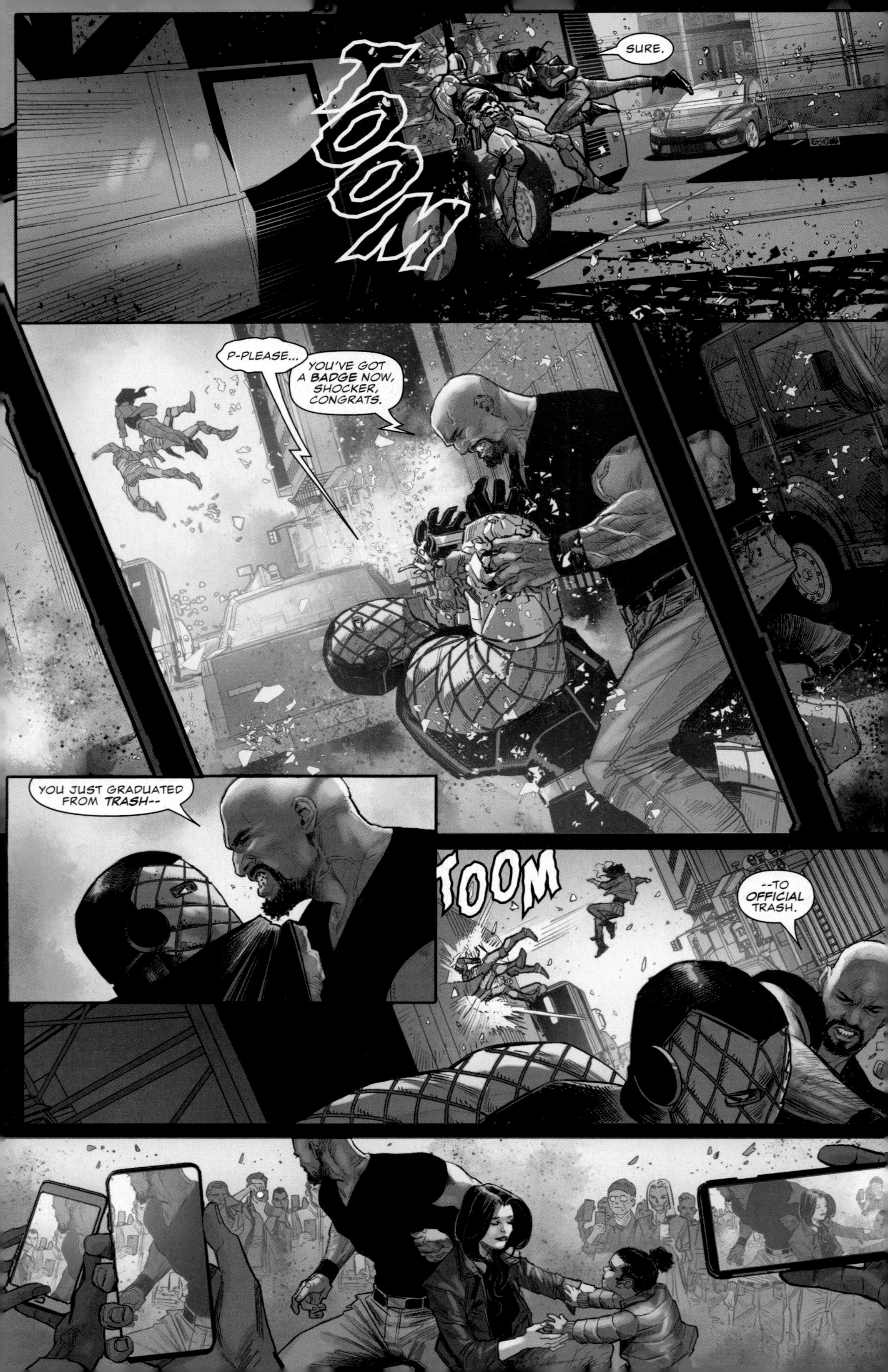
TOOOM
SURE.
P-PLEASE...
YOU'VE GOT A BADGE NOW, SHOCKER, CONGRATS.
YOU JUST GRADUATED FROM TRASH--
TOOM
--TO OFFICIAL TRASH.

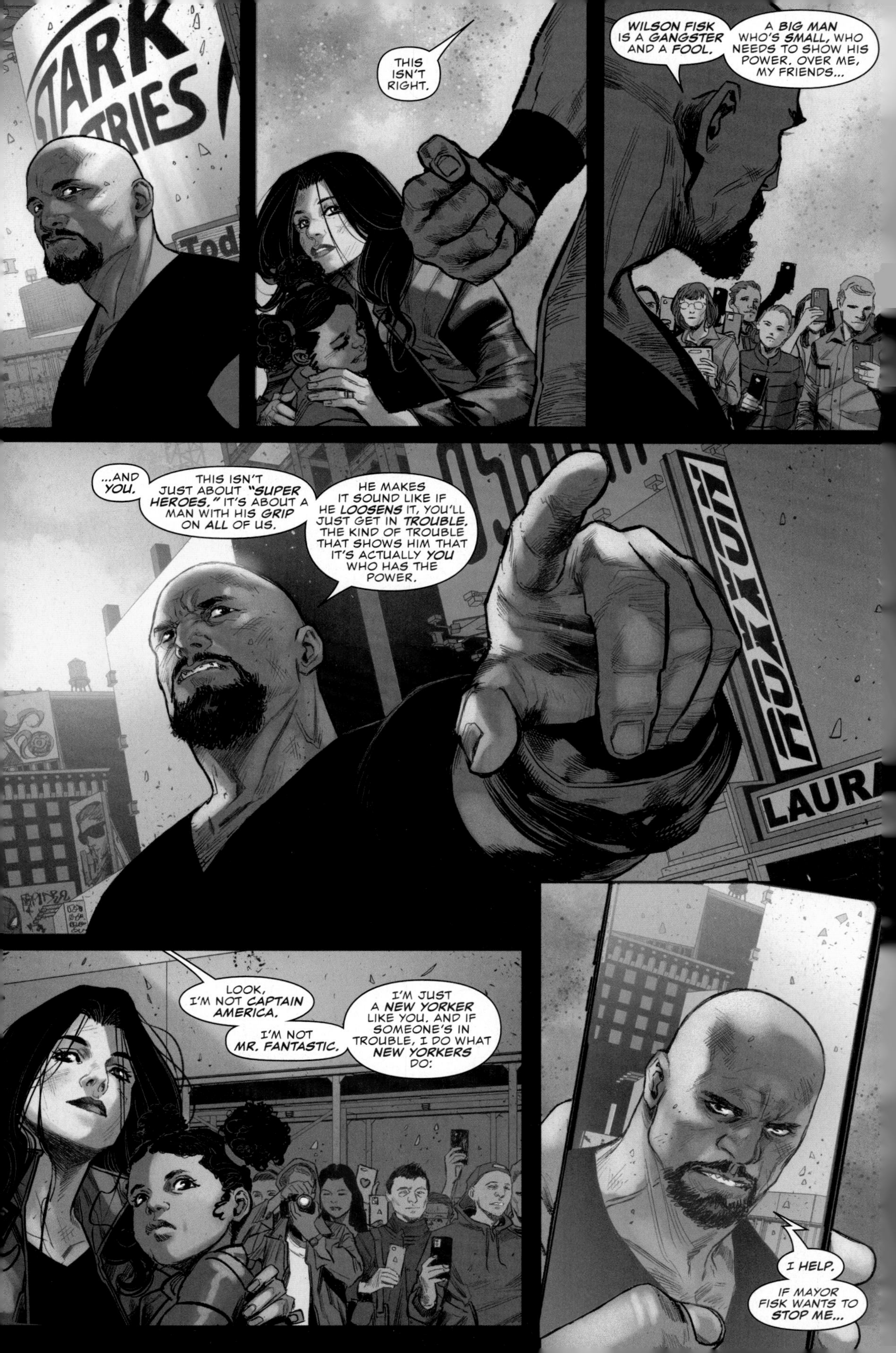
STARK
TRIES
THIS ISN'T RIGHT.
WILSON FISK IS A GANGSTER AND A FOOL.
A BIG MAN WHO'S SMALL, WHO NEEDS TO SHOW HIS POWER. OVER ME, MY FRIENDS...
...AND YOU.
THIS ISN'T JUST ABOUT "SUPER HEROES." IT'S ABOUT A MAN WITH HIS GRIP ON ALL OF US.
HE MAKES IT SOUND LIKE IF HE LOOSENS IT, YOU'LL JUST GET IN TROUBLE. THE KIND OF TROUBLE THAT SHOWS HIM THAT IT'S ACTUALLY YOU WHO HAS THE POWER.
LAURA
LOOK, I'M NOT CAPTAIN AMERICA.
I'M NOT MR. FANTASTIC.
I'M JUST A NEW YORKER LIKE YOU. AND IF SOMEONE'S IN TROUBLE, I DO WHAT NEW YORKERS DO:
I HELP.
IF MAYOR FISK WANTS TO STOP ME...

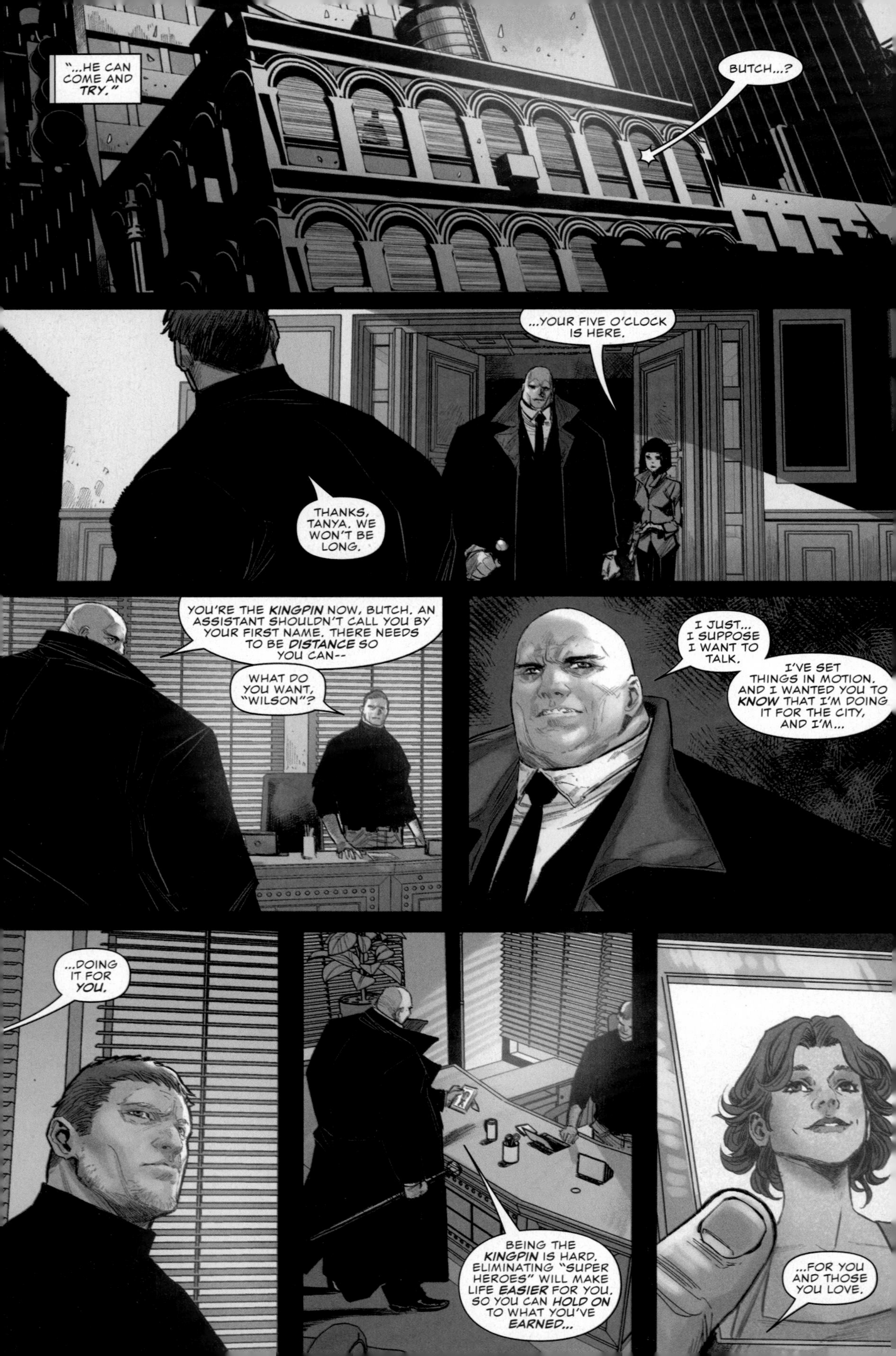
"...HE CAN COME AND TRY."
BUTCH...?
...YOUR FIVE O'CLOCK IS HERE.
THANKS, TANYA. WE WON'T BE LONG.
YOU'RE THE KINGPIN NOW, BUTCH. AN ASSISTANT SHOULDN'T CALL YOU BY YOUR FIRST NAME. THERE NEEDS TO BE DISTANCE SO YOU CAN--
WHAT DO YOU WANT, "WILSON"?
I JUST... I SUPPOSE I WANT TO TALK.
I'VE SET THINGS IN MOTION. AND I WANTED YOU TO KNOW THAT I'M DOING IT FOR THE CITY, AND I'M...
...DOING IT FOR YOU.
BEING THE KINGPIN IS HARD. ELIMINATING "SUPER HEROES" WILL MAKE LIFE EASIER FOR YOU, SO YOU CAN HOLD ON TO WHAT YOU'VE EARNED...
...FOR YOU AND THOSE YOU LOVE.

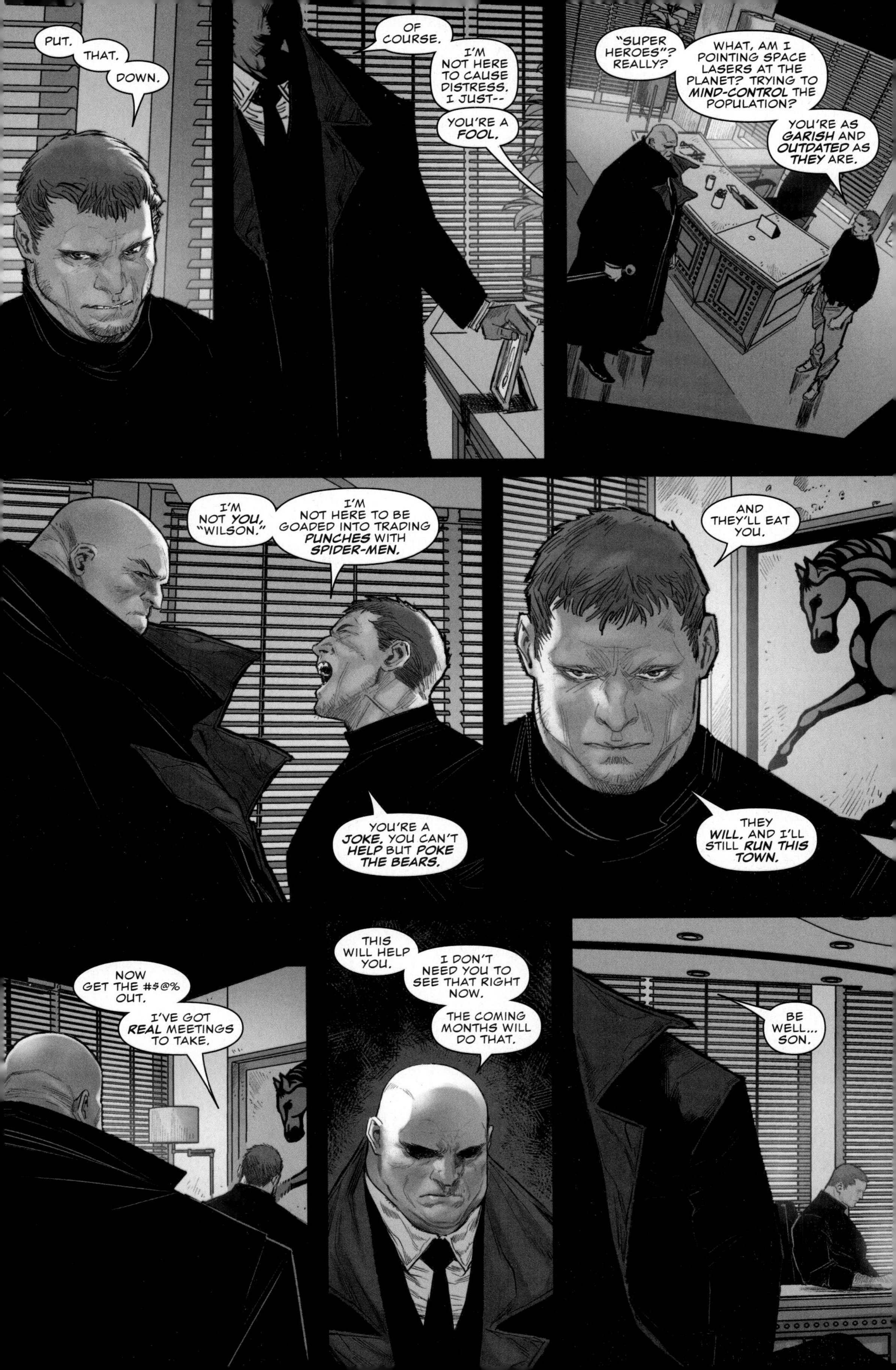
PUT.
THAT.
DOWN.
OF COURSE.
I'M NOT HERE TO CAUSE DISTRESS. I JUST--
YOU'RE A FOOL.
"SUPER HEROES"? REALLY?
WHAT, AM I POINTING SPACE LASERS AT THE PLANET? TRYING TO MIND-CONTROL THE POPULATION?
YOU'RE AS GARISH AND OUTDATED AS THEY ARE.
I'M NOT YOU, "WILSON."
I'M NOT HERE TO BE GOADED INTO TRADING PUNCHES WITH SPIDER-MEN.
YOU'RE A JOKE. YOU CAN'T HELP BUT POKE THE BEARS.
AND THEY'LL EAT YOU.
THEY WILL, AND I'LL STILL RUN THIS TOWN.
NOW GET THE #$@% OUT.
I'VE GOT REAL MEETINGS TO TAKE.
THIS WILL HELP YOU.
I DON'T NEED YOU TO SEE THAT RIGHT NOW.
THE COMING MONTHS WILL DO THAT.
BE WELL... SON.

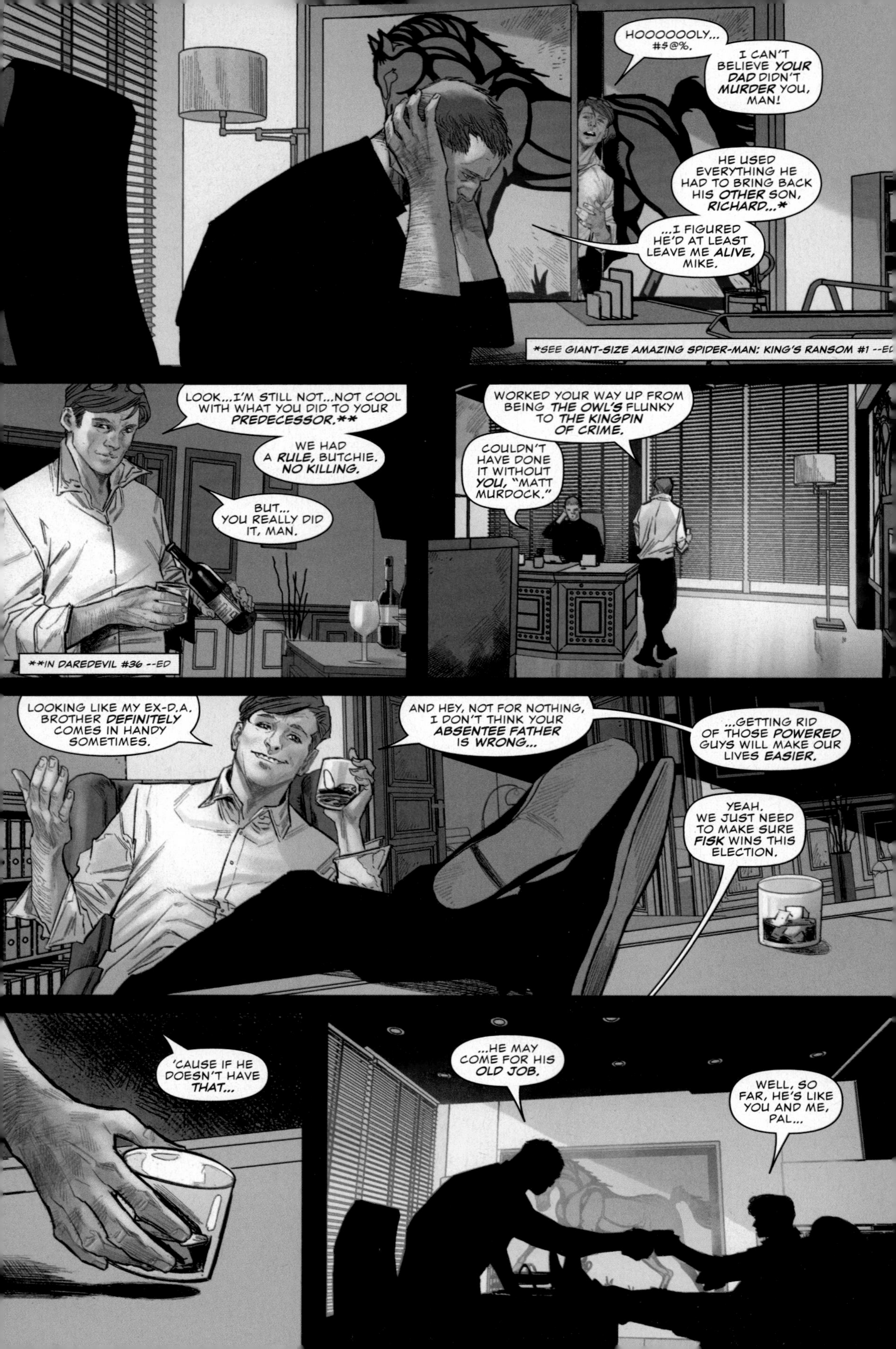
HOOOOOOLY... #$@%.
I CAN'T BELIEVE YOUR DAD DIDN'T MURDER YOU, MAN!
HE USED EVERYTHING HE HAD TO BRING BACK HIS OTHER SON, RICHARD...*
...I FIGURED HE'D AT LEAST LEAVE ME ALIVE, MIKE.
*SEE GIANT-SIZE AMAZING SPIDER-MAN: KING'S RANSOM #1 --ED
LOOK...I'M STILL NOT...NOT COOL WITH WHAT YOU DID TO YOUR PREDECESSOR.**
WE HAD A RULE, BUTCHIE. NO KILLING.
BUT... YOU REALLY DID IT, MAN.
**IN DAREDEVIL #36 --ED
WORKED YOUR WAY UP FROM BEING THE OWL'S FLUNKY TO THE KINGPIN OF CRIME.
COULDN'T HAVE DONE IT WITHOUT YOU, "MATT MURDOCK."
LOOKING LIKE MY EX-D.A. BROTHER DEFINITELY COMES IN HANDY SOMETIMES.
AND HEY, NOT FOR NOTHING, I DON'T THINK YOUR ABSENTEE FATHER IS WRONG...
...GETTING RID OF THOSE POWERED GUYS WILL MAKE OUR LIVES EASIER.
YEAH. WE JUST NEED TO MAKE SURE FISK WINS THIS ELECTION.
'CAUSE IF HE DOESN'T HAVE THAT...
...HE MAY COME FOR HIS OLD JOB.
WELL, SO FAR, HE'S LIKE YOU AND ME, PAL...

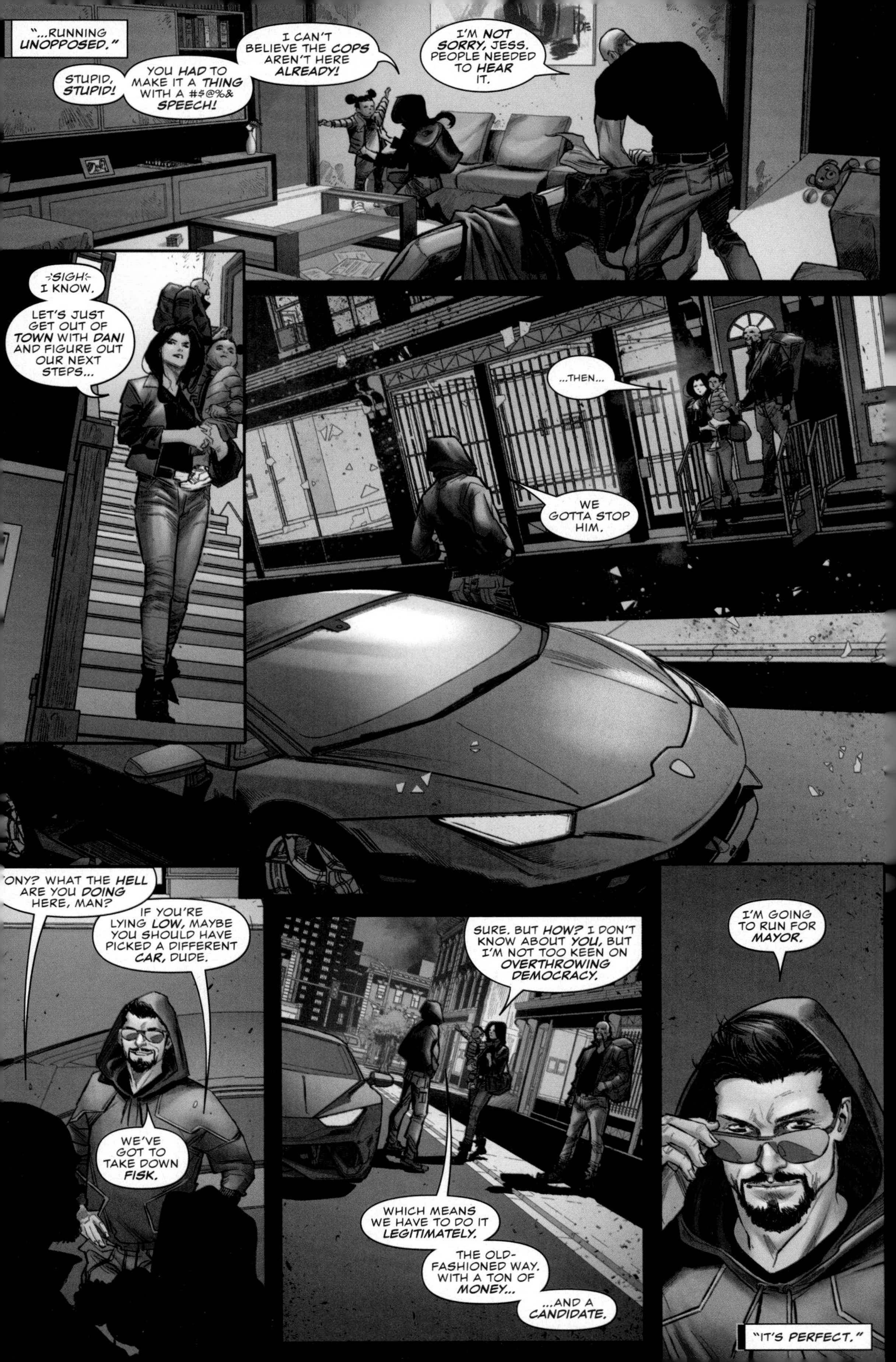
"...RUNNING UNOPPOSED."
STUPID, STUPID!
YOU HAD TO MAKE IT A THING WITH A #$@%& SPEECH!
I CAN'T BELIEVE THE COPS AREN'T HERE ALREADY!
I'M NOT SORRY, JESS. PEOPLE NEEDED TO HEAR IT.
SIGH I KNOW.
LET'S JUST GET OUT OF TOWN WITH DANI AND FIGURE OUT OUR NEXT STEPS...
...THEN...
WE GOTTA STOP HIM.
TONY? WHAT THE HELL ARE YOU DOING HERE, MAN?
IF YOU'RE LYING LOW, MAYBE YOU SHOULD HAVE PICKED A DIFFERENT CAR, DUDE.
WE'VE GOT TO TAKE DOWN FISK.
SURE. BUT HOW? I DON'T KNOW ABOUT YOU, BUT I'M NOT TOO KEEN ON OVERTHROWING DEMOCRACY.
WHICH MEANS WE HAVE TO DO IT LEGITIMATELY.
THE OLD-FASHIONED WAY. WITH A TON OF MONEY...
...AND A CANDIDATE.
I'M GOING TO RUN FOR MAYOR.
"IT'S PERFECT."

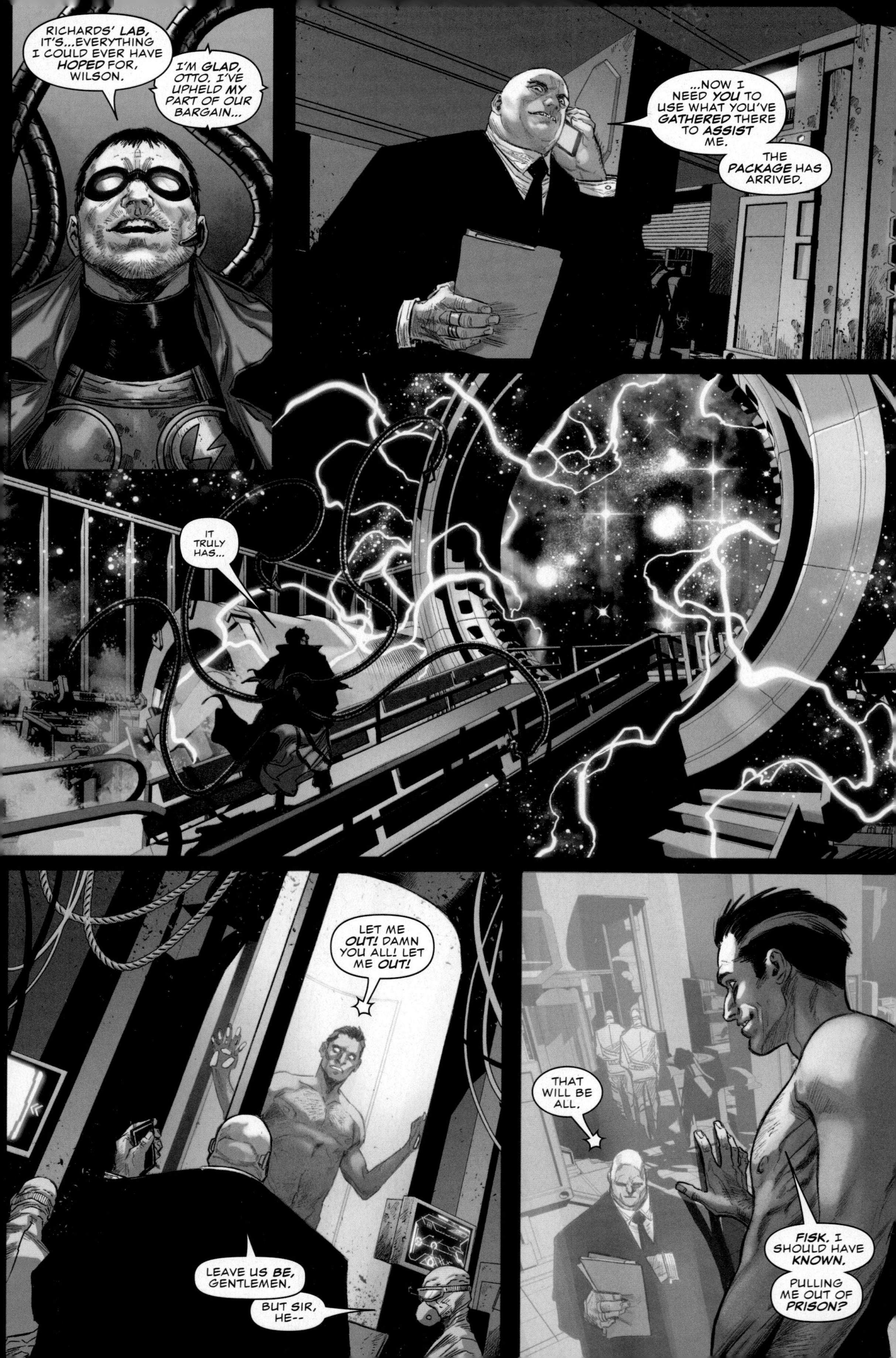
RICHARDS' LAB, IT'S...EVERYTHING I COULD EVER HAVE HOPED FOR, WILSON.
I'M GLAD, OTTO. I'VE UPHELD MY PART OF OUR BARGAIN...
...NOW I NEED YOU TO USE WHAT YOU'VE GATHERED THERE TO ASSIST ME.
THE PACKAGE HAS ARRIVED.
IT TRULY HAS...
LET ME OUT! DAMN YOU ALL! LET ME OUT!
LEAVE US BE, GENTLEMEN.
BUT SIR, HE--
THAT WILL BE ALL.
FISK. I SHOULD HAVE KNOWN.
PULLING ME OUT OF PRISON?

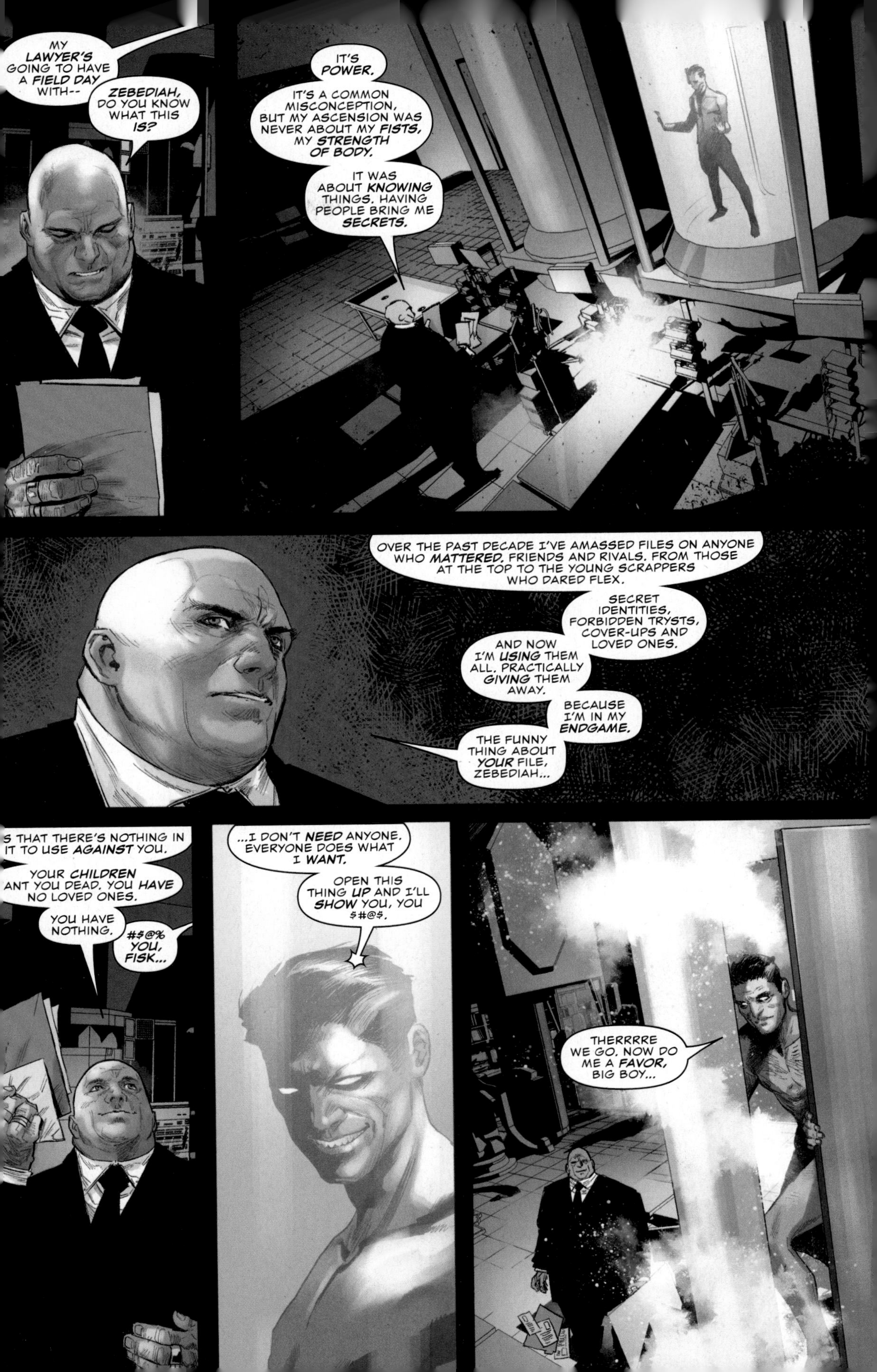

MY LAWYER'S GOING TO HAVE A FIELD DAY WITH--
ZEBEDIAH, DO YOU KNOW WHAT THIS IS?
IT'S POWER.
IT'S A COMMON MISCONCEPTION, BUT MY ASCENSION WAS NEVER ABOUT MY FISTS, MY STRENGTH OF BODY.
IT WAS ABOUT KNOWING THINGS. HAVING PEOPLE BRING ME SECRETS.
OVER THE PAST DECADE I'VE AMASSED FILES ON ANYONE WHO MATTERED. FRIENDS AND RIVALS. FROM THOSE AT THE TOP TO THE YOUNG SCRAPPERS WHO DARED FLEX.
SECRET IDENTITIES, FORBIDDEN TRYSTS, COVER-UPS AND LOVED ONES.
AND NOW I'M USING THEM ALL. PRACTICALLY GIVING THEM AWAY.
BECAUSE I'M IN MY ENDGAME.
THE FUNNY THING ABOUT YOUR FILE, ZEBEDIAH...
S THAT THERE'S NOTHING IN IT TO USE AGAINST YOU.
YOUR CHILDREN ANT YOU DEAD. YOU HAVE NO LOVED ONES.
YOU HAVE NOTHING.
#$@% YOU, FISK...
...I DON'T NEED ANYONE. EVERYONE DOES WHAT I WANT.
OPEN THIS THING UP AND I'LL SHOW YOU, YOU $#@$.
THERRRRE WE GO. NOW DO ME A FAVOR, BIG BOY...

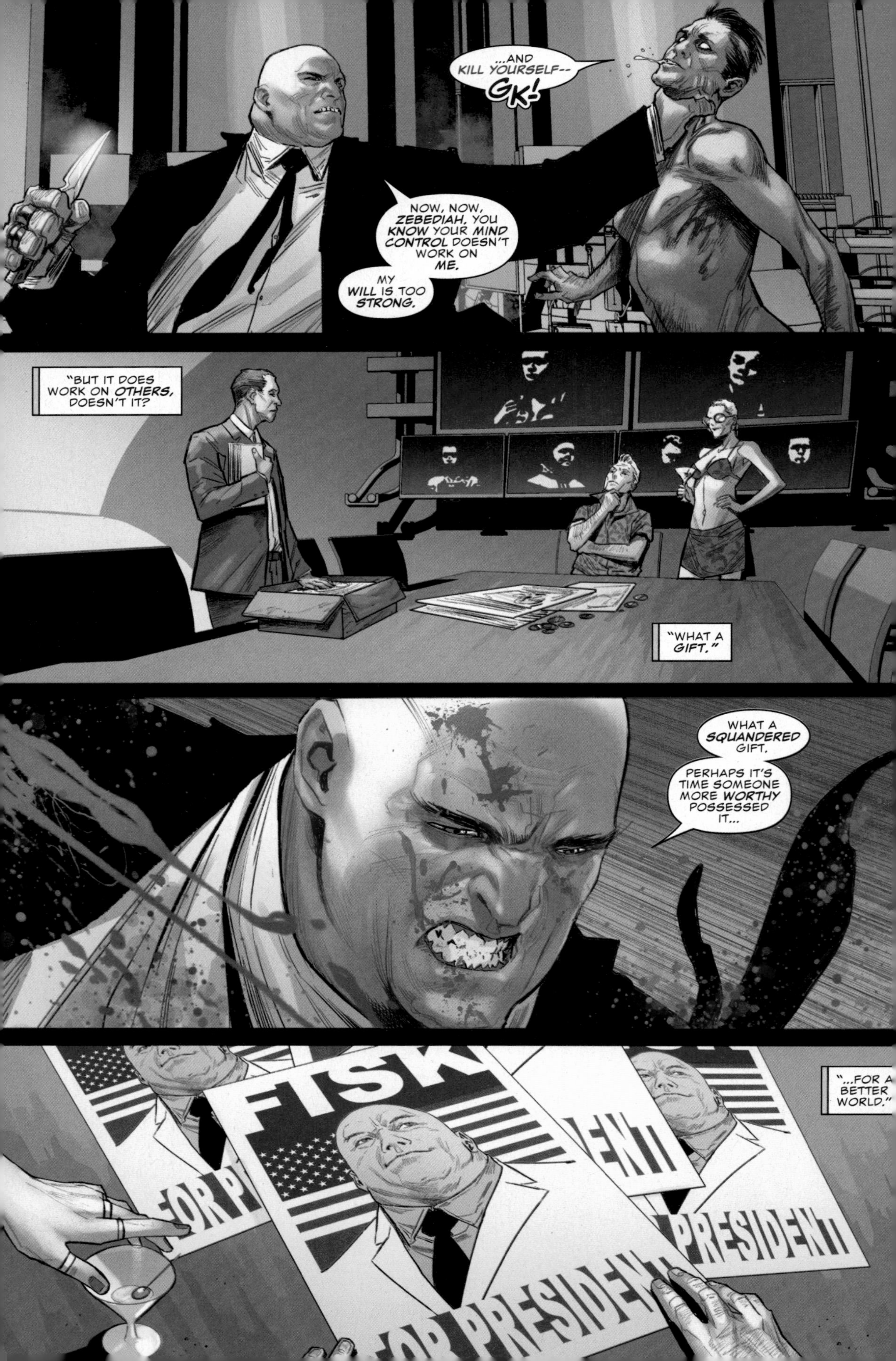
...AND KILL YOURSELF-- GK!
NOW, NOW, ZEBEDIAH, YOU KNOW YOUR MIND CONTROL DOESN'T WORK ON ME.
MY WILL IS TOO STRONG.
"BUT IT DOES WORK ON OTHERS, DOESN'T IT?
"WHAT A GIFT."
WHAT A SQUANDERED GIFT.
PERHAPS IT'S TIME SOMEONE MORE WORTHY POSSESSED IT...
FISK
FOR PRESIDENT
PRESIDENT
"...FOR A BETTER WORLD."

2

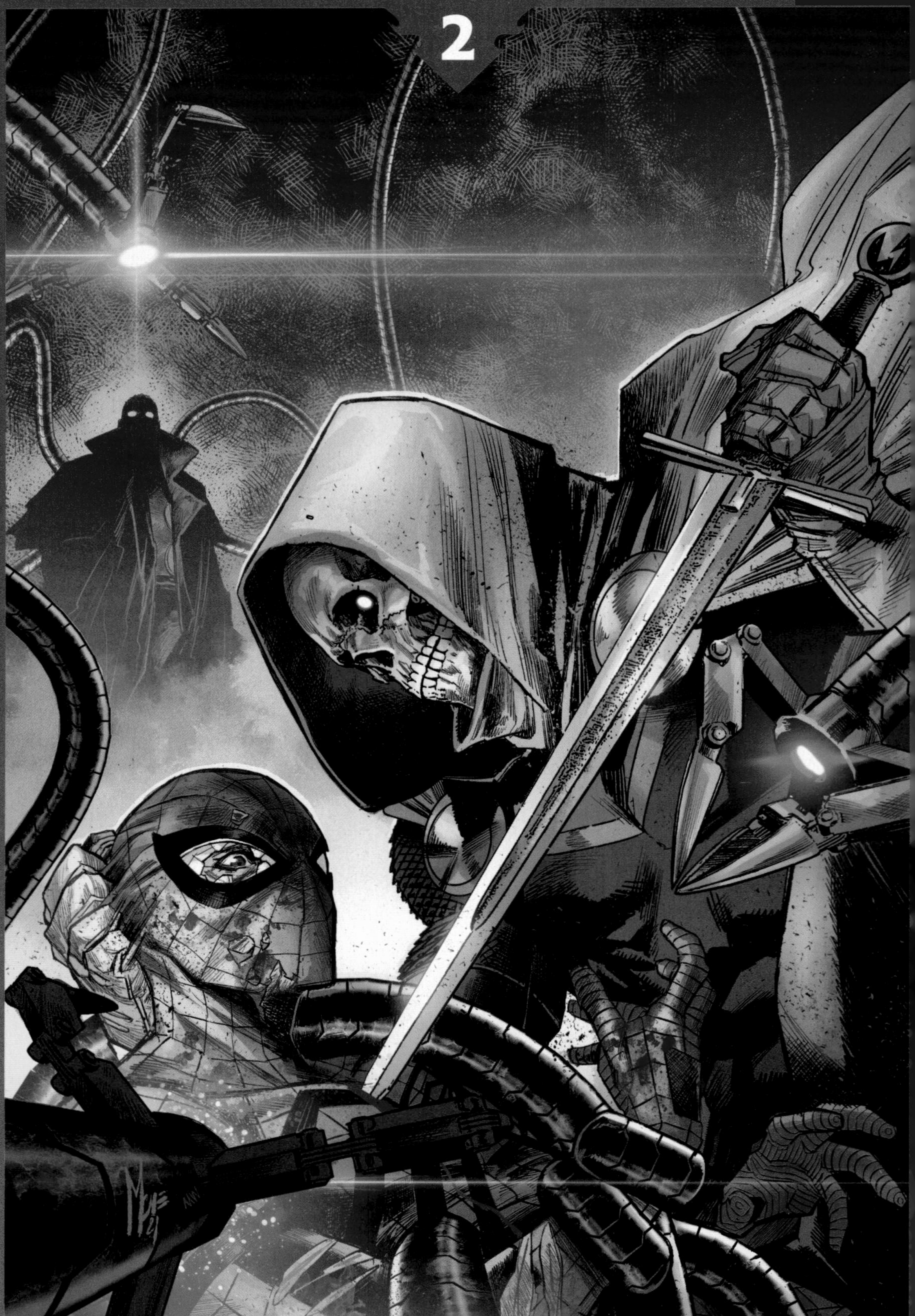

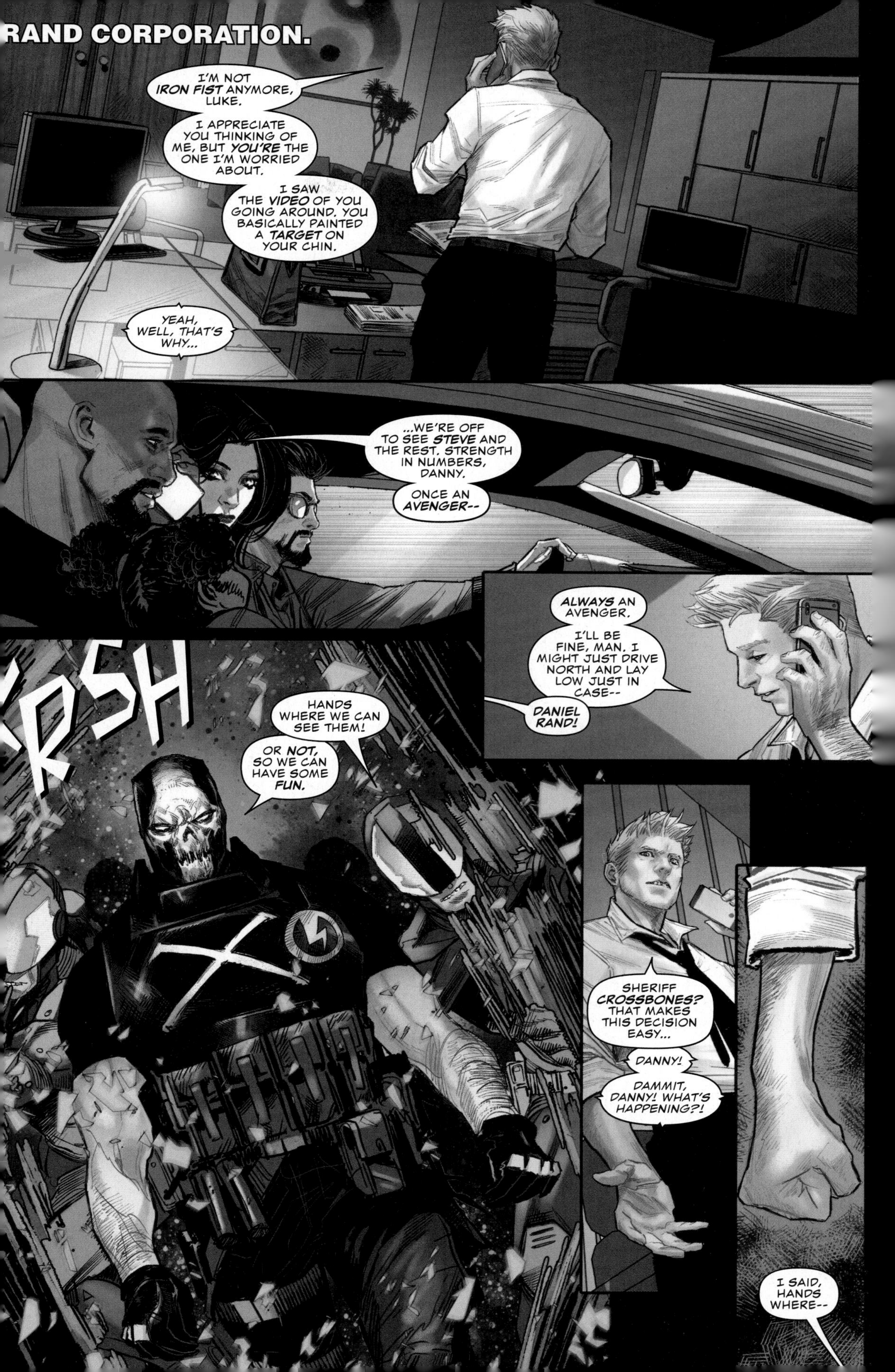
RAND CORPORATION.
I'M NOT IRON FIST ANYMORE, LUKE.
I APPRECIATE YOU THINKING OF ME, BUT YOU'RE THE ONE I'M WORRIED ABOUT.
I SAW THE VIDEO OF YOU GOING AROUND. YOU BASICALLY PAINTED A TARGET ON YOUR CHIN.
YEAH, WELL, THAT'S WHY...
...WE'RE OFF TO SEE STEVE AND THE REST. STRENGTH IN NUMBERS, DANNY.
ONCE AN AVENGER--
ALWAYS AN AVENGER.
I'LL BE FINE, MAN. I MIGHT JUST DRIVE NORTH AND LAY LOW JUST IN CASE--
DANIEL RAND!
KRSH
HANDS WHERE WE CAN SEE THEM!
OR NOT, SO WE CAN HAVE SOME FUN.
SHERIFF CROSSBONES? THAT MAKES THIS DECISION EASY...
DANNY!
DAMMIT, DANNY! WHAT'S HAPPENING?!
I SAID, HANDS WHERE--

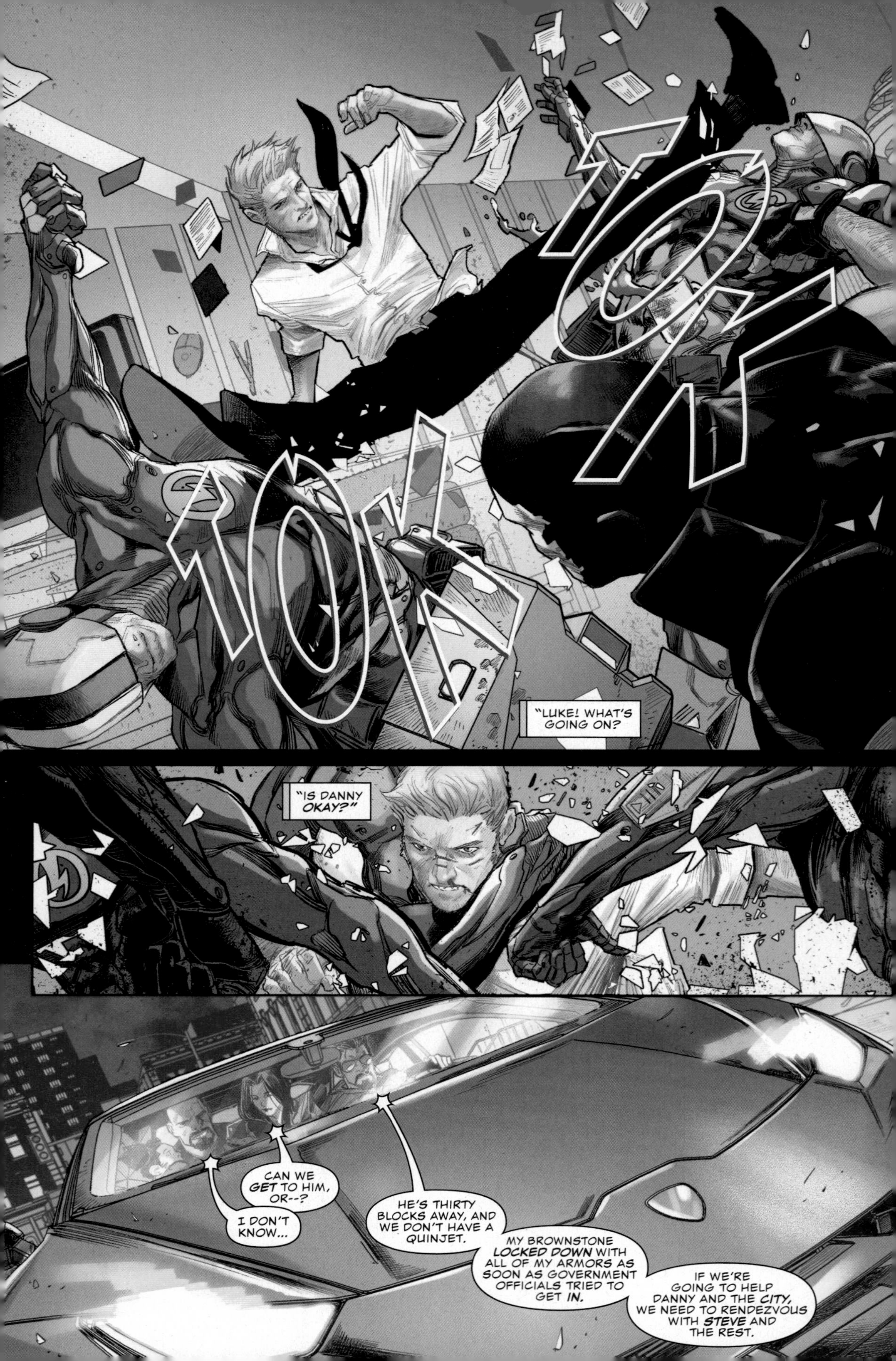
TOK
TOK
"LUKE! WHAT'S GOING ON?
"IS DANNY OKAY?"
CAN WE GET TO HIM, OR--?
I DON'T KNOW...
HE'S THIRTY BLOCKS AWAY, AND WE DON'T HAVE A QUINJET.
MY BROWNSTONE LOCKED DOWN WITH ALL OF MY ARMORS AS SOON AS GOVERNMENT OFFICIALS TRIED TO GET IN.
IF WE'RE GOING TO HELP DANNY AND THE CITY, WE NEED TO RENDEZVOUS WITH STEVE AND THE REST.

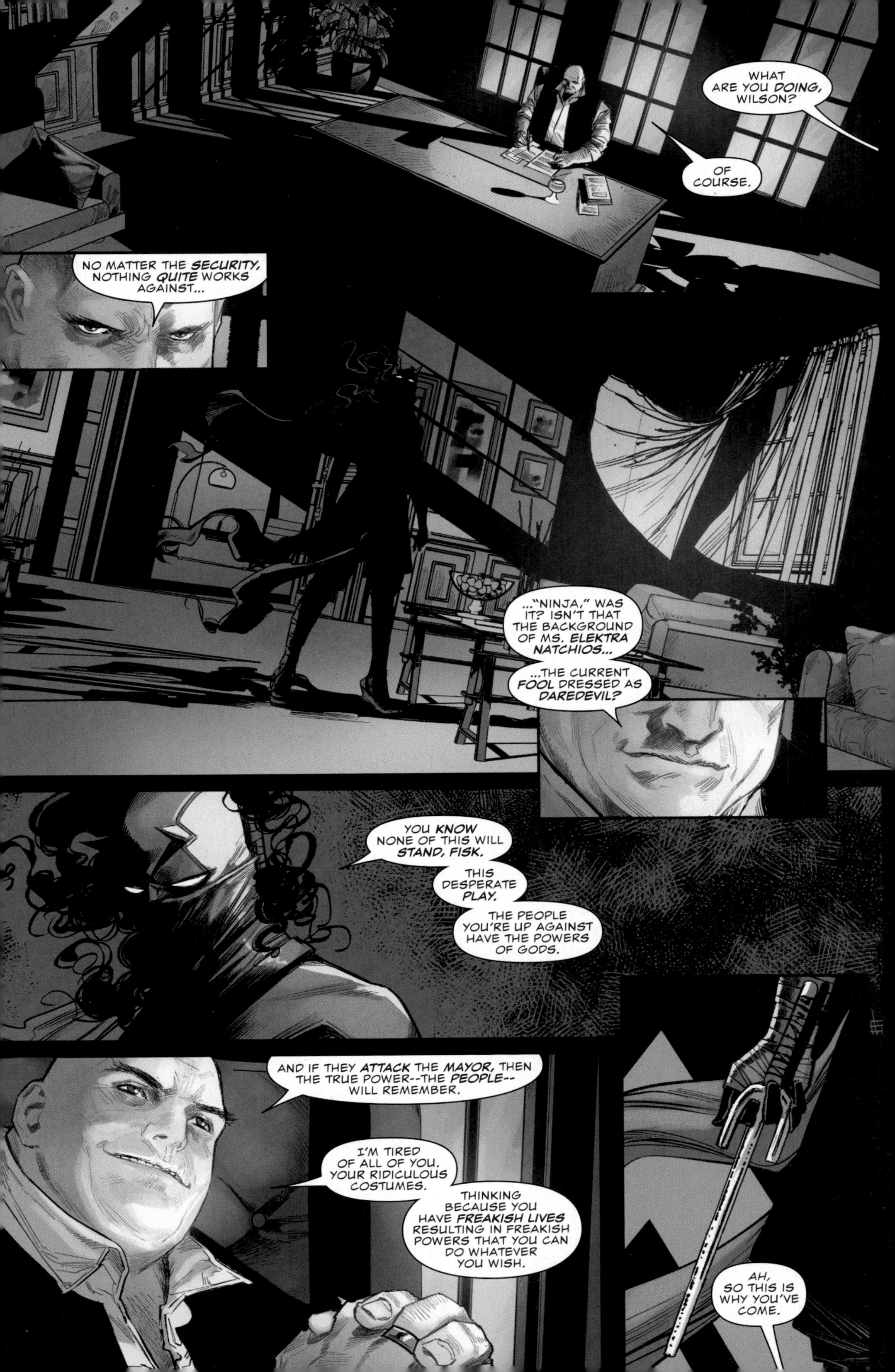
WHAT ARE YOU DOING, WILSON?
OF COURSE.
NO MATTER THE SECURITY, NOTHING QUITE WORKS AGAINST...
..."NINJA," WAS IT? ISN'T THAT THE BACKGROUND OF MS. ELEKTRA NATCHIOS...
...THE CURRENT FOOL DRESSED AS DAREDEVIL?
YOU KNOW NONE OF THIS WILL STAND, FISK.
THIS DESPERATE PLAY.
THE PEOPLE YOU'RE UP AGAINST HAVE THE POWERS OF GODS.
AND IF THEY ATTACK THE MAYOR, THEN THE TRUE POWER--THE PEOPLE--WILL REMEMBER.
I'M TIRED OF ALL OF YOU. YOUR RIDICULOUS COSTUMES.
THINKING BECAUSE YOU HAVE FREAKISH LIVES RESULTING IN FREAKISH POWERS THAT YOU CAN DO WHATEVER YOU WISH.
AH, SO THIS IS WHY YOU'VE COME.

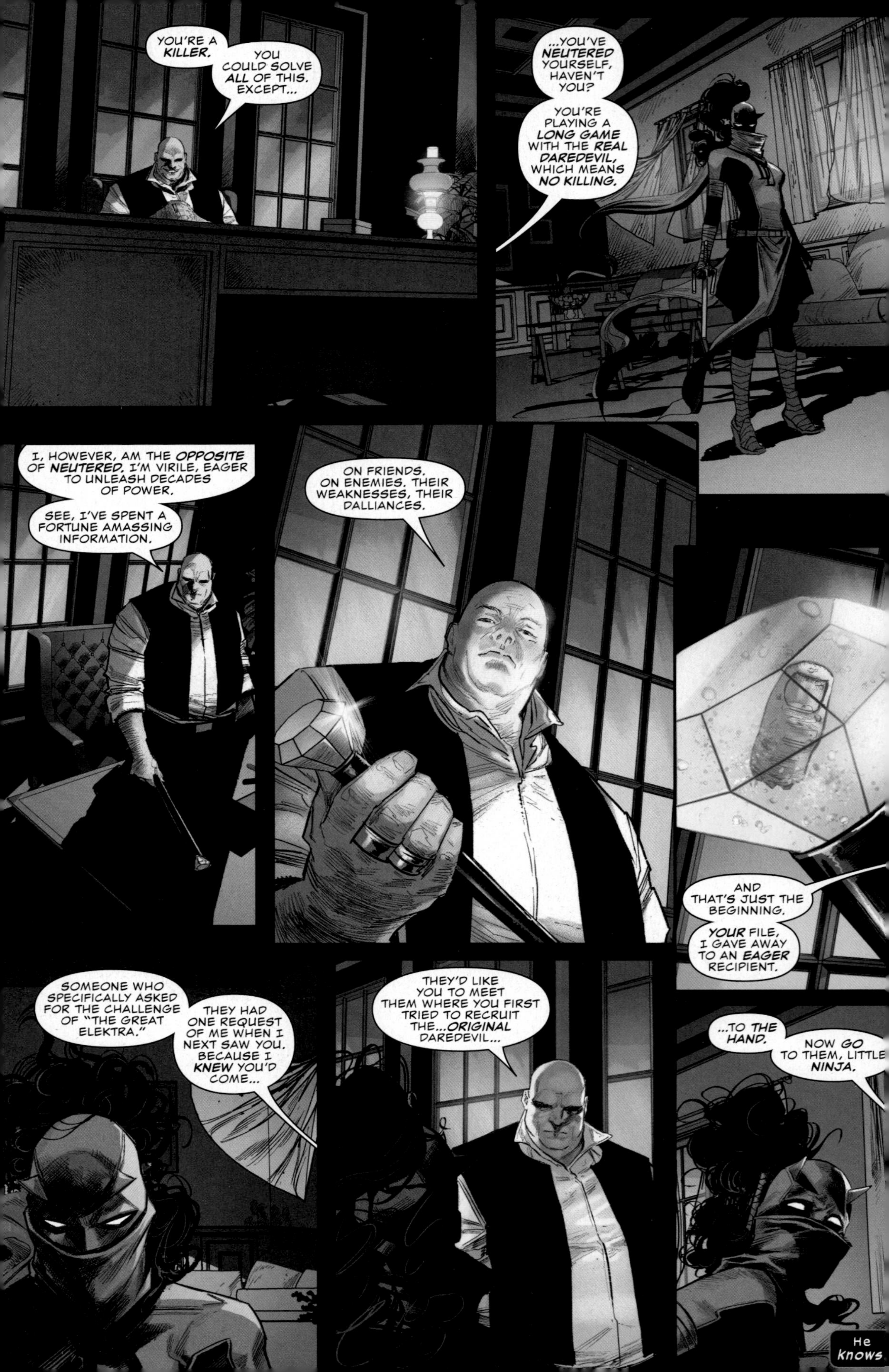
YOU'RE A KILLER.
YOU COULD SOLVE ALL OF THIS. EXCEPT...
...YOU'VE NEUTERED YOURSELF, HAVEN'T YOU?
YOU'RE PLAYING A LONG GAME WITH THE REAL DAREDEVIL, WHICH MEANS NO KILLING.
I, HOWEVER, AM THE OPPOSITE OF NEUTERED. I'M VIRILE, EAGER TO UNLEASH DECADES OF POWER.
SEE, I'VE SPENT A FORTUNE AMASSING INFORMATION.
ON FRIENDS. ON ENEMIES. THEIR WEAKNESSES, THEIR DALLIANCES.
AND THAT'S JUST THE BEGINNING.
YOUR FILE, I GAVE AWAY TO AN EAGER RECIPIENT.
SOMEONE WHO SPECIFICALLY ASKED FOR THE CHALLENGE OF "THE GREAT ELEKTRA."
THEY HAD ONE REQUEST OF ME WHEN I NEXT SAW YOU. BECAUSE I KNEW YOU'D COME...
THEY'D LIKE YOU TO MEET THEM WHERE YOU FIRST TRIED TO RECRUIT THE...ORIGINAL DAREDEVIL...
...TO THE HAND.
NOW GO TO THEM, LITTLE NINJA.
He knows

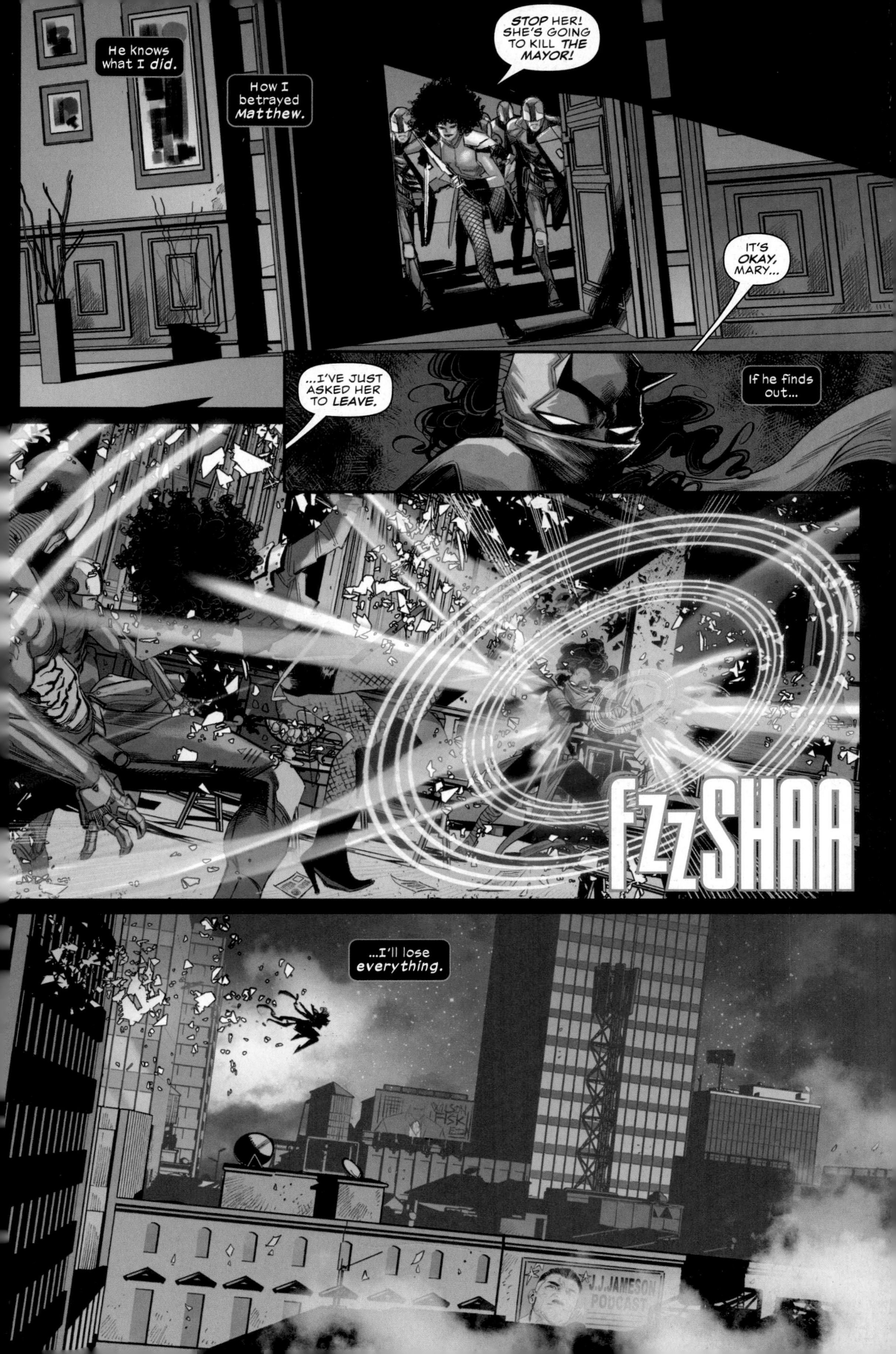
He knows what I did.
How I betrayed Matthew.
STOP HER! SHE'S GOING TO KILL THE MAYOR!
IT'S OKAY, MARY...
...I'VE JUST ASKED HER TO LEAVE.
If he finds out...
FZZSHAA
...I'll lose everything.
J.J. JAMESON PODCAST

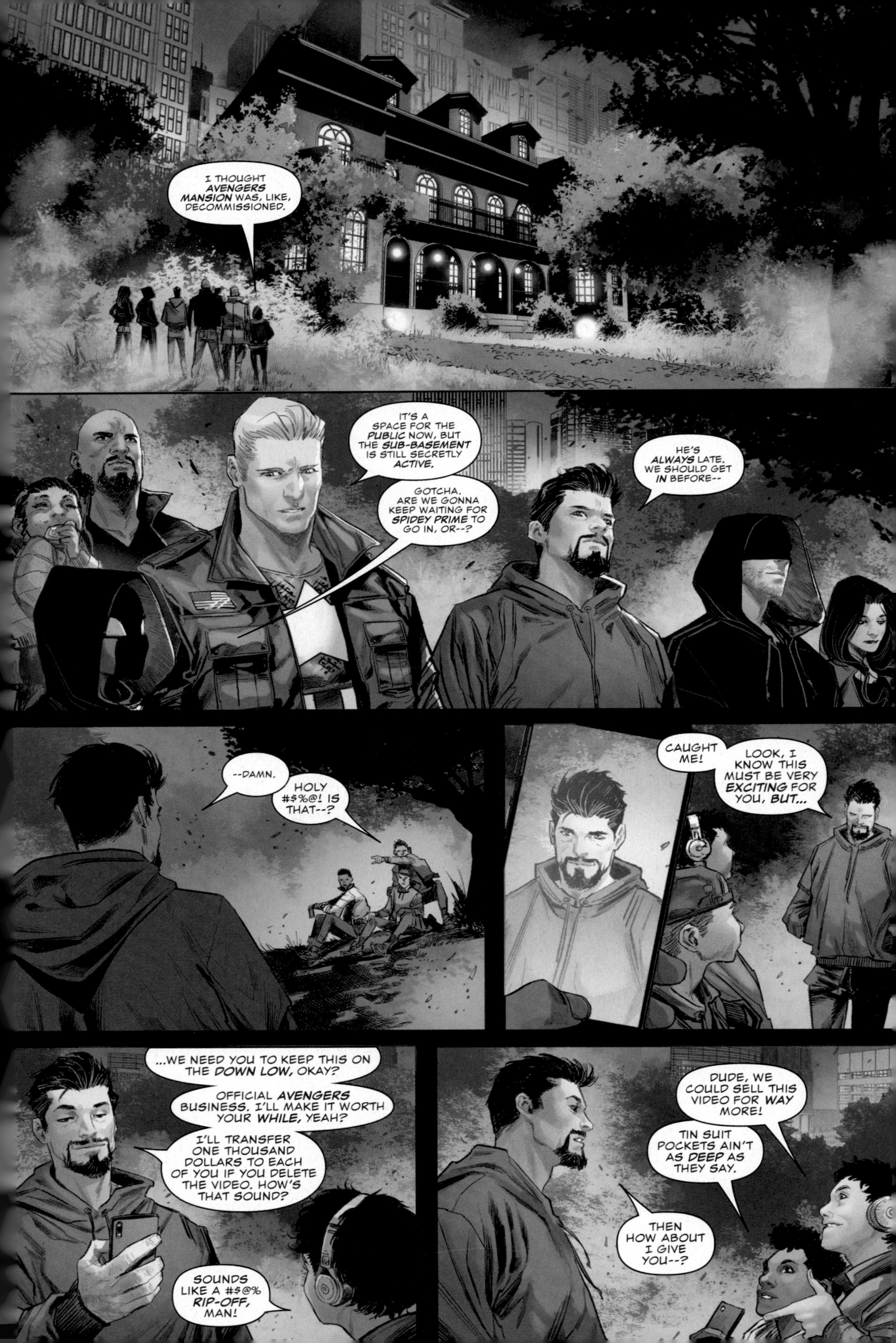
I THOUGHT AVENGERS MANSION WAS, LIKE, DECOMMISSIONED.
IT'S A SPACE FOR THE PUBLIC NOW, BUT THE SUB-BASEMENT IS STILL SECRETLY ACTIVE.
GOTCHA. ARE WE GONNA KEEP WAITING FOR SPIDEY PRIME TO GO IN, OR--?
HE'S ALWAYS LATE. WE SHOULD GET IN BEFORE--
--DAMN.
HOLY #$%@! IS THAT--?
CAUGHT ME!
LOOK, I KNOW THIS MUST BE VERY EXCITING FOR YOU, BUT...
...WE NEED YOU TO KEEP THIS ON THE DOWN LOW, OKAY?
OFFICIAL AVENGERS BUSINESS. I'LL MAKE IT WORTH YOUR WHILE, YEAH?
I'LL TRANSFER ONE THOUSAND DOLLARS TO EACH OF YOU IF YOU DELETE THE VIDEO. HOW'S THAT SOUND?
SOUNDS LIKE A #$@% RIP-OFF, MAN!
DUDE, WE COULD SELL THIS VIDEO FOR WAY MORE!
TIN SUIT POCKETS AIN'T AS DEEP AS THEY SAY.
THEN HOW ABOUT I GIVE YOU--?

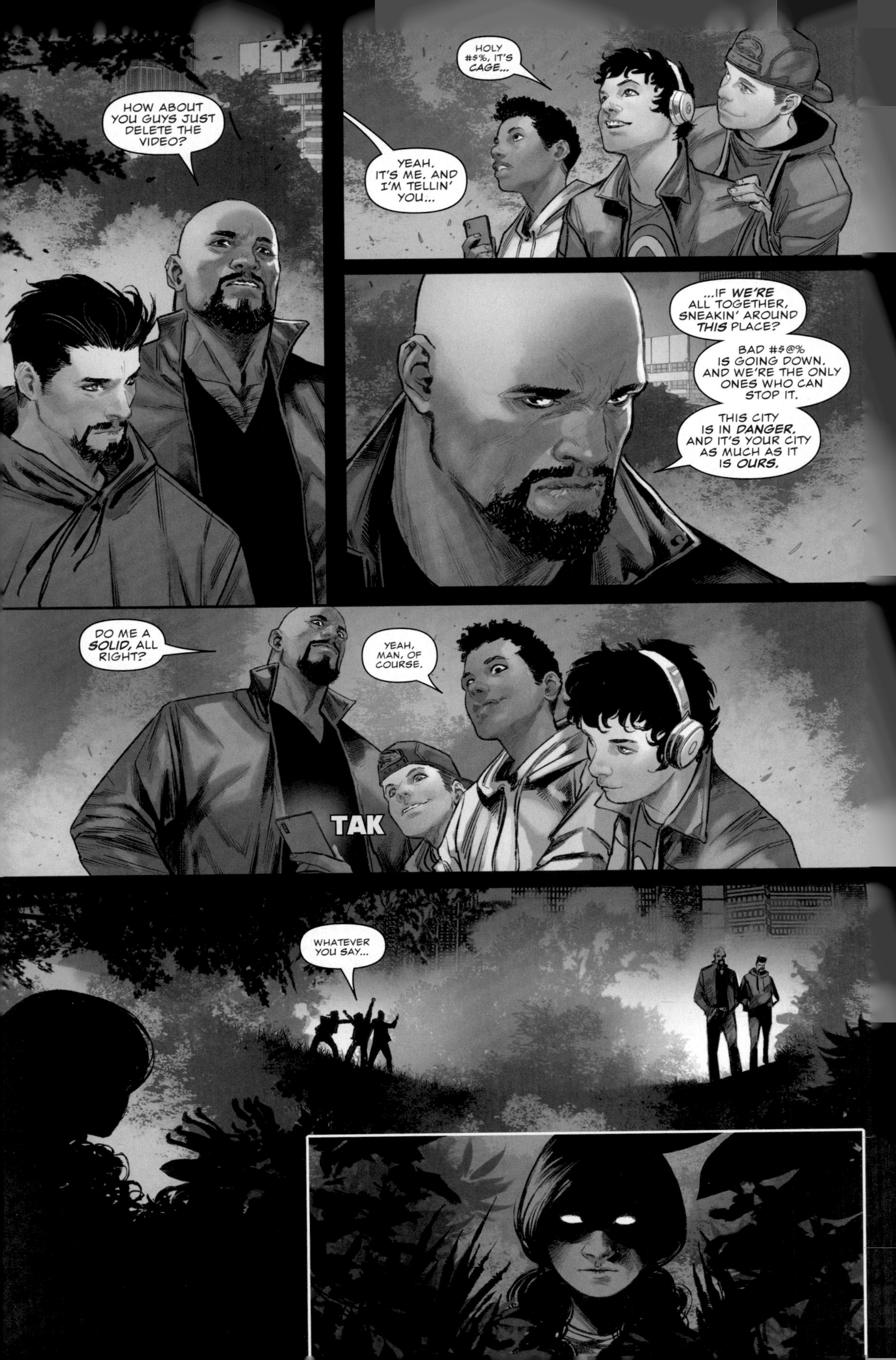
HOW ABOUT YOU GUYS JUST DELETE THE VIDEO?
HOLY #$%, IT'S CAGE...
YEAH, IT'S ME. AND I'M TELLIN' YOU...
...IF WE'RE ALL TOGETHER, SNEAKIN' AROUND THIS PLACE?
BAD #$@% IS GOING DOWN. AND WE'RE THE ONLY ONES WHO CAN STOP IT.
THIS CITY IS IN DANGER. AND IT'S YOUR CITY AS MUCH AS IT IS OURS.
DO ME A SOLID, ALL RIGHT?
YEAH, MAN, OF COURSE.
TAK
WHATEVER YOU SAY...

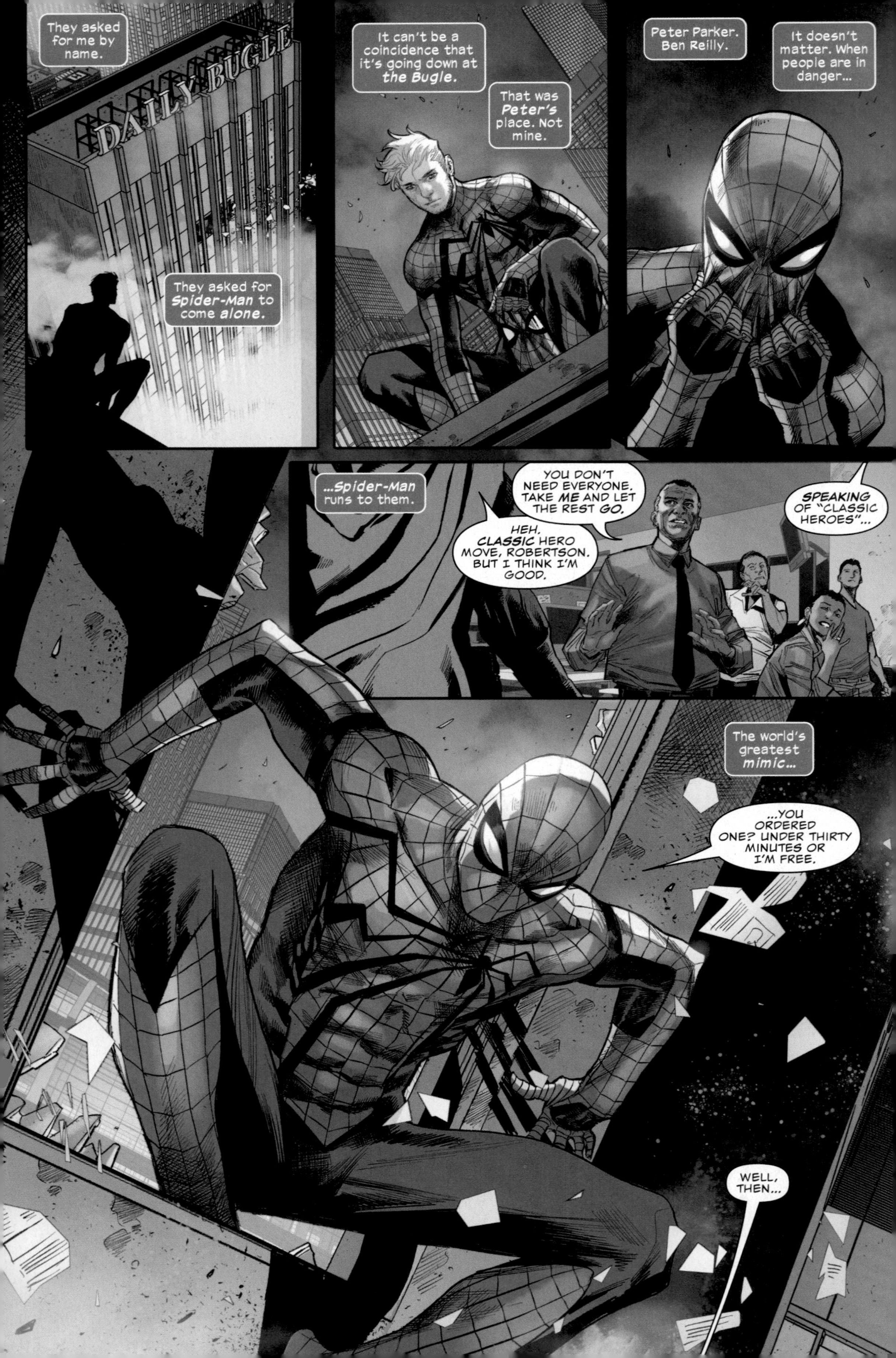

They asked for me by name.
They asked for Spider-Man to come alone.
It can't be a coincidence that it's going down at the Bugle.
That was Peter's place. Not mine.
Peter Parker. Ben Reilly.
It doesn't matter. When people are in danger...
DAILY BUGLE
...Spider-Man runs to them.
YOU DON'T NEED EVERYONE. TAKE ME AND LET THE REST GO.
HEH. CLASSIC HERO MOVE, ROBERTSON. BUT I THINK I'M GOOD.
SPEAKING OF "CLASSIC HEROES"...
The world's greatest mimic...
...YOU ORDERED ONE? UNDER THIRTY MINUTES OR I'M FREE.
WELL, THEN...

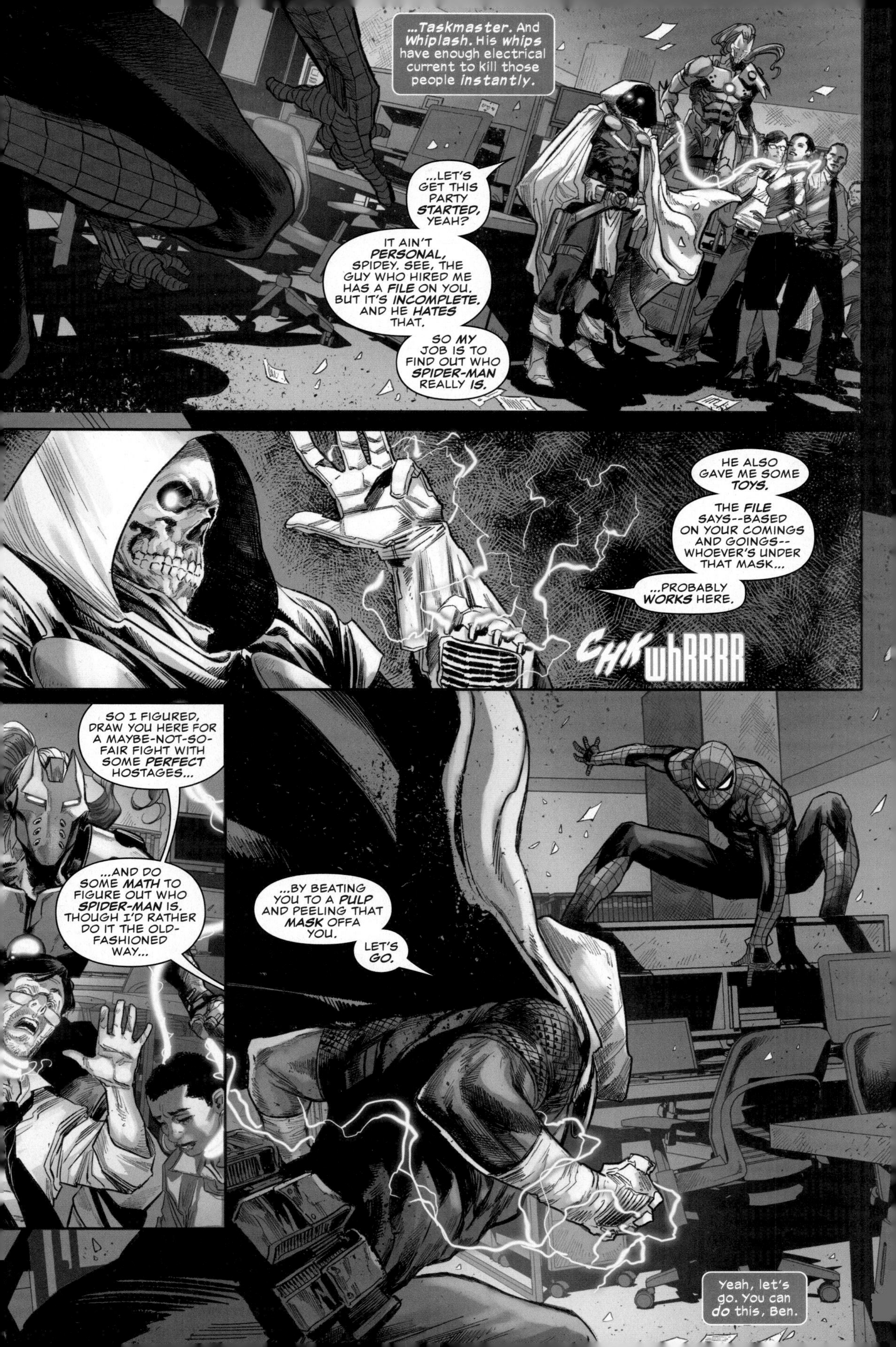
...Taskmaster. And Whiplash. His whips have enough electrical current to kill those people instantly.
...LET'S GET THIS PARTY STARTED, YEAH?
IT AIN'T PERSONAL, SPIDEY. SEE, THE GUY WHO HIRED ME HAS A FILE ON YOU. BUT IT'S INCOMPLETE, AND HE HATES THAT.
SO MY JOB IS TO FIND OUT WHO SPIDER-MAN REALLY IS.
HE ALSO GAVE ME SOME TOYS.
THE FILE SAYS--BASED ON YOUR COMINGS AND GOINGS--WHOEVER'S UNDER THAT MASK...
...PROBABLY WORKS HERE.
CHK whRRRR
SO I FIGURED, DRAW YOU HERE FOR A MAYBE-NOT-SO-FAIR FIGHT WITH SOME PERFECT HOSTAGES...
...AND DO SOME MATH TO FIGURE OUT WHO SPIDER-MAN IS. THOUGH I'D RATHER DO IT THE OLD-FASHIONED WAY...
...BY BEATING YOU TO A PULP AND PEELING THAT MASK OFFA YOU.
LET'S GO.
Yeah, let's go. You can do this, Ben.

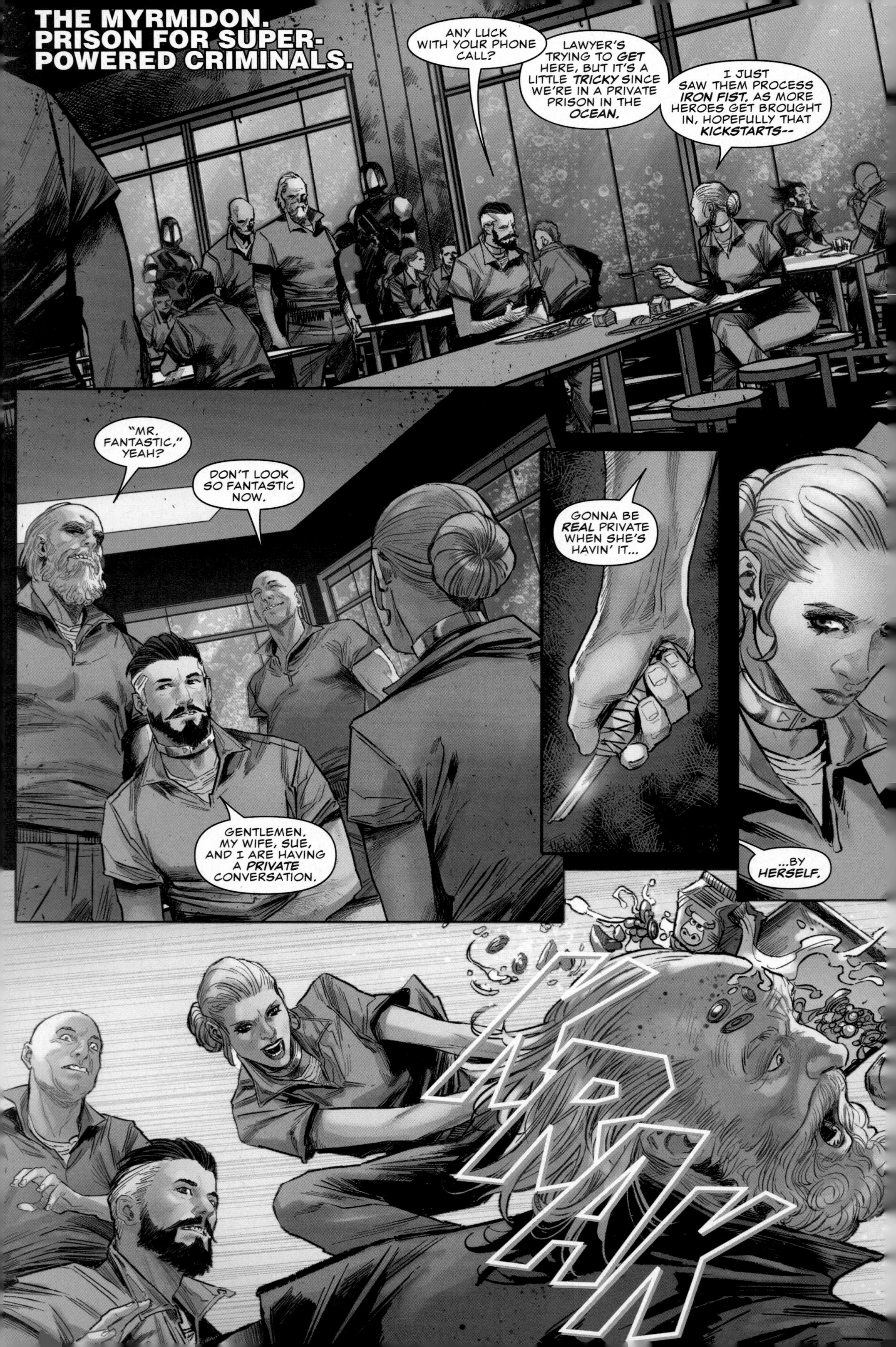
THE MYRMIDON. PRISON FOR SUPER-POWERED CRIMINALS.
ANY LUCK WITH YOUR PHONE CALL?
LAWYER'S TRYING TO GET HERE, BUT IT'S A LITTLE TRICKY SINCE WE'RE IN A PRIVATE PRISON IN THE OCEAN.
I JUST SAW THEM PROCESS IRON FIST. AS MORE HEROES GET BROUGHT IN, HOPEFULLY THAT KICKSTARTS--
"MR. FANTASTIC," YEAH?
DON'T LOOK SO FANTASTIC NOW.
GENTLEMEN. MY WIFE, SUE, AND I ARE HAVING A PRIVATE CONVERSATION.
GONNA BE REAL PRIVATE WHEN SHE'S HAVIN' IT...
...BY HERSELF.

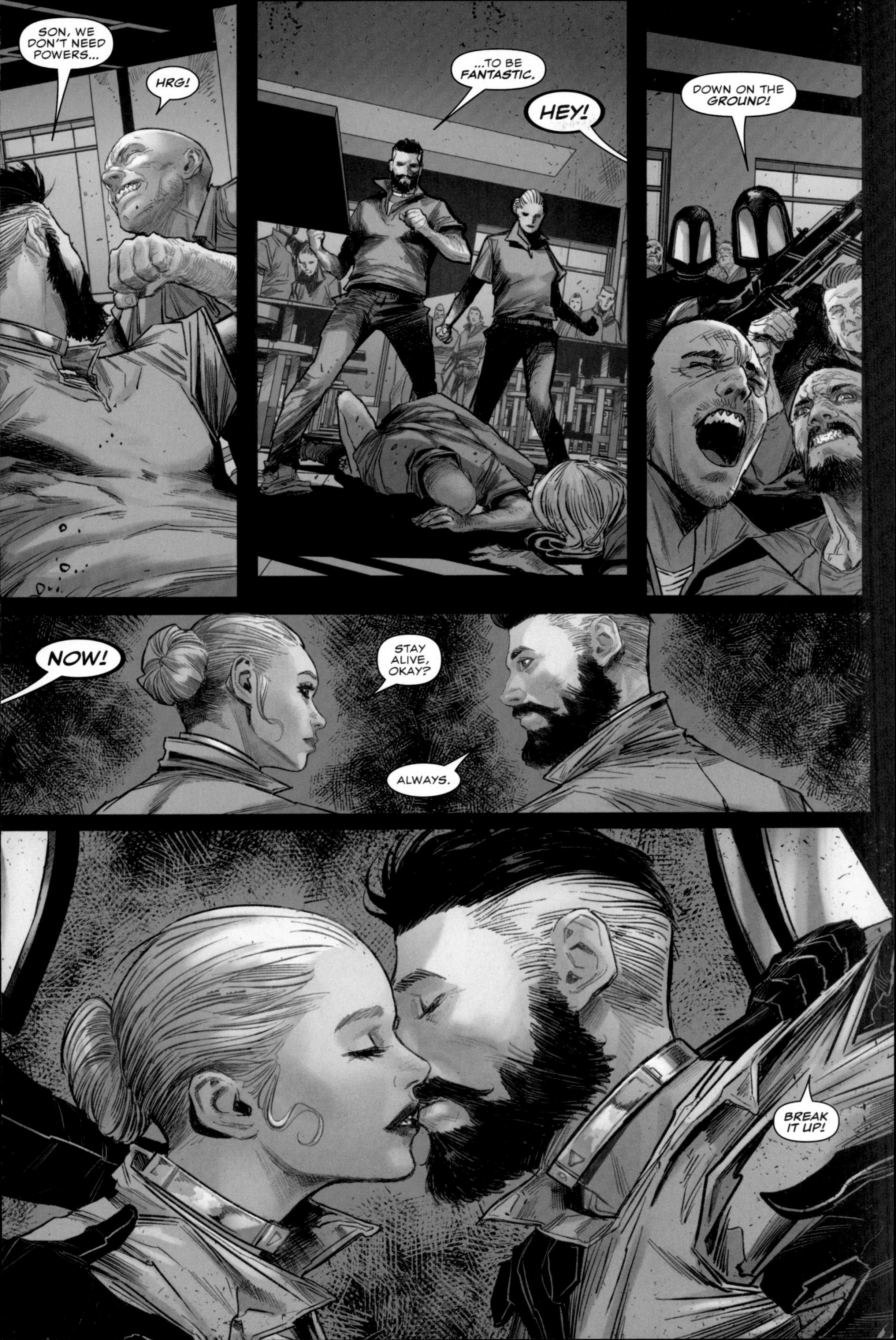
SON, WE DON'T NEED POWERS...
HRG!
...TO BE FANTASTIC.
HEY!
DOWN ON THE GROUND!
NOW!
STAY ALIVE, OKAY?
ALWAYS.
BREAK IT UP!

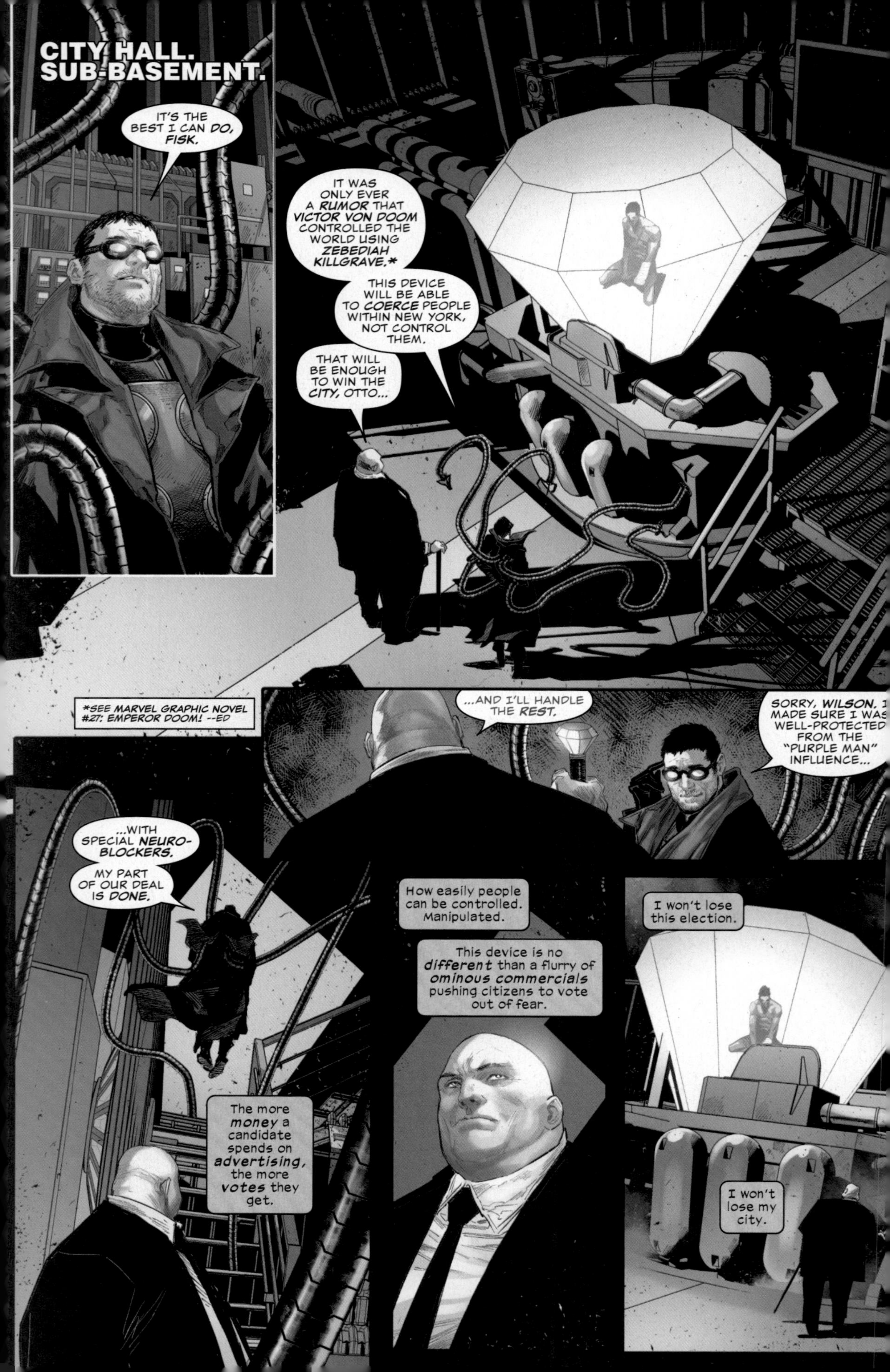
CITY HALL. SUB-BASEMENT.
IT'S THE BEST I CAN DO, FISK.
IT WAS ONLY EVER A RUMOR THAT VICTOR VON DOOM CONTROLLED THE WORLD USING ZEBEDIAH KILLGRAVE.*
THIS DEVICE WILL BE ABLE TO COERCE PEOPLE WITHIN NEW YORK, NOT CONTROL THEM.
THAT WILL BE ENOUGH TO WIN THE CITY, OTTO...
*SEE MARVEL GRAPHIC NOVEL #27: EMPEROR DOOM! --ED
...AND I'LL HANDLE THE REST.
SORRY, WILSON. I MADE SURE I WAS WELL-PROTECTED FROM THE "PURPLE MAN" INFLUENCE...
...WITH SPECIAL NEURO-BLOCKERS.
MY PART OF OUR DEAL IS DONE.
The more money a candidate spends on advertising, the more votes they get.
How easily people can be controlled. Manipulated.
This device is no different than a flurry of ominous commercials pushing citizens to vote out of fear.
I won't lose this election.
I won't lose my city.

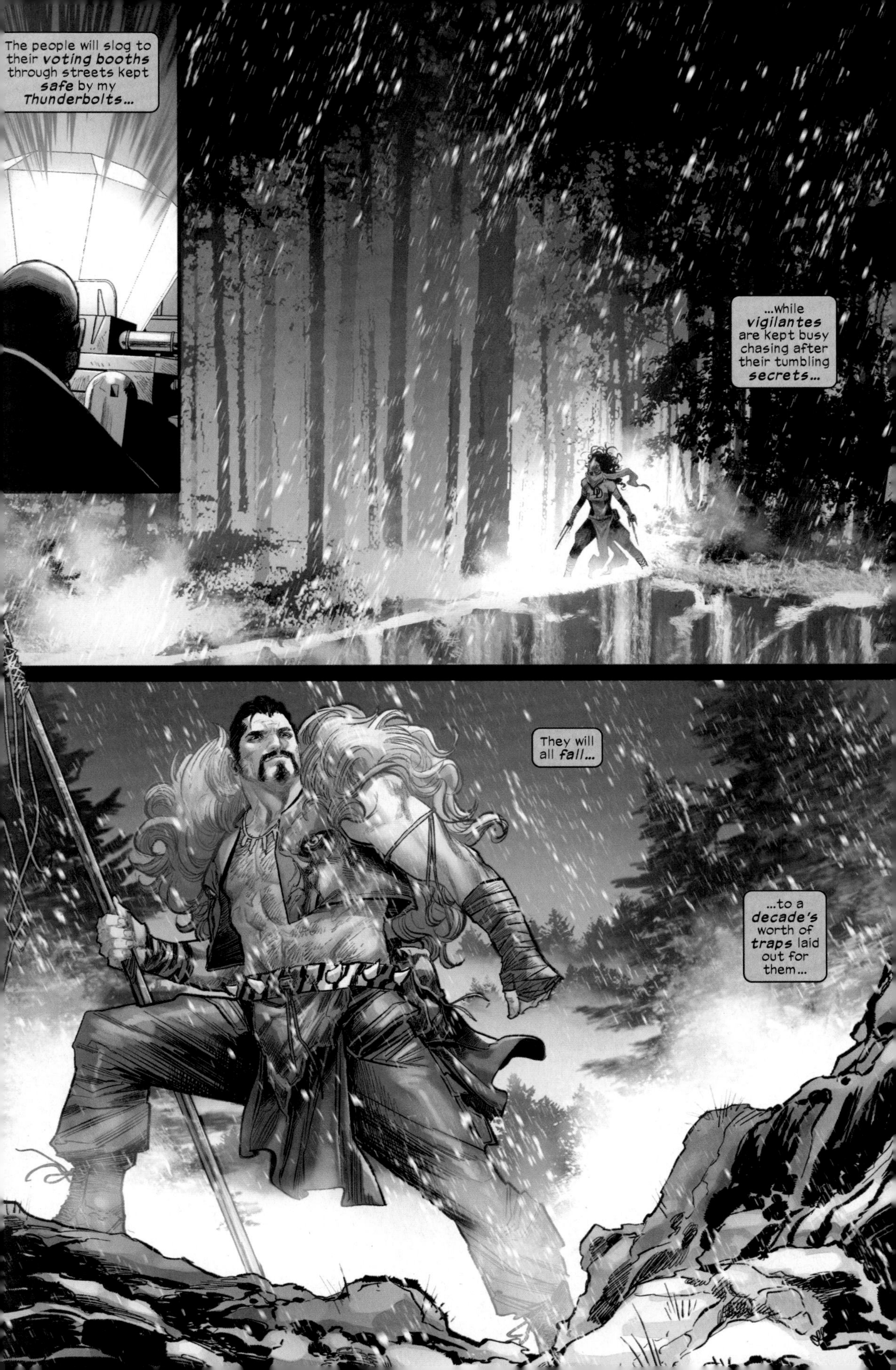
The people will slog to their *voting booths* through streets kept *safe* by my *Thunderbolts*...
...while *vigilantes* are kept busy chasing after their tumbling *secrets*...
They will all *fall*...
...to a *decade's* worth of *traps* laid out for them...

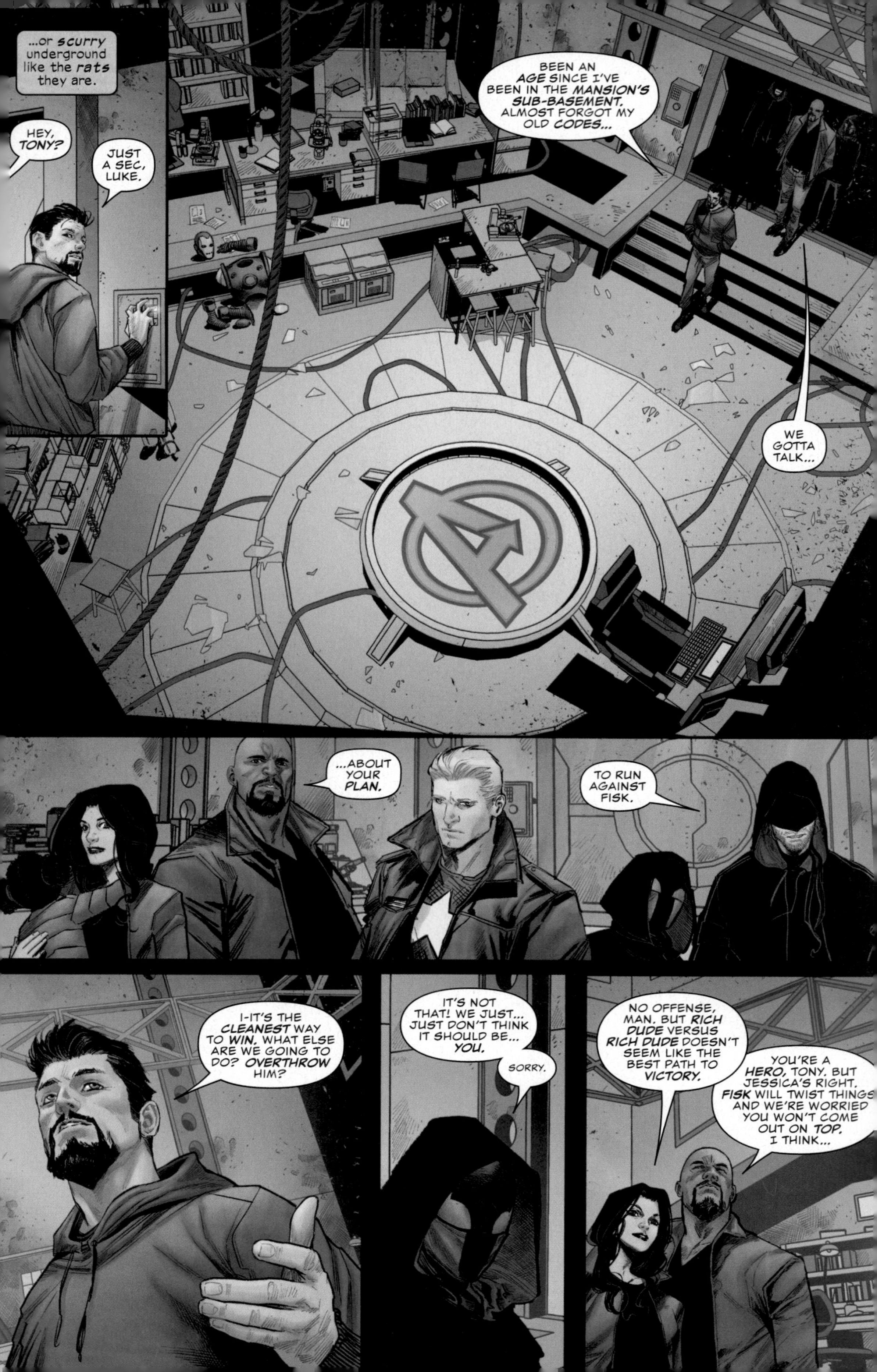
...or scurry underground like the rats they are.
HEY, TONY?
JUST A SEC, LUKE.
BEEN AN AGE SINCE I'VE BEEN IN THE MANSION'S SUB-BASEMENT. ALMOST FORGOT MY OLD CODES...
WE GOTTA TALK...
...ABOUT YOUR PLAN.
TO RUN AGAINST FISK.
I-IT'S THE CLEANEST WAY TO WIN. WHAT ELSE ARE WE GOING TO DO? OVERTHROW HIM?
IT'S NOT THAT! WE JUST... JUST DON'T THINK IT SHOULD BE... YOU.
SORRY.
NO OFFENSE, MAN. BUT RICH DUDE VERSUS RICH DUDE DOESN'T SEEM LIKE THE BEST PATH TO VICTORY.
YOU'RE A HERO, TONY. BUT JESSICA'S RIGHT. FISK WILL TWIST THINGS AND WE'RE WORRIED YOU WON'T COME OUT ON TOP. I THINK...

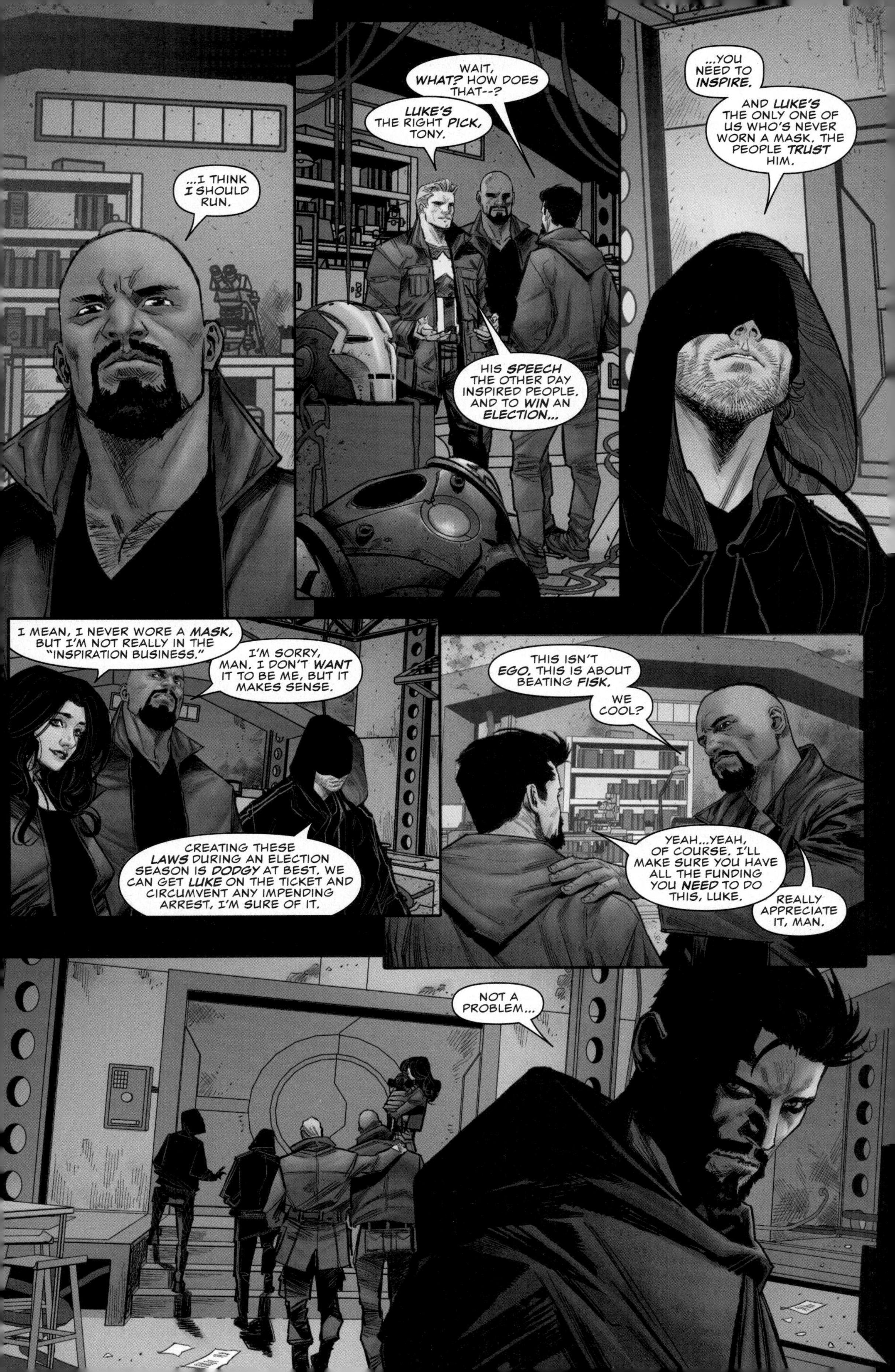

...I THINK I SHOULD RUN.
WAIT, WHAT? HOW DOES THAT--?
LUKE'S THE RIGHT PICK, TONY.
HIS SPEECH THE OTHER DAY INSPIRED PEOPLE. AND TO WIN AN ELECTION...
...YOU NEED TO INSPIRE.
AND LUKE'S THE ONLY ONE OF US WHO'S NEVER WORN A MASK. THE PEOPLE TRUST HIM.
I MEAN, I NEVER WORE A MASK, BUT I'M NOT REALLY IN THE "INSPIRATION BUSINESS."
I'M SORRY, MAN. I DON'T WANT IT TO BE ME, BUT IT MAKES SENSE.
CREATING THESE LAWS DURING AN ELECTION SEASON IS DODGY AT BEST. WE CAN GET LUKE ON THE TICKET AND CIRCUMVENT ANY IMPENDING ARREST, I'M SURE OF IT.
THIS ISN'T EGO. THIS IS ABOUT BEATING FISK.
WE COOL?
YEAH...YEAH, OF COURSE. I'LL MAKE SURE YOU HAVE ALL THE FUNDING YOU NEED TO DO THIS, LUKE.
REALLY APPRECIATE IT, MAN.
NOT A PROBLEM...

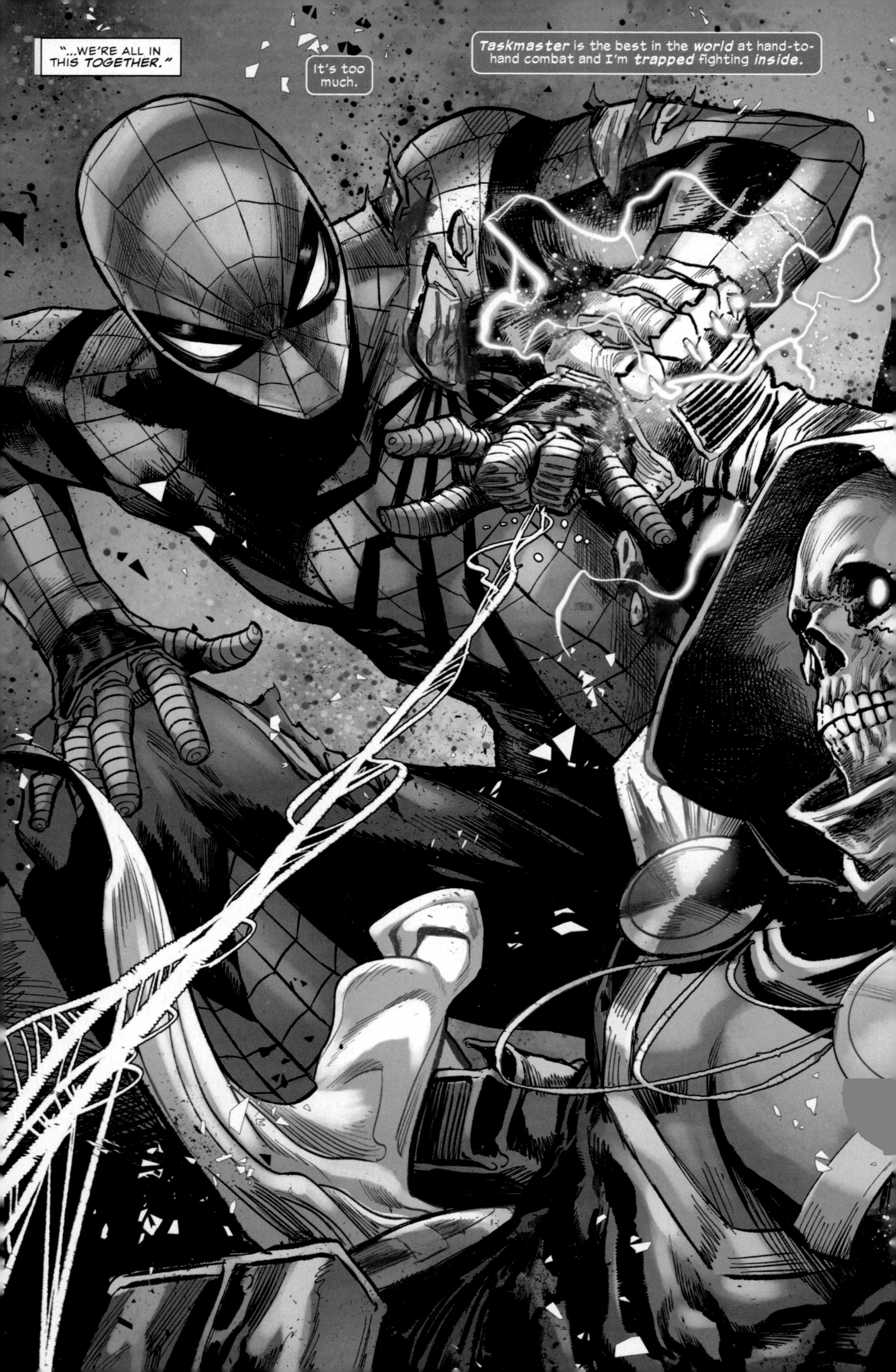
"...WE'RE ALL IN THIS TOGETHER."
It's too much.
Taskmaster is the best in the world at hand-to-hand combat and I'm trapped fighting inside.

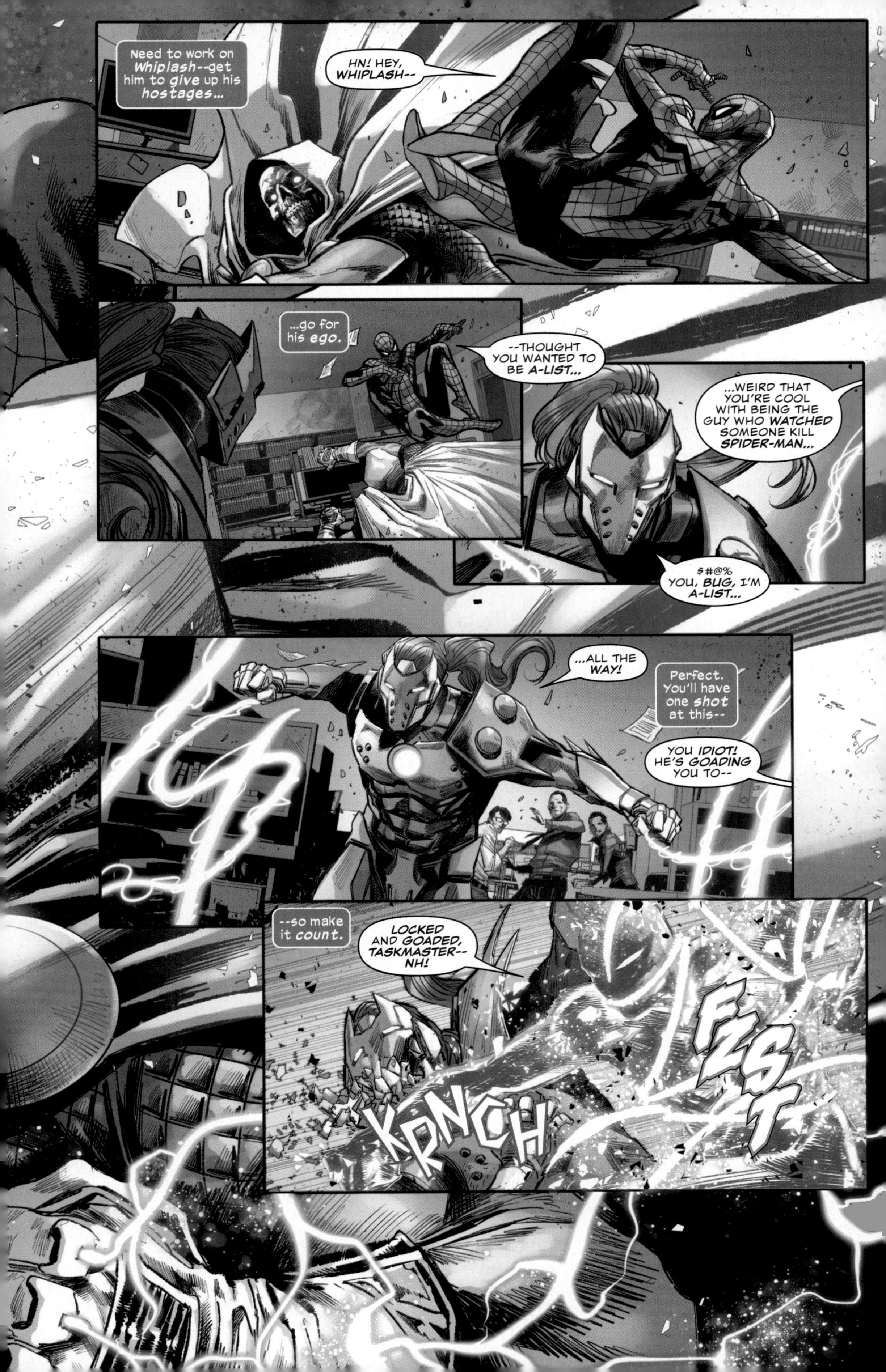

Need to work on Whiplash--get him to give up his hostages...
HN! HEY, WHIPLASH--
...go for his ego.
--THOUGHT YOU WANTED TO BE A-LIST...
...WEIRD THAT YOU'RE COOL WITH BEING THE GUY WHO WATCHED SOMEONE KILL SPIDER-MAN...
$#@% YOU, BUG, I'M A-LIST...
...ALL THE WAY!
Perfect. You'll have one shot at this--
YOU IDIOT! HE'S GOADING YOU TO--
--so make it count.
LOCKED AND GOADED, TASKMASTER--NH!
FZST
KRNCH

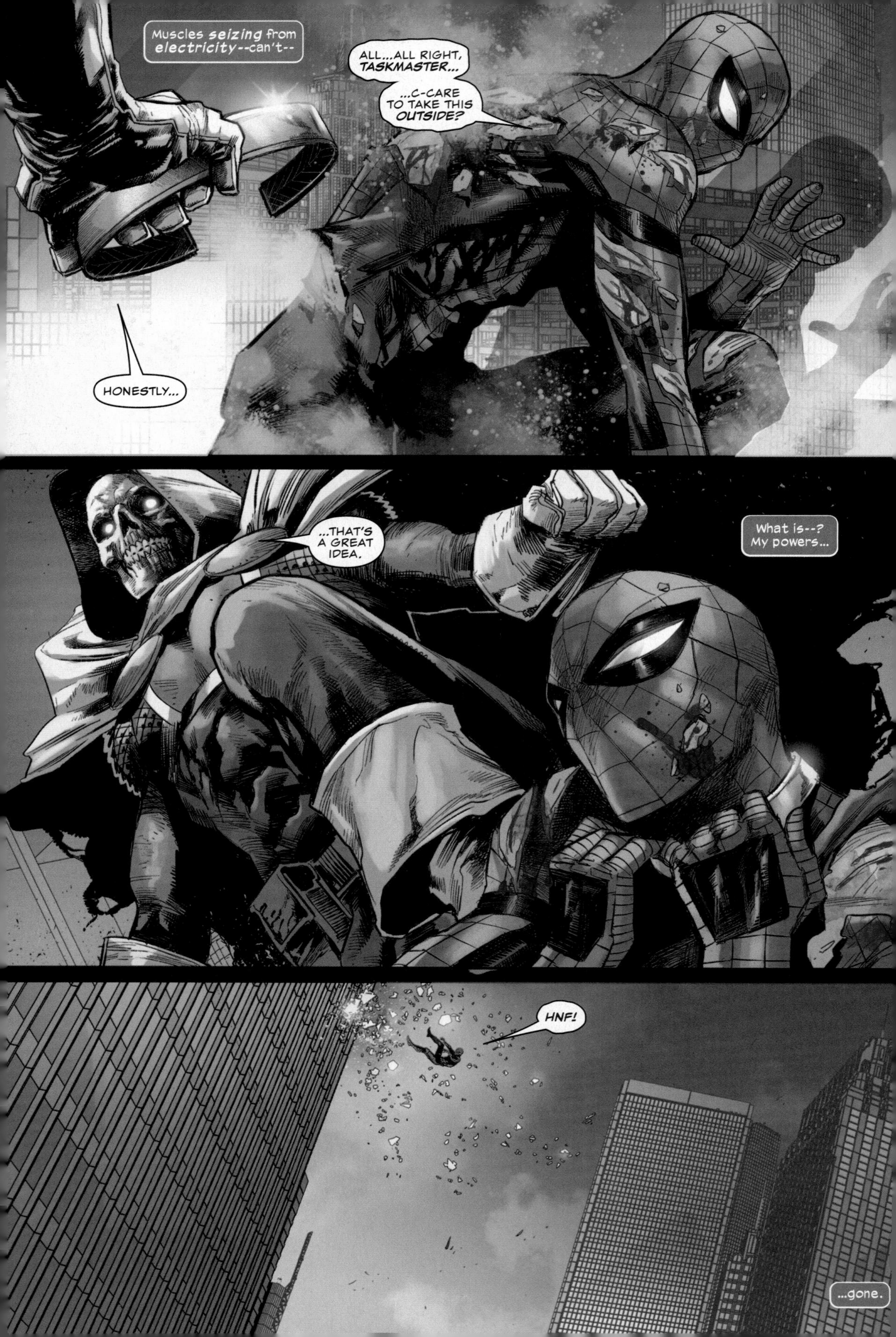
Muscles seizing from electricity--can't--
ALL...ALL RIGHT, TASKMASTER...
...C-CARE TO TAKE THIS OUTSIDE?
HONESTLY...
...THAT'S A GREAT IDEA.
What is--? My powers...
HNF!
...gone.

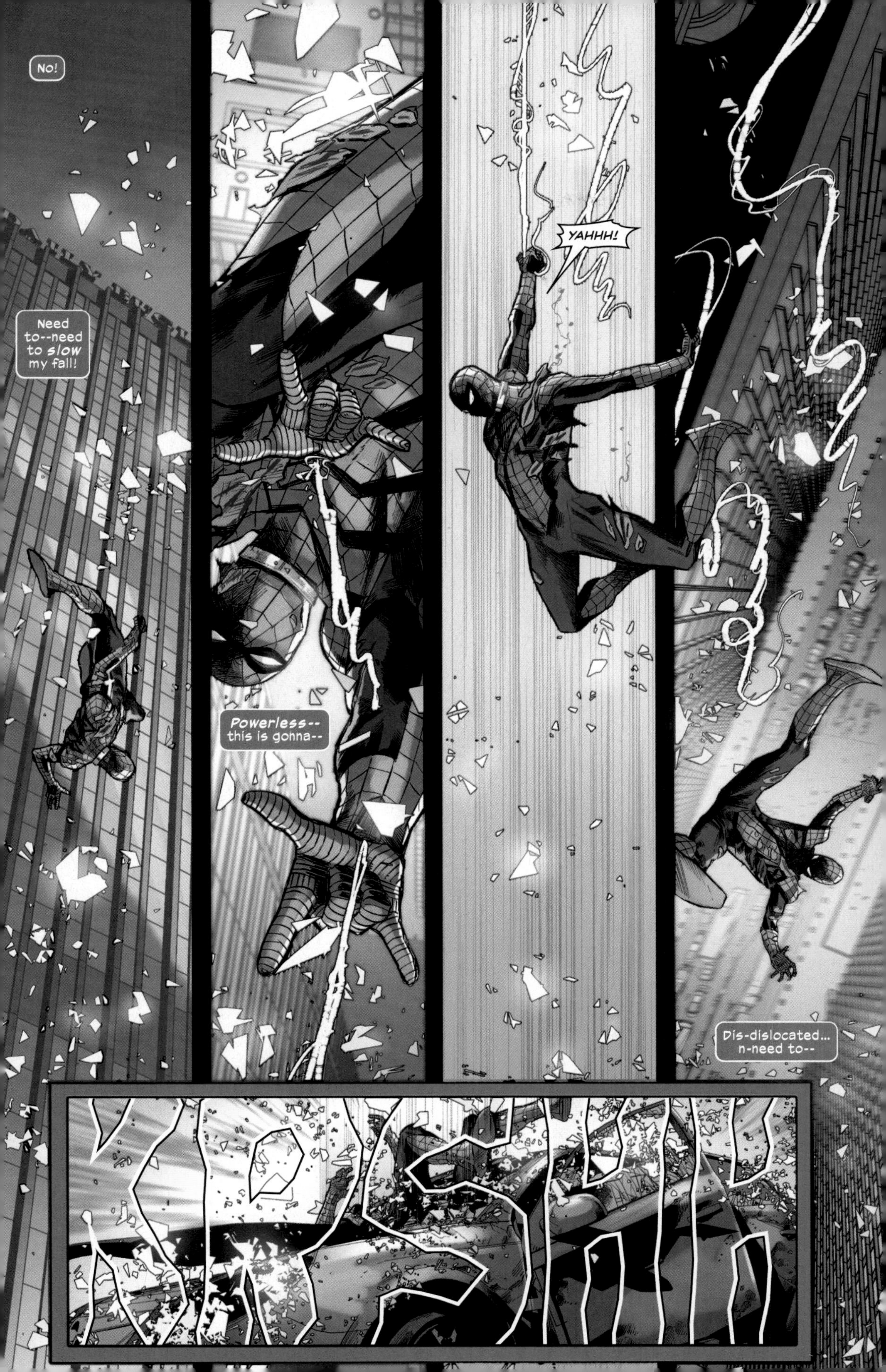
No!
Need to--need to *slow* my fall!
Powerless--this is gonna--
YAHHH!
Dis-dislocated... n-need to--

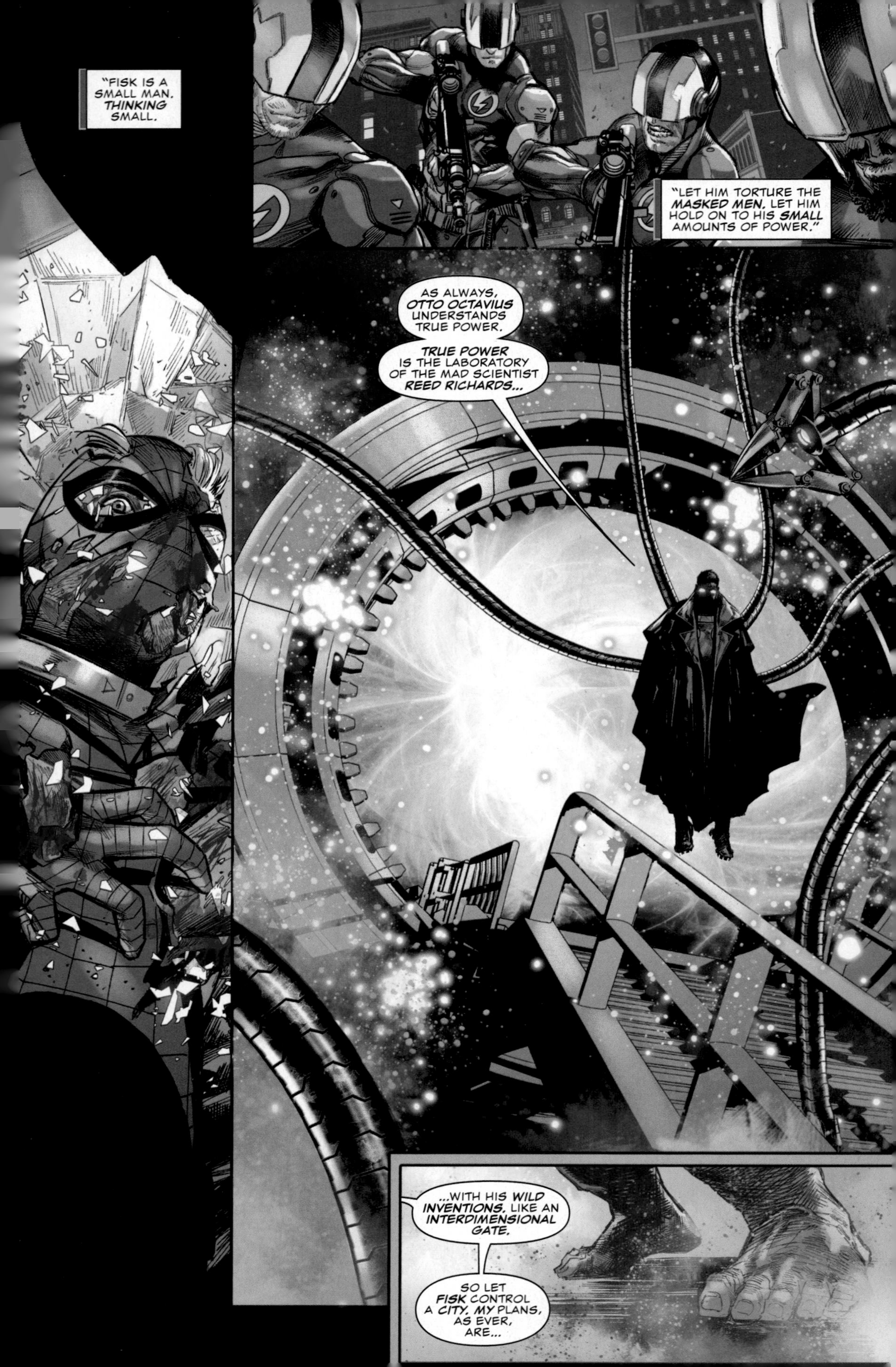
"FISK IS A SMALL MAN. THINKING SMALL.
"LET HIM TORTURE THE MASKED MEN. LET HIM HOLD ON TO HIS SMALL AMOUNTS OF POWER."
AS ALWAYS, OTTO OCTAVIUS UNDERSTANDS TRUE POWER.
TRUE POWER IS THE LABORATORY OF THE MAD SCIENTIST REED RICHARDS...
...WITH HIS WILD INVENTIONS, LIKE AN INTERDIMENSIONAL GATE.
SO LET FISK CONTROL A CITY. MY PLANS, AS EVER, ARE...

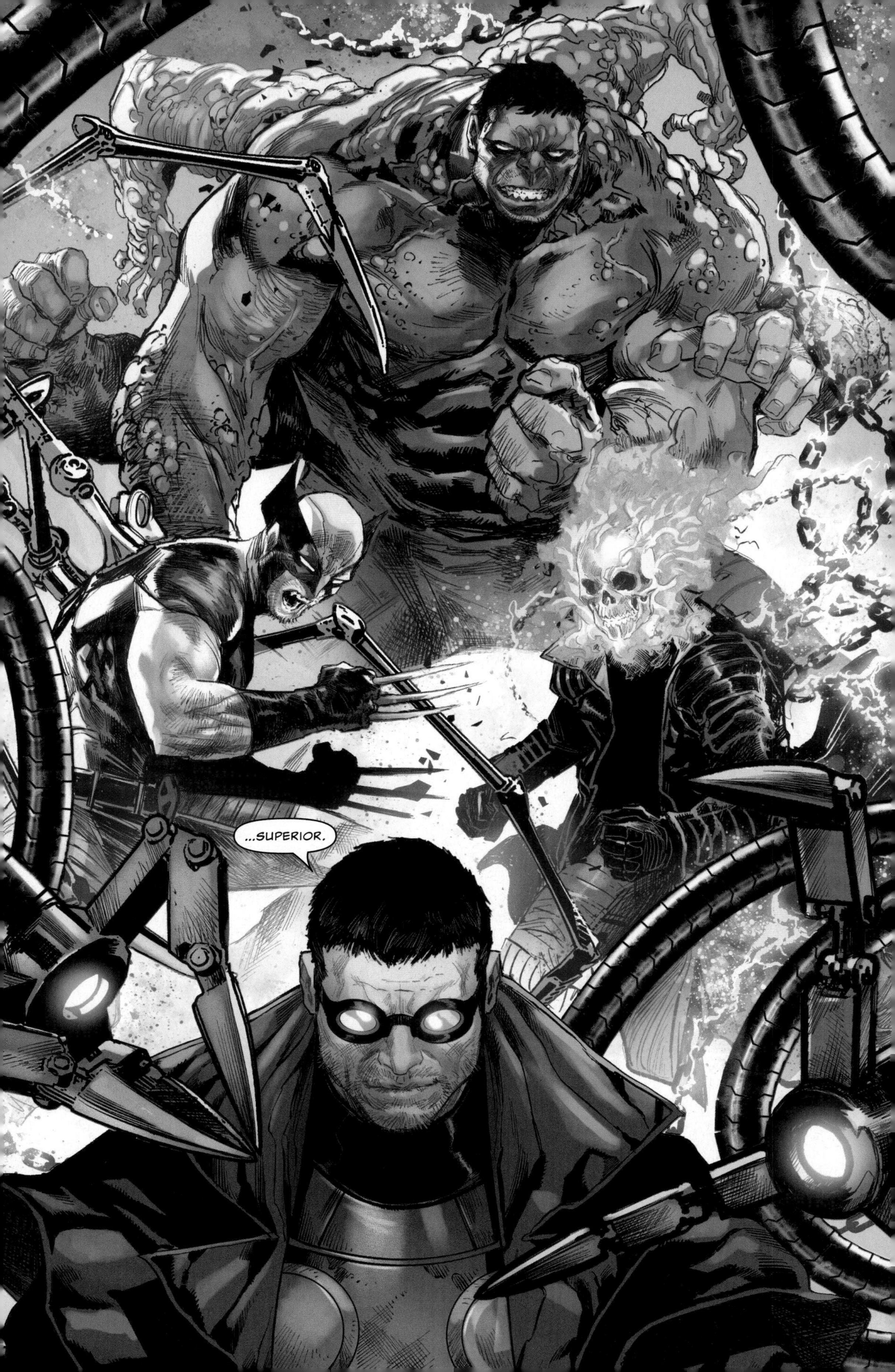
...SUPERIOR.

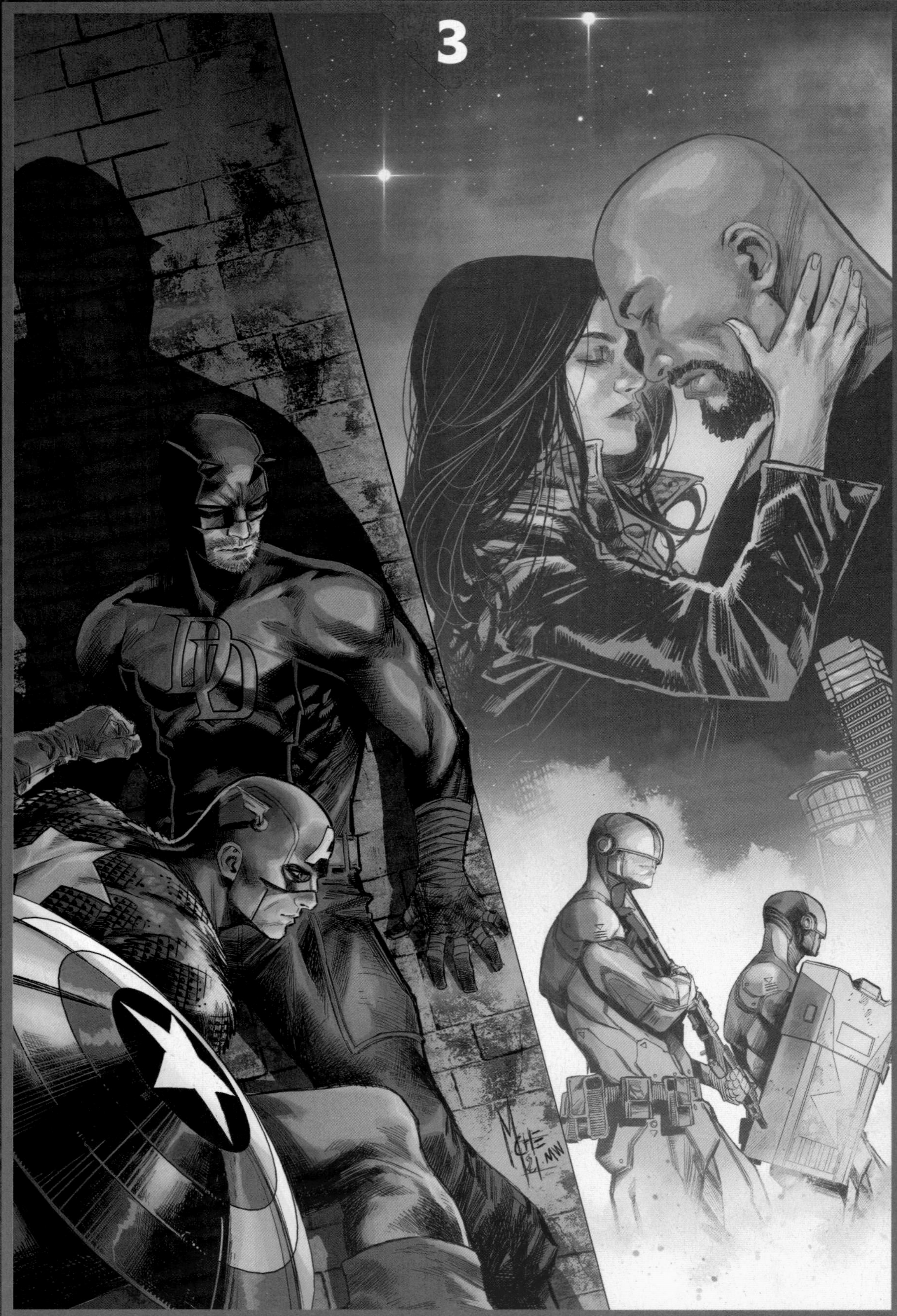
3

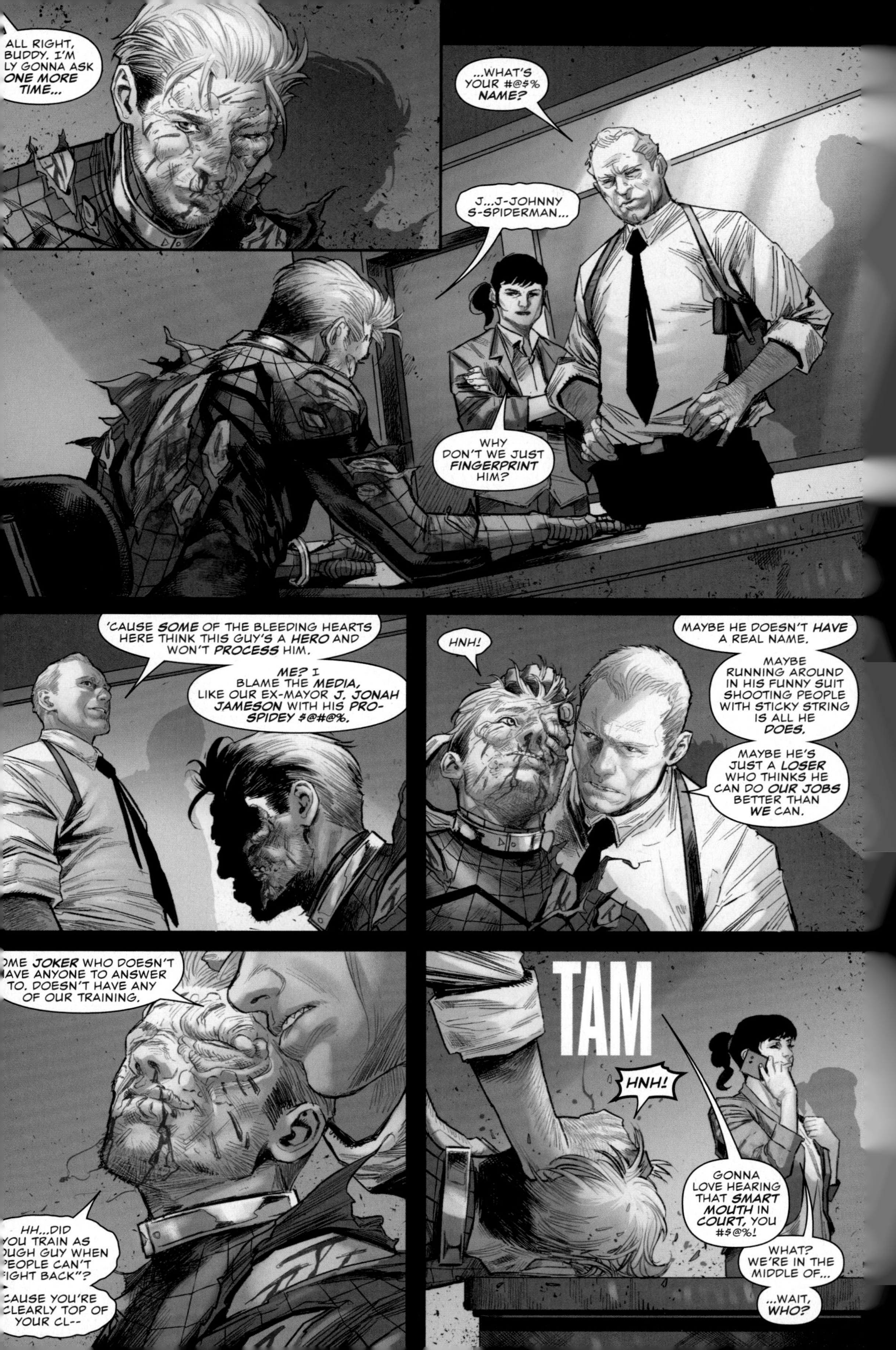
ALL RIGHT, BUDDY. I'M LY GONNA ASK ONE MORE TIME...
...WHAT'S YOUR #@$% NAME?
J...J-JOHNNY S-SPIDERMAN...
WHY DON'T WE JUST FINGERPRINT HIM?
'CAUSE SOME OF THE BLEEDING HEARTS HERE THINK THIS GUY'S A HERO AND WON'T PROCESS HIM.
ME? I BLAME THE MEDIA, LIKE OUR EX-MAYOR J. JONAH JAMESON WITH HIS PRO-SPIDEY $@#@%.
HNH!
MAYBE HE DOESN'T HAVE A REAL NAME.
MAYBE RUNNING AROUND IN HIS FUNNY SUIT SHOOTING PEOPLE WITH STICKY STRING IS ALL HE DOES.
MAYBE HE'S JUST A LOSER WHO THINKS HE CAN DO OUR JOBS BETTER THAN WE CAN.
OME JOKER WHO DOESN'T AVE ANYONE TO ANSWER TO. DOESN'T HAVE ANY OF OUR TRAINING.
HH...DID YOU TRAIN AS OUGH GUY WHEN PEOPLE CAN'T FIGHT BACK"?
CAUSE YOU'RE CLEARLY TOP OF YOUR CL--
TAM
HNH!
GONNA LOVE HEARING THAT SMART MOUTH IN COURT, YOU #$@%!
WHAT? WE'RE IN THE MIDDLE OF...
...WAIT, WHO?

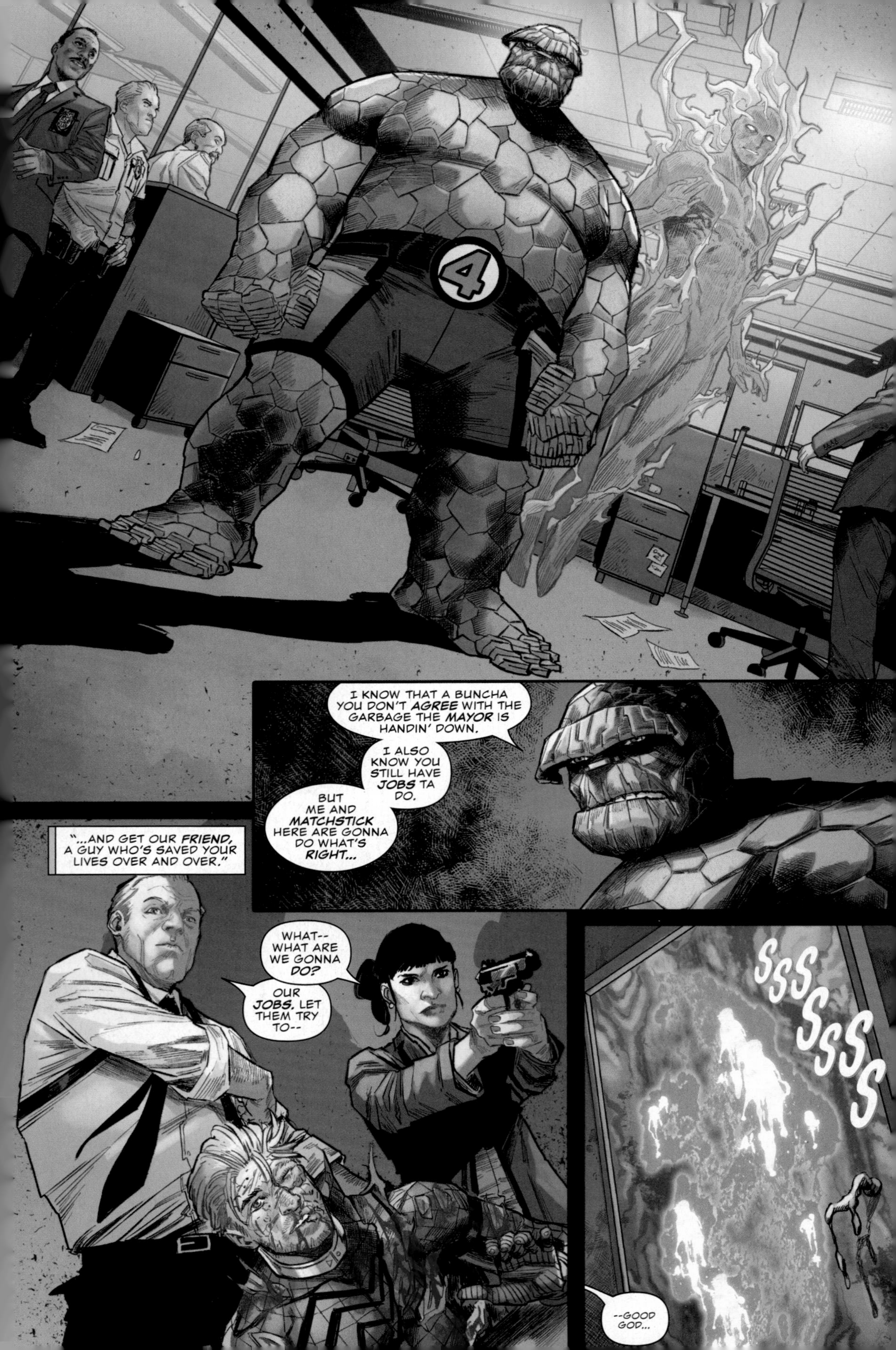
I KNOW THAT A BUNCHA YOU DON'T AGREE WITH THE GARBAGE THE MAYOR IS HANDIN' DOWN.
I ALSO KNOW YOU STILL HAVE JOBS TA DO.
BUT ME AND MATCHSTICK HERE ARE GONNA DO WHAT'S RIGHT...
"...AND GET OUR FRIEND, A GUY WHO'S SAVED YOUR LIVES OVER AND OVER."
WHAT-- WHAT ARE WE GONNA DO?
OUR JOBS. LET THEM TRY TO--
SSSSSSSS
--GOOD GOD...

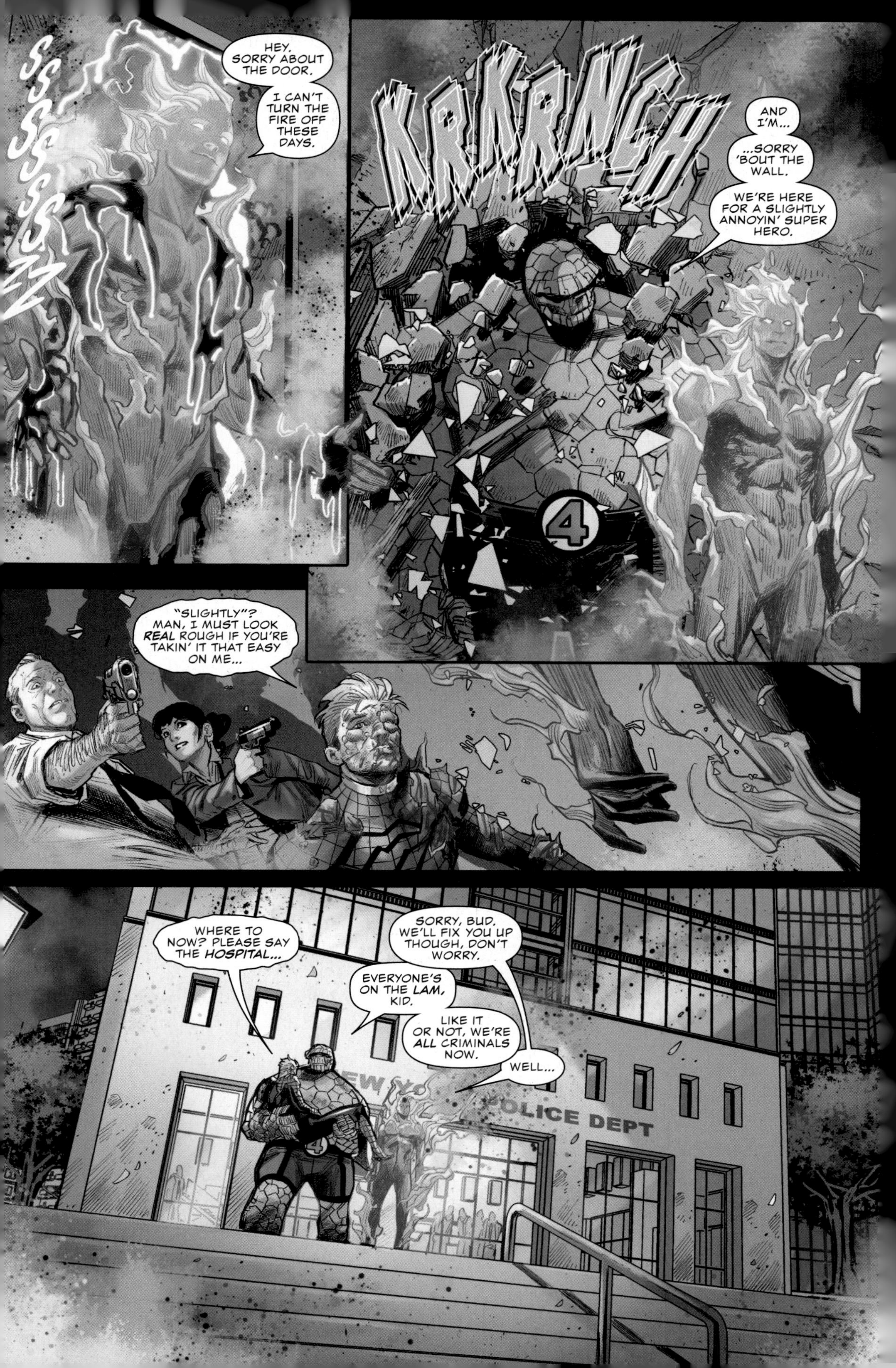
SSSSSSSSZZ
HEY. SORRY ABOUT THE DOOR.
I CAN'T TURN THE FIRE OFF THESE DAYS.
KRKRNCH
AND I'M...
...SORRY 'BOUT THE WALL.
WE'RE HERE FOR A SLIGHTLY ANNOYIN' SUPER HERO.
4
"SLIGHTLY"? MAN, I MUST LOOK **REAL** ROUGH IF YOU'RE TAKIN' IT THAT EASY ON ME...
WHERE TO NOW? PLEASE SAY THE ***HOSPITAL...***
SORRY, BUD. WE'LL FIX YOU UP THOUGH, DON'T WORRY.
EVERYONE'S ON THE ***LAM,*** KID.
LIKE IT OR NOT, WE'RE ***ALL*** CRIMINALS NOW.
WELL...
POLICE DEPT

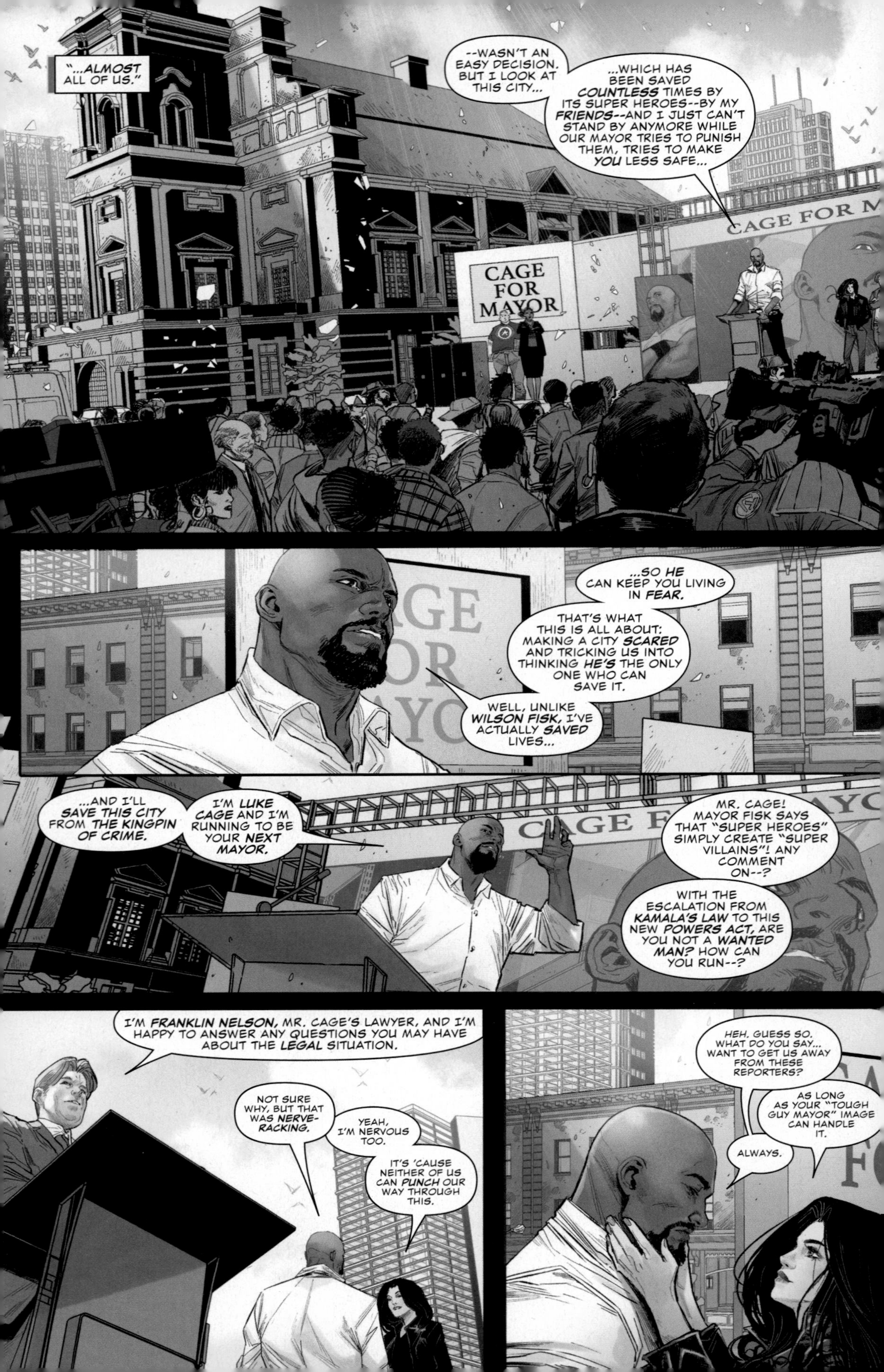
"...ALMOST ALL OF US."
--WASN'T AN EASY DECISION. BUT I LOOK AT THIS CITY...
...WHICH HAS BEEN SAVED COUNTLESS TIMES BY ITS SUPER HEROES--BY MY FRIENDS--AND I JUST CAN'T STAND BY ANYMORE WHILE OUR MAYOR TRIES TO PUNISH THEM, TRIES TO MAKE YOU LESS SAFE...
CAGE FOR MAYOR
...SO HE CAN KEEP YOU LIVING IN FEAR.
THAT'S WHAT THIS IS ALL ABOUT: MAKING A CITY SCARED AND TRICKING US INTO THINKING HE'S THE ONLY ONE WHO CAN SAVE IT.
WELL, UNLIKE WILSON FISK, I'VE ACTUALLY SAVED LIVES...
...AND I'LL SAVE THIS CITY FROM THE KINGPIN OF CRIME.
I'M LUKE CAGE AND I'M RUNNING TO BE YOUR NEXT MAYOR.
MR. CAGE! MAYOR FISK SAYS THAT "SUPER HEROES" SIMPLY CREATE "SUPER VILLAINS"! ANY COMMENT ON--?
WITH THE ESCALATION FROM KAMALA'S LAW TO THIS NEW POWERS ACT, ARE YOU NOT A WANTED MAN? HOW CAN YOU RUN--?
I'M FRANKLIN NELSON, MR. CAGE'S LAWYER, AND I'M HAPPY TO ANSWER ANY QUESTIONS YOU MAY HAVE ABOUT THE LEGAL SITUATION.
NOT SURE WHY, BUT THAT WAS NERVE-RACKING.
YEAH, I'M NERVOUS TOO.
IT'S 'CAUSE NEITHER OF US CAN PUNCH OUR WAY THROUGH THIS.
HEH. GUESS SO. WHAT DO YOU SAY... WANT TO GET US AWAY FROM THESE REPORTERS?
AS LONG AS YOUR "TOUGH GUY MAYOR" IMAGE CAN HANDLE IT.
ALWAYS.

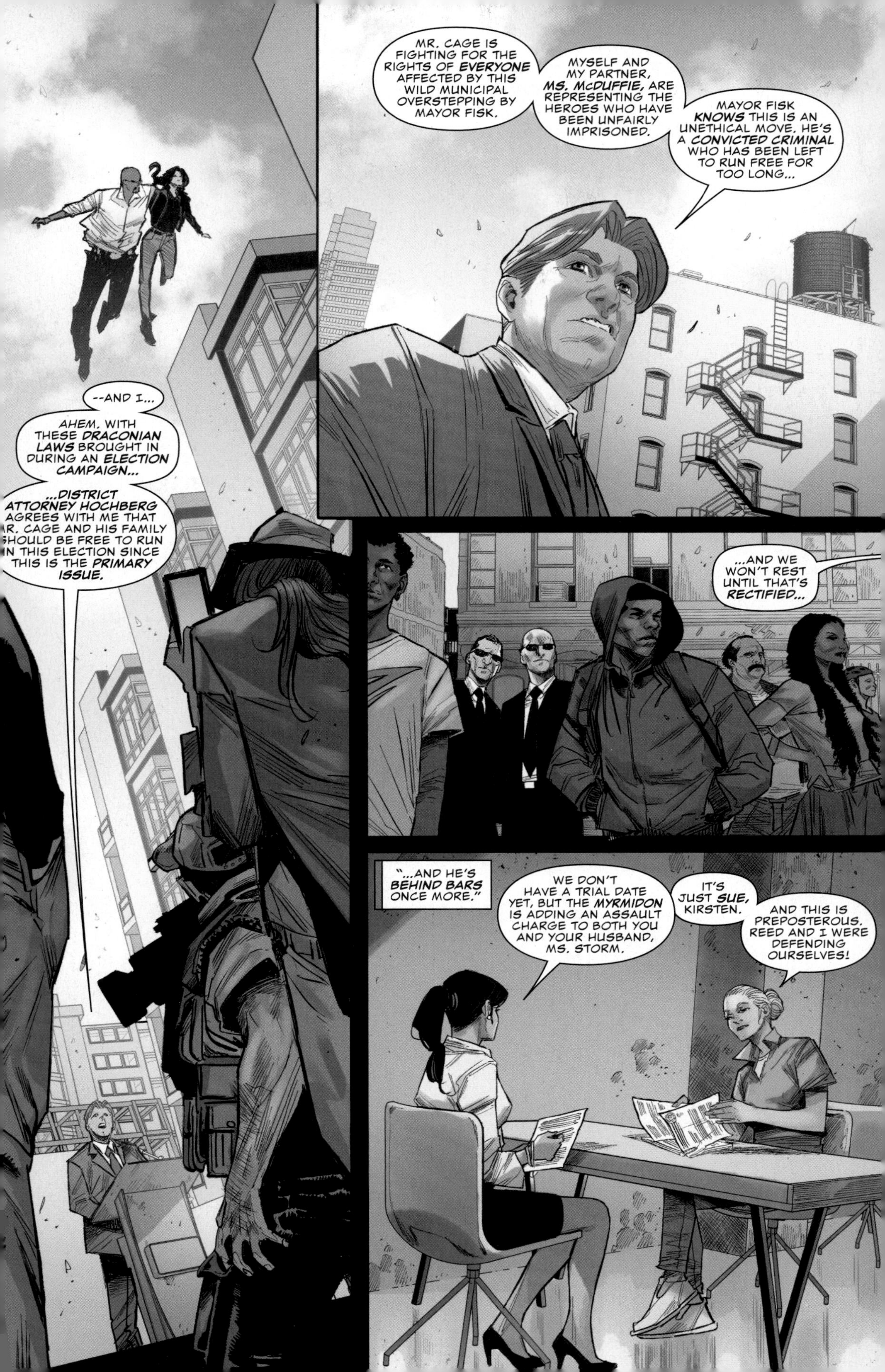
MR. CAGE IS FIGHTING FOR THE RIGHTS OF EVERYONE AFFECTED BY THIS WILD MUNICIPAL OVERSTEPPING BY MAYOR FISK.
MYSELF AND MY PARTNER, MS. McDUFFIE, ARE REPRESENTING THE HEROES WHO HAVE BEEN UNFAIRLY IMPRISONED.
MAYOR FISK KNOWS THIS IS AN UNETHICAL MOVE. HE'S A CONVICTED CRIMINAL WHO HAS BEEN LEFT TO RUN FREE FOR TOO LONG...
--AND I...
AHEM. WITH THESE DRACONIAN LAWS BROUGHT IN DURING AN ELECTION CAMPAIGN...
...DISTRICT ATTORNEY HOCHBERG AGREES WITH ME THAT R. CAGE AND HIS FAMILY SHOULD BE FREE TO RUN N THIS ELECTION SINCE THIS IS THE PRIMARY ISSUE.
...AND WE WON'T REST UNTIL THAT'S RECTIFIED...
"...AND HE'S BEHIND BARS ONCE MORE."
WE DON'T HAVE A TRIAL DATE YET, BUT THE MYRMIDON IS ADDING AN ASSAULT CHARGE TO BOTH YOU AND YOUR HUSBAND, MS. STORM.
IT'S JUST SUE, KIRSTEN.
AND THIS IS PREPOSTEROUS. REED AND I WERE DEFENDING OURSELVES!

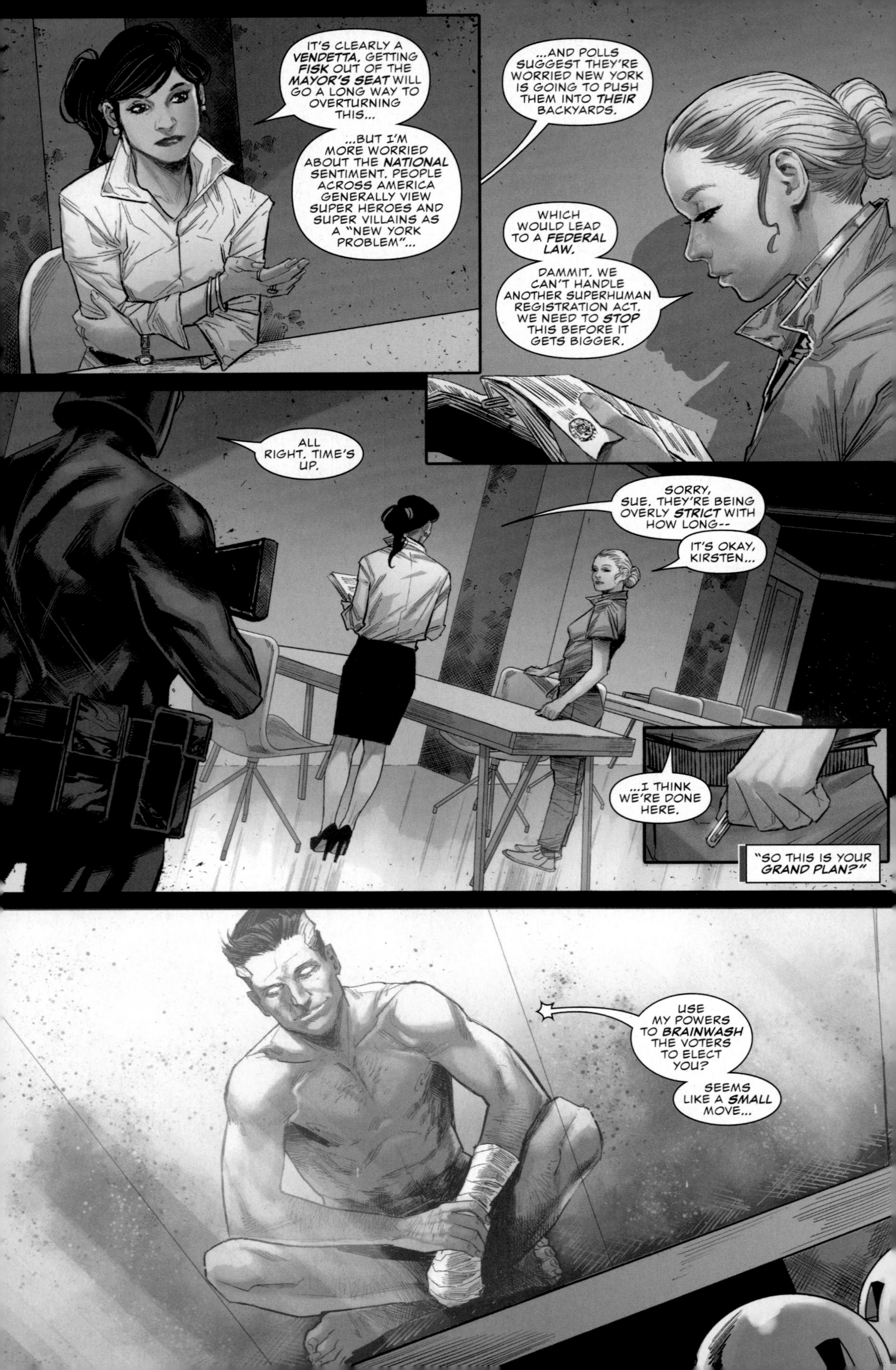
IT'S CLEARLY A VENDETTA. GETTING FISK OUT OF THE MAYOR'S SEAT WILL GO A LONG WAY TO OVERTURNING THIS...
...BUT I'M MORE WORRIED ABOUT THE NATIONAL SENTIMENT. PEOPLE ACROSS AMERICA GENERALLY VIEW SUPER HEROES AND SUPER VILLAINS AS A "NEW YORK PROBLEM"...
...AND POLLS SUGGEST THEY'RE WORRIED NEW YORK IS GOING TO PUSH THEM INTO THEIR BACKYARDS.
WHICH WOULD LEAD TO A FEDERAL LAW.
DAMMIT. WE CAN'T HANDLE ANOTHER SUPERHUMAN REGISTRATION ACT. WE NEED TO STOP THIS BEFORE IT GETS BIGGER.
ALL RIGHT. TIME'S UP.
SORRY, SUE. THEY'RE BEING OVERLY STRICT WITH HOW LONG--
IT'S OKAY, KIRSTEN...
...I THINK WE'RE DONE HERE.
"SO THIS IS YOUR GRAND PLAN?"
USE MY POWERS TO BRAINWASH THE VOTERS TO ELECT YOU?
SEEMS LIKE A SMALL MOVE...

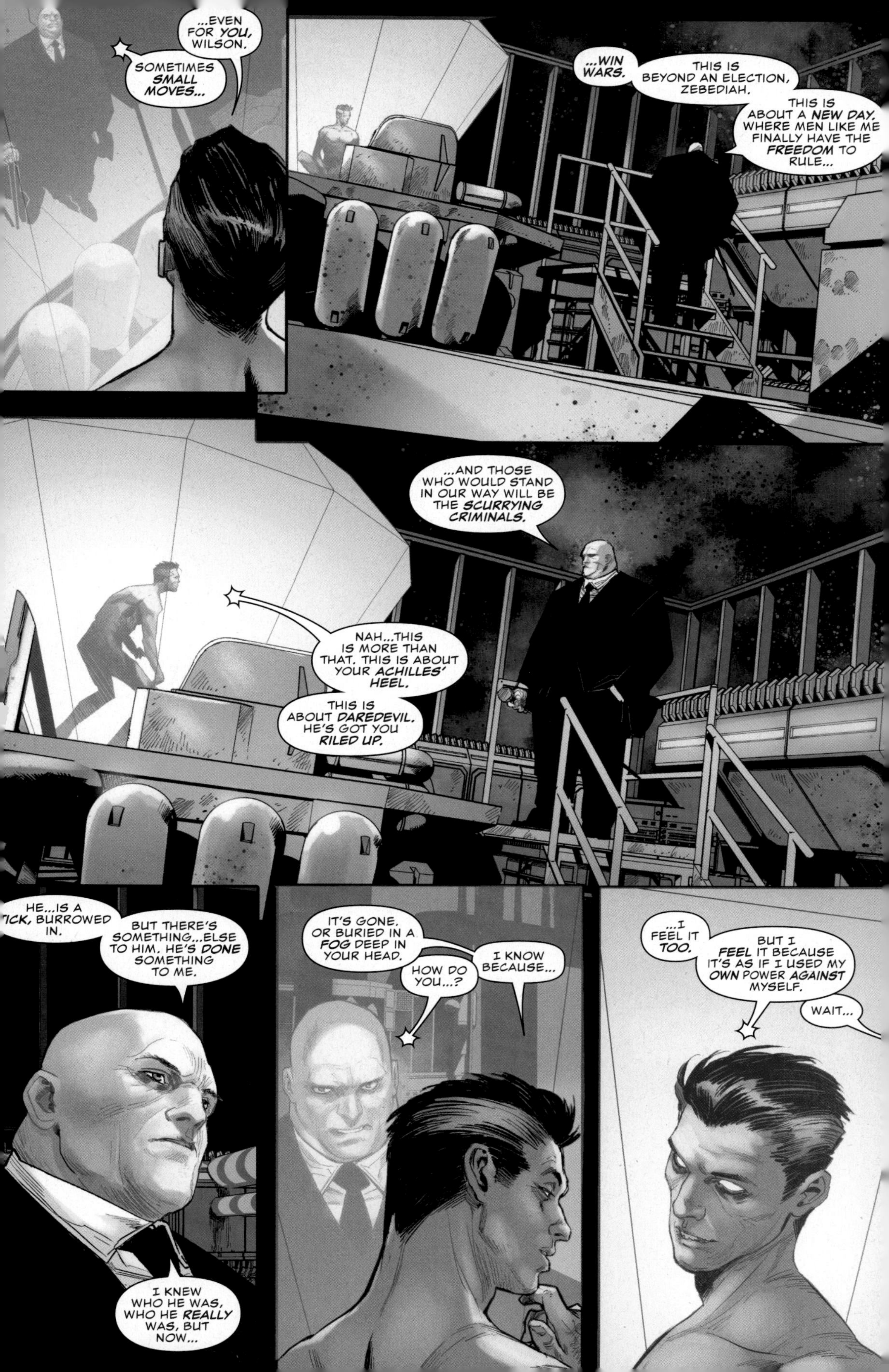
...EVEN FOR YOU, WILSON.
SOMETIMES SMALL MOVES...
...WIN WARS.
THIS IS BEYOND AN ELECTION, ZEBEDIAH.
THIS IS ABOUT A NEW DAY, WHERE MEN LIKE ME FINALLY HAVE THE FREEDOM TO RULE...
...AND THOSE WHO WOULD STAND IN OUR WAY WILL BE THE SCURRYING CRIMINALS.
NAH...THIS IS MORE THAN THAT. THIS IS ABOUT YOUR ACHILLES' HEEL.
THIS IS ABOUT DAREDEVIL. HE'S GOT YOU RILED UP.
HE...IS A TICK, BURROWED IN.
BUT THERE'S SOMETHING...ELSE TO HIM. HE'S DONE SOMETHING TO ME.
I KNEW WHO HE WAS, WHO HE REALLY WAS, BUT NOW...
IT'S GONE. OR BURIED IN A FOG DEEP IN YOUR HEAD.
HOW DO YOU...?
I KNOW BECAUSE...
...I FEEL IT TOO.
BUT I FEEL IT BECAUSE IT'S AS IF I USED MY OWN POWER AGAINST MYSELF.
WAIT...

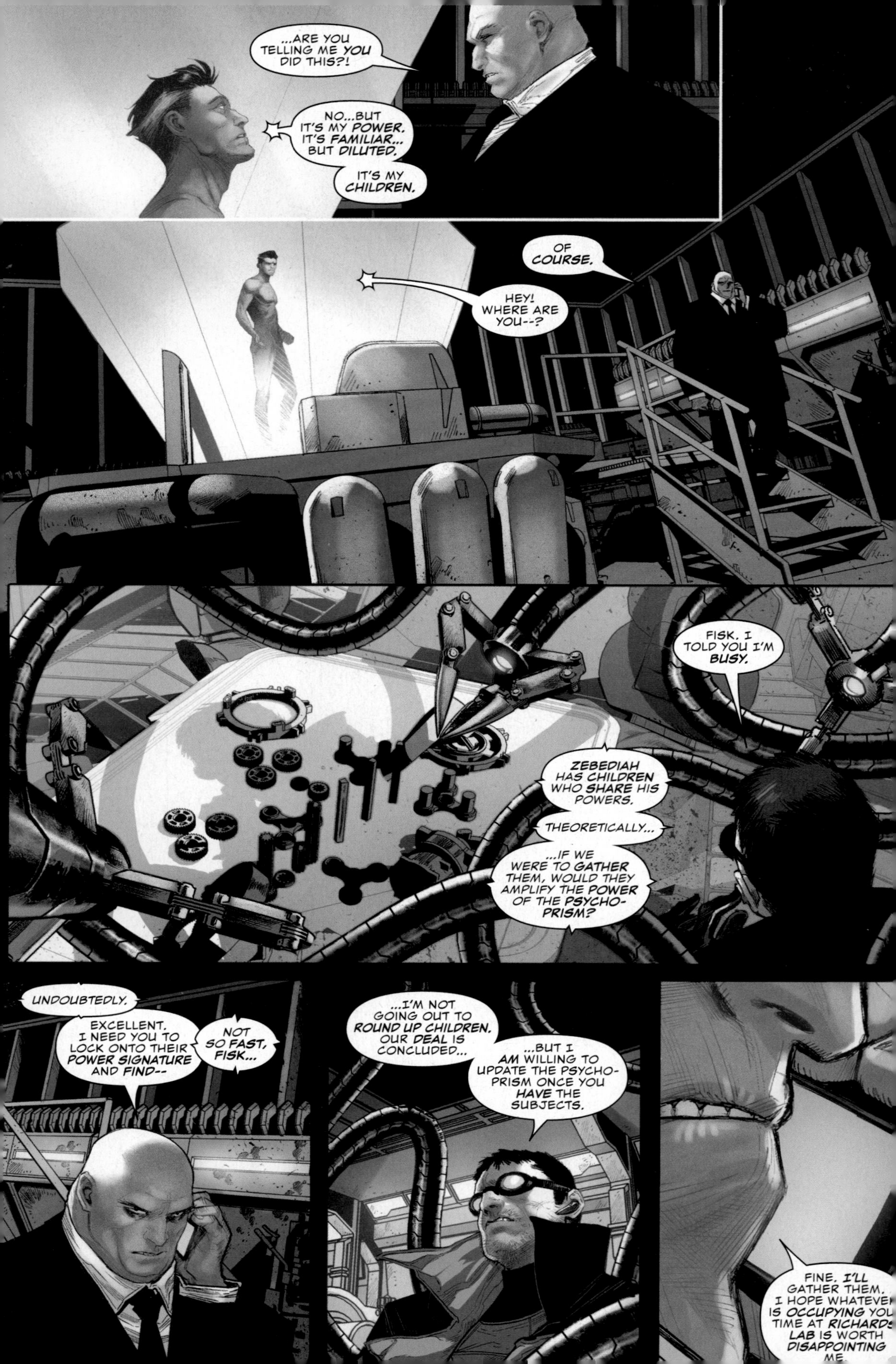
...ARE YOU TELLING ME YOU DID THIS?!
NO...BUT IT'S MY POWER. IT'S FAMILIAR... BUT DILUTED.
IT'S MY CHILDREN.
OF COURSE.
HEY! WHERE ARE YOU--?
FISK. I TOLD YOU I'M BUSY.
ZEBEDIAH HAS CHILDREN WHO SHARE HIS POWERS.
THEORETICALLY...
...IF WE WERE TO GATHER THEM, WOULD THEY AMPLIFY THE POWER OF THE PSYCHO-PRISM?
UNDOUBTEDLY.
EXCELLENT. I NEED YOU TO LOCK ONTO THEIR POWER SIGNATURE AND FIND--
NOT SO FAST, FISK...
...I'M NOT GOING OUT TO ROUND UP CHILDREN. OUR DEAL IS CONCLUDED...
...BUT I AM WILLING TO UPDATE THE PSYCHO-PRISM ONCE YOU HAVE THE SUBJECTS.
FINE. I'LL GATHER THEM. I HOPE WHATEVER IS OCCUPYING YOUR TIME AT RICHARDS LAB IS WORTH DISAPPOINTING ME.

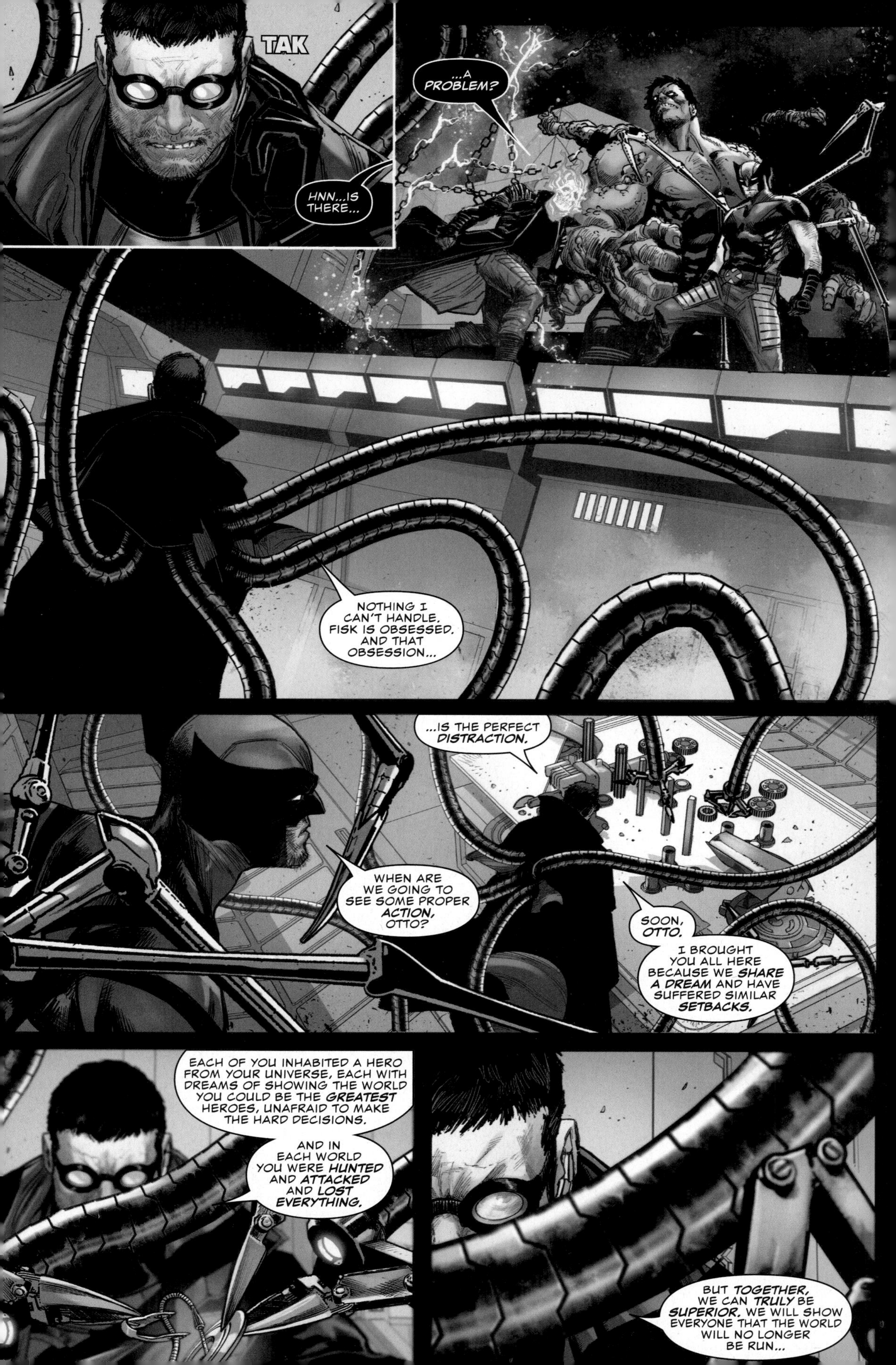
TAK
...A PROBLEM?
HNN...IS THERE...
NOTHING I CAN'T HANDLE. FISK IS OBSESSED. AND THAT OBSESSION...
...IS THE PERFECT DISTRACTION.
WHEN ARE WE GOING TO SEE SOME PROPER ACTION, OTTO?
SOON, OTTO.
I BROUGHT YOU ALL HERE BECAUSE WE SHARE A DREAM AND HAVE SUFFERED SIMILAR SETBACKS.
EACH OF YOU INHABITED A HERO FROM YOUR UNIVERSE, EACH WITH DREAMS OF SHOWING THE WORLD YOU COULD BE THE GREATEST HEROES, UNAFRAID TO MAKE THE HARD DECISIONS.
AND IN EACH WORLD YOU WERE HUNTED AND ATTACKED AND LOST EVERYTHING.
BUT TOGETHER, WE CAN TRULY BE SUPERIOR. WE WILL SHOW EVERYONE THAT THE WORLD WILL NO LONGER BE RUN...

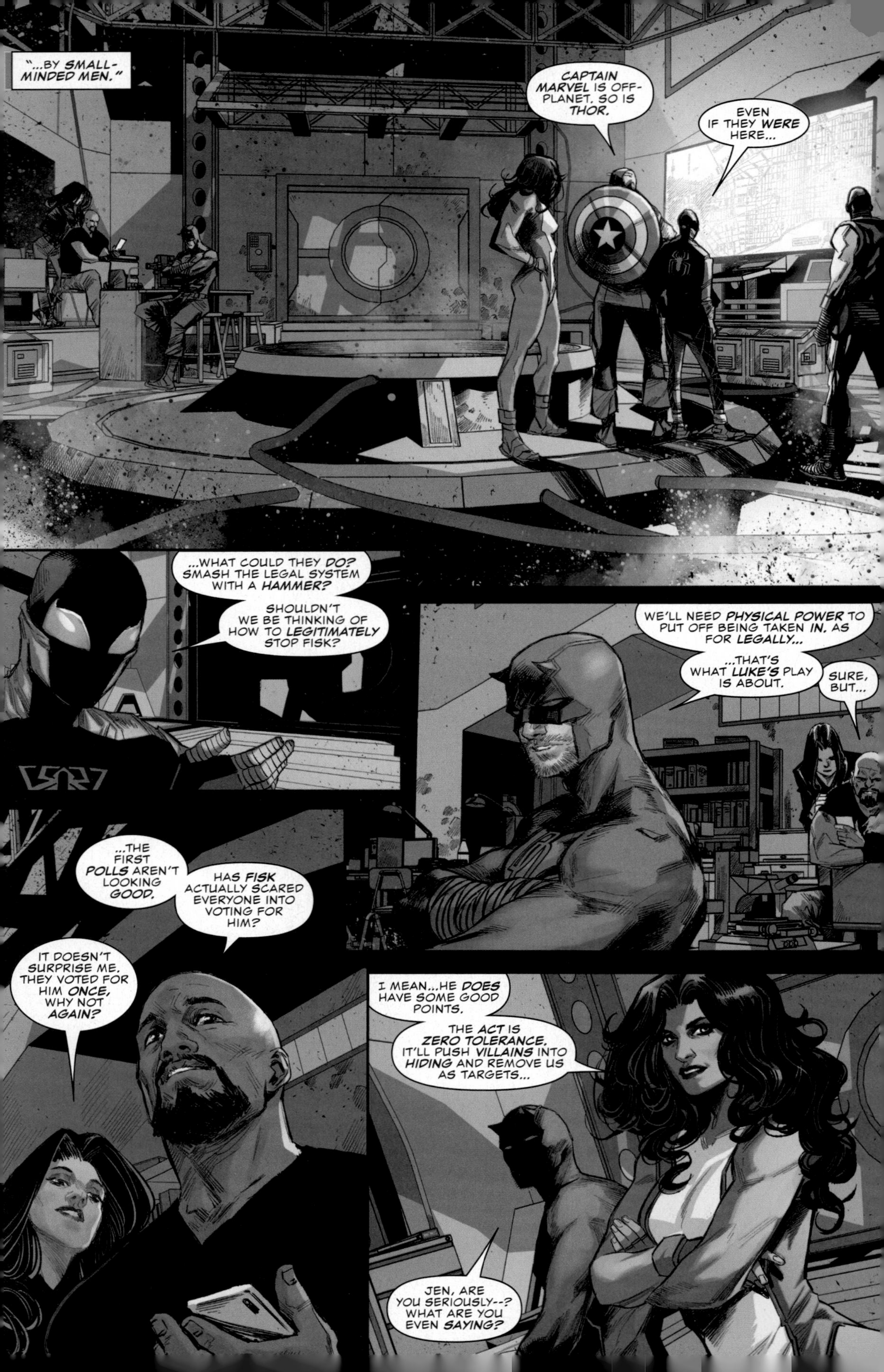
"...BY SMALL-MINDED MEN."
CAPTAIN MARVEL IS OFF-PLANET. SO IS THOR.
EVEN IF THEY WERE HERE...
...WHAT COULD THEY DO? SMASH THE LEGAL SYSTEM WITH A HAMMER?
SHOULDN'T WE BE THINKING OF HOW TO LEGITIMATELY STOP FISK?
WE'LL NEED PHYSICAL POWER TO PUT OFF BEING TAKEN IN. AS FOR LEGALLY...
...THAT'S WHAT LUKE'S PLAY IS ABOUT.
SURE, BUT...
...THE FIRST POLLS AREN'T LOOKING GOOD.
HAS FISK ACTUALLY SCARED EVERYONE INTO VOTING FOR HIM?
IT DOESN'T SURPRISE ME. THEY VOTED FOR HIM ONCE, WHY NOT AGAIN?
I MEAN...HE DOES HAVE SOME GOOD POINTS.
THE ACT IS ZERO TOLERANCE. IT'LL PUSH VILLAINS INTO HIDING AND REMOVE US AS TARGETS...
JEN, ARE YOU SERIOUSLY--? WHAT ARE YOU EVEN SAYING?

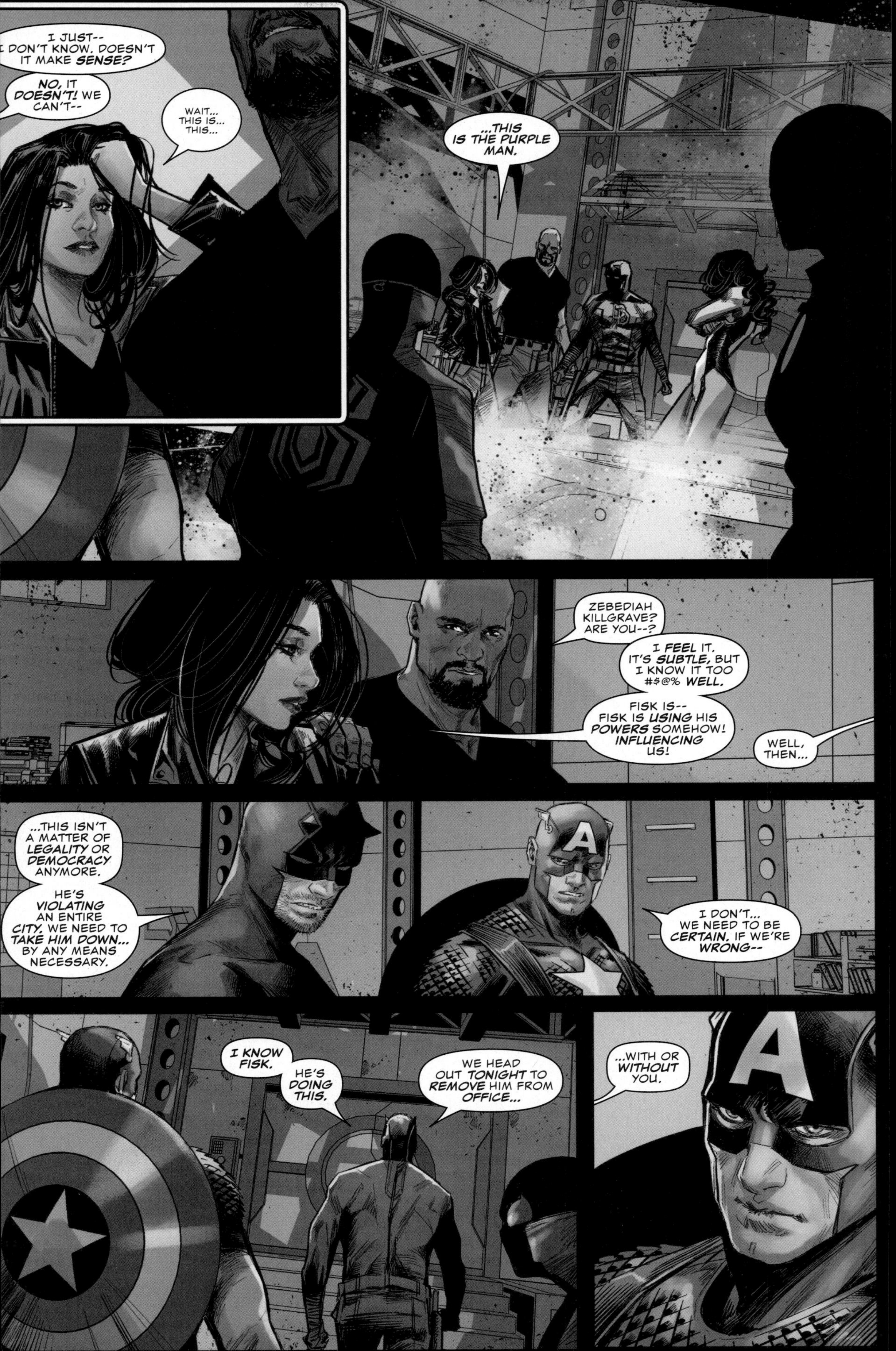
I JUST-- I DON'T KNOW. DOESN'T IT MAKE SENSE?
NO, IT DOESN'T! WE CAN'T--
WAIT... THIS IS... THIS...
...THIS IS THE PURPLE MAN.
ZEBEDIAH KILLGRAVE? ARE YOU--?
I FEEL IT. IT'S SUBTLE, BUT I KNOW IT TOO #$@% WELL.
FISK IS-- FISK IS USING HIS POWERS SOMEHOW! INFLUENCING US!
WELL, THEN...
...THIS ISN'T A MATTER OF LEGALITY OR DEMOCRACY ANYMORE.
HE'S VIOLATING AN ENTIRE CITY. WE NEED TO TAKE HIM DOWN... BY ANY MEANS NECESSARY.
I DON'T... WE NEED TO BE CERTAIN. IF WE'RE WRONG--
I KNOW FISK.
HE'S DOING THIS.
WE HEAD OUT TONIGHT TO REMOVE HIM FROM OFFICE...
...WITH OR WITHOUT YOU.

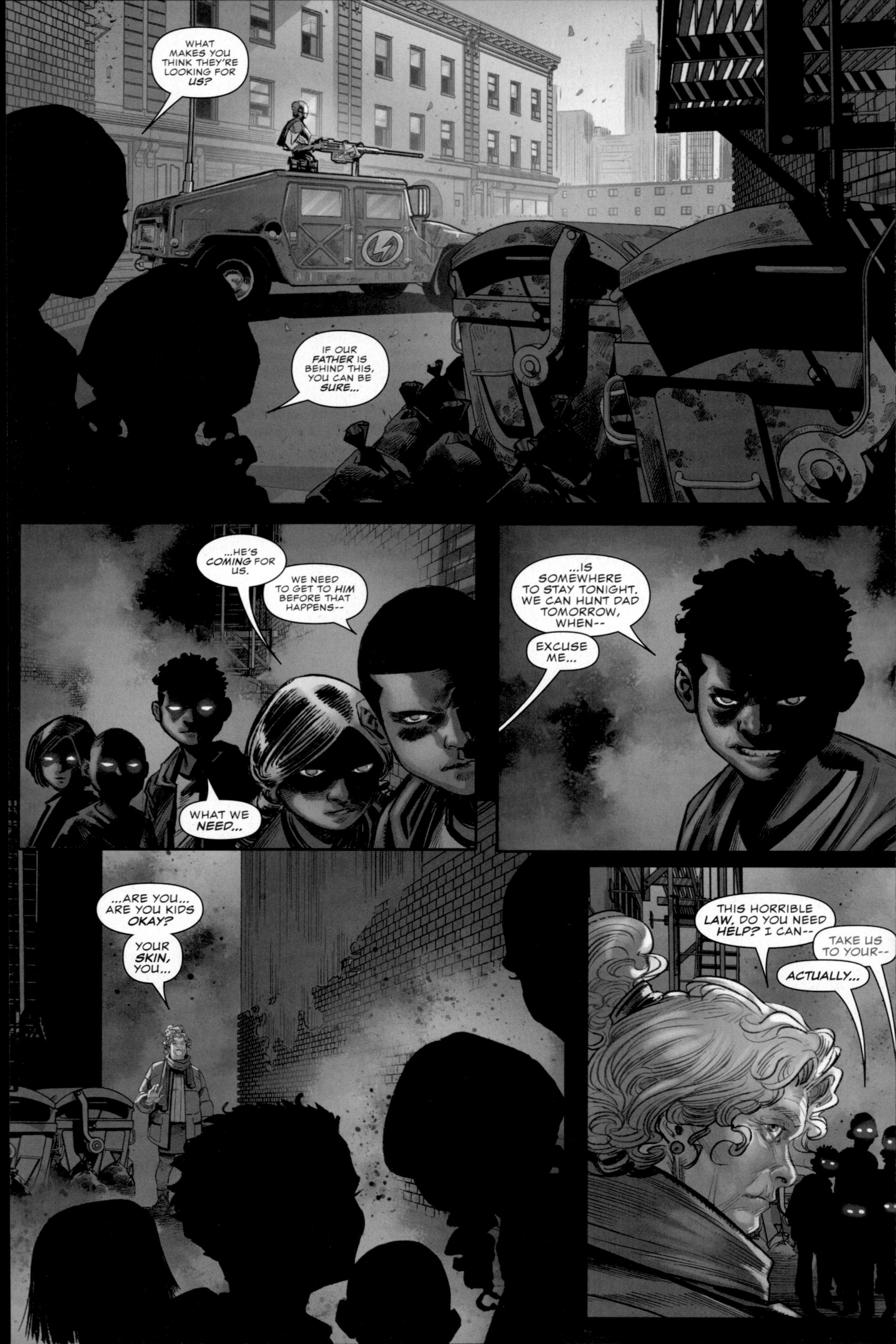
WHAT MAKES YOU THINK THEY'RE LOOKING FOR US?
IF OUR FATHER IS BEHIND THIS, YOU CAN BE SURE...
...HE'S COMING FOR US.
WE NEED TO GET TO HIM BEFORE THAT HAPPENS--
WHAT WE NEED...
...IS SOMEWHERE TO STAY TONIGHT. WE CAN HUNT DAD TOMORROW, WHEN--
EXCUSE ME...
...ARE YOU... ARE YOU KIDS OKAY?
YOUR SKIN, YOU...
THIS HORRIBLE LAW. DO YOU NEED HELP? I CAN--
TAKE US TO YOUR--
ACTUALLY...

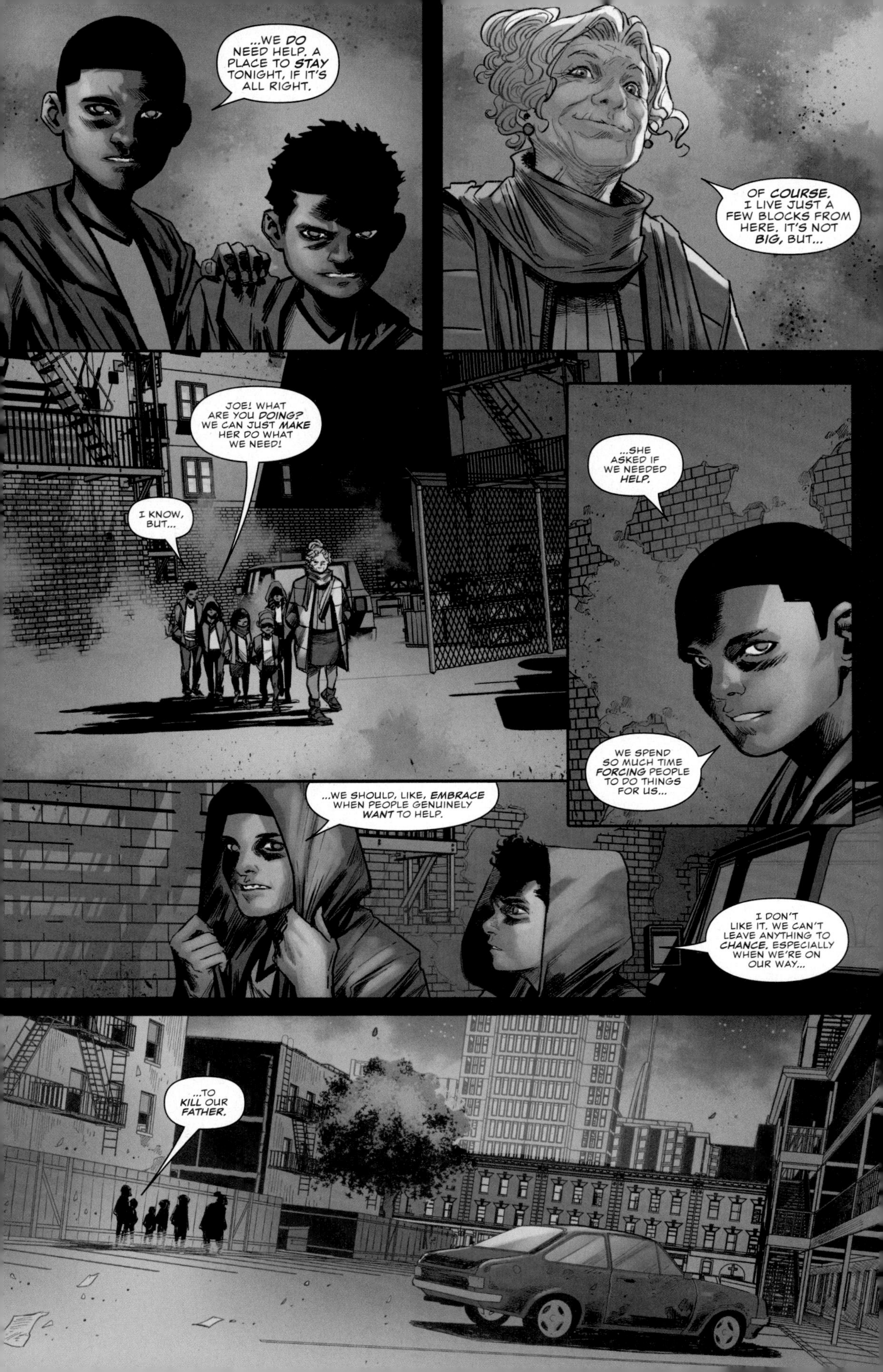
...WE DO NEED HELP. A PLACE TO STAY TONIGHT, IF IT'S ALL RIGHT.
OF COURSE. I LIVE JUST A FEW BLOCKS FROM HERE. IT'S NOT BIG, BUT...
JOE! WHAT ARE YOU DOING? WE CAN JUST MAKE HER DO WHAT WE NEED!
I KNOW, BUT...
...SHE ASKED IF WE NEEDED HELP.
WE SPEND SO MUCH TIME FORCING PEOPLE TO DO THINGS FOR US...
...WE SHOULD, LIKE, EMBRACE WHEN PEOPLE GENUINELY WANT TO HELP.
I DON'T LIKE IT. WE CAN'T LEAVE ANYTHING TO CHANCE. ESPECIALLY WHEN WE'RE ON OUR WAY...
...TO KILL OUR FATHER.

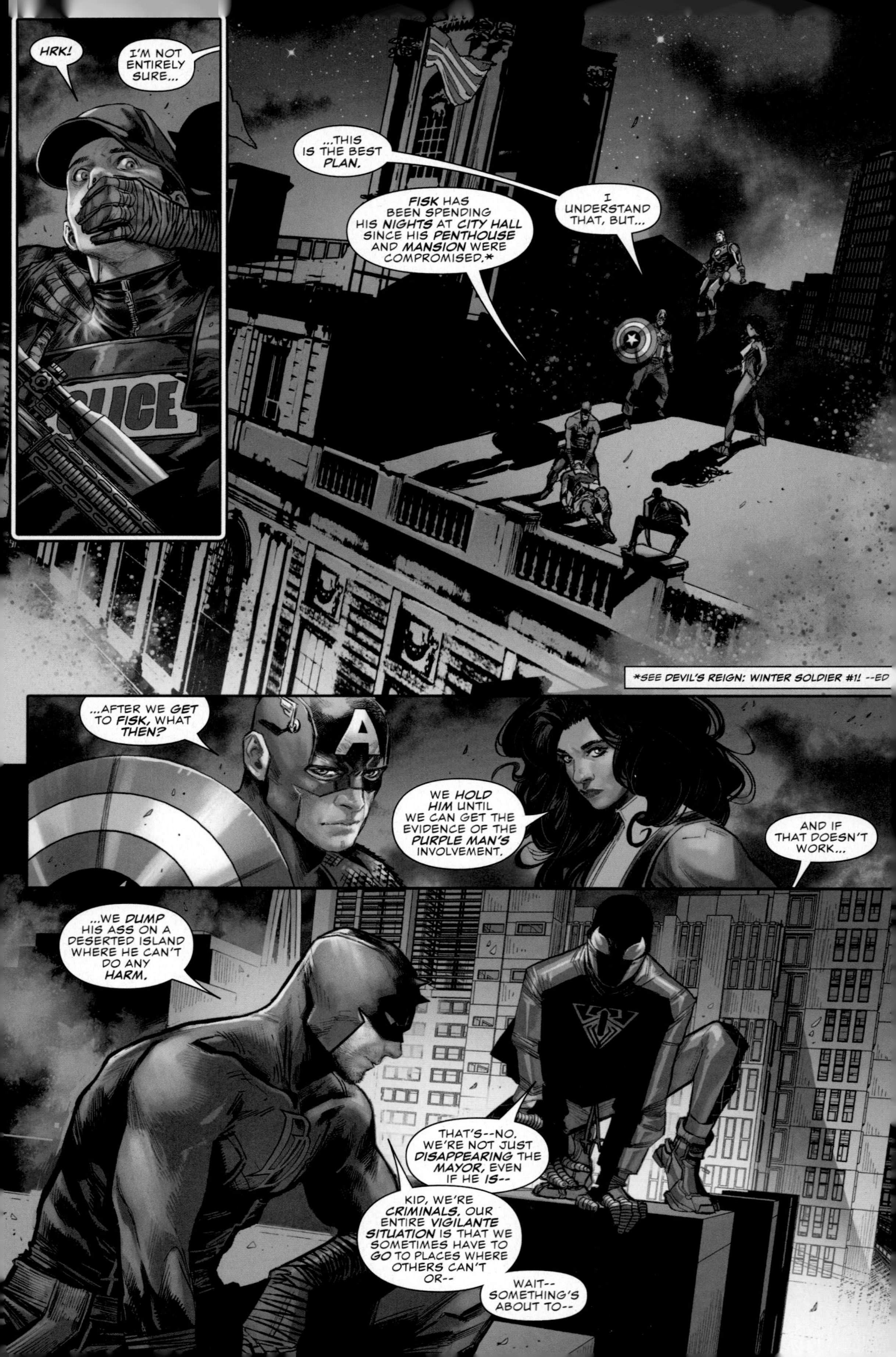
HRK!
I'M NOT ENTIRELY SURE...
...THIS IS THE BEST PLAN.
FISK HAS BEEN SPENDING HIS NIGHTS AT CITY HALL SINCE HIS PENTHOUSE AND MANSION WERE COMPROMISED.*
I UNDERSTAND THAT, BUT...
*SEE DEVIL'S REIGN: WINTER SOLDIER #1! --ED
...AFTER WE GET TO FISK, WHAT THEN?
WE HOLD HIM UNTIL WE CAN GET THE EVIDENCE OF THE PURPLE MAN'S INVOLVEMENT.
AND IF THAT DOESN'T WORK...
...WE DUMP HIS ASS ON A DESERTED ISLAND WHERE HE CAN'T DO ANY HARM.
THAT'S--NO. WE'RE NOT JUST DISAPPEARING THE MAYOR, EVEN IF HE IS--
KID, WE'RE CRIMINALS. OUR ENTIRE VIGILANTE SITUATION IS THAT WE SOMETIMES HAVE TO GO TO PLACES WHERE OTHERS CAN'T OR--
WAIT-- SOMETHING'S ABOUT TO--

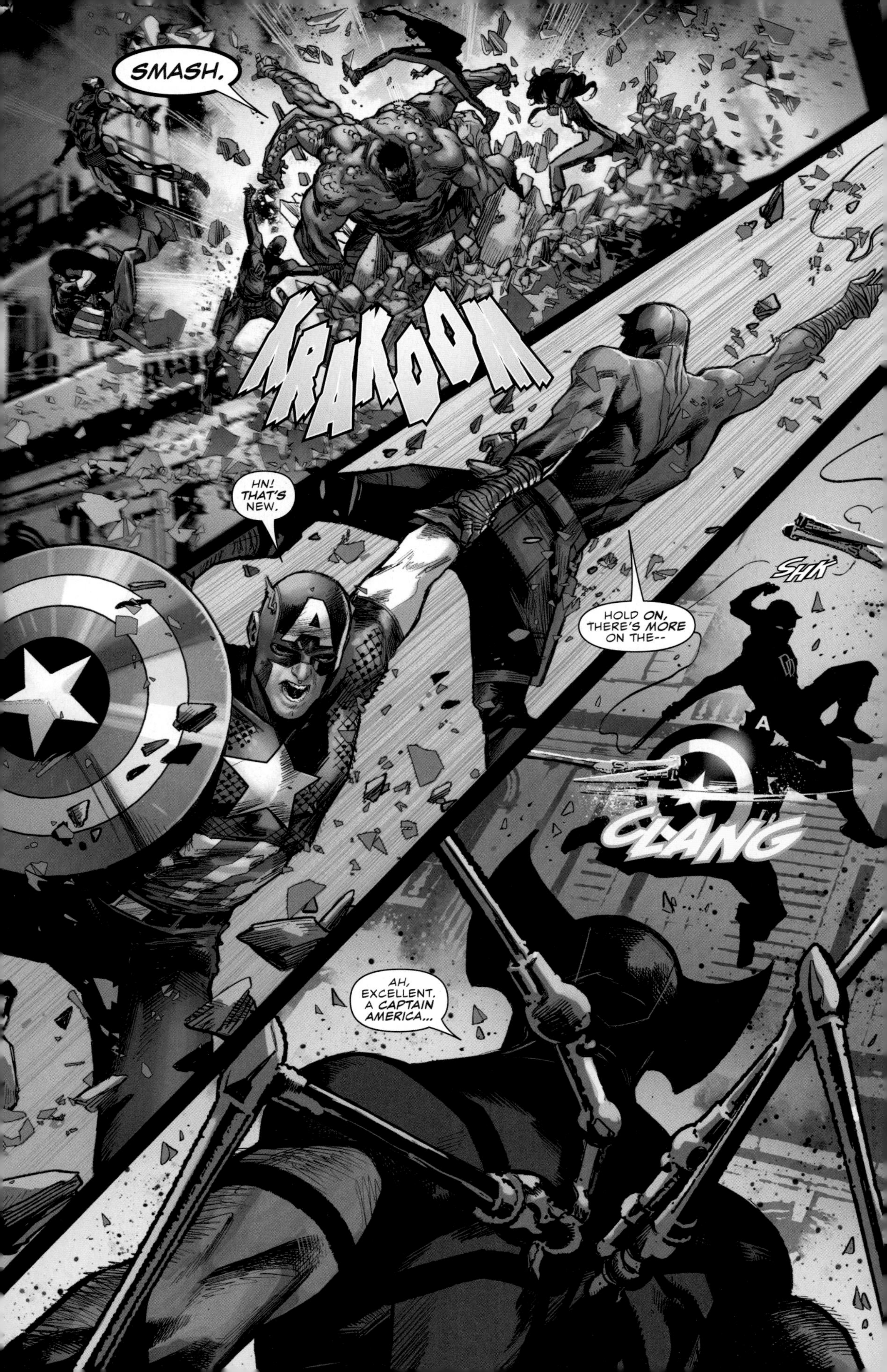
SMASH.
KRAKOOM
HN! THAT'S NEW.
HOLD ON, THERE'S MORE ON THE--
SHK
CLANG
AH, EXCELLENT. A CAPTAIN AMERICA...

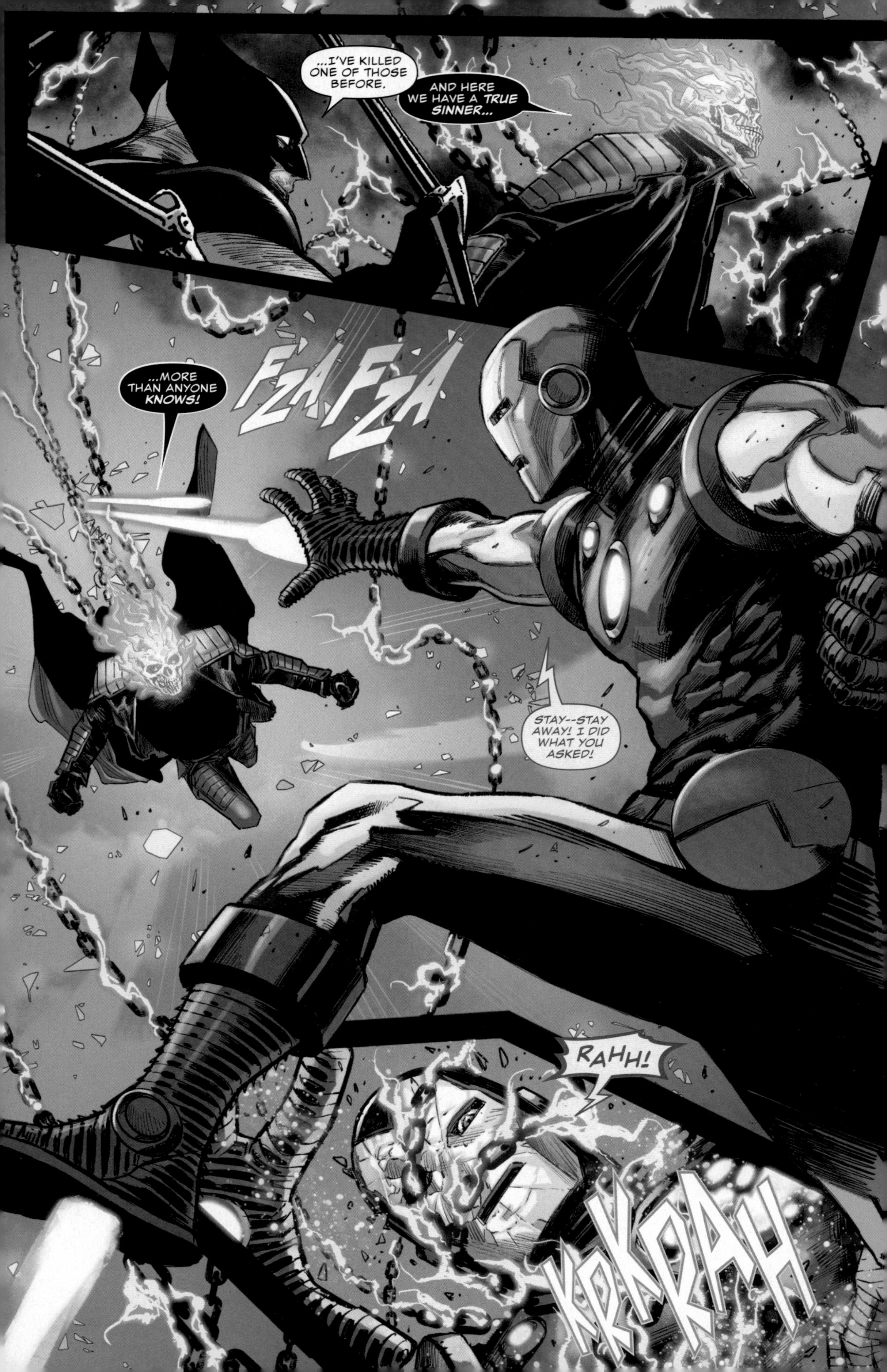

...I'VE KILLED ONE OF THOSE BEFORE.
AND HERE WE HAVE A TRUE SINNER...
...MORE THAN ANYONE KNOWS!
FZA FZA
STAY--STAY AWAY! I DID WHAT YOU ASKED!
RAHH!
KRKRAH

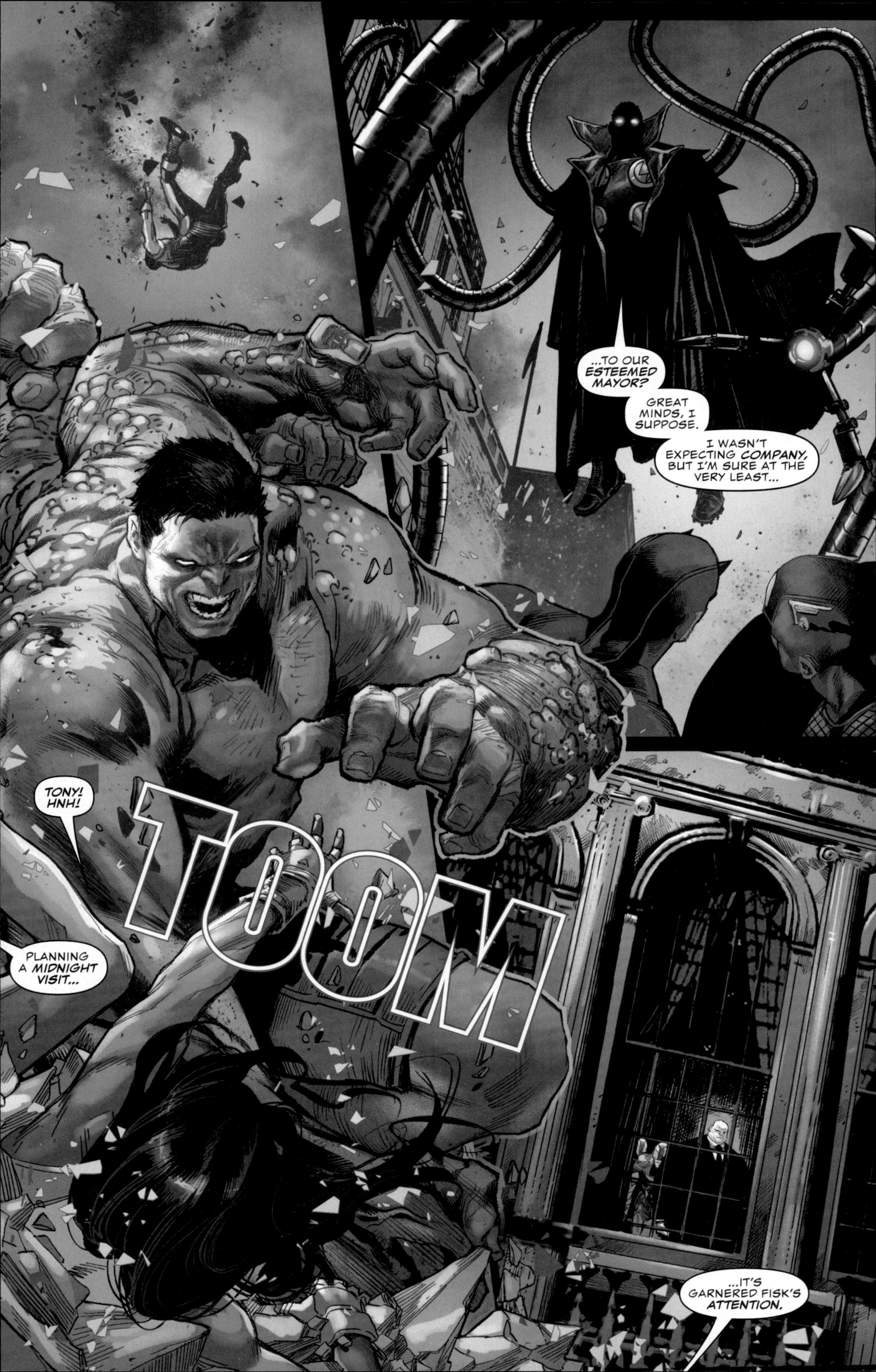
...TO OUR ESTEEMED MAYOR?
GREAT MINDS, I SUPPOSE.
I WASN'T EXPECTING COMPANY, BUT I'M SURE AT THE VERY LEAST...
TONY! HNH!
TOOM
PLANNING A MIDNIGHT VISIT...
...IT'S GARNERED FISK'S ATTENTION.

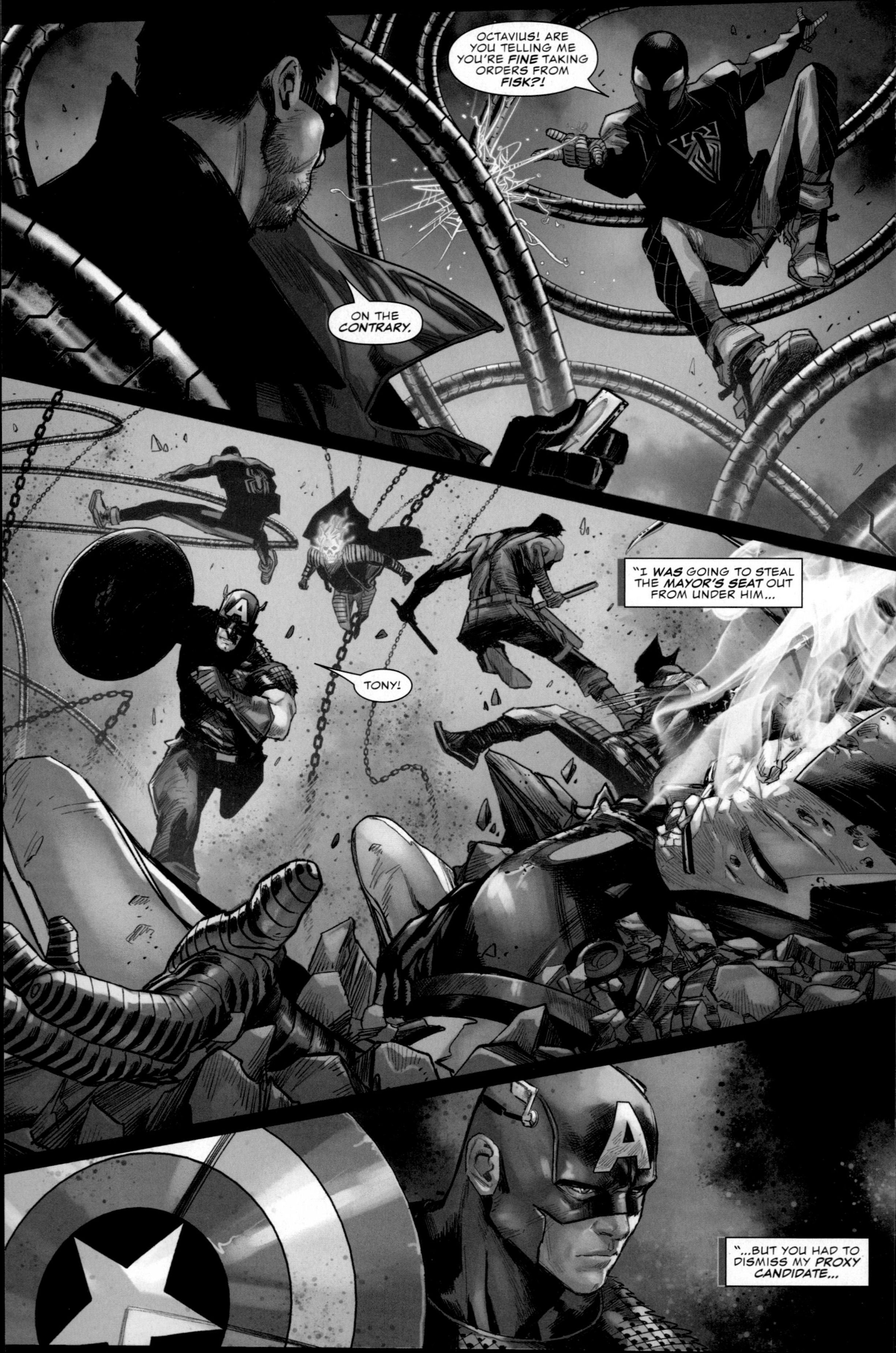
OCTAVIUS! ARE YOU TELLING ME YOU'RE FINE TAKING ORDERS FROM FISK?!
ON THE CONTRARY.
"I WAS GOING TO STEAL THE MAYOR'S SEAT OUT FROM UNDER HIM...
TONY!
"...BUT YOU HAD TO DISMISS MY PROXY CANDIDATE...

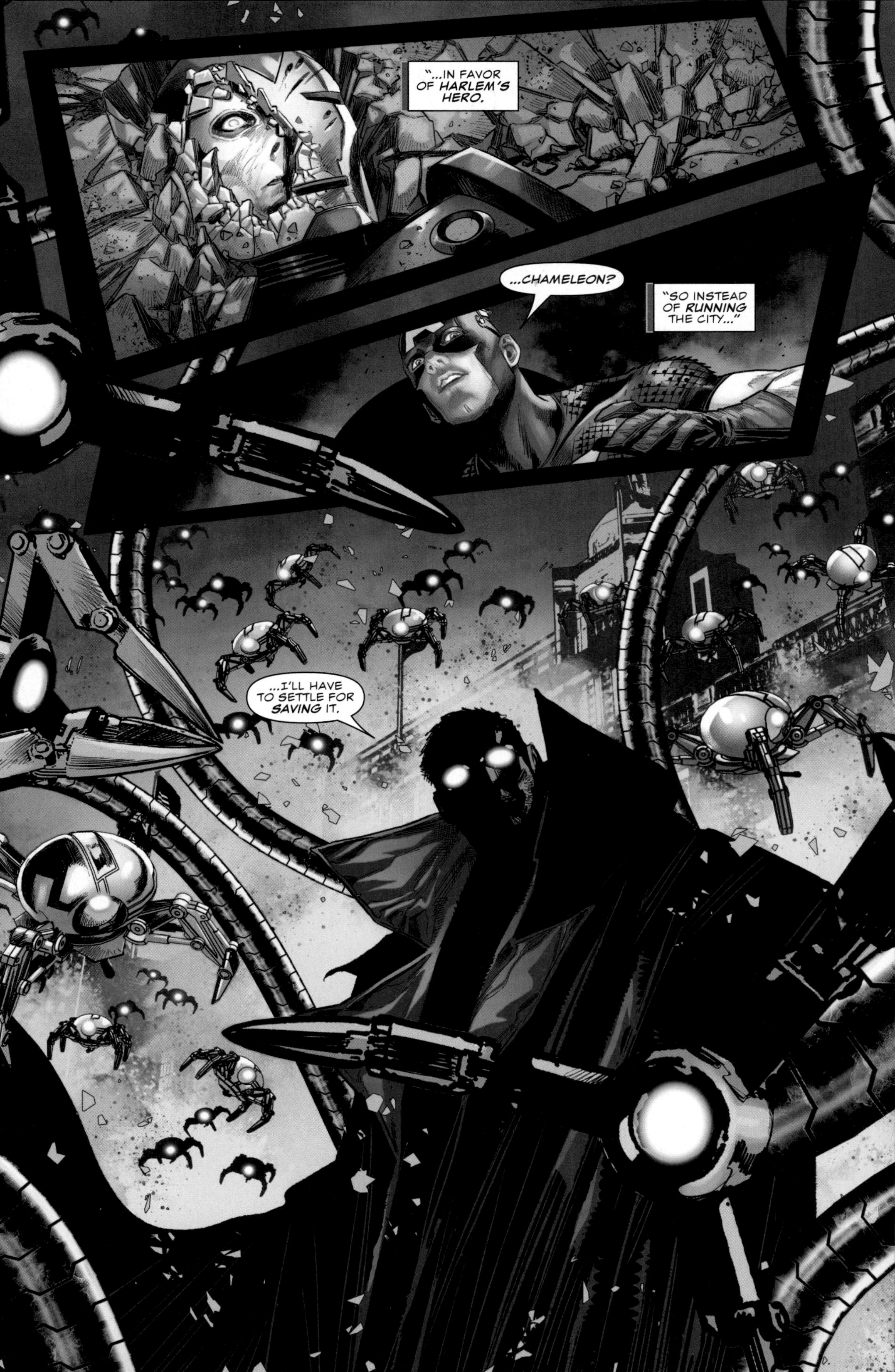
"...IN FAVOR OF HARLEM'S HERO.
...CHAMELEON?
"SO INSTEAD OF RUNNING THE CITY..."
...I'LL HAVE TO SETTLE FOR SAVING IT.

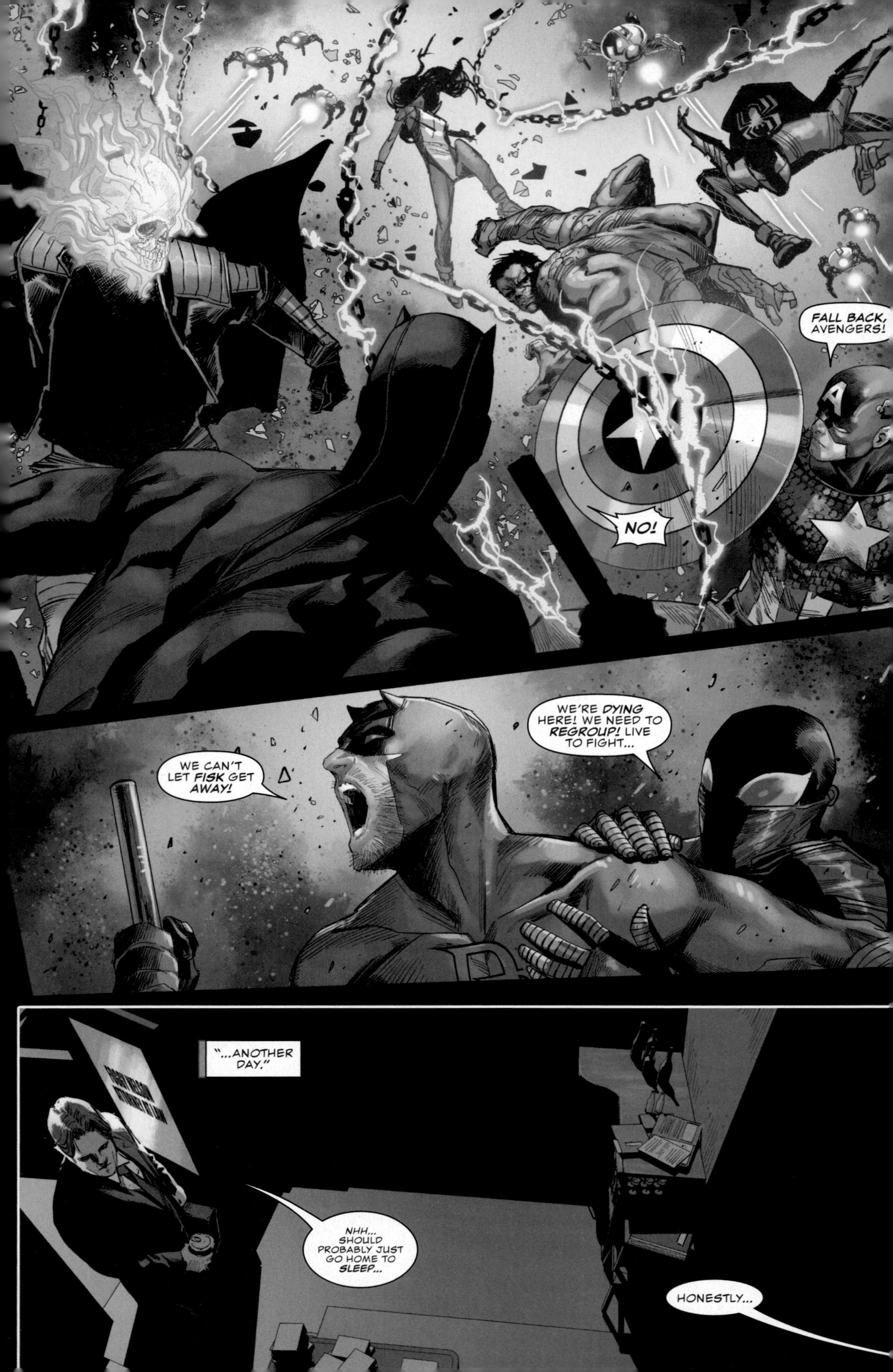
FALL BACK, AVENGERS!
NO!
WE CAN'T LET FISK GET AWAY!
WE'RE DYING HERE! WE NEED TO REGROUP! LIVE TO FIGHT...
"...ANOTHER DAY."
NHH... SHOULD PROBABLY JUST GO HOME TO SLEEP...
HONESTLY...

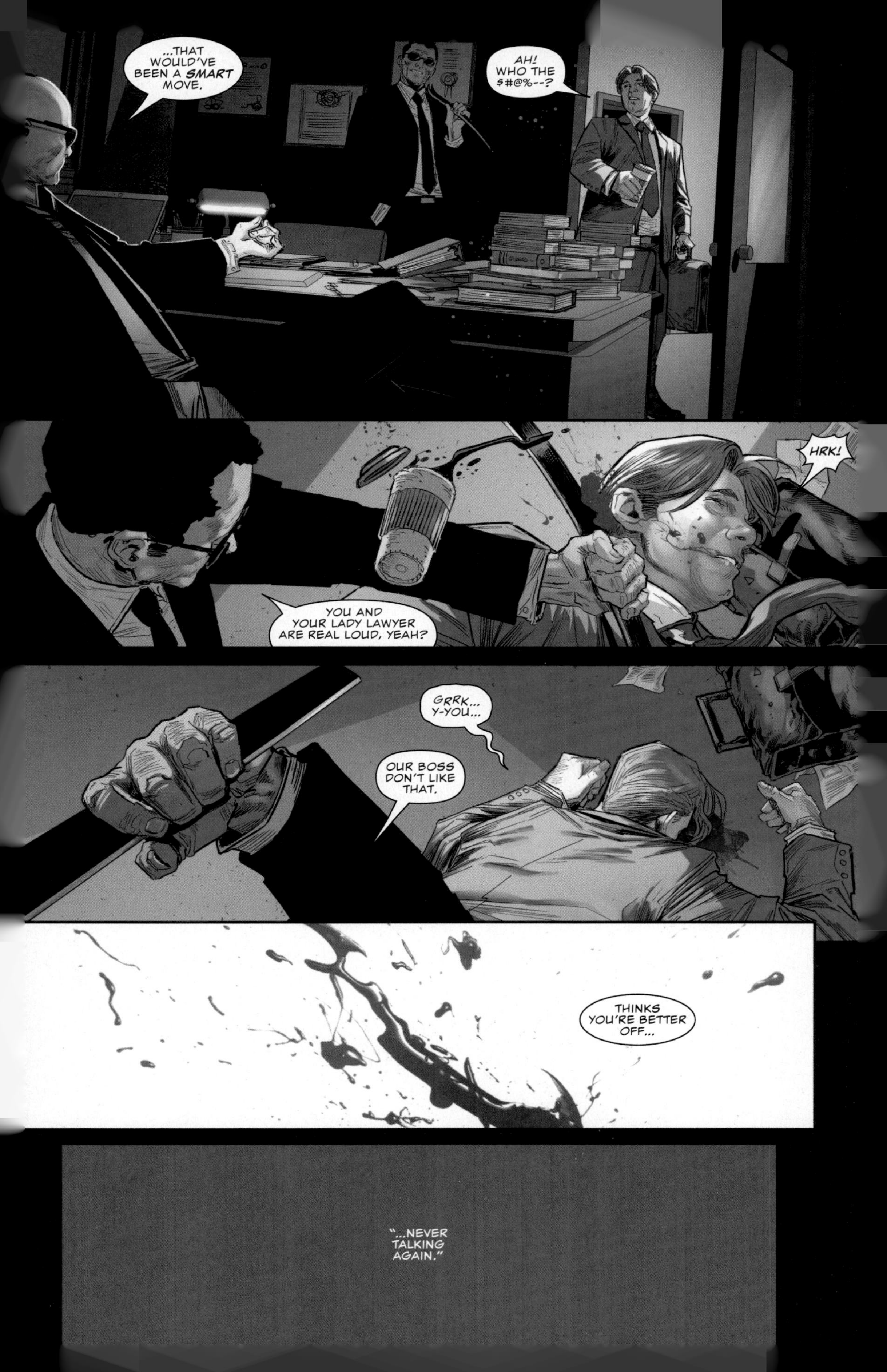
...THAT WOULD'VE BEEN A SMART MOVE.
AH! WHO THE $#@%--?
HRK!
YOU AND YOUR LADY LAWYER ARE REAL LOUD, YEAH?
GRRK... Y-YOU...
OUR BOSS DON'T LIKE THAT.
THINKS YOU'RE BETTER OFF...
"...NEVER TALKING AGAIN."

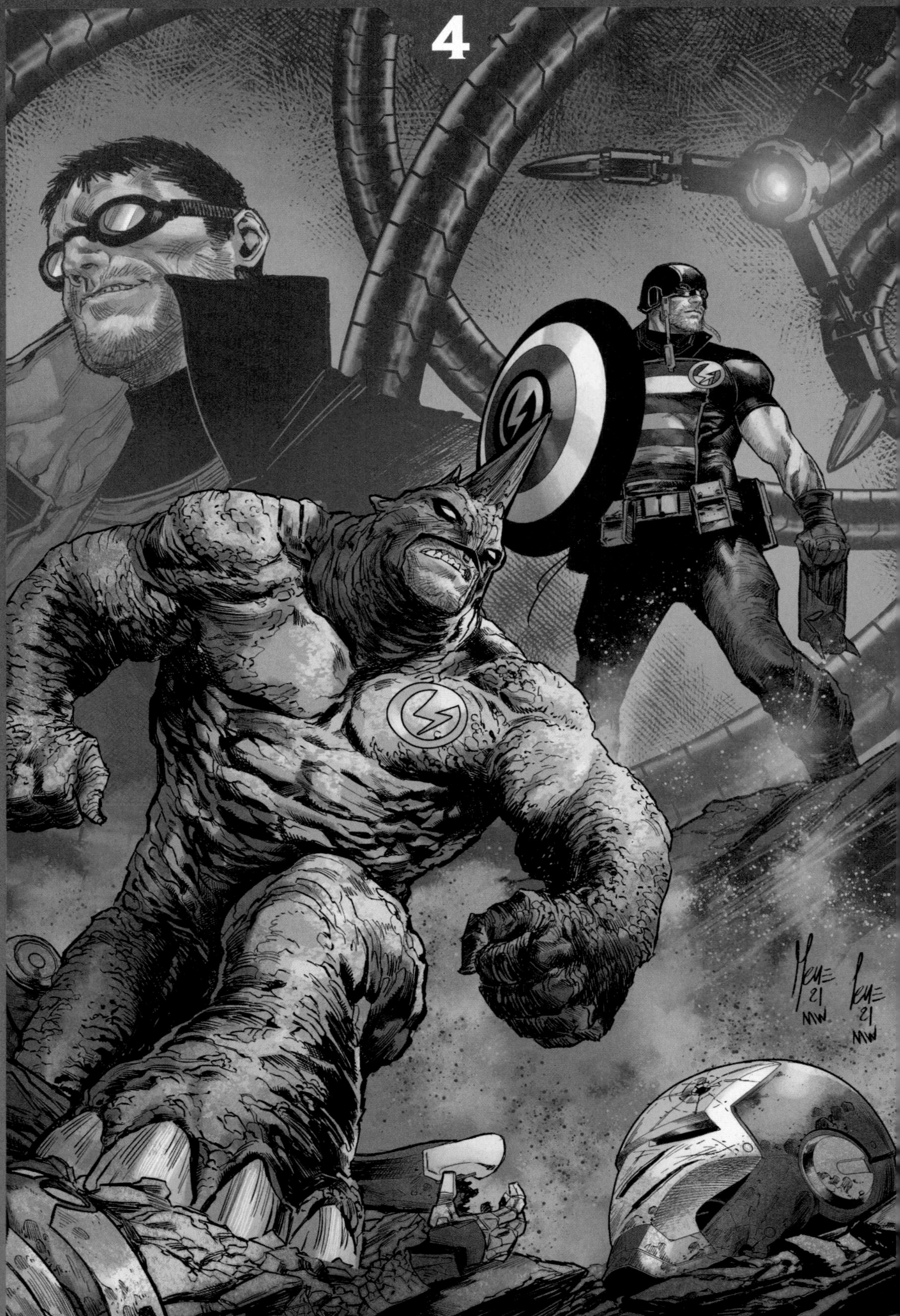
4

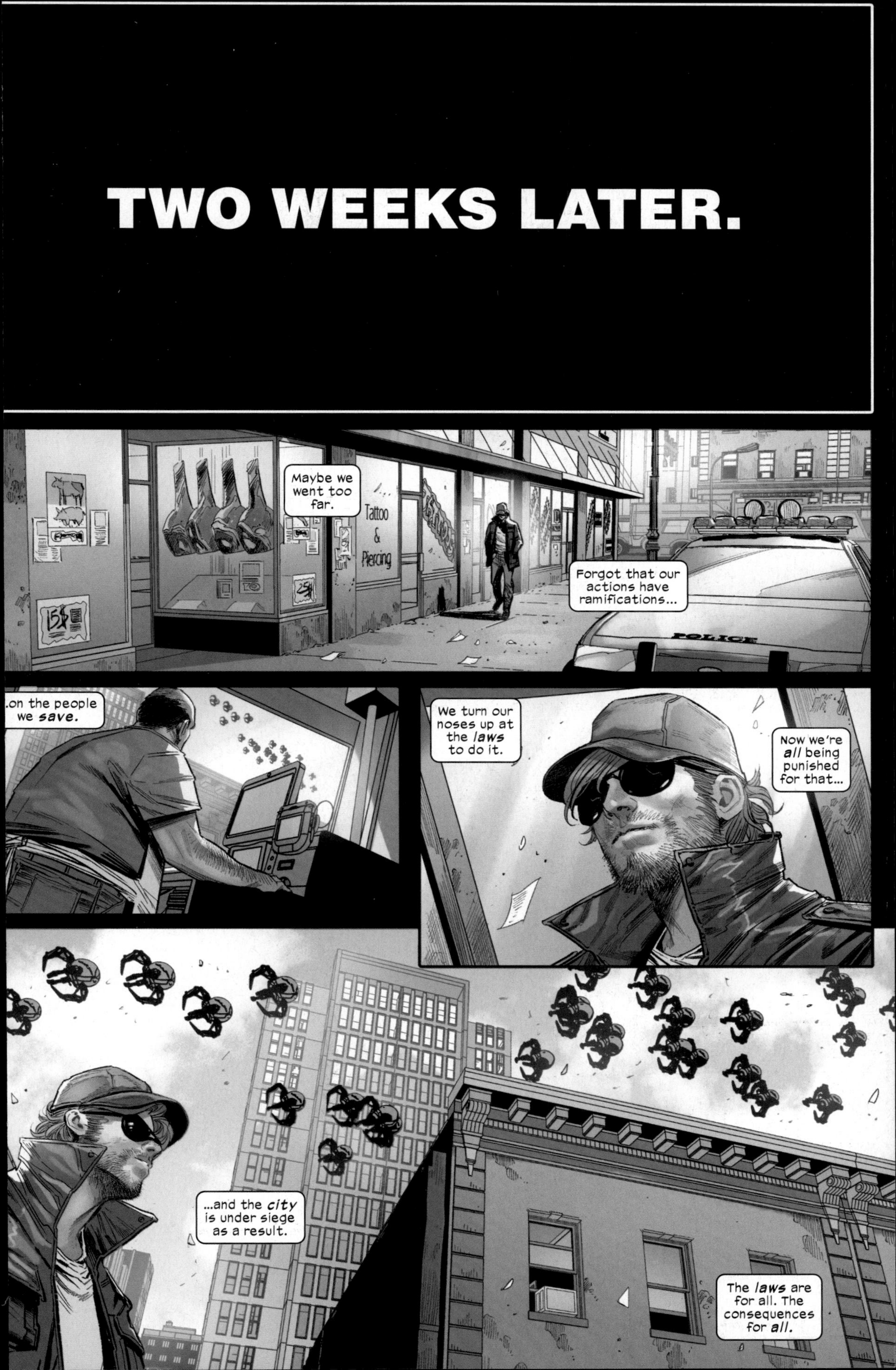
TWO WEEKS LATER.
Maybe we went too far.
Tattoo & Piercing
Forgot that our actions have ramifications...
POLICE
...on the people we *save.*
We turn our noses up at the *laws* to do it.
Now we're *all* being punished for that...
...and the *city* is under siege as a result.
The *laws* are for all. The consequences for *all.*

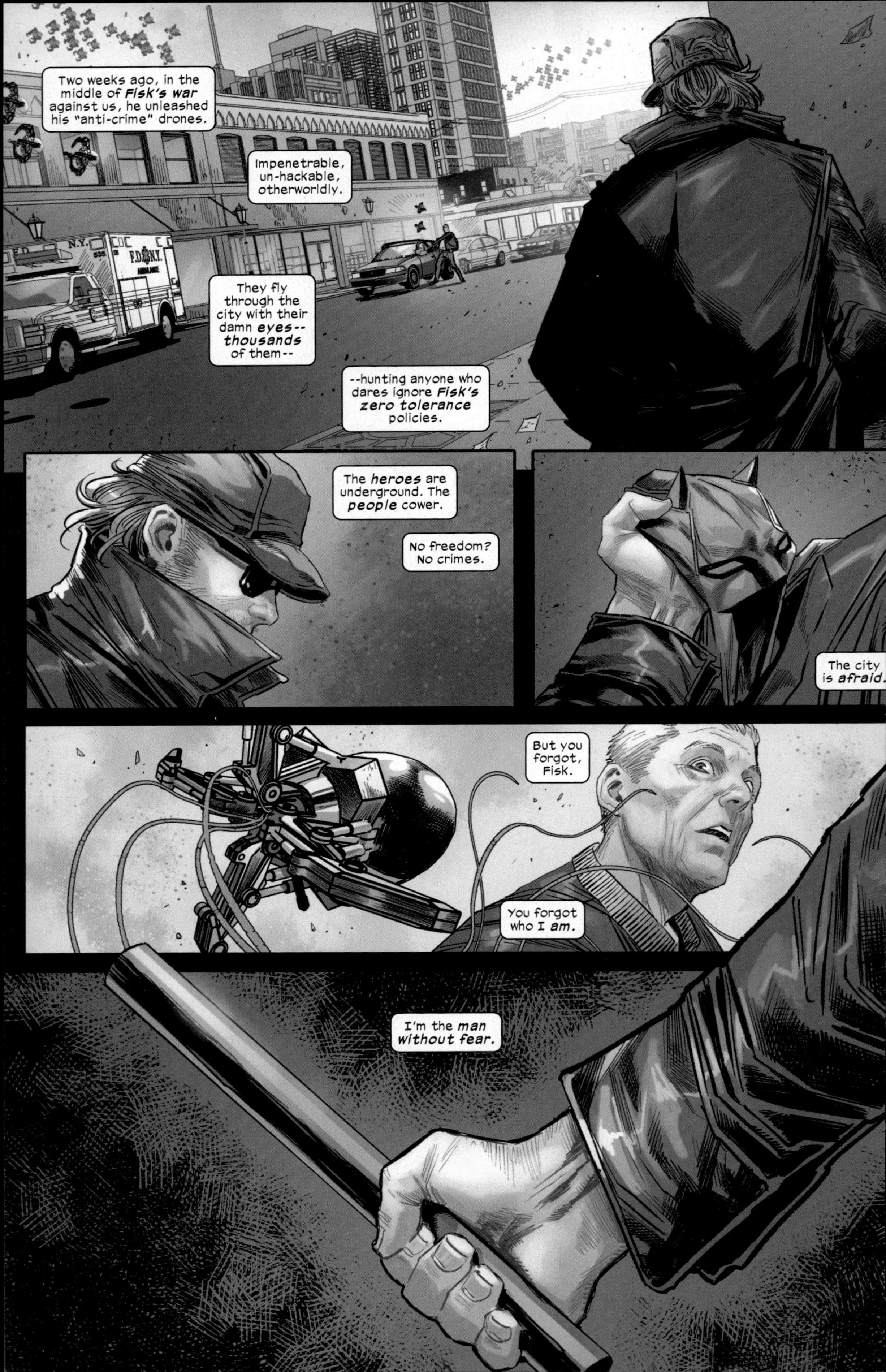
Two weeks ago, in the middle of Fisk's war against us, he unleashed his "anti-crime" drones.
Impenetrable, un-hackable, otherworldly.
They fly through the city with their damn eyes-- thousands of them--
--hunting anyone who dares ignore Fisk's zero tolerance policies.
The heroes are underground. The people cower.
No freedom? No crimes.
The city is afraid.
But you forgot, Fisk.
You forgot who I am.
I'm the man without fear.

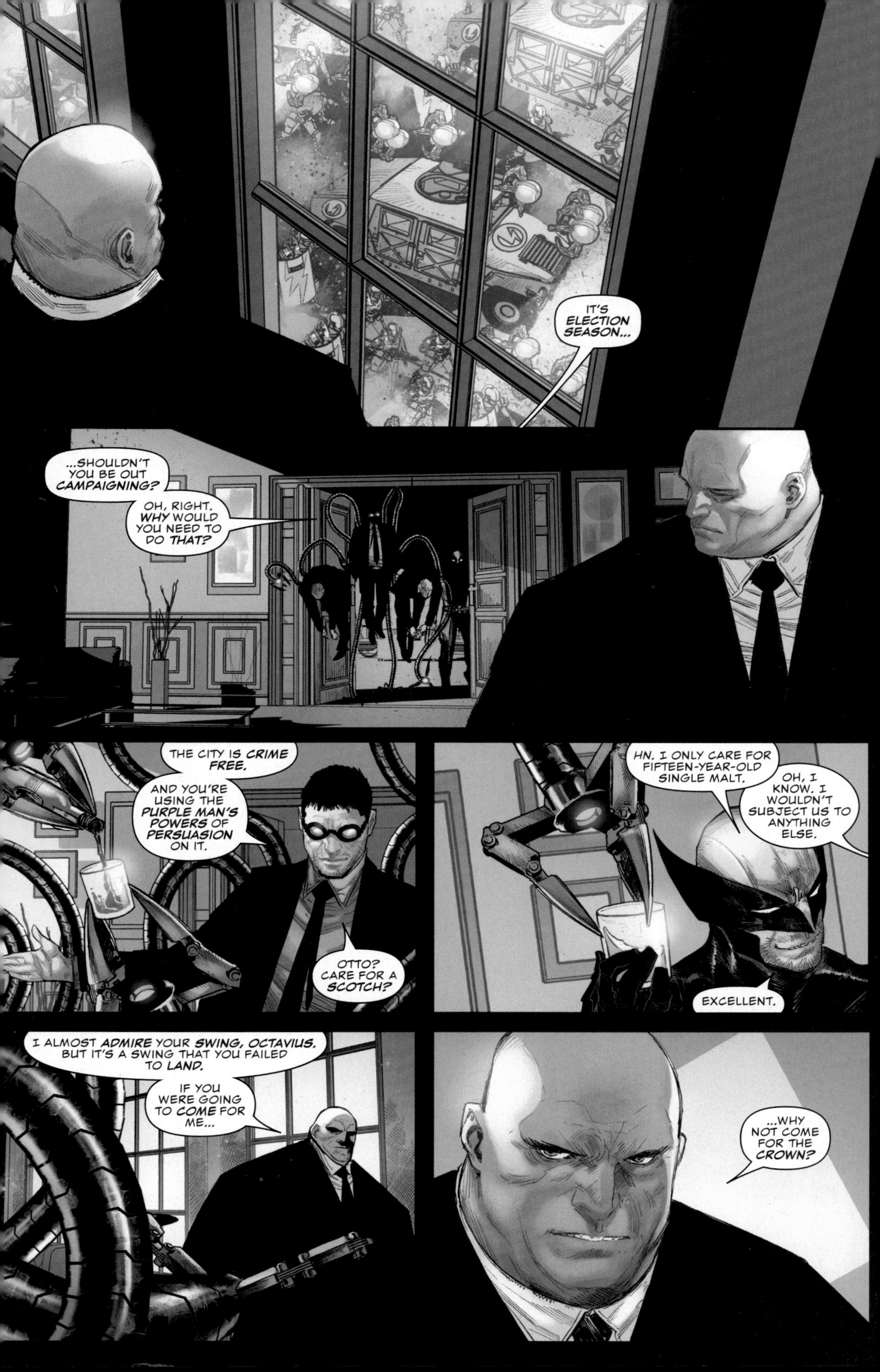
IT'S ELECTION SEASON...
...SHOULDN'T YOU BE OUT CAMPAIGNING?
OH, RIGHT. WHY WOULD YOU NEED TO DO THAT?
THE CITY IS CRIME FREE.
AND YOU'RE USING THE PURPLE MAN'S POWERS OF PERSUASION ON IT.
OTTO? CARE FOR A SCOTCH?
HN. I ONLY CARE FOR FIFTEEN-YEAR-OLD SINGLE MALT.
OH, I KNOW. I WOULDN'T SUBJECT US TO ANYTHING ELSE.
EXCELLENT.
I ALMOST ADMIRE YOUR SWING, OCTAVIUS. BUT IT'S A SWING THAT YOU FAILED TO LAND.
IF YOU WERE GOING TO COME FOR ME...
...WHY NOT COME FOR THE CROWN?

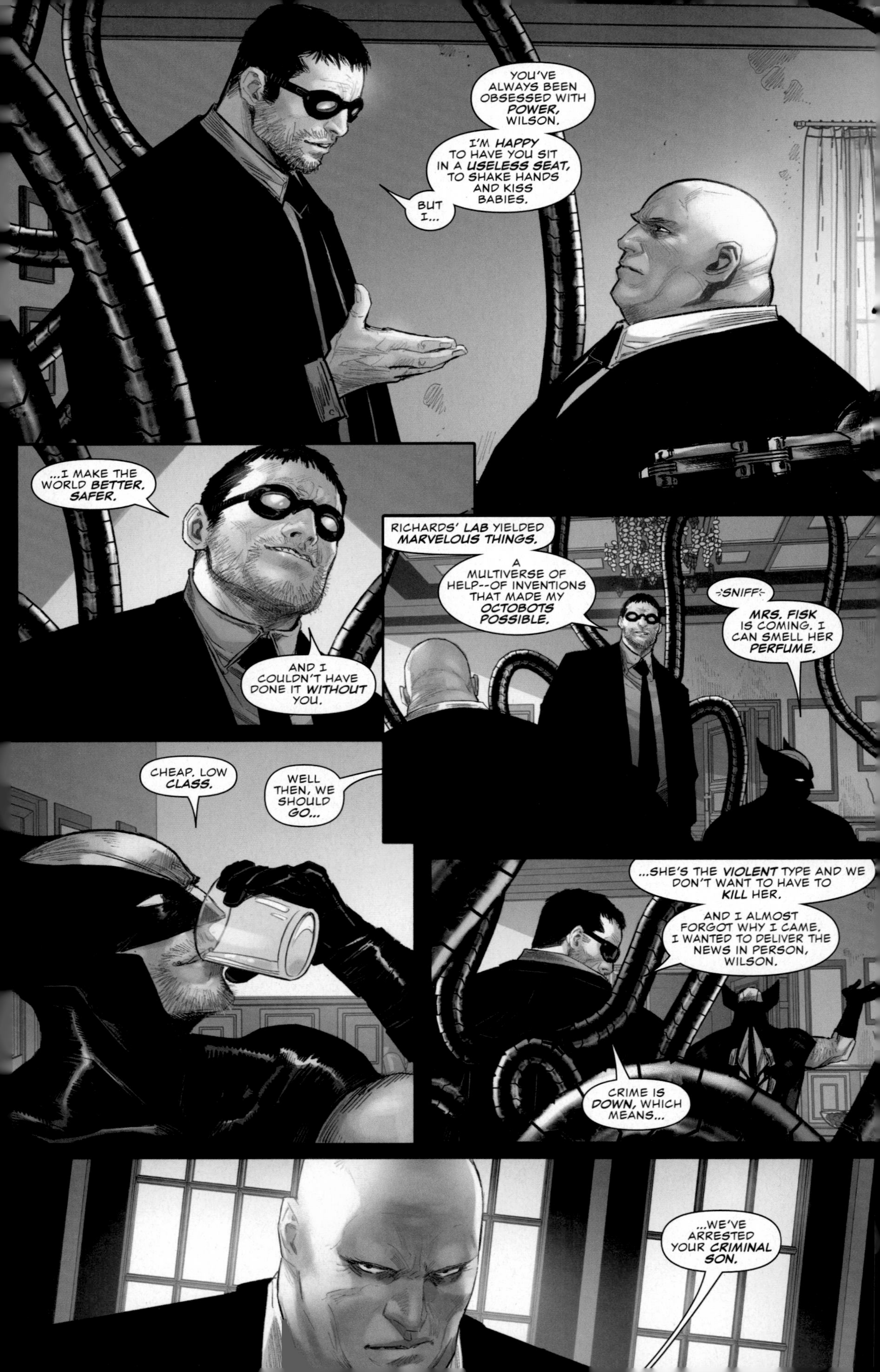
YOU'VE ALWAYS BEEN OBSESSED WITH POWER, WILSON.
I'M HAPPY TO HAVE YOU SIT IN A USELESS SEAT, TO SHAKE HANDS AND KISS BABIES.
BUT I...
...I MAKE THE WORLD BETTER. SAFER.
AND I COULDN'T HAVE DONE IT WITHOUT YOU.
RICHARDS' LAB YIELDED MARVELOUS THINGS.
A MULTIVERSE OF HELP--OF INVENTIONS THAT MADE MY OCTOBOTS POSSIBLE.
SNIFF
MRS. FISK IS COMING. I CAN SMELL HER PERFUME.
CHEAP. LOW CLASS.
WELL THEN, WE SHOULD GO...
...SHE'S THE VIOLENT TYPE AND WE DON'T WANT TO HAVE TO KILL HER.
AND I ALMOST FORGOT WHY I CAME. I WANTED TO DELIVER THE NEWS IN PERSON, WILSON.
CRIME IS DOWN, WHICH MEANS...
...WE'VE ARRESTED YOUR CRIMINAL SON.

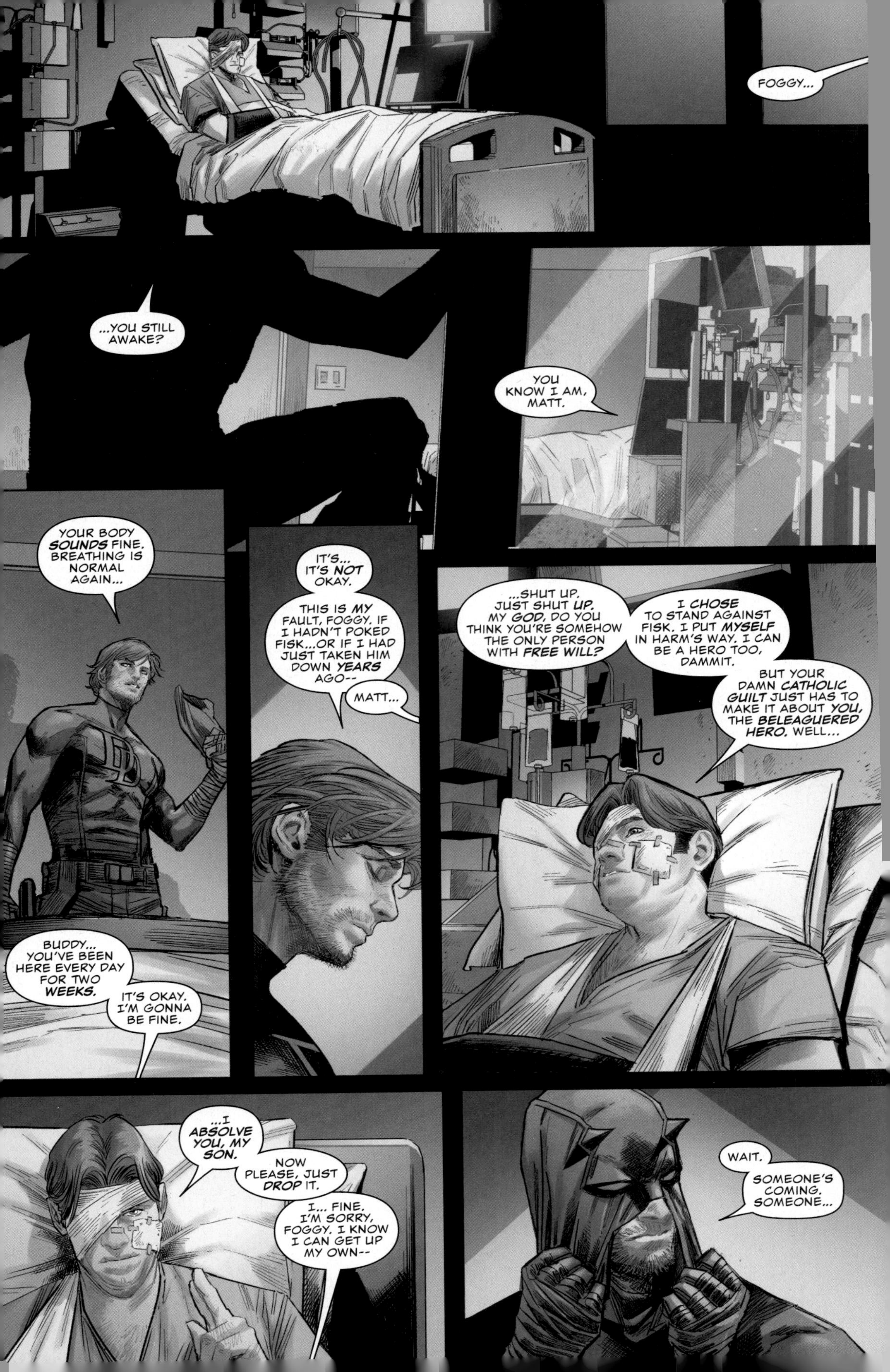
FOGGY...
...YOU STILL AWAKE?
YOU KNOW I AM, MATT.
YOUR BODY SOUNDS FINE. BREATHING IS NORMAL AGAIN...
BUDDY... YOU'VE BEEN HERE EVERY DAY FOR TWO WEEKS.
IT'S OKAY. I'M GONNA BE FINE.
IT'S... IT'S NOT OKAY.
THIS IS MY FAULT, FOGGY. IF I HADN'T POKED FISK...OR IF I HAD JUST TAKEN HIM DOWN YEARS AGO--
MATT...
...SHUT UP. JUST SHUT UP. MY GOD, DO YOU THINK YOU'RE SOMEHOW THE ONLY PERSON WITH FREE WILL?
I CHOSE TO STAND AGAINST FISK. I PUT MYSELF IN HARM'S WAY. I CAN BE A HERO TOO, DAMMIT.
BUT YOUR DAMN CATHOLIC GUILT JUST HAS TO MAKE IT ABOUT YOU, THE BELEAGUERED HERO. WELL...
...I ABSOLVE YOU, MY SON.
NOW PLEASE, JUST DROP IT.
I... FINE. I'M SORRY, FOGGY. I KNOW I CAN GET UP MY OWN--
WAIT.
SOMEONE'S COMING. SOMEONE...

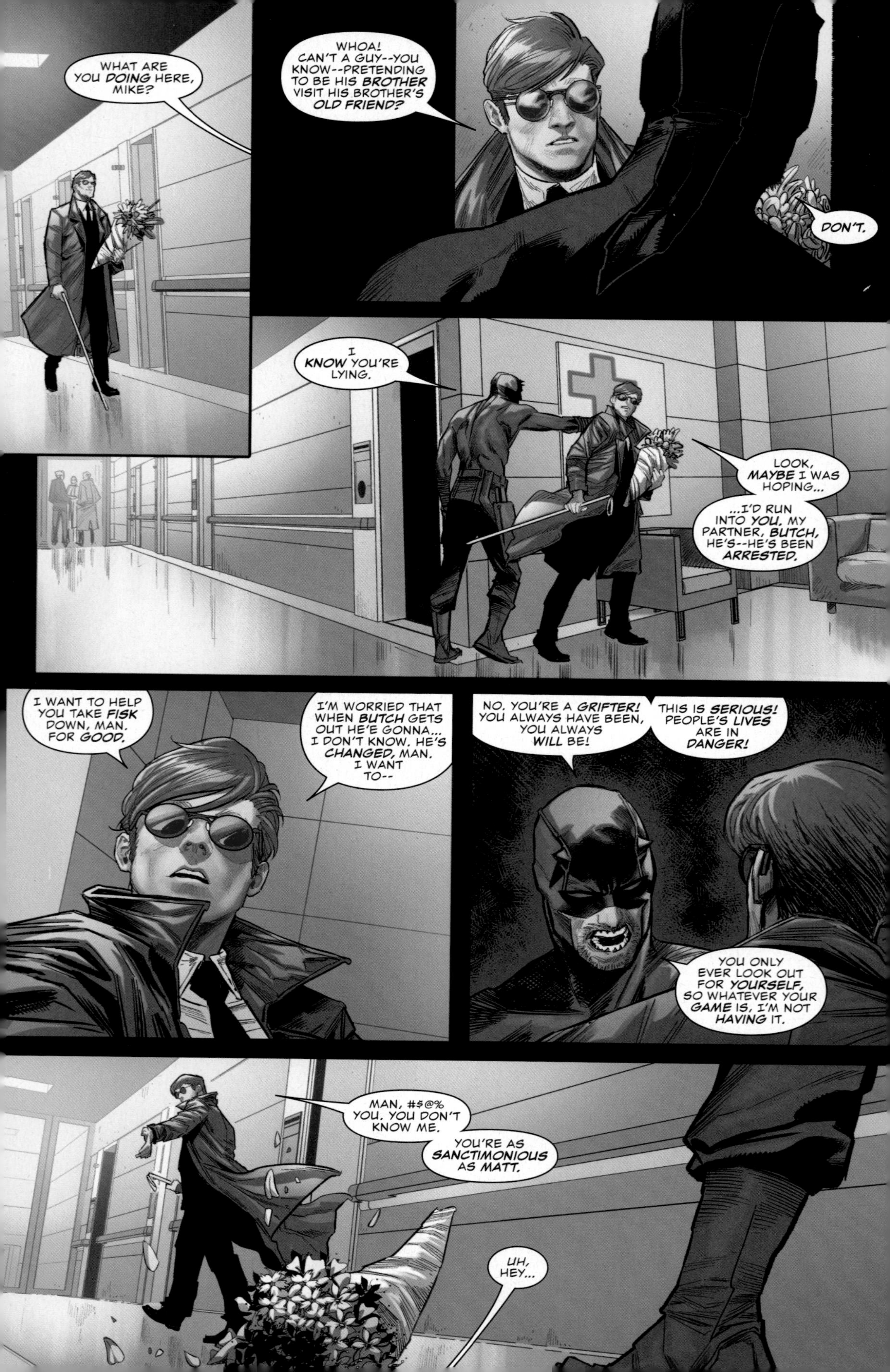
WHAT ARE YOU DOING HERE, MIKE?
WHOA! CAN'T A GUY--YOU KNOW--PRETENDING TO BE HIS BROTHER VISIT HIS BROTHER'S OLD FRIEND?
DON'T.
I KNOW YOU'RE LYING.
LOOK, MAYBE I WAS HOPING...
...I'D RUN INTO YOU. MY PARTNER, BUTCH, HE'S--HE'S BEEN ARRESTED.
I WANT TO HELP YOU TAKE FISK DOWN, MAN. FOR GOOD.
I'M WORRIED THAT WHEN BUTCH GETS OUT HE'E GONNA... I DON'T KNOW. HE'S CHANGED, MAN. I WANT TO--
NO. YOU'RE A GRIFTER! YOU ALWAYS HAVE BEEN, YOU ALWAYS WILL BE!
THIS IS SERIOUS! PEOPLE'S LIVES ARE IN DANGER!
YOU ONLY EVER LOOK OUT FOR YOURSELF, SO WHATEVER YOUR GAME IS, I'M NOT HAVING IT.
MAN, #$@% YOU. YOU DON'T KNOW ME.
YOU'RE AS SANCTIMONIOUS AS MATT.
UH, HEY...

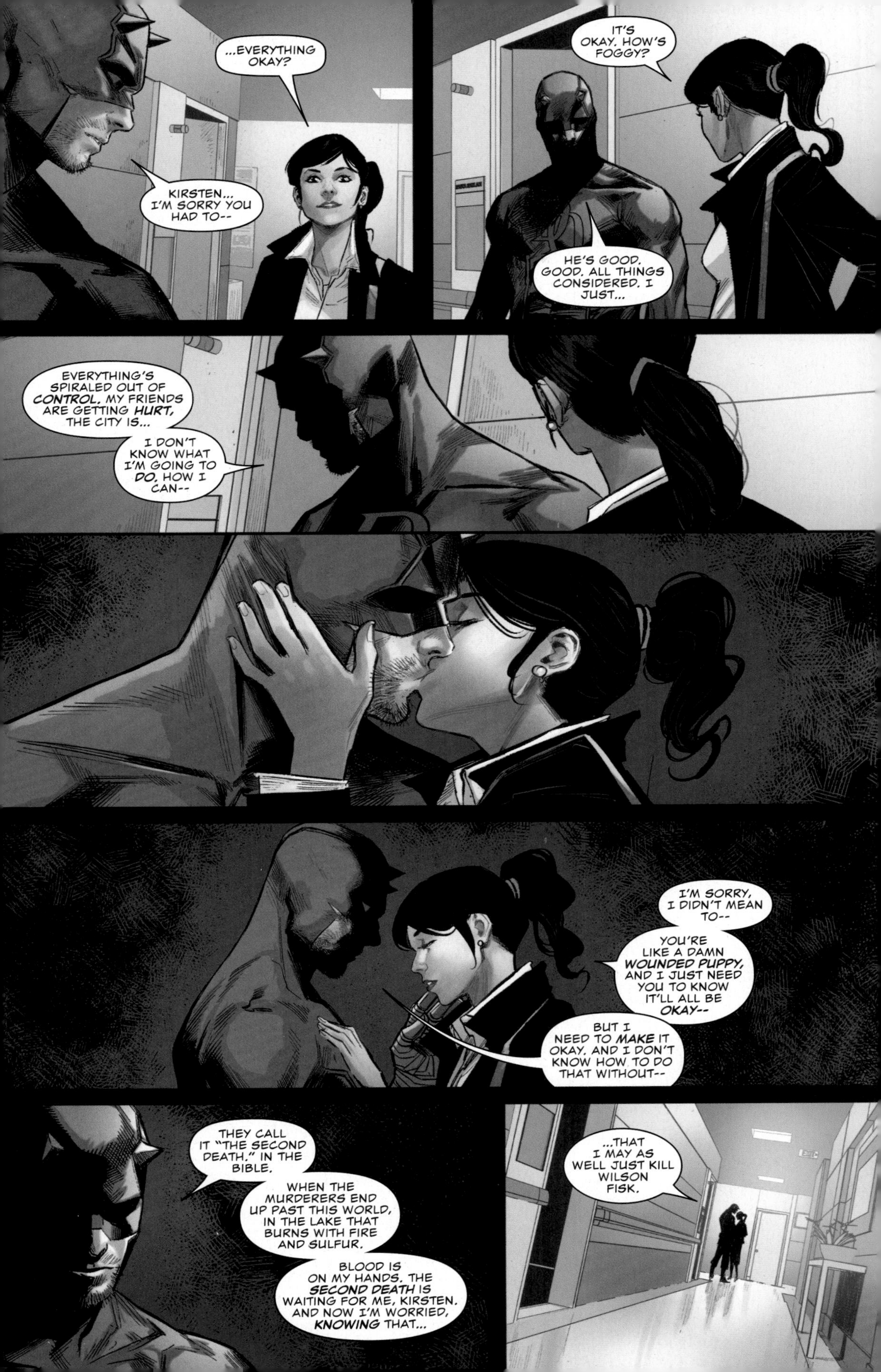
...EVERYTHING OKAY?
KIRSTEN... I'M SORRY YOU HAD TO--
IT'S OKAY. HOW'S FOGGY?
HE'S GOOD. GOOD. ALL THINGS CONSIDERED. I JUST...
EVERYTHING'S SPIRALED OUT OF CONTROL. MY FRIENDS ARE GETTING HURT, THE CITY IS...
I DON'T KNOW WHAT I'M GOING TO DO, HOW I CAN--
I'M SORRY, I DIDN'T MEAN TO--
YOU'RE LIKE A DAMN WOUNDED PUPPY, AND I JUST NEED YOU TO KNOW IT'LL ALL BE OKAY--
BUT I NEED TO MAKE IT OKAY. AND I DON'T KNOW HOW TO DO THAT WITHOUT--
THEY CALL IT "THE SECOND DEATH." IN THE BIBLE.
WHEN THE MURDERERS END UP PAST THIS WORLD, IN THE LAKE THAT BURNS WITH FIRE AND SULFUR.
BLOOD IS ON MY HANDS. THE SECOND DEATH IS WAITING FOR ME, KIRSTEN. AND NOW I'M WORRIED, KNOWING THAT...
...THAT I MAY AS WELL JUST KILL WILSON FISK.

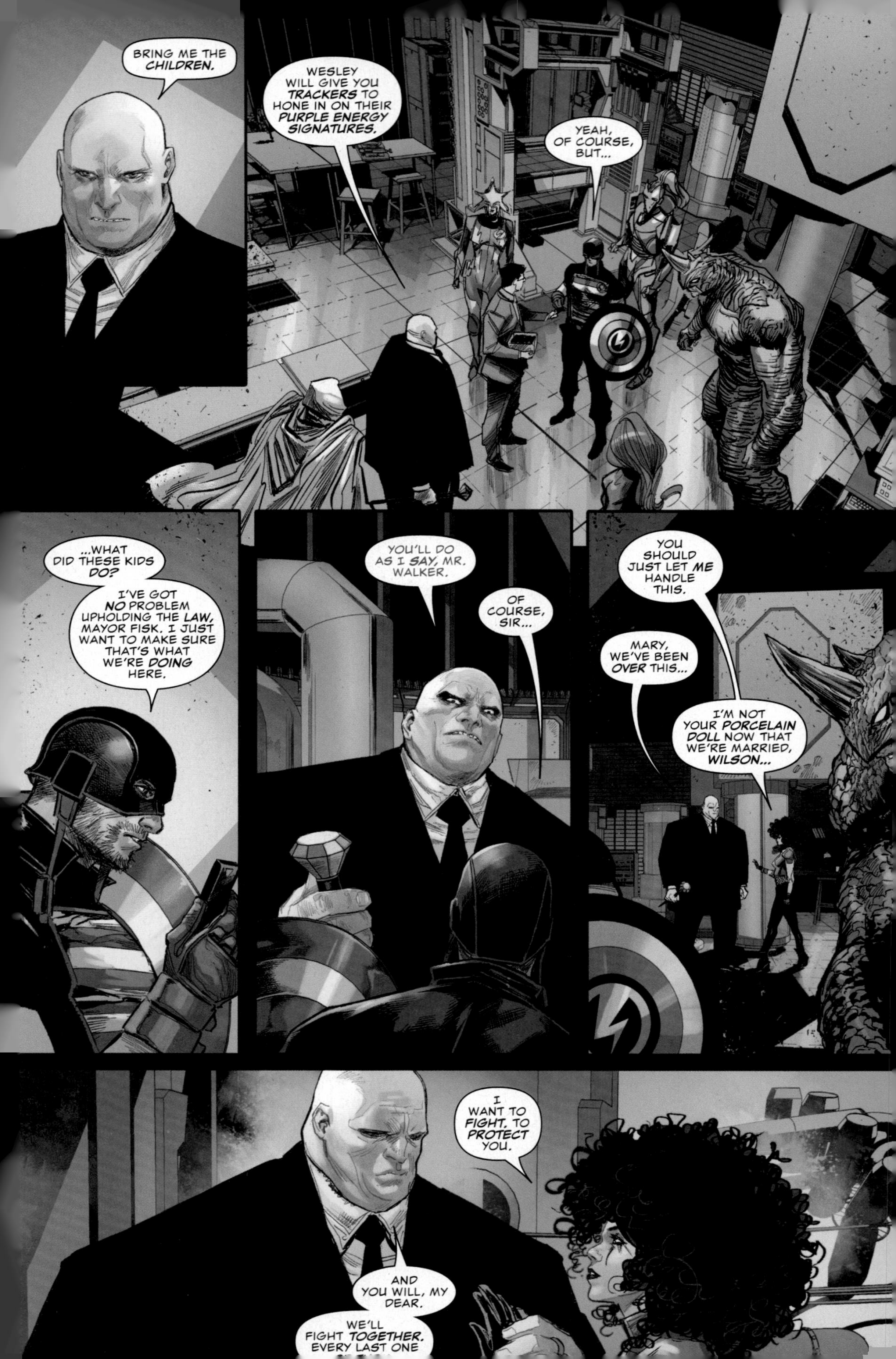
BRING ME THE CHILDREN.
WESLEY WILL GIVE YOU TRACKERS TO HONE IN ON THEIR PURPLE ENERGY SIGNATURES.
YEAH, OF COURSE, BUT...
...WHAT DID THESE KIDS DO?
I'VE GOT NO PROBLEM UPHOLDING THE LAW, MAYOR FISK. I JUST WANT TO MAKE SURE THAT'S WHAT WE'RE DOING HERE.
YOU'LL DO AS I SAY, MR. WALKER.
OF COURSE, SIR...
YOU SHOULD JUST LET ME HANDLE THIS.
MARY, WE'VE BEEN OVER THIS...
I'M NOT YOUR PORCELAIN DOLL NOW THAT WE'RE MARRIED, WILSON...
I WANT TO FIGHT, TO PROTECT YOU.
AND YOU WILL, MY DEAR.
WE'LL FIGHT TOGETHER. EVERY LAST ONE

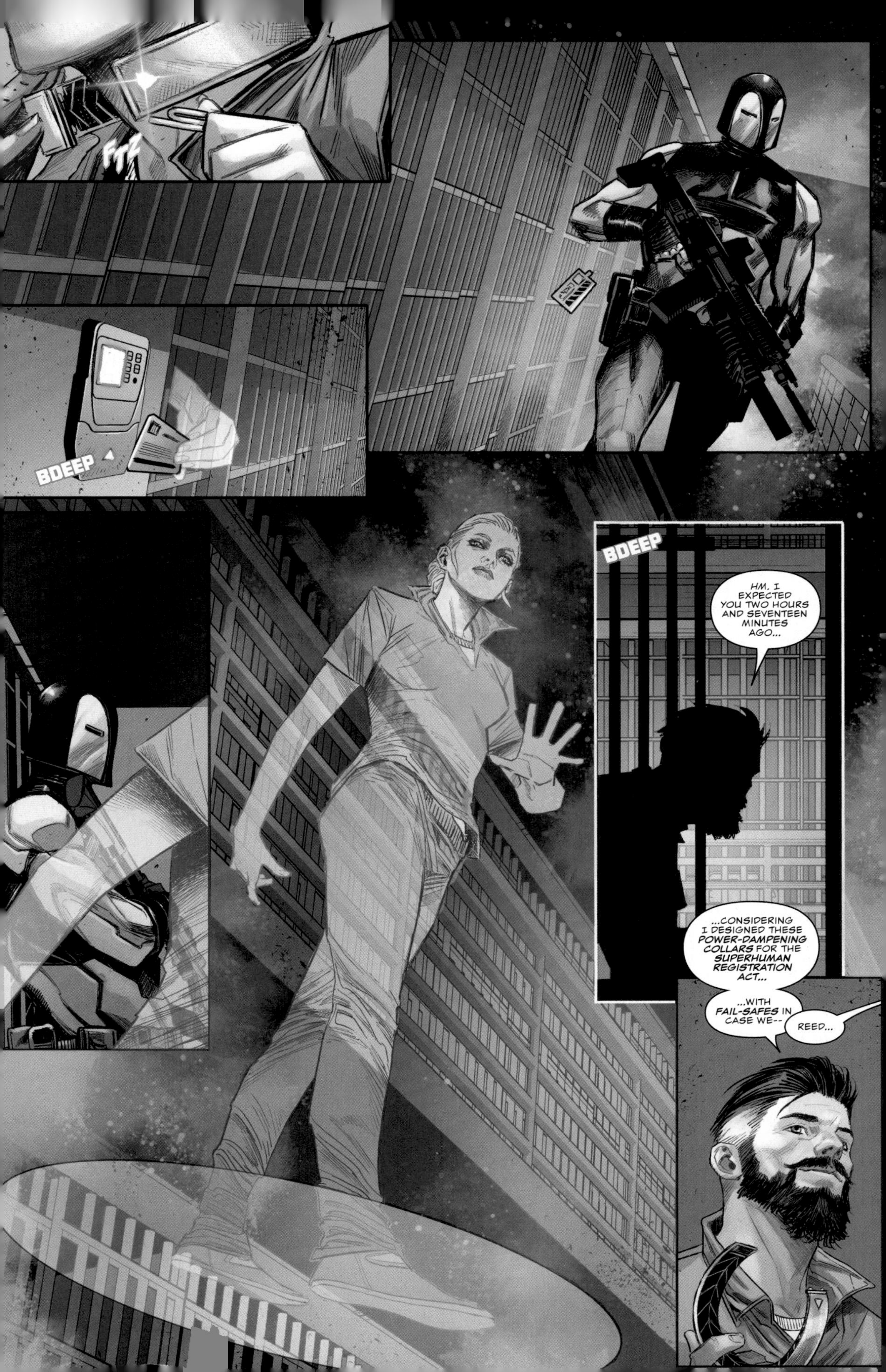
FTZ
BDEEP
BDEEP
HM. I EXPECTED YOU TWO HOURS AND SEVENTEEN MINUTES AGO...
...CONSIDERING I DESIGNED THESE POWER-DAMPENING COLLARS FOR THE SUPERHUMAN REGISTRATION ACT...
...WITH FAIL-SAFES IN CASE WE--
REED...

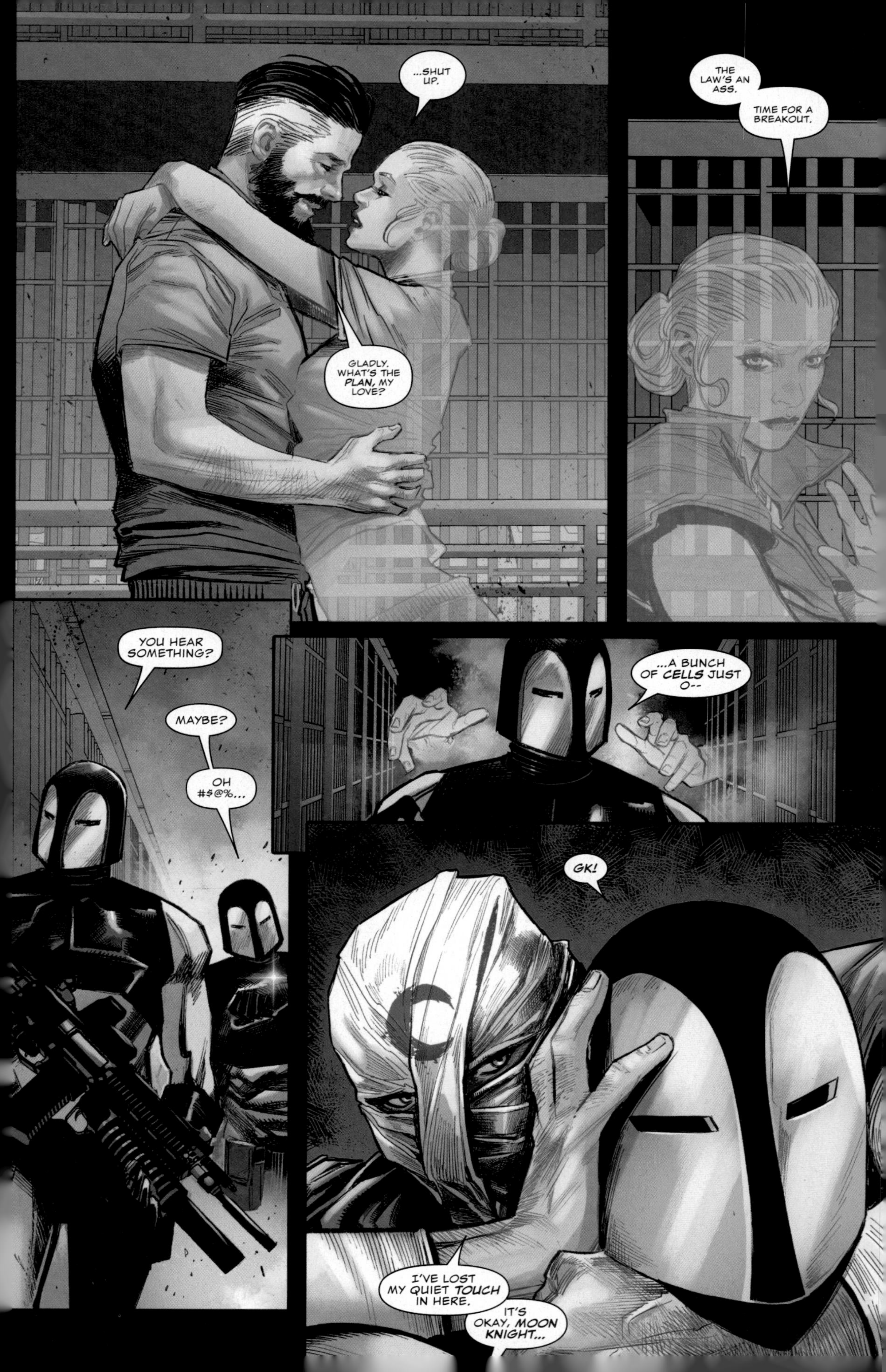
...SHUT UP.
GLADLY. WHAT'S THE PLAN, MY LOVE?
THE LAW'S AN ASS.
TIME FOR A BREAKOUT.
YOU HEAR SOMETHING?
MAYBE?
OH #$@%...
...A BUNCH OF CELLS JUST O--
GK!
I'VE LOST MY QUIET TOUCH IN HERE.
IT'S OKAY, MOON KNIGHT...

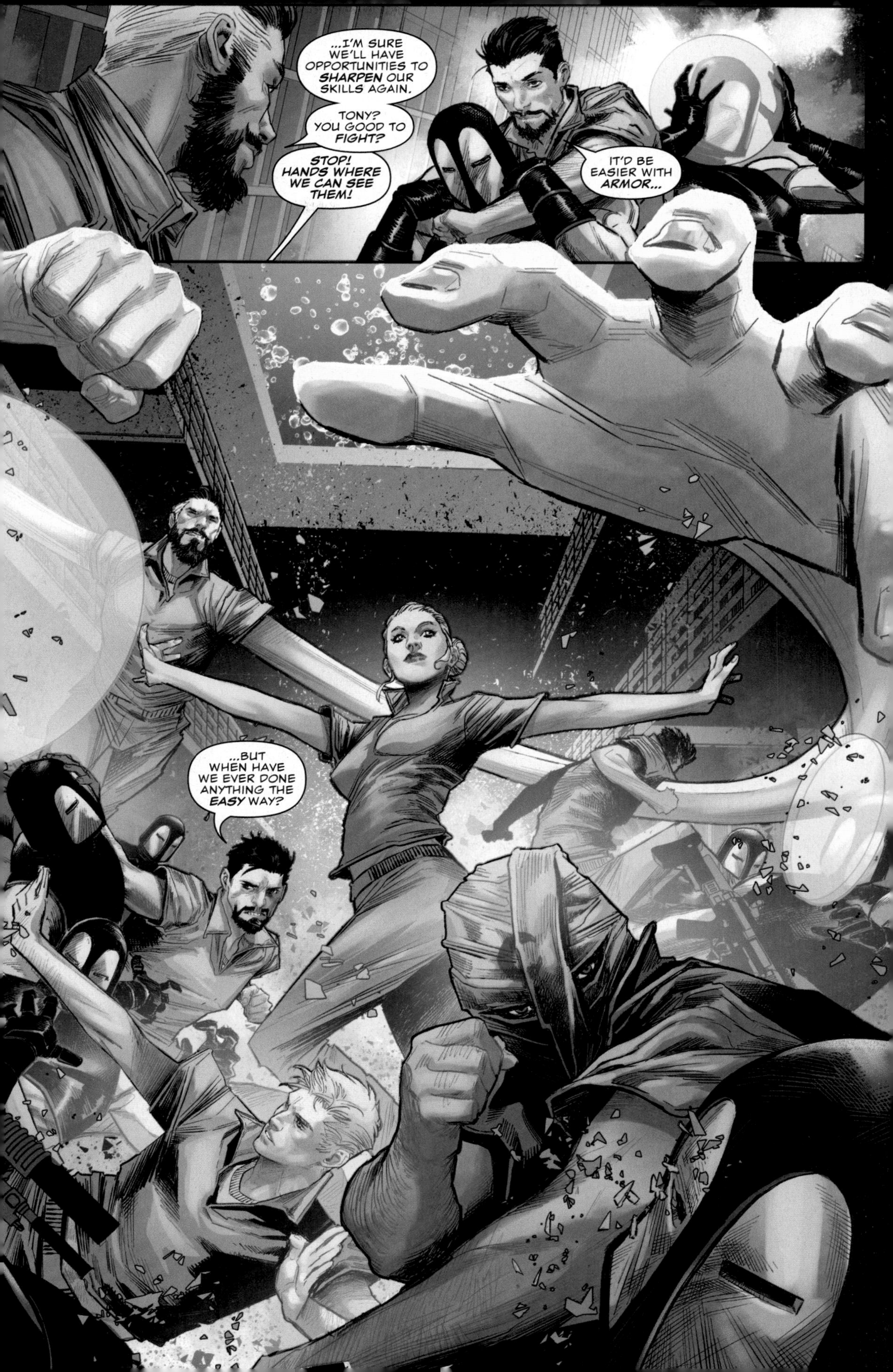
...I'M SURE WE'LL HAVE OPPORTUNITIES TO SHARPEN OUR SKILLS AGAIN.
TONY? YOU GOOD TO FIGHT?
STOP! HANDS WHERE WE CAN SEE THEM!
IT'D BE EASIER WITH ARMOR...
...BUT WHEN HAVE WE EVER DONE ANYTHING THE EASY WAY?

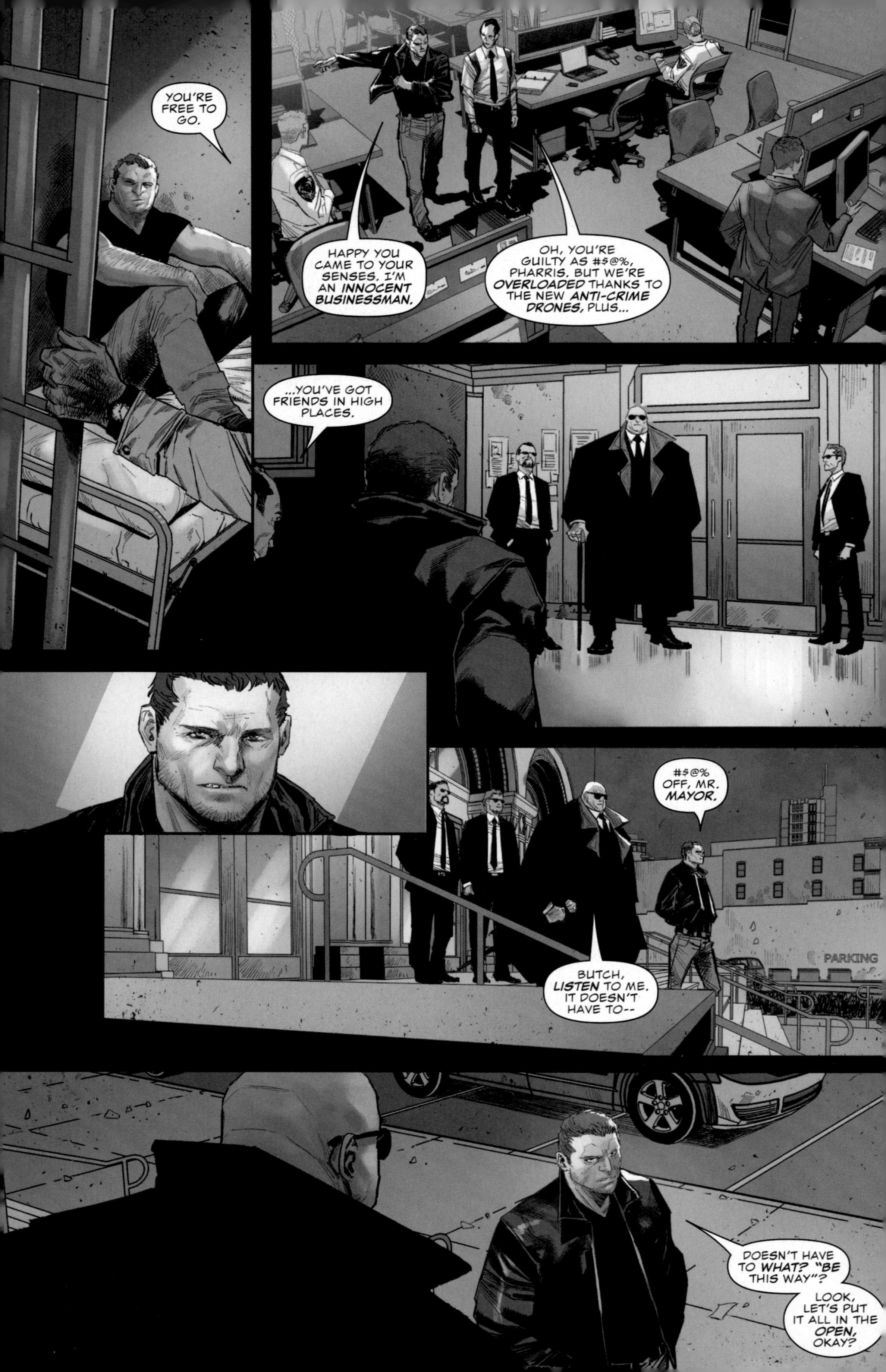
YOU'RE FREE TO GO.
HAPPY YOU CAME TO YOUR SENSES. I'M AN INNOCENT BUSINESSMAN.
OH, YOU'RE GUILTY AS #$@%, PHARRIS. BUT WE'RE OVERLOADED THANKS TO THE NEW ANTI-CRIME DRONES, PLUS...
...YOU'VE GOT FRIENDS IN HIGH PLACES.
#$@% OFF, MR. MAYOR.
PARKING
BUTCH, LISTEN TO ME. IT DOESN'T HAVE TO--
DOESN'T HAVE TO WHAT? "BE THIS WAY"?
LOOK, LET'S PUT IT ALL IN THE OPEN, OKAY?

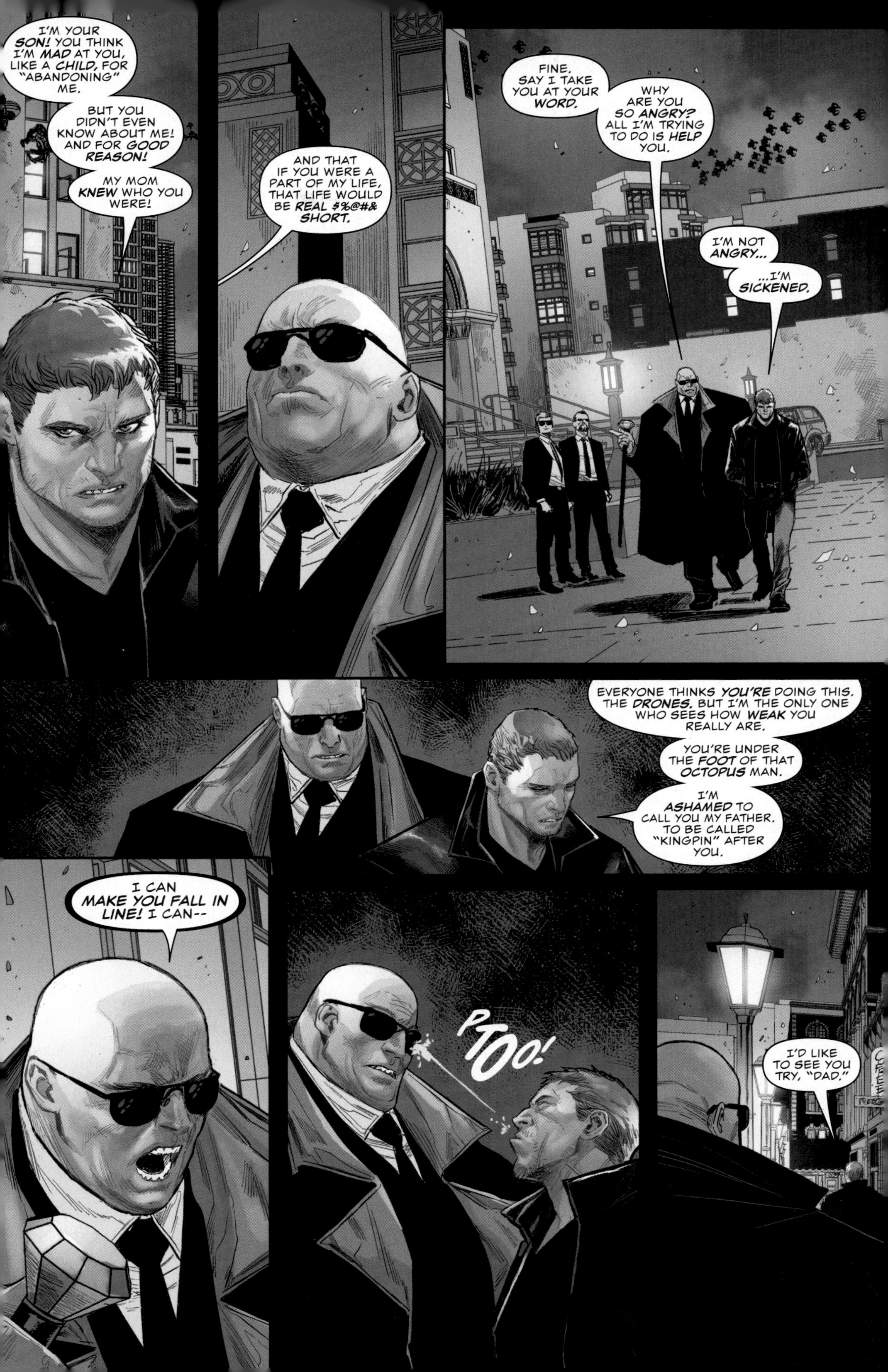

I'M YOUR SON! YOU THINK I'M MAD AT YOU, LIKE A CHILD, FOR "ABANDONING" ME.
BUT YOU DIDN'T EVEN KNOW ABOUT ME! AND FOR GOOD REASON!
MY MOM KNEW WHO YOU WERE!
AND THAT IF YOU WERE A PART OF MY LIFE, THAT LIFE WOULD BE REAL $%@#& SHORT.
FINE. SAY I TAKE YOU AT YOUR WORD.
WHY ARE YOU SO ANGRY? ALL I'M TRYING TO DO IS HELP YOU.
I'M NOT ANGRY...
...I'M SICKENED.
EVERYONE THINKS YOU'RE DOING THIS. THE DRONES. BUT I'M THE ONLY ONE WHO SEES HOW WEAK YOU REALLY ARE.
YOU'RE UNDER THE FOOT OF THAT OCTOPUS MAN.
I'M ASHAMED TO CALL YOU MY FATHER. TO BE CALLED "KINGPIN" AFTER YOU.
I CAN MAKE YOU FALL IN LINE! I CAN--
PTOO!
I'D LIKE TO SEE YOU TRY, "DAD."

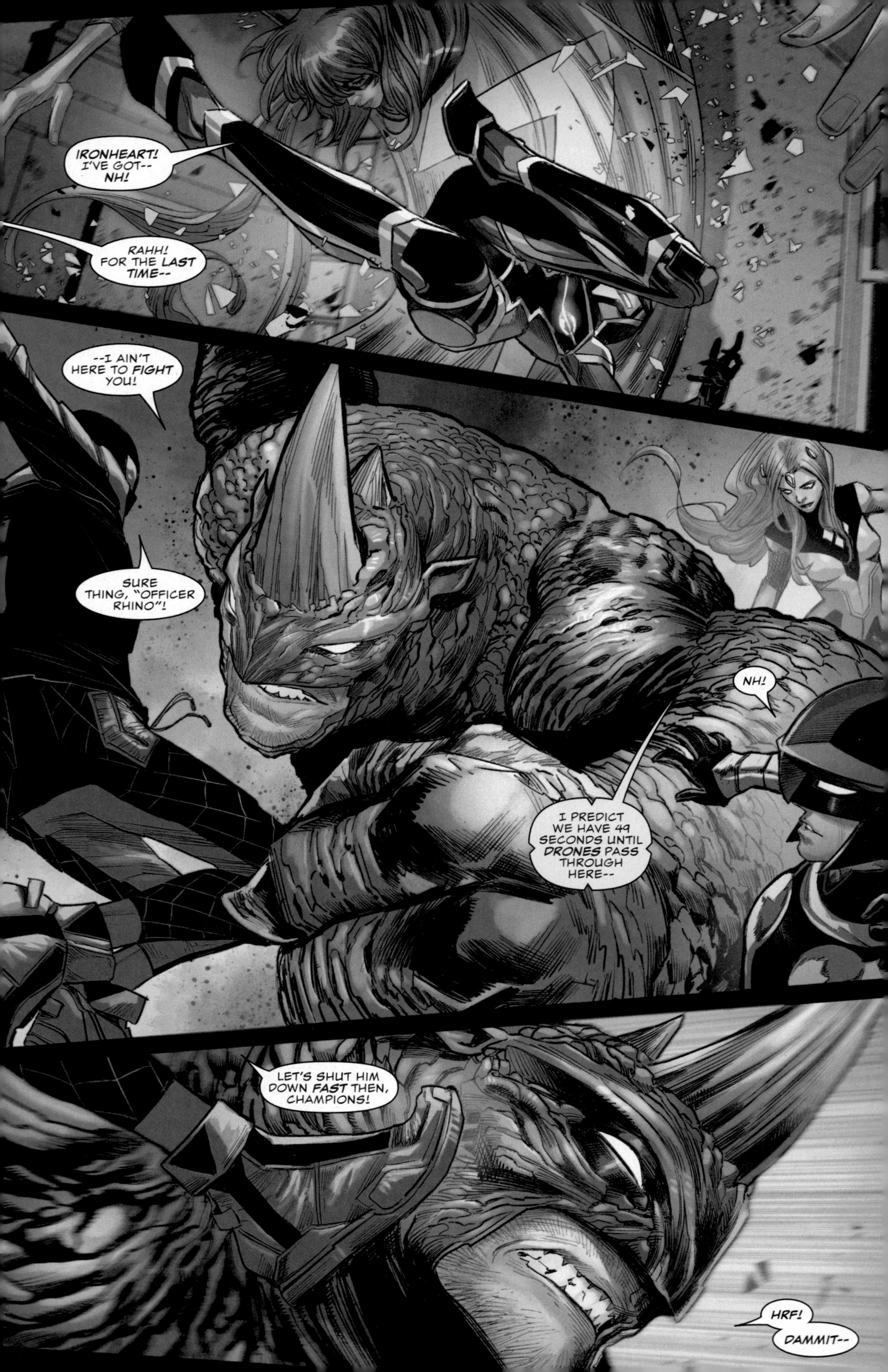
IRONHEART! I'VE GOT-- NH!
RAHH! FOR THE LAST TIME--
--I AIN'T HERE TO FIGHT YOU!
SURE THING, "OFFICER RHINO"!
NH!
I PREDICT WE HAVE 49 SECONDS UNTIL DRONES PASS THROUGH HERE--
LET'S SHUT HIM DOWN FAST THEN, CHAMPIONS!
HRF!
DAMMIT--

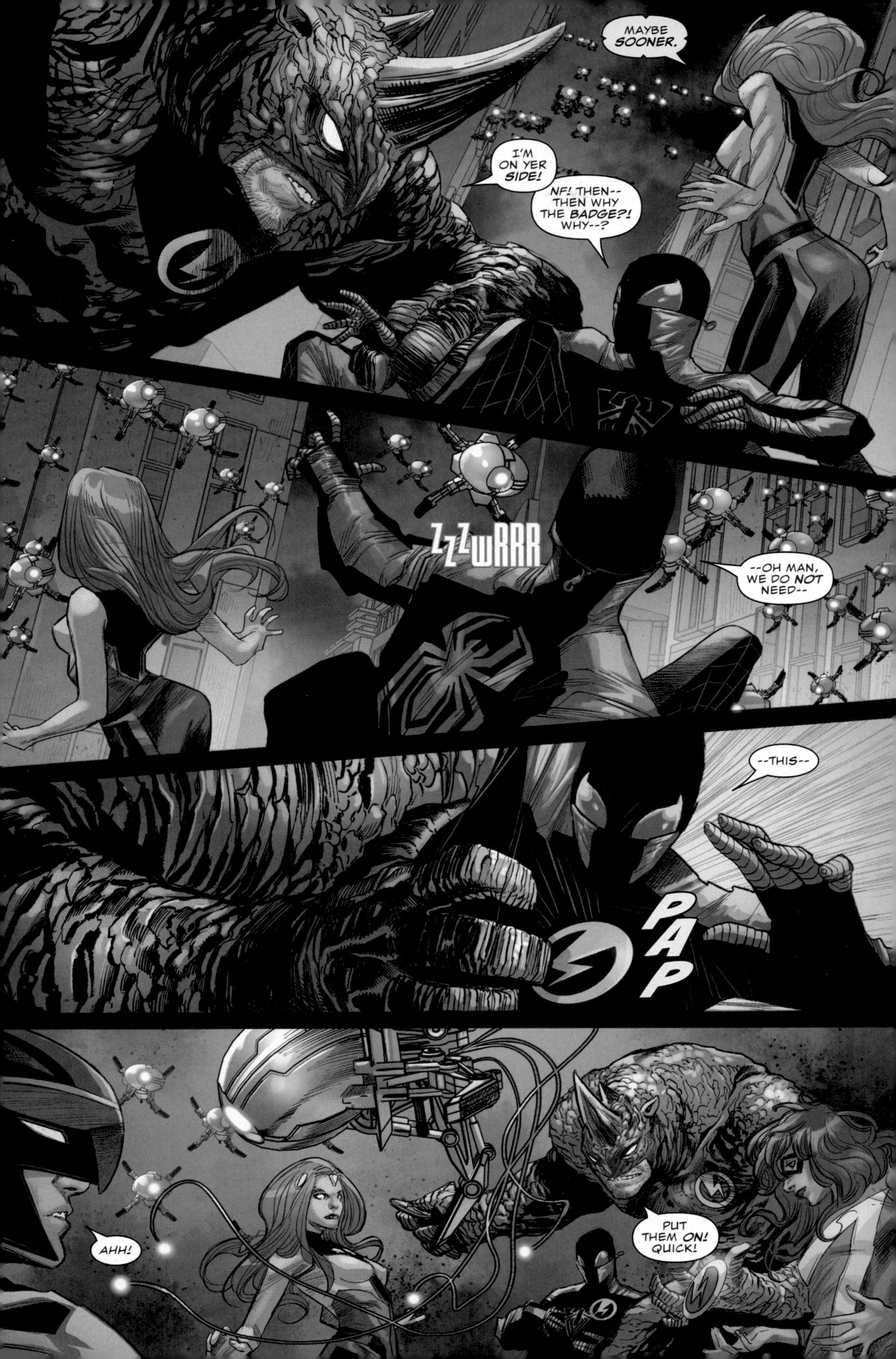
MAYBE SOONER.
I'M ON YER SIDE!
NF! THEN-- THEN WHY THE BADGE?! WHY--?
ZZZWRRR
--OH MAN, WE DO NOT NEED--
--THIS--
PAP PAP
AHH!
PUT THEM ON! QUICK!

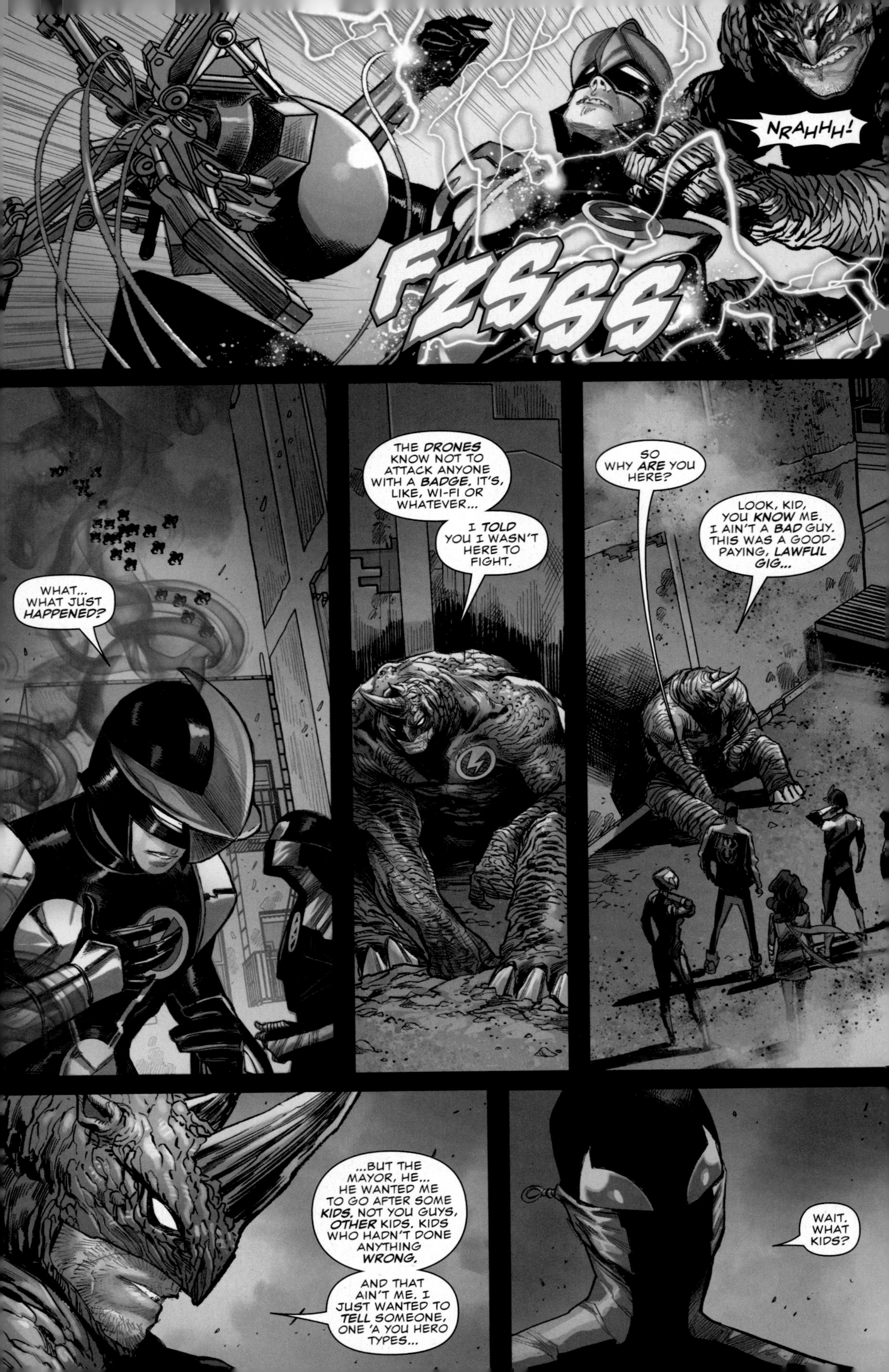
NRAHHH!
FZSSS
WHAT... WHAT JUST HAPPENED?
THE DRONES KNOW NOT TO ATTACK ANYONE WITH A BADGE. IT'S, LIKE, WI-FI OR WHATEVER...
I TOLD YOU I WASN'T HERE TO FIGHT.
SO WHY ARE YOU HERE?
LOOK, KID, YOU KNOW ME. I AIN'T A BAD GUY. THIS WAS A GOOD-PAYING, LAWFUL GIG...
...BUT THE MAYOR, HE... HE WANTED ME TO GO AFTER SOME KIDS. NOT YOU GUYS, OTHER KIDS. KIDS WHO HADN'T DONE ANYTHING WRONG.
AND THAT AIN'T ME. I JUST WANTED TO TELL SOMEONE, ONE 'A YOU HERO TYPES...
WAIT. WHAT KIDS?

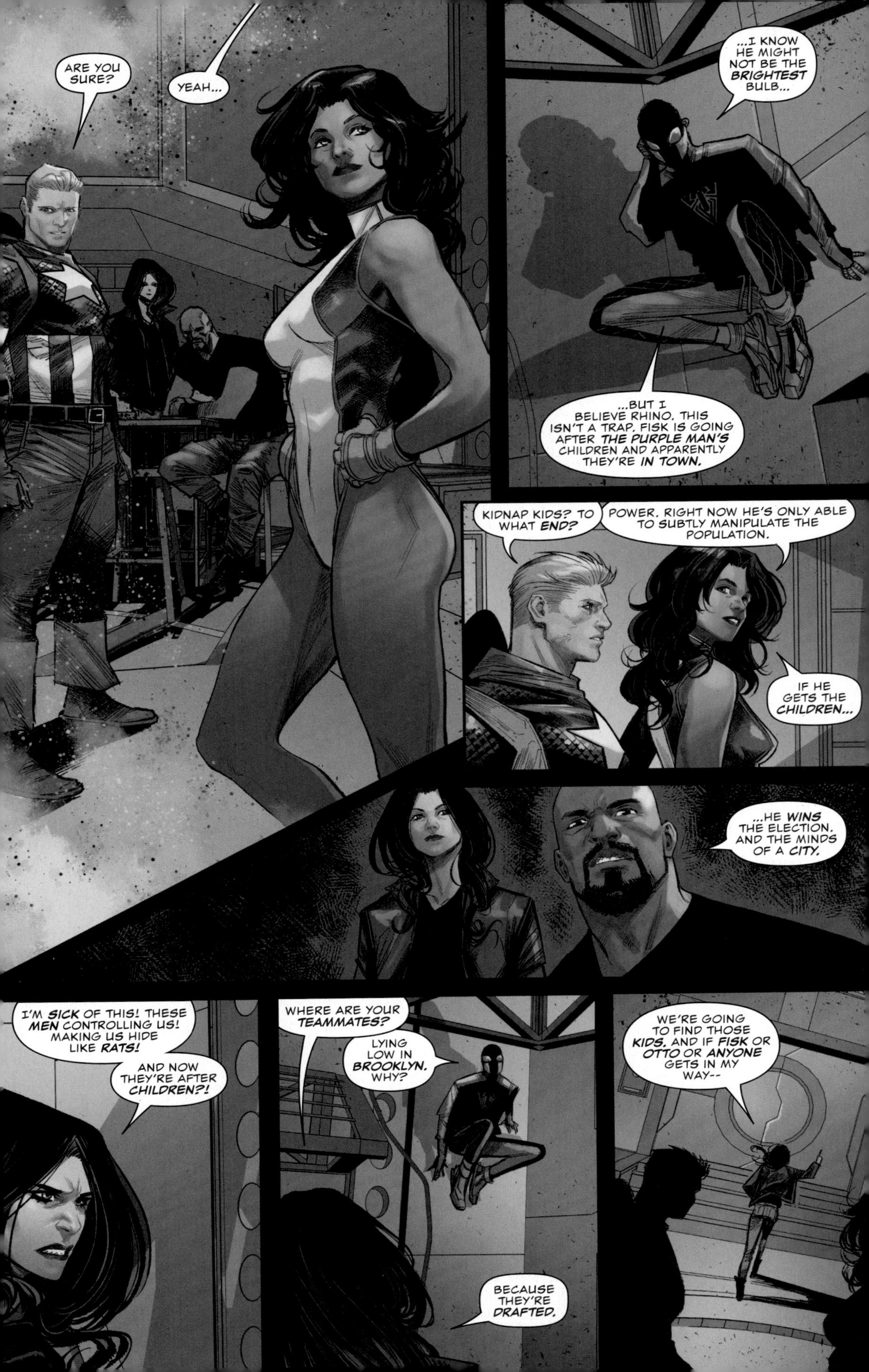
ARE YOU SURE?
YEAH...
...I KNOW HE MIGHT NOT BE THE BRIGHTEST BULB...
...BUT I BELIEVE RHINO. THIS ISN'T A TRAP. FISK IS GOING AFTER THE PURPLE MAN'S CHILDREN AND APPARENTLY THEY'RE IN TOWN.
KIDNAP KIDS? TO WHAT END?
POWER. RIGHT NOW HE'S ONLY ABLE TO SUBTLY MANIPULATE THE POPULATION.
IF HE GETS THE CHILDREN...
...HE WINS THE ELECTION. AND THE MINDS OF A CITY.
I'M SICK OF THIS! THESE MEN CONTROLLING US! MAKING US HIDE LIKE RATS!
AND NOW THEY'RE AFTER CHILDREN?!
WHERE ARE YOUR TEAMMATES?
LYING LOW IN BROOKLYN. WHY?
BECAUSE THEY'RE DRAFTED.
WE'RE GOING TO FIND THOSE KIDS, AND IF FISK OR OTTO OR ANYONE GETS IN MY WAY--

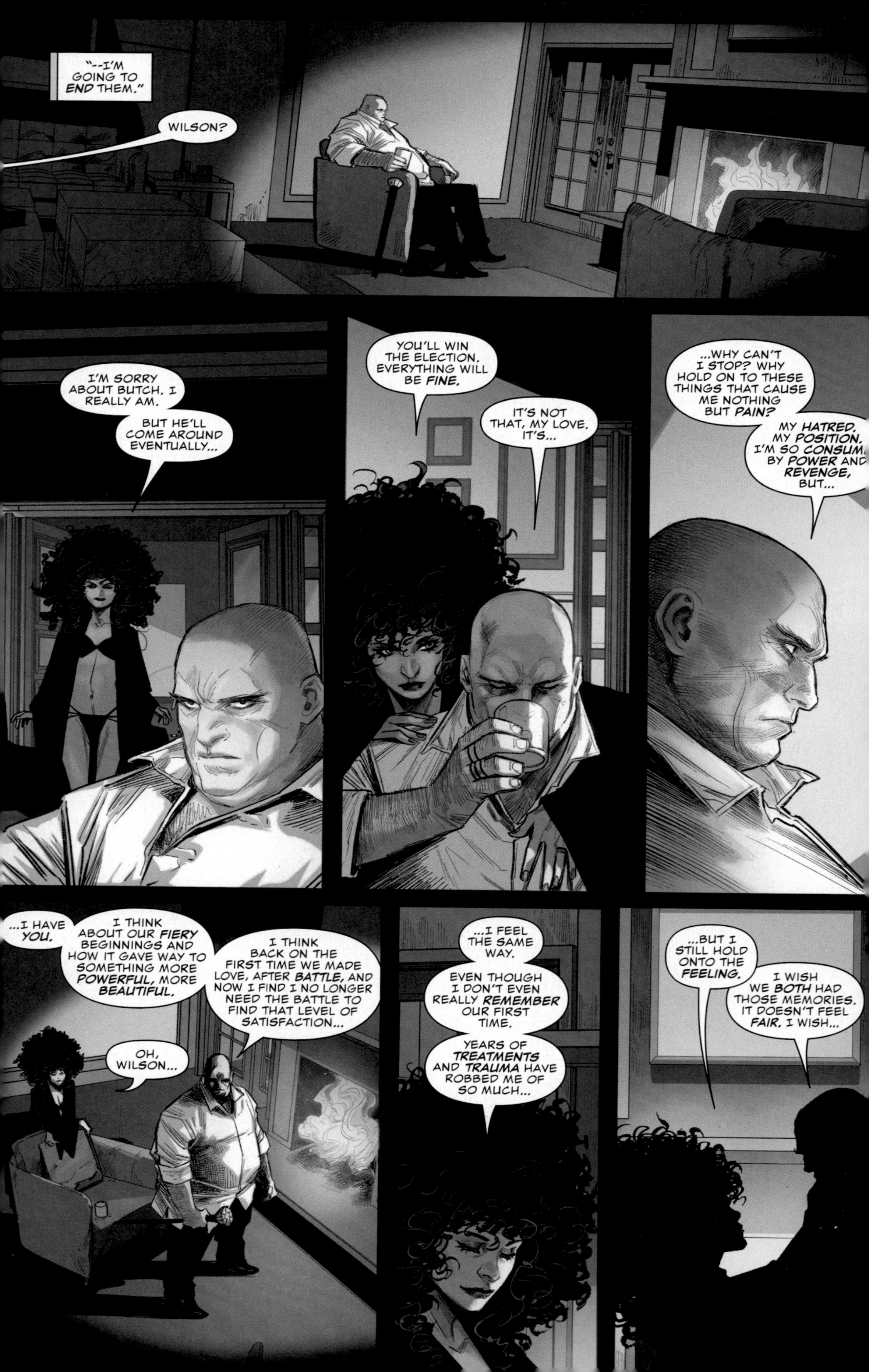
"--I'M GOING TO END THEM."
WILSON?
I'M SORRY ABOUT BUTCH. I REALLY AM.
BUT HE'LL COME AROUND EVENTUALLY...
YOU'LL WIN THE ELECTION. EVERYTHING WILL BE FINE.
IT'S NOT THAT, MY LOVE. IT'S...
...WHY CAN'T I STOP? WHY HOLD ON TO THESE THINGS THAT CAUSE ME NOTHING BUT PAIN?
MY HATRED. MY POSITION. I'M SO CONSUM BY POWER AND REVENGE, BUT...
...I HAVE YOU.
I THINK ABOUT OUR FIERY BEGINNINGS AND HOW IT GAVE WAY TO SOMETHING MORE POWERFUL, MORE BEAUTIFUL.
I THINK BACK ON THE FIRST TIME WE MADE LOVE, AFTER BATTLE, AND NOW I FIND I NO LONGER NEED THE BATTLE TO FIND THAT LEVEL OF SATISFACTION...
OH, WILSON...
...I FEEL THE SAME WAY.
EVEN THOUGH I DON'T EVEN REALLY REMEMBER OUR FIRST TIME.
YEARS OF TREATMENTS AND TRAUMA HAVE ROBBED ME OF SO MUCH...
...BUT I STILL HOLD ONTO THE FEELING.
I WISH WE BOTH HAD THOSE MEMORIES. IT DOESN'T FEEL FAIR. I WISH...

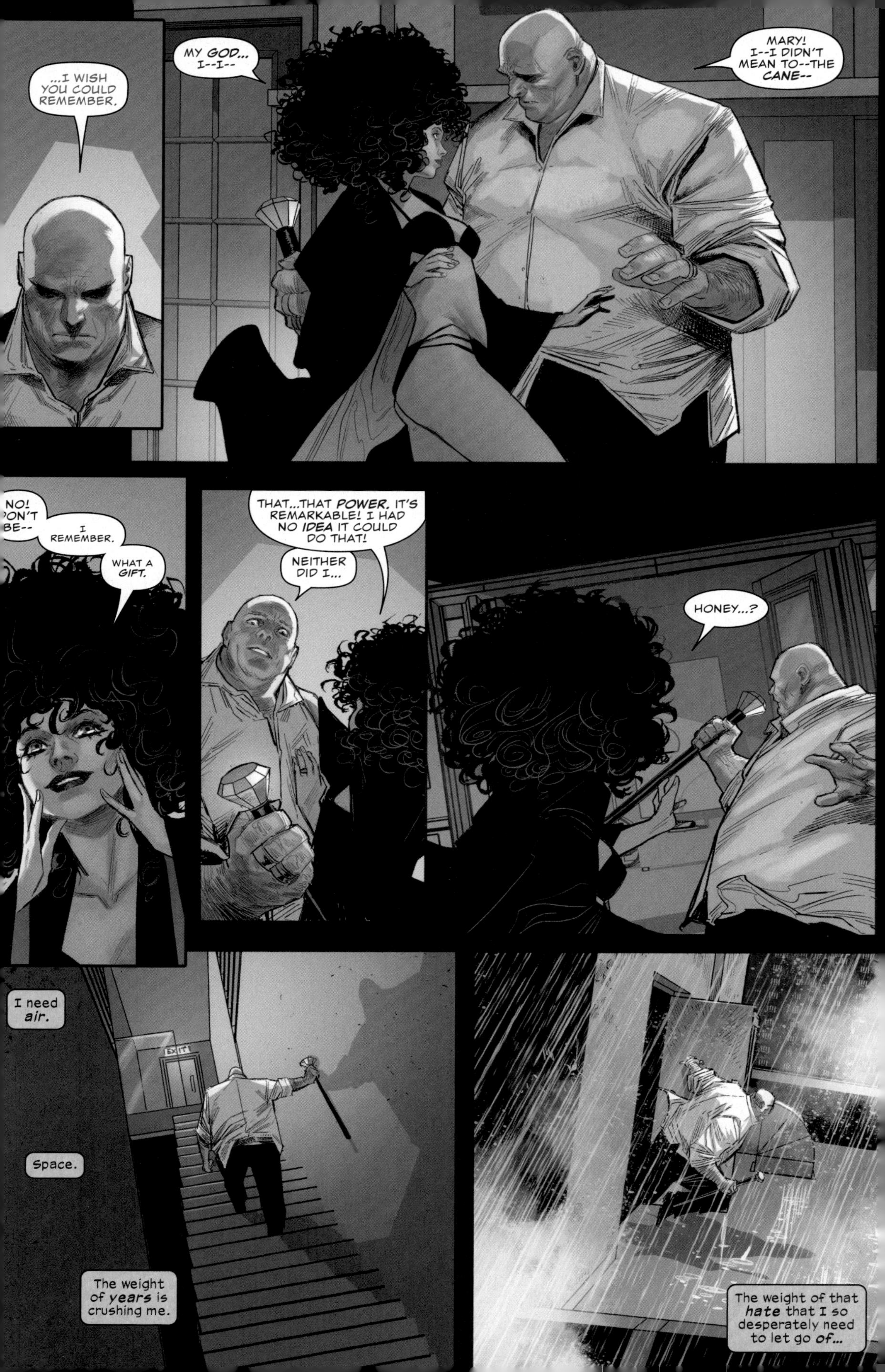
...I WISH YOU COULD REMEMBER.
MY GOD... I--I--
MARY! I--I DIDN'T MEAN TO--THE CANE--
NO! DON'T BE--
I REMEMBER.
WHAT A GIFT.
THAT...THAT POWER. IT'S REMARKABLE! I HAD NO IDEA IT COULD DO THAT!
NEITHER DID I...
HONEY...?
I need air.
EXIT
Space.
The weight of years is crushing me.
The weight of that hate that I so desperately need to let go of...

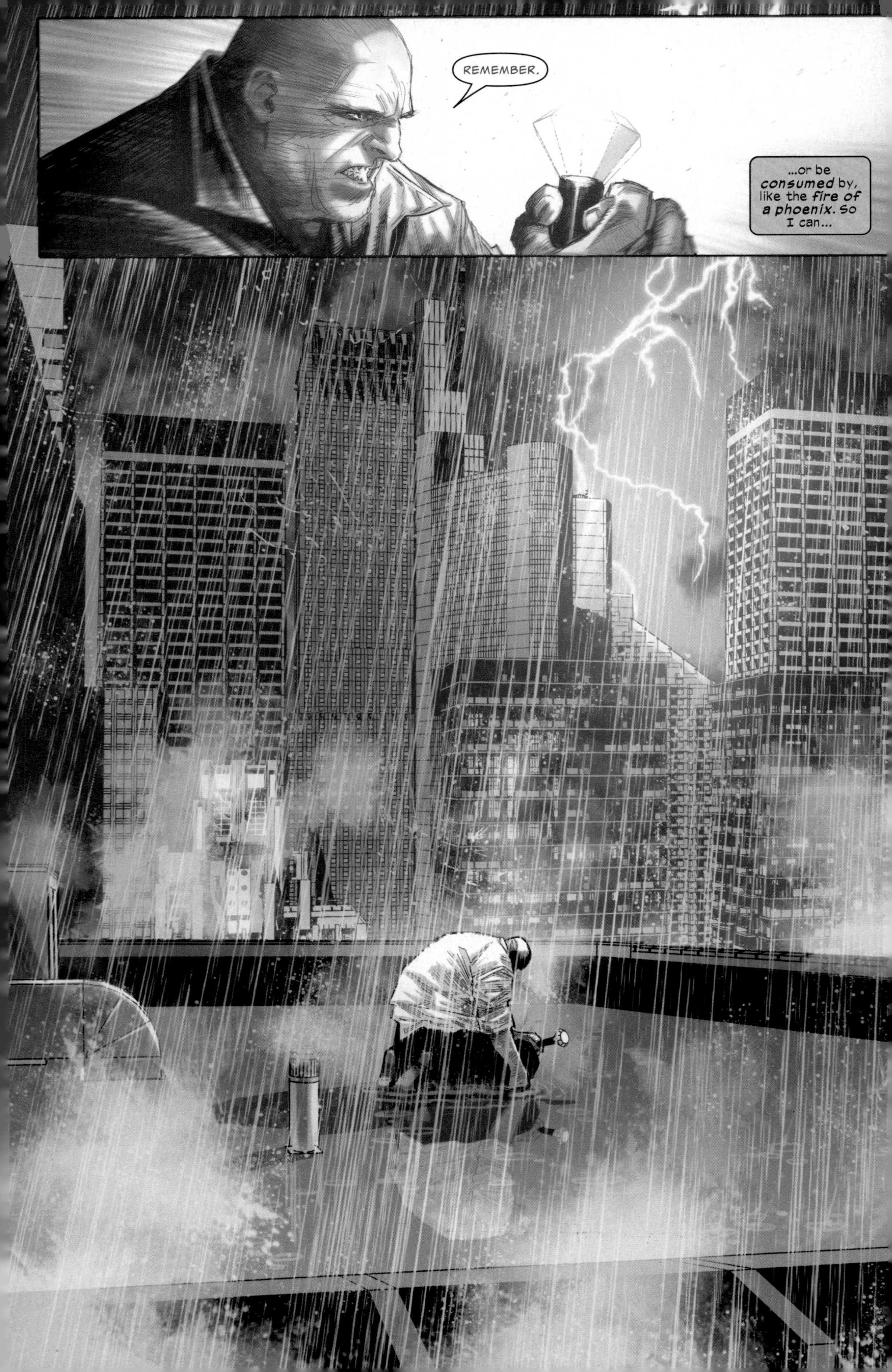
REMEMBER.
...or be consumed by, like the fire of a phoenix. So I can...

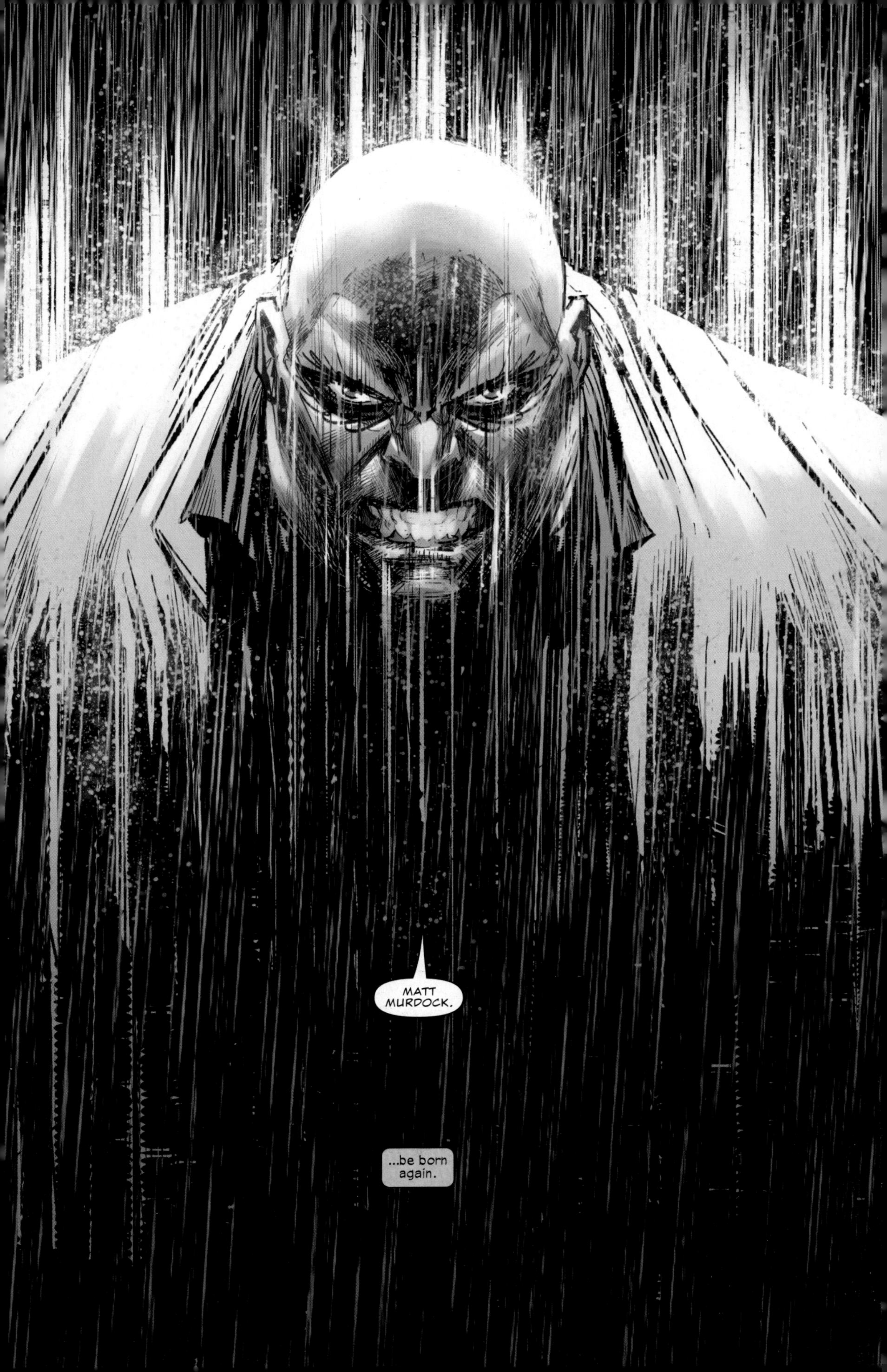
MATT MURDOCK.
...be born again.

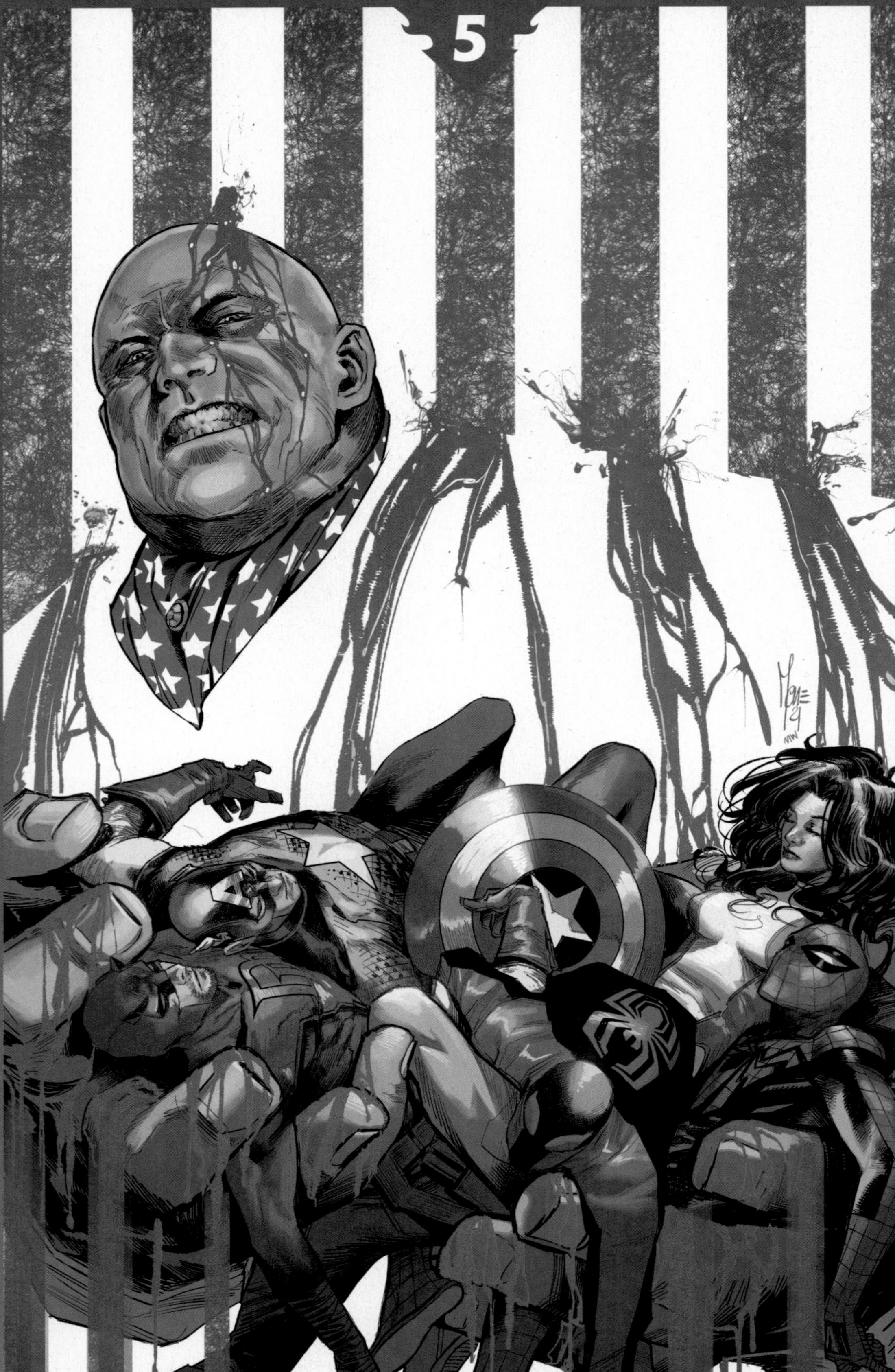
5

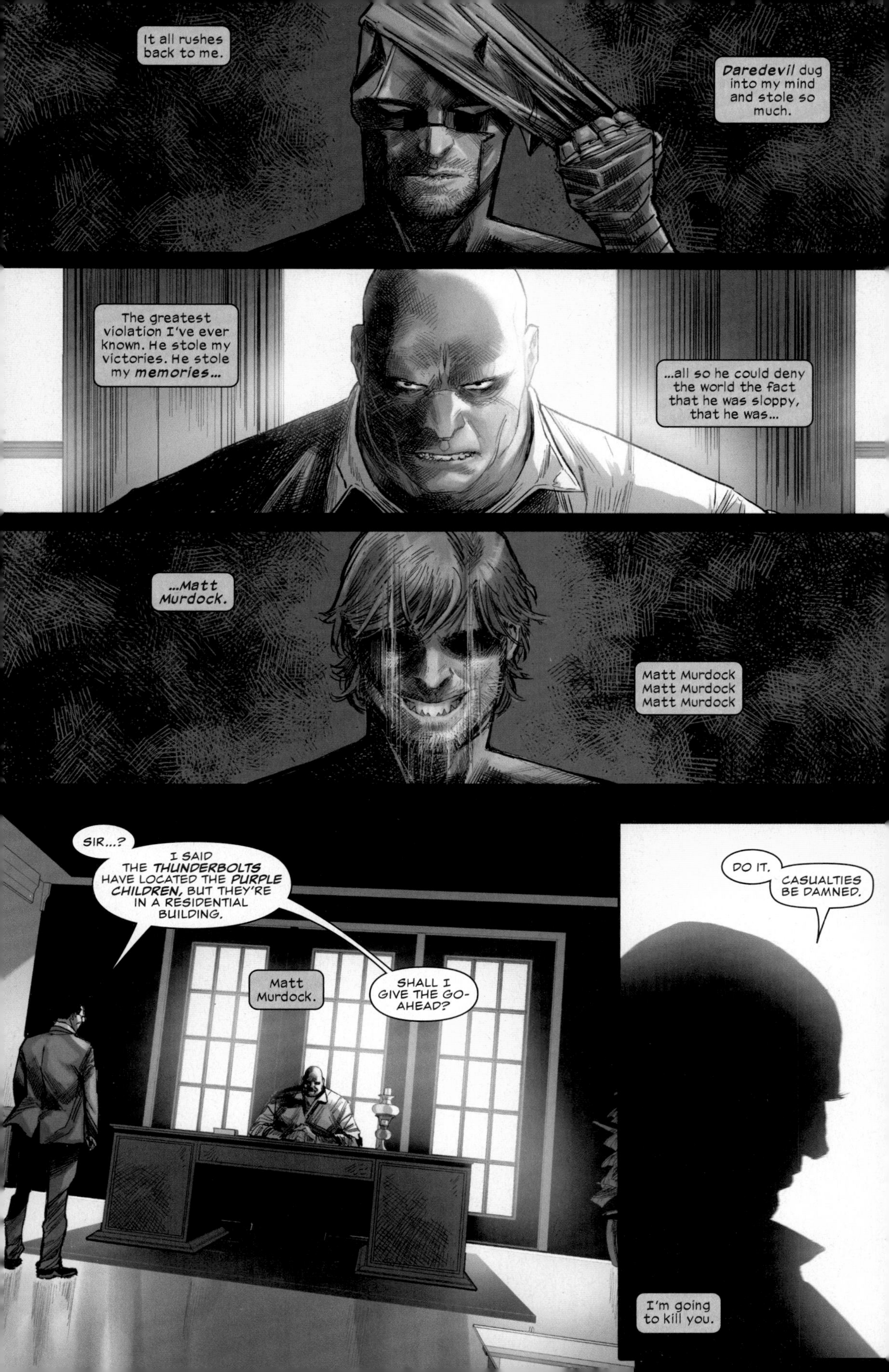

It all rushes back to me.
Daredevil dug into my mind and stole so much.
The greatest violation I've ever known. He stole my victories. He stole my memories...
...all so he could deny the world the fact that he was sloppy, that he was...
...Matt Murdock.
Matt Murdock
Matt Murdock
Matt Murdock
SIR...?
I SAID THE THUNDERBOLTS HAVE LOCATED THE PURPLE CHILDREN, BUT THEY'RE IN A RESIDENTIAL BUILDING.
Matt Murdock.
SHALL I GIVE THE GO-AHEAD?
DO IT.
CASUALTIES BE DAMNED.
I'm going to kill you.

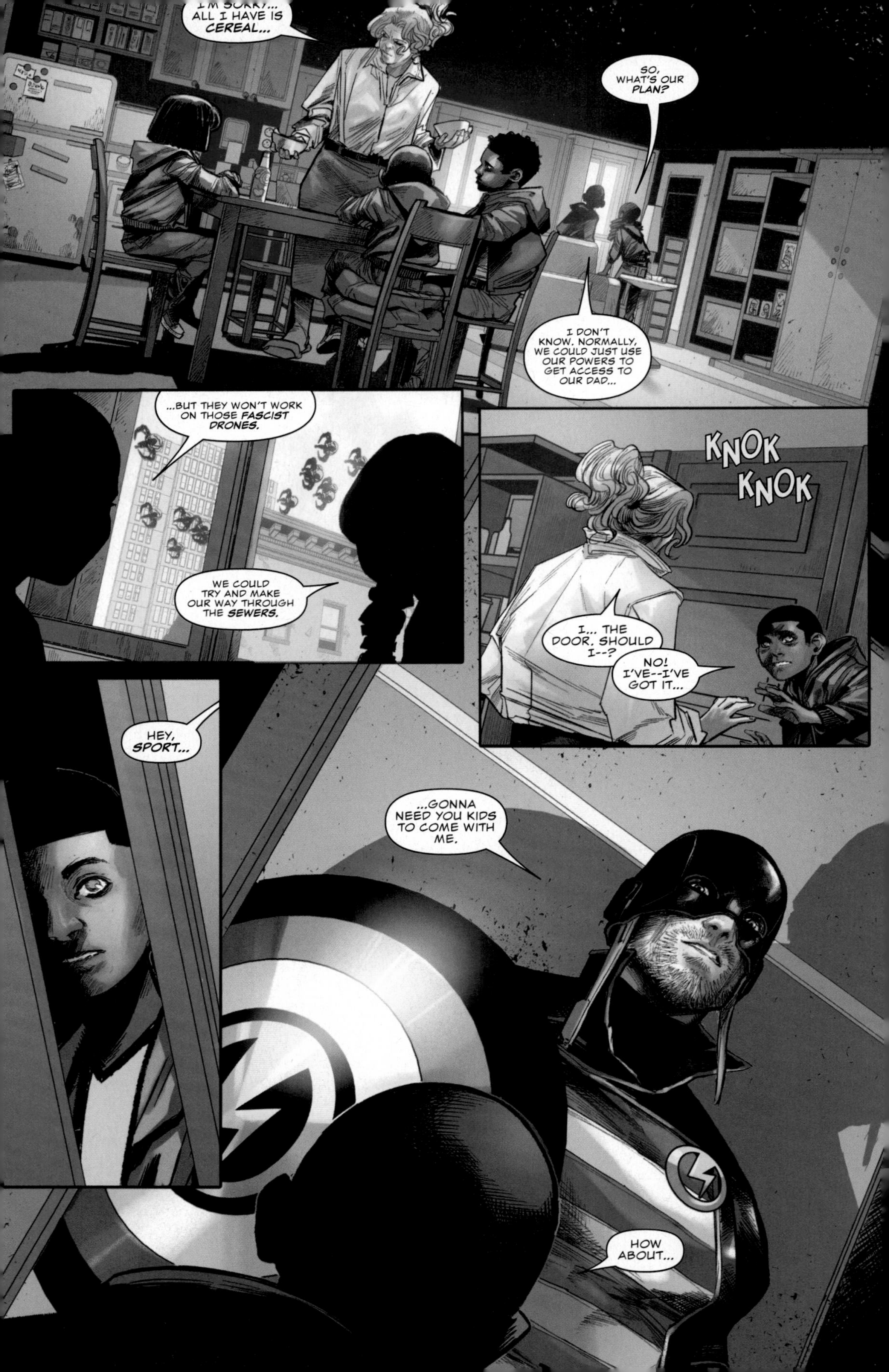
I'M SORRY... ALL I HAVE IS CEREAL...
SO, WHAT'S OUR PLAN?
I DON'T KNOW. NORMALLY, WE COULD JUST USE OUR POWERS TO GET ACCESS TO OUR DAD...
...BUT THEY WON'T WORK ON THOSE FASCIST DRONES.
WE COULD TRY AND MAKE OUR WAY THROUGH THE SEWERS.
KNOK KNOK
I... THE DOOR. SHOULD I--?
NO! I'VE--I'VE GOT IT...
HEY, SPORT...
...GONNA NEED YOU KIDS TO COME WITH ME.
HOW ABOUT...

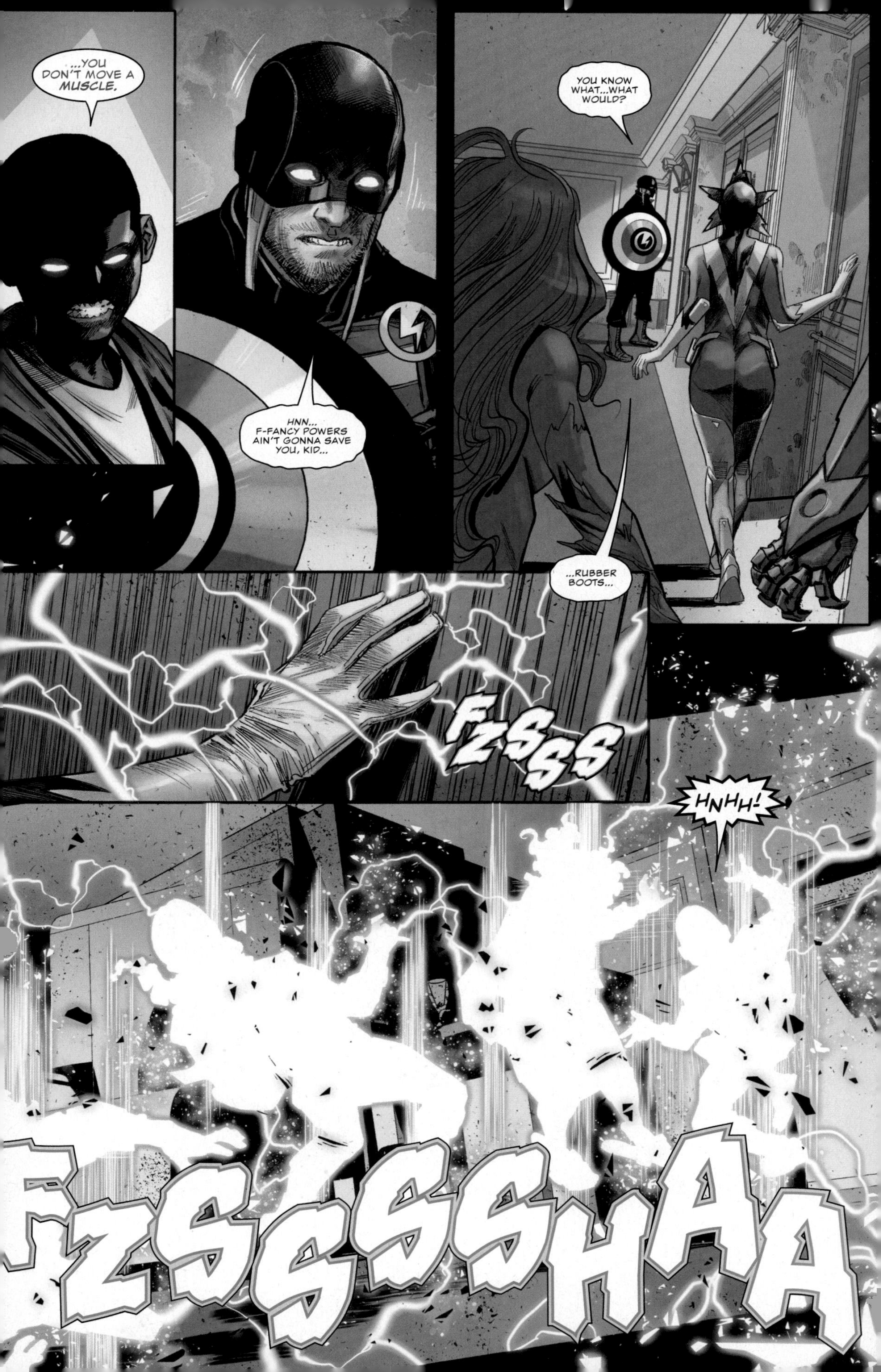
...YOU DON'T MOVE A MUSCLE.
HNN... F-FANCY POWERS AIN'T GONNA SAVE YOU, KID...
YOU KNOW WHAT...WHAT WOULD?
...RUBBER BOOTS...
FZSSSS
HNHH!
FZSSSSHAA

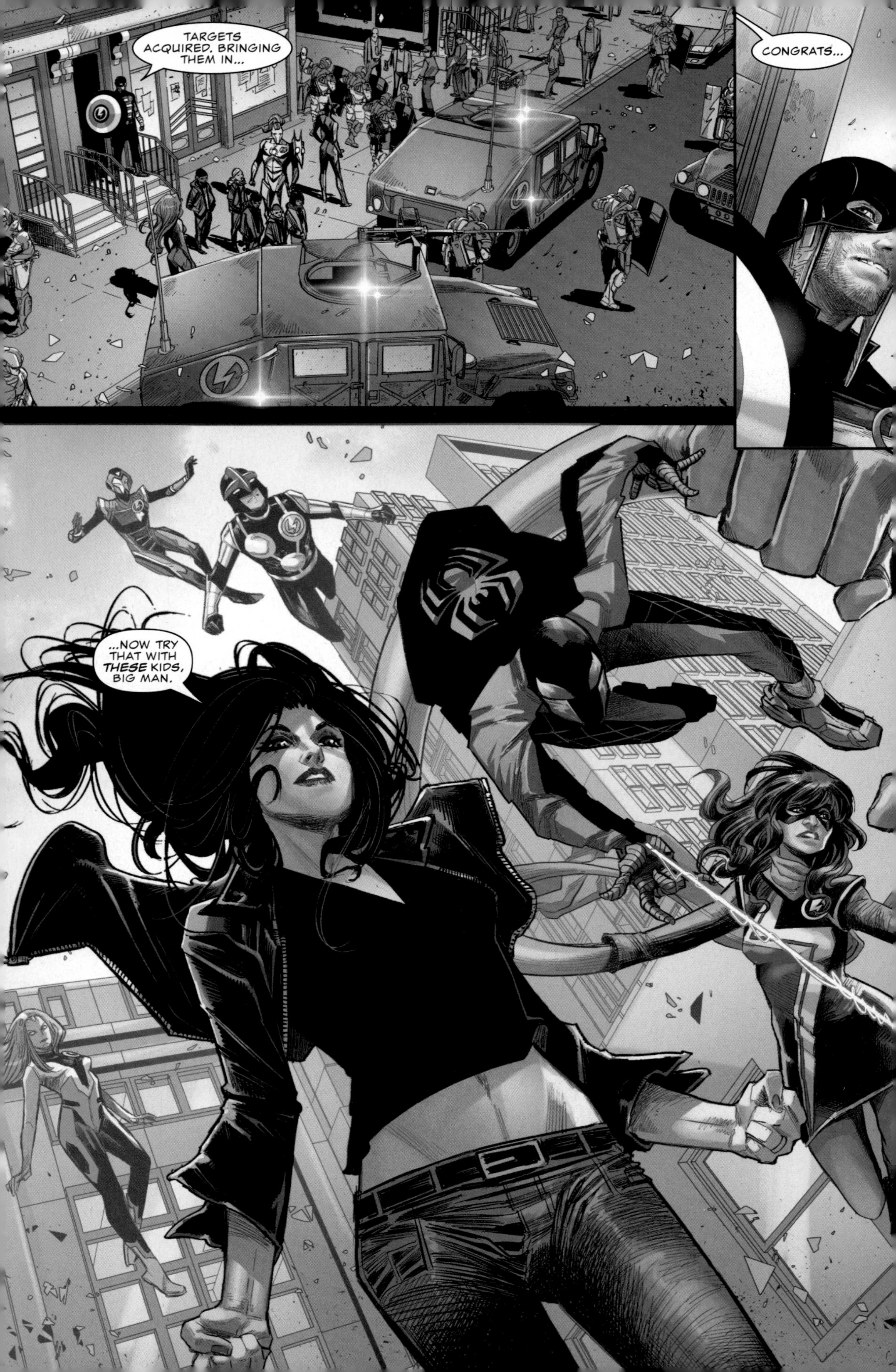
TARGETS ACQUIRED. BRINGING THEM IN...
CONGRATS...
...NOW TRY THAT WITH THESE KIDS, BIG MAN.

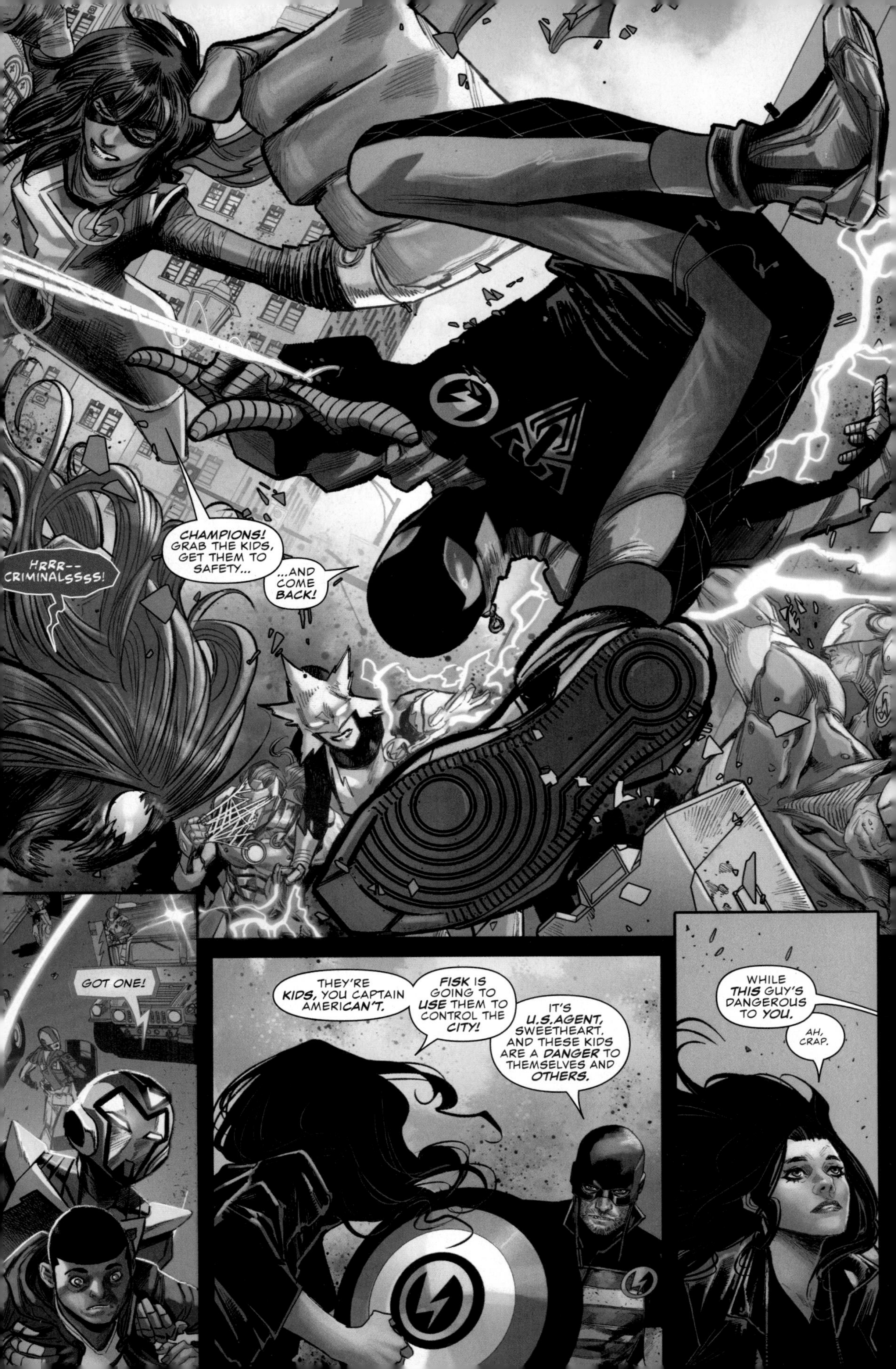
HRRR--
CRIMINALSSSS!
CHAMPIONS! GRAB THE KIDS, GET THEM TO SAFETY...
...AND COME BACK!
GOT ONE!
THEY'RE KIDS, YOU CAPTAIN AMERICAN'T.
FISK IS GOING TO USE THEM TO CONTROL THE CITY!
IT'S U.S.AGENT, SWEETHEART, AND THESE KIDS ARE A DANGER TO THEMSELVES AND OTHERS.
WHILE THIS GUY'S DANGEROUS TO YOU.
AH, CRAP.

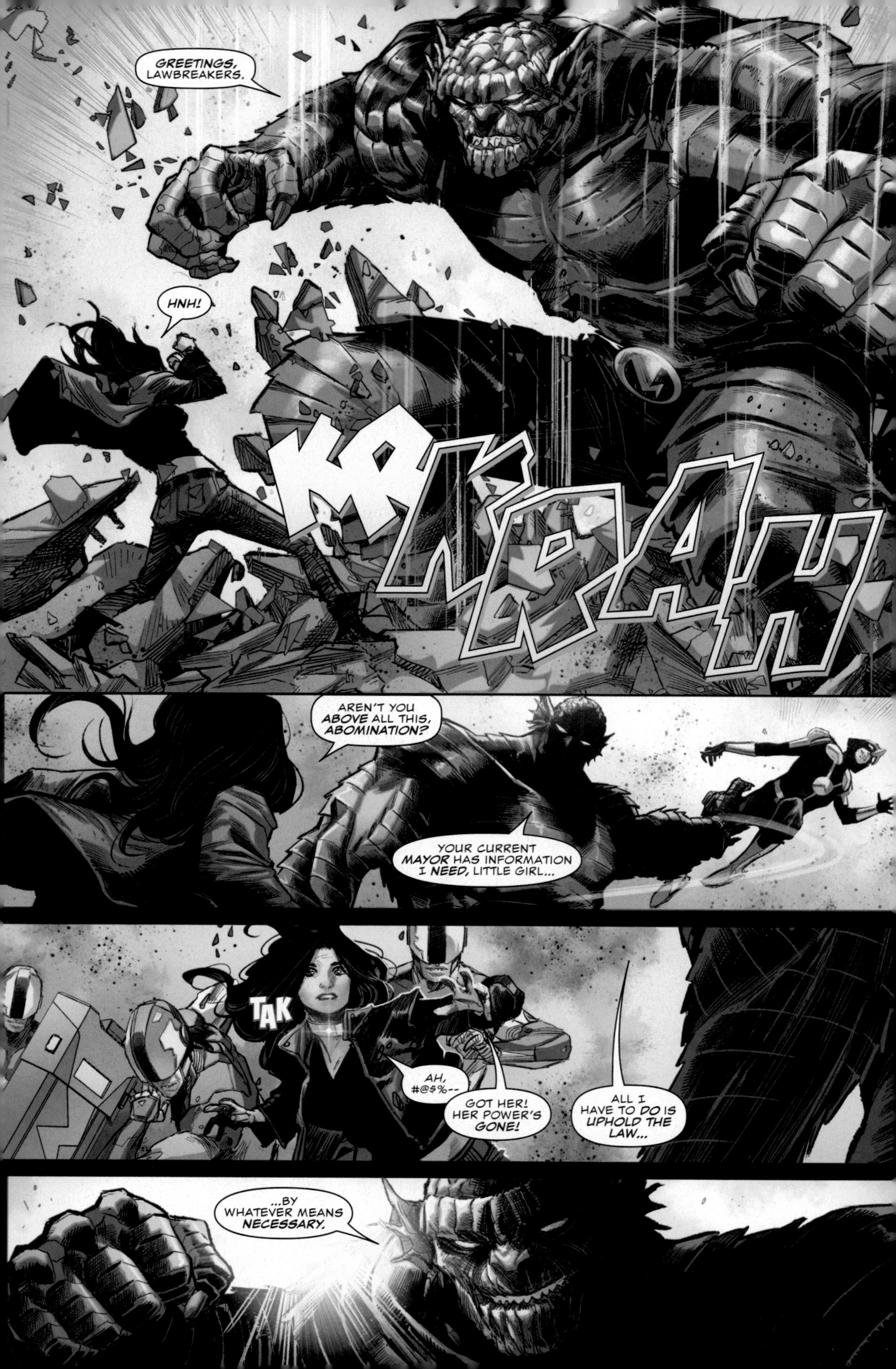
GREETINGS, LAWBREAKERS.
HNH!
KRAKAAH
AREN'T YOU ABOVE ALL THIS, ABOMINATION?
YOUR CURRENT MAYOR HAS INFORMATION I NEED, LITTLE GIRL...
TAK
AH, #@$%--
GOT HER! HER POWER'S GONE!
ALL I HAVE TO DO IS UPHOLD THE LAW...
...BY WHATEVER MEANS NECESSARY.

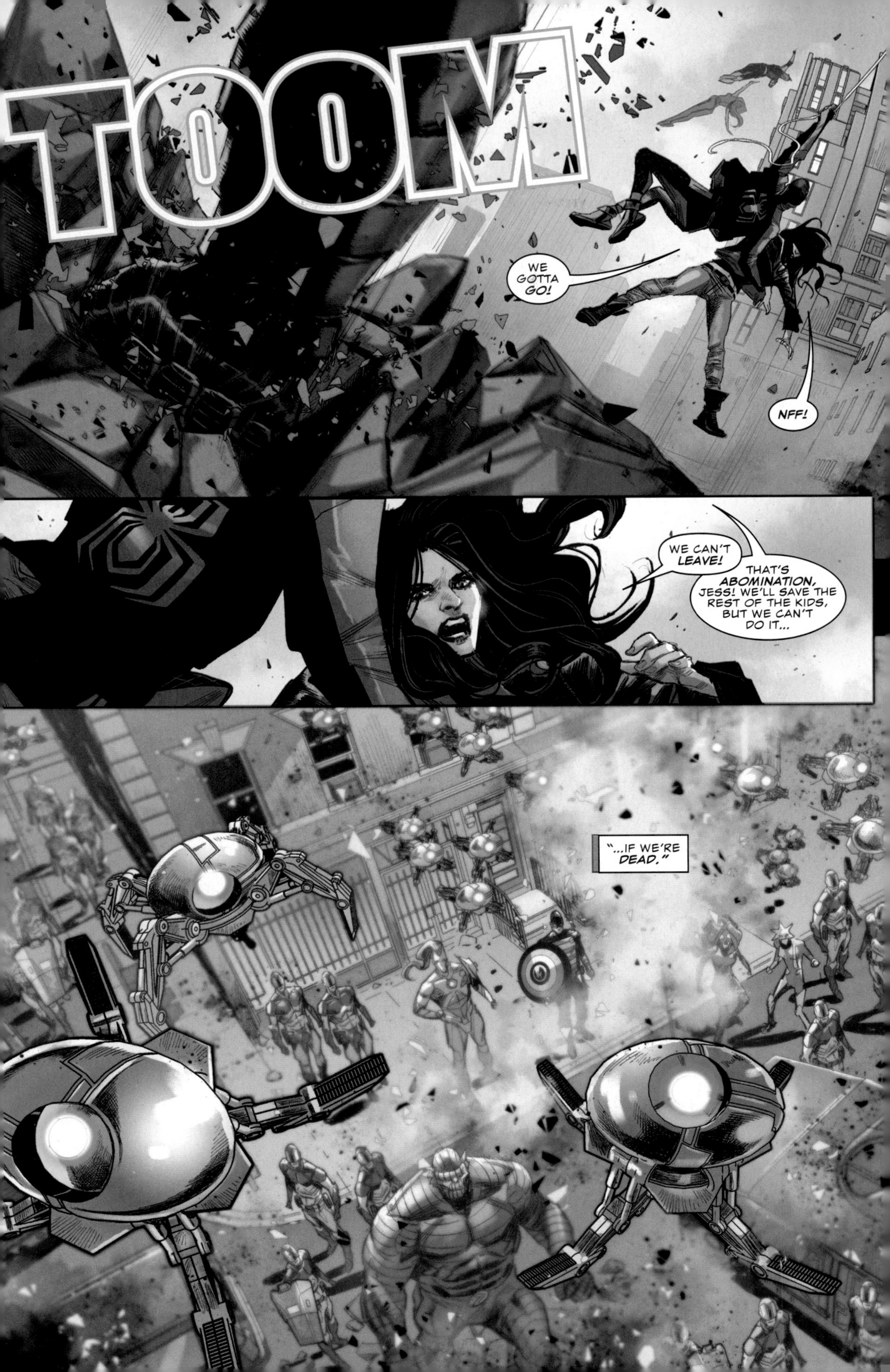
TOOM
WE GOTTA GO!
NFF!
WE CAN'T LEAVE!
THAT'S ABOMINATION, JESS! WE'LL SAVE THE REST OF THE KIDS, BUT WE CAN'T DO IT...
"...IF WE'RE DEAD."

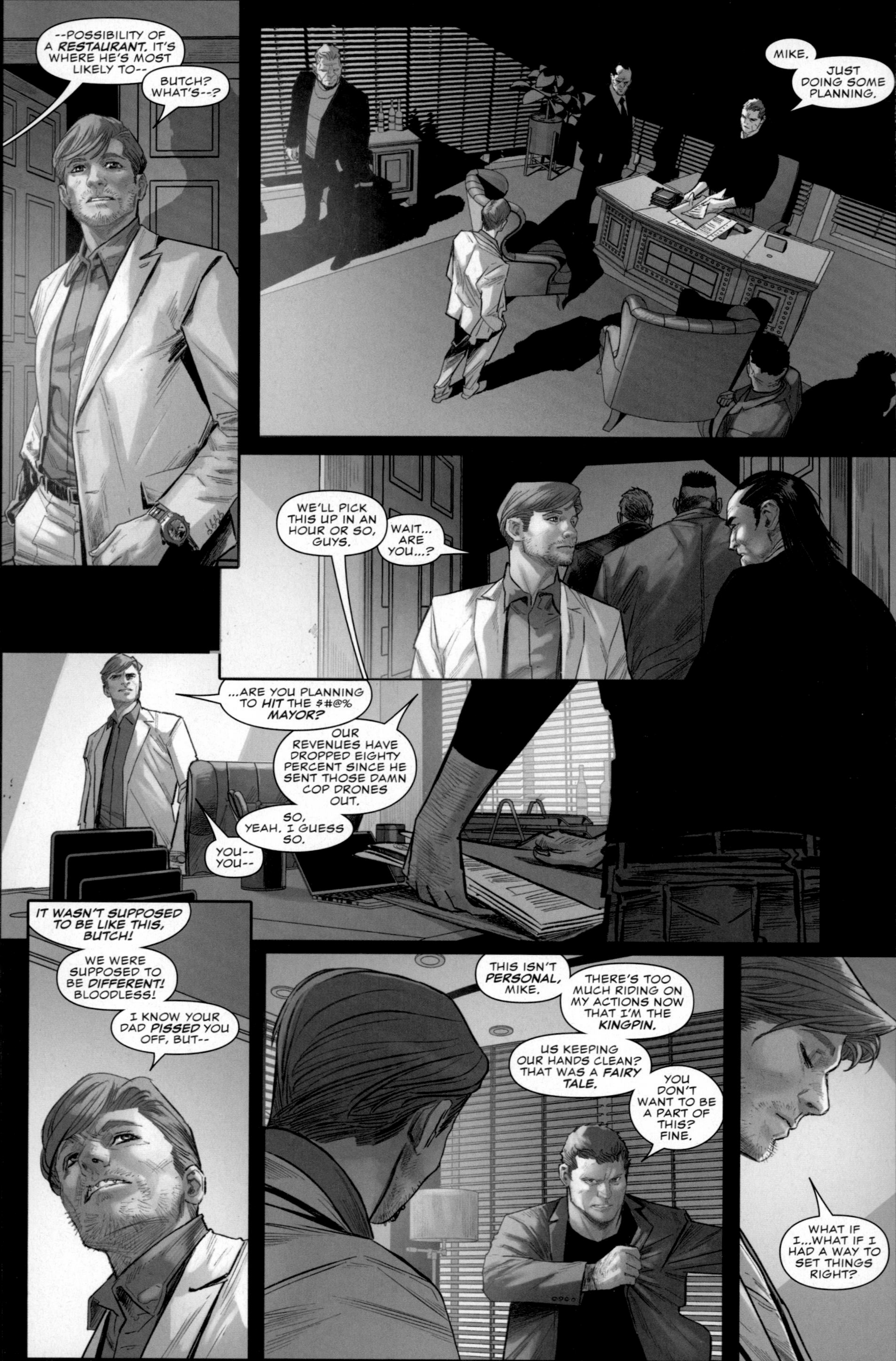
--POSSIBILITY OF A RESTAURANT. IT'S WHERE HE'S MOST LIKELY TO--
BUTCH? WHAT'S--?
MIKE. JUST DOING SOME PLANNING.
WE'LL PICK THIS UP IN AN HOUR OR SO, GUYS.
WAIT... ARE YOU...?
...ARE YOU PLANNING TO HIT THE $#@% MAYOR?
OUR REVENUES HAVE DROPPED EIGHTY PERCENT SINCE HE SENT THOSE DAMN COP DRONES OUT.
SO, YEAH. I GUESS SO.
YOU-- YOU--
IT WASN'T SUPPOSED TO BE LIKE THIS, BUTCH!
WE WERE SUPPOSED TO BE DIFFERENT! BLOODLESS!
I KNOW YOUR DAD PISSED YOU OFF, BUT--
THIS ISN'T PERSONAL, MIKE.
THERE'S TOO MUCH RIDING ON MY ACTIONS NOW THAT I'M THE KINGPIN.
US KEEPING OUR HANDS CLEAN? THAT WAS A FAIRY TALE.
YOU DON'T WANT TO BE A PART OF THIS? FINE.
WHAT IF I...WHAT IF I HAD A WAY TO SET THINGS RIGHT?

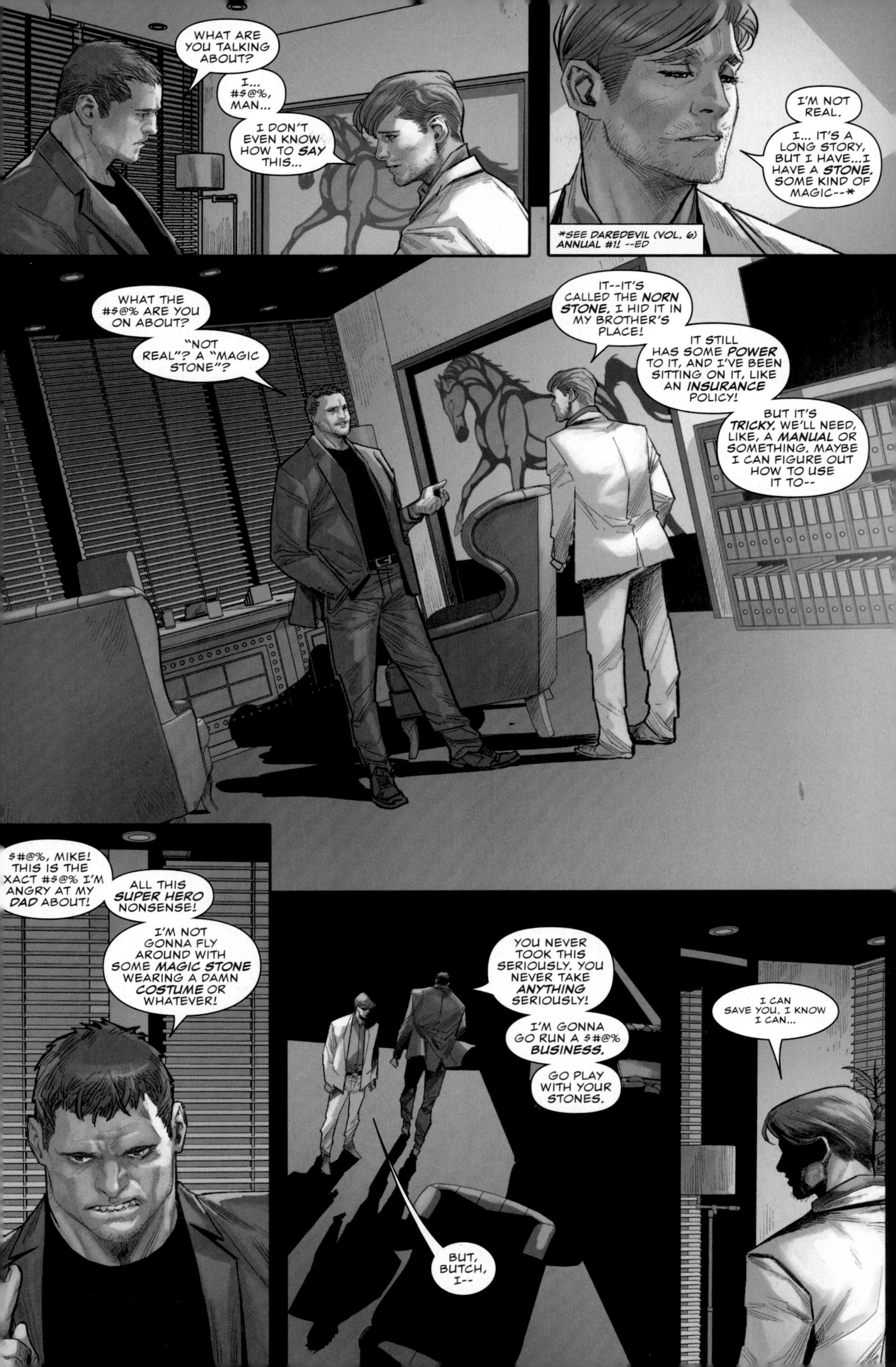
WHAT ARE YOU TALKING ABOUT?
I... #$@%, MAN...
I DON'T EVEN KNOW HOW TO SAY THIS...
I'M NOT REAL.
I... IT'S A LONG STORY, BUT I HAVE...I HAVE A STONE. SOME KIND OF MAGIC--*
*SEE DAREDEVIL (VOL. 6) ANNUAL #1! --ED
WHAT THE #$@% ARE YOU ON ABOUT?
"NOT REAL"? A "MAGIC STONE"?
IT--IT'S CALLED THE NORN STONE. I HID IT IN MY BROTHER'S PLACE!
IT STILL HAS SOME POWER TO IT, AND I'VE BEEN SITTING ON IT, LIKE AN INSURANCE POLICY!
BUT IT'S TRICKY. WE'LL NEED, LIKE, A MANUAL OR SOMETHING. MAYBE I CAN FIGURE OUT HOW TO USE IT TO--
$#@%, MIKE! THIS IS THE XACT #$@% I'M ANGRY AT MY DAD ABOUT!
ALL THIS SUPER HERO NONSENSE!
I'M NOT GONNA FLY AROUND WITH SOME MAGIC STONE WEARING A DAMN COSTUME OR WHATEVER!
YOU NEVER TOOK THIS SERIOUSLY. YOU NEVER TAKE ANYTHING SERIOUSLY!
I'M GONNA GO RUN A $#@% BUSINESS.
GO PLAY WITH YOUR STONES.
BUT, BUTCH, I--
I CAN SAVE YOU. I KNOW I CAN...

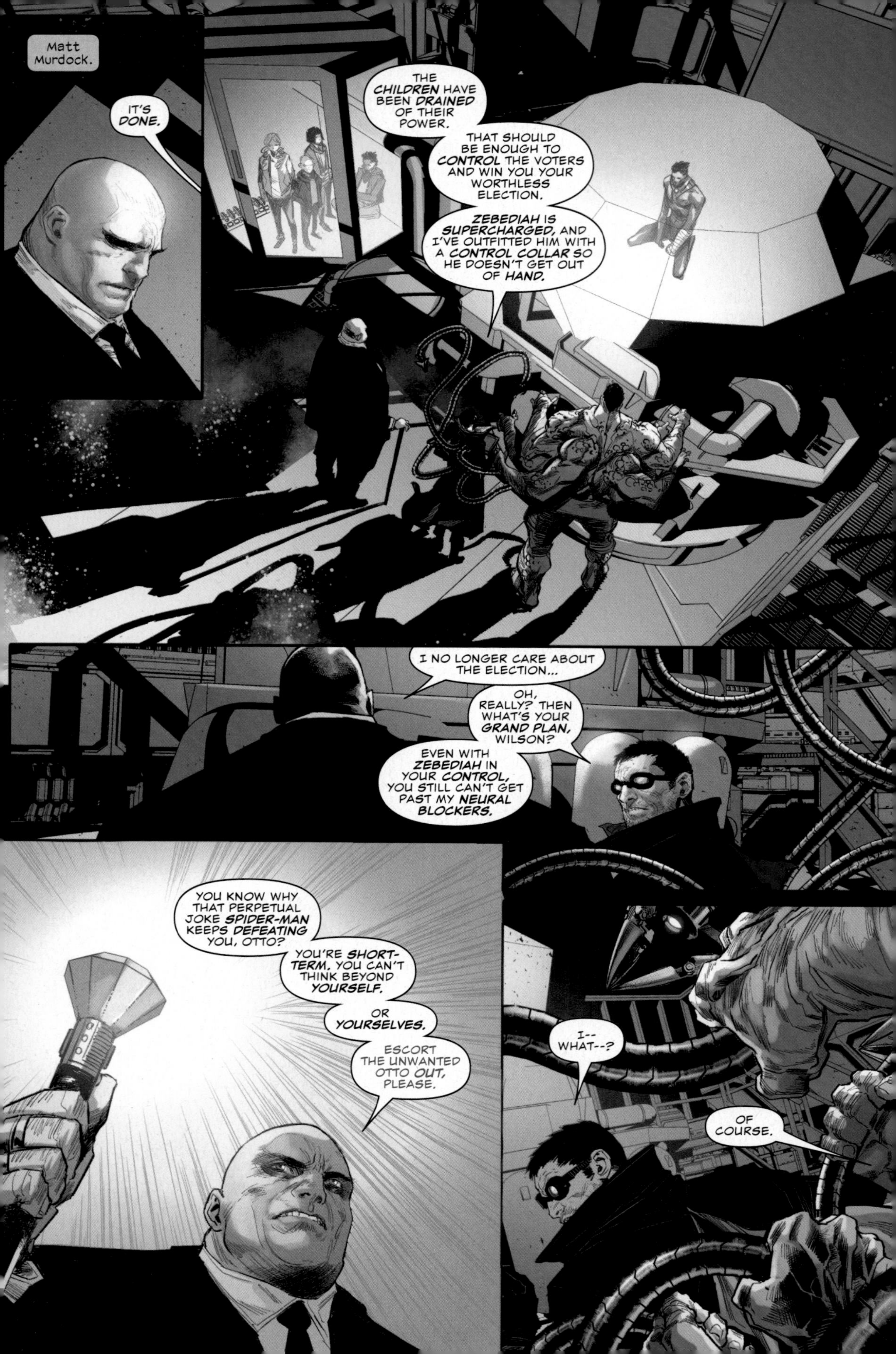
Matt Murdock.
IT'S DONE.
THE CHILDREN HAVE BEEN DRAINED OF THEIR POWER.
THAT SHOULD BE ENOUGH TO CONTROL THE VOTERS AND WIN YOU YOUR WORTHLESS ELECTION.
ZEBEDIAH IS SUPERCHARGED, AND I'VE OUTFITTED HIM WITH A CONTROL COLLAR SO HE DOESN'T GET OUT OF HAND.
I NO LONGER CARE ABOUT THE ELECTION...
OH, REALLY? THEN WHAT'S YOUR GRAND PLAN, WILSON?
EVEN WITH ZEBEDIAH IN YOUR CONTROL, YOU STILL CAN'T GET PAST MY NEURAL BLOCKERS.
YOU KNOW WHY THAT PERPETUAL JOKE SPIDER-MAN KEEPS DEFEATING YOU, OTTO?
YOU'RE SHORT-TERM. YOU CAN'T THINK BEYOND YOURSELF.
OR YOURSELVES.
ESCORT THE UNWANTED OTTO OUT, PLEASE.
I-- WHAT--?
OF COURSE.

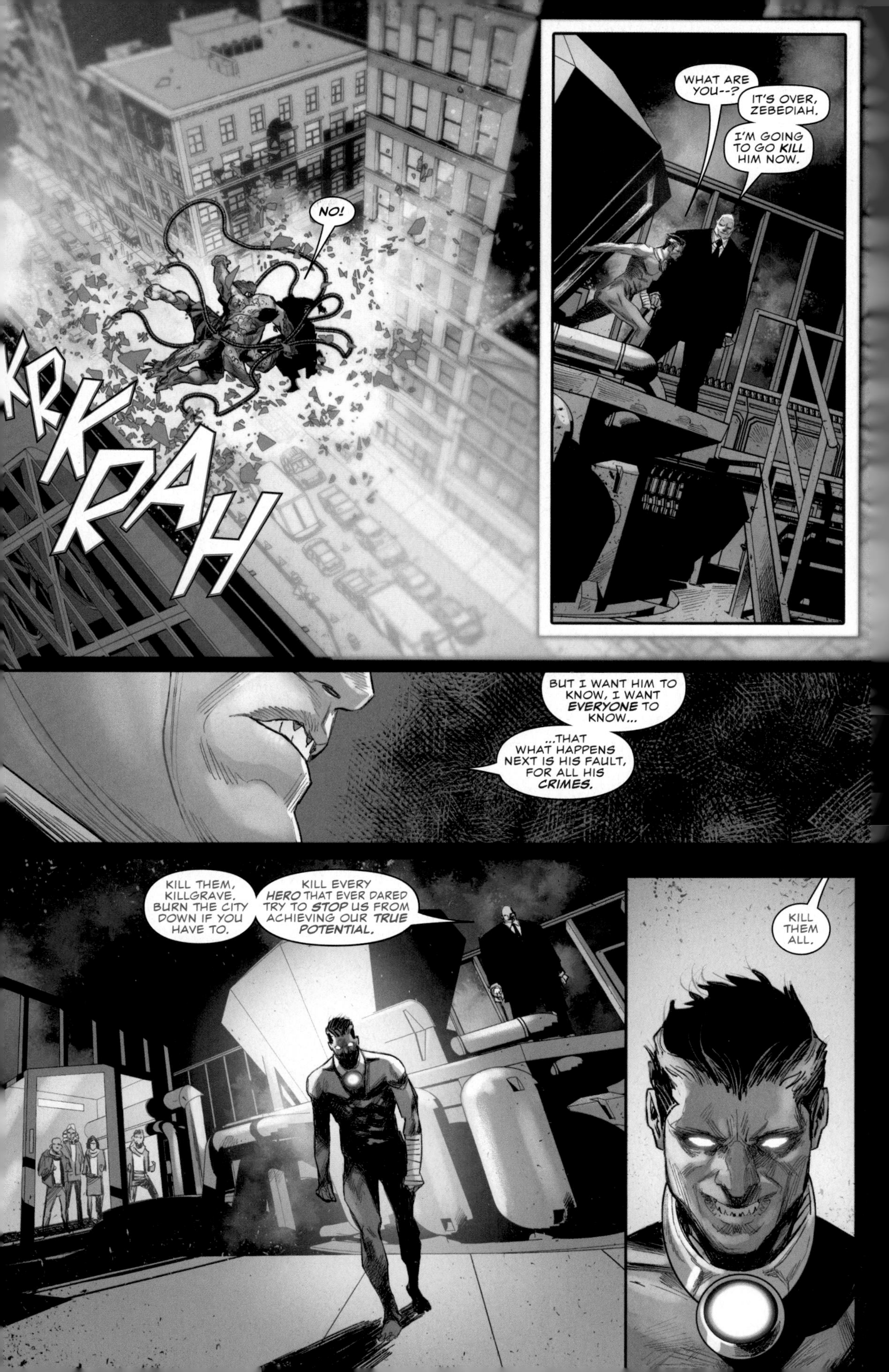
KRKRAH
NO!
WHAT ARE YOU--?
IT'S OVER, ZEBEDIAH.
I'M GOING TO GO KILL HIM NOW.
BUT I WANT HIM TO KNOW, I WANT EVERYONE TO KNOW...
...THAT WHAT HAPPENS NEXT IS HIS FAULT, FOR ALL HIS CRIMES.
KILL THEM, KILLGRAVE. BURN THE CITY DOWN IF YOU HAVE TO.
KILL EVERY HERO THAT EVER DARED TRY TO STOP US FROM ACHIEVING OUR TRUE POTENTIAL.
KILL THEM ALL.

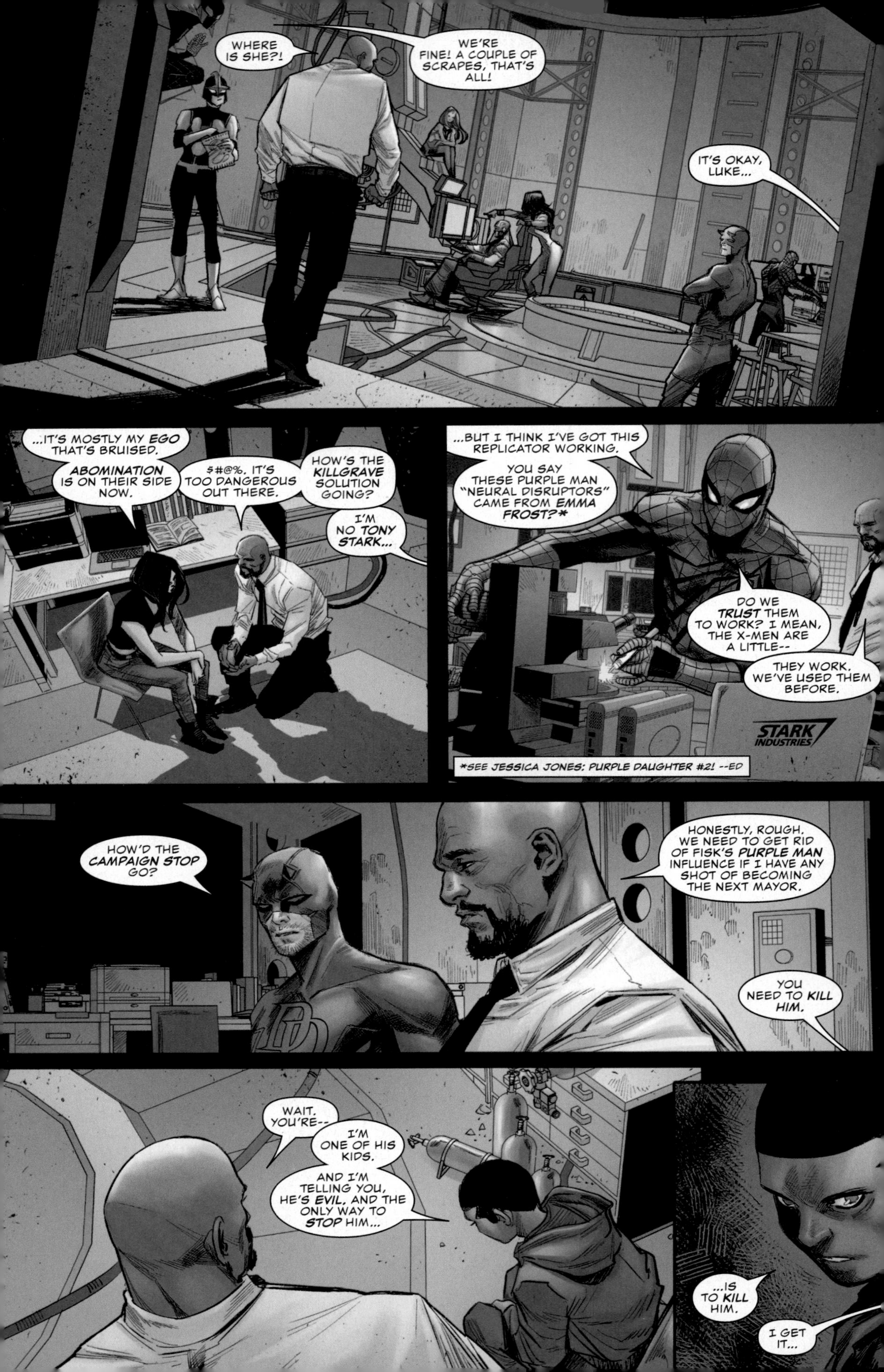
WHERE IS SHE?!
WE'RE FINE! A COUPLE OF SCRAPES, THAT'S ALL!
IT'S OKAY, LUKE...
...IT'S MOSTLY MY EGO THAT'S BRUISED.
ABOMINATION IS ON THEIR SIDE NOW.
$#@%. IT'S TOO DANGEROUS OUT THERE.
HOW'S THE KILLGRAVE SOLUTION GOING?
I'M NO TONY STARK...
...BUT I THINK I'VE GOT THIS REPLICATOR WORKING.
YOU SAY THESE PURPLE MAN "NEURAL DISRUPTORS" CAME FROM EMMA FROST?*
DO WE TRUST THEM TO WORK? I MEAN, THE X-MEN ARE A LITTLE--
THEY WORK. WE'VE USED THEM BEFORE.
STARK INDUSTRIES
*SEE JESSICA JONES: PURPLE DAUGHTER #2! --ED
HOW'D THE CAMPAIGN STOP GO?
HONESTLY, ROUGH. WE NEED TO GET RID OF FISK'S PURPLE MAN INFLUENCE IF I HAVE ANY SHOT OF BECOMING THE NEXT MAYOR.
YOU NEED TO KILL HIM.
WAIT. YOU'RE--
I'M ONE OF HIS KIDS.
AND I'M TELLING YOU, HE'S EVIL, AND THE ONLY WAY TO STOP HIM...
...IS TO KILL HIM.
I GET IT...

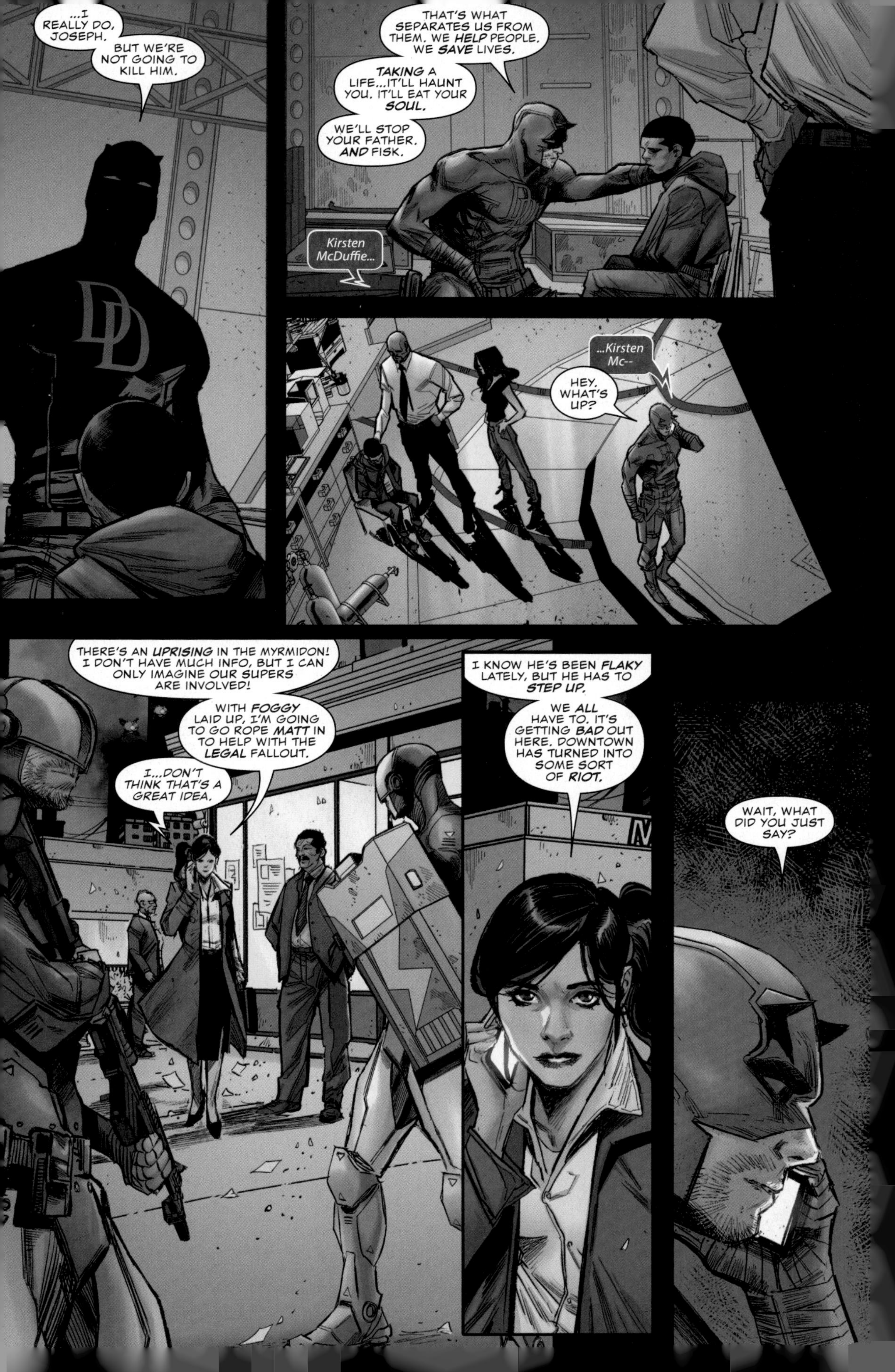

...I REALLY DO, JOSEPH.
BUT WE'RE NOT GOING TO KILL HIM.
THAT'S WHAT SEPARATES US FROM THEM. WE HELP PEOPLE. WE SAVE LIVES.
TAKING A LIFE...IT'LL HAUNT YOU. IT'LL EAT YOUR SOUL.
WE'LL STOP YOUR FATHER. AND FISK.
Kirsten McDuffie...
...Kirsten Mc--
HEY. WHAT'S UP?
THERE'S AN UPRISING IN THE MYRMIDON! I DON'T HAVE MUCH INFO, BUT I CAN ONLY IMAGINE OUR SUPERS ARE INVOLVED!
WITH FOGGY LAID UP, I'M GOING TO GO ROPE MATT IN TO HELP WITH THE LEGAL FALLOUT.
I...DON'T THINK THAT'S A GREAT IDEA.
I KNOW HE'S BEEN FLAKY LATELY, BUT HE HAS TO STEP UP.
WE ALL HAVE TO. IT'S GETTING BAD OUT HERE. DOWNTOWN HAS TURNED INTO SOME SORT OF RIOT.
WAIT, WHAT DID YOU JUST SAY?

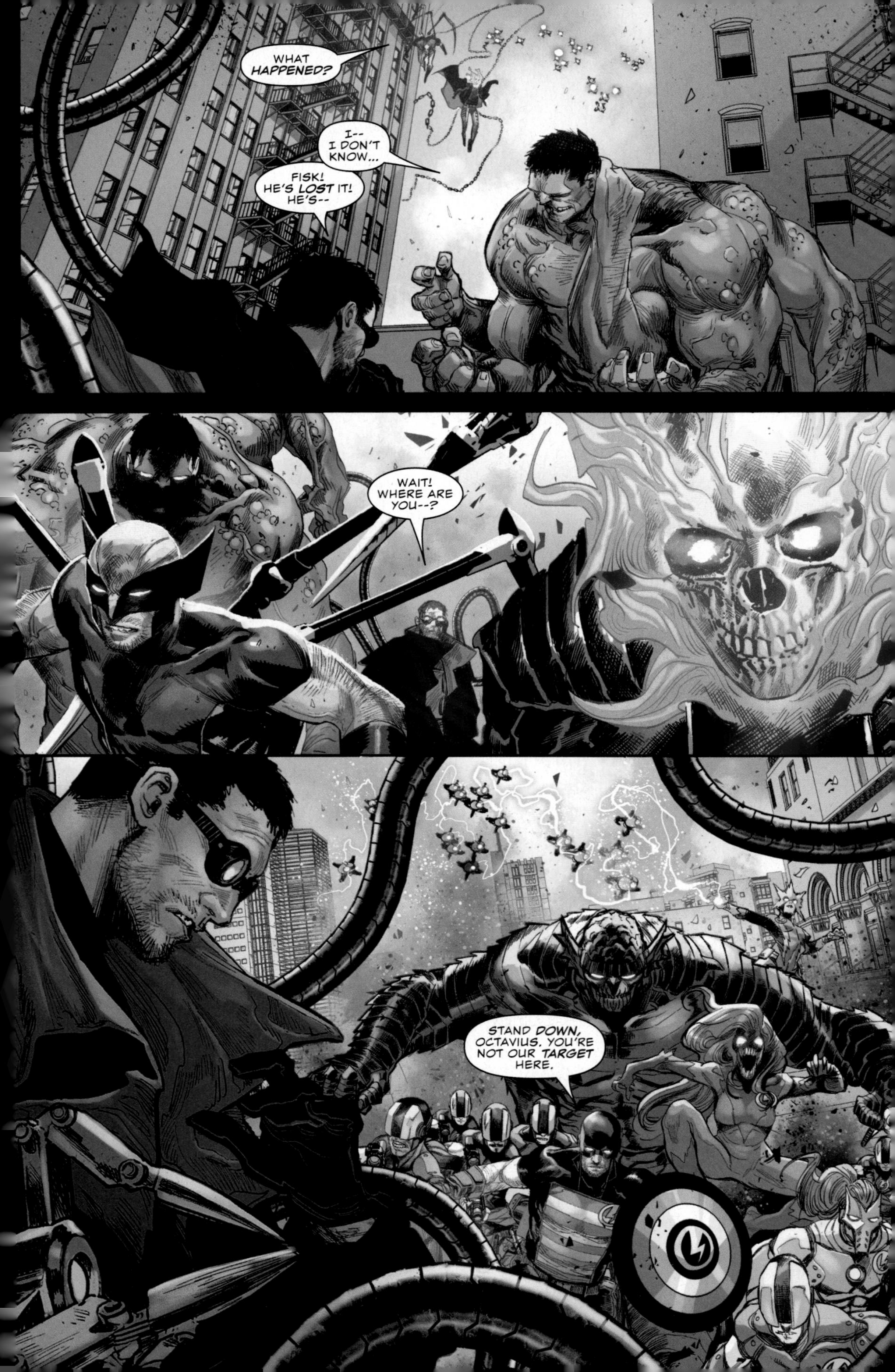
WHAT HAPPENED?
I-- I DON'T KNOW...
FISK! HE'S LOST IT! HE'S--
WAIT! WHERE ARE YOU--?
STAND DOWN, OCTAVIUS. YOU'RE NOT OUR TARGET HERE.

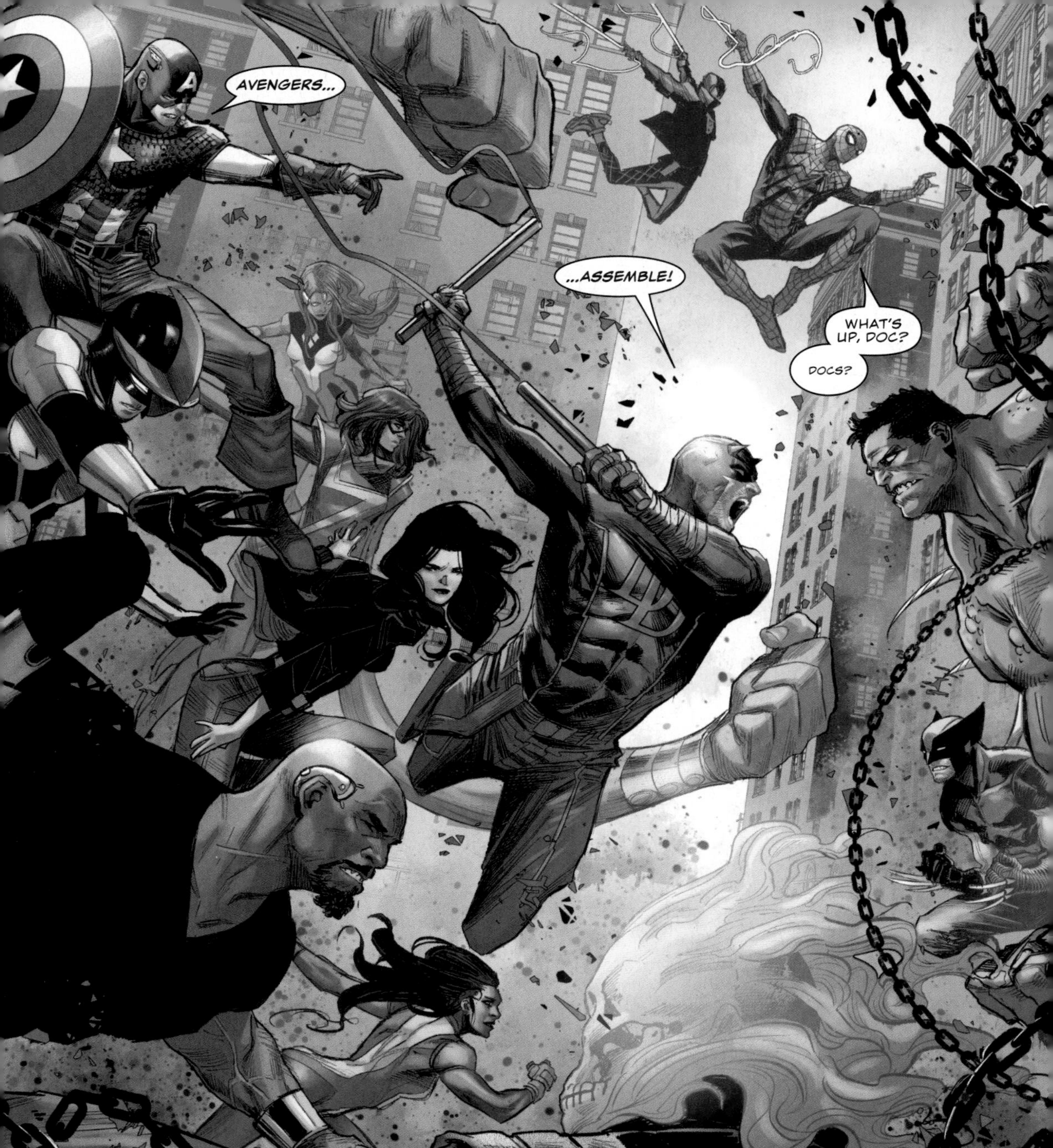
AVENGERS...
...ASSEMBLE!
WHAT'S UP, DOC?
DOCS?

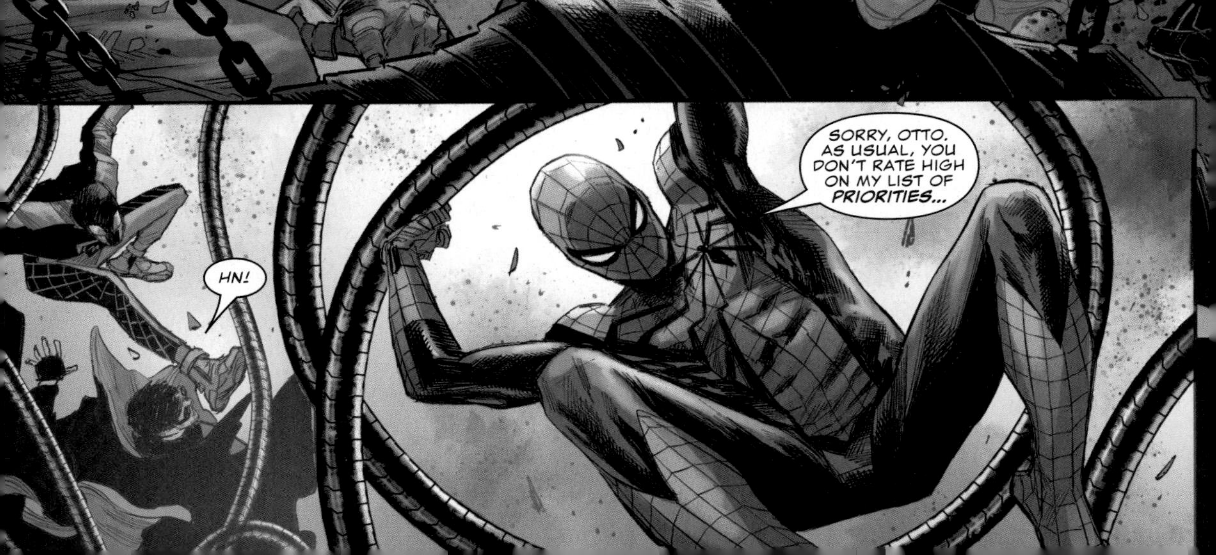
SORRY, OTTO. AS USUAL, YOU DON'T RATE HIGH ON MY LIST OF PRIORITIES...
HN!

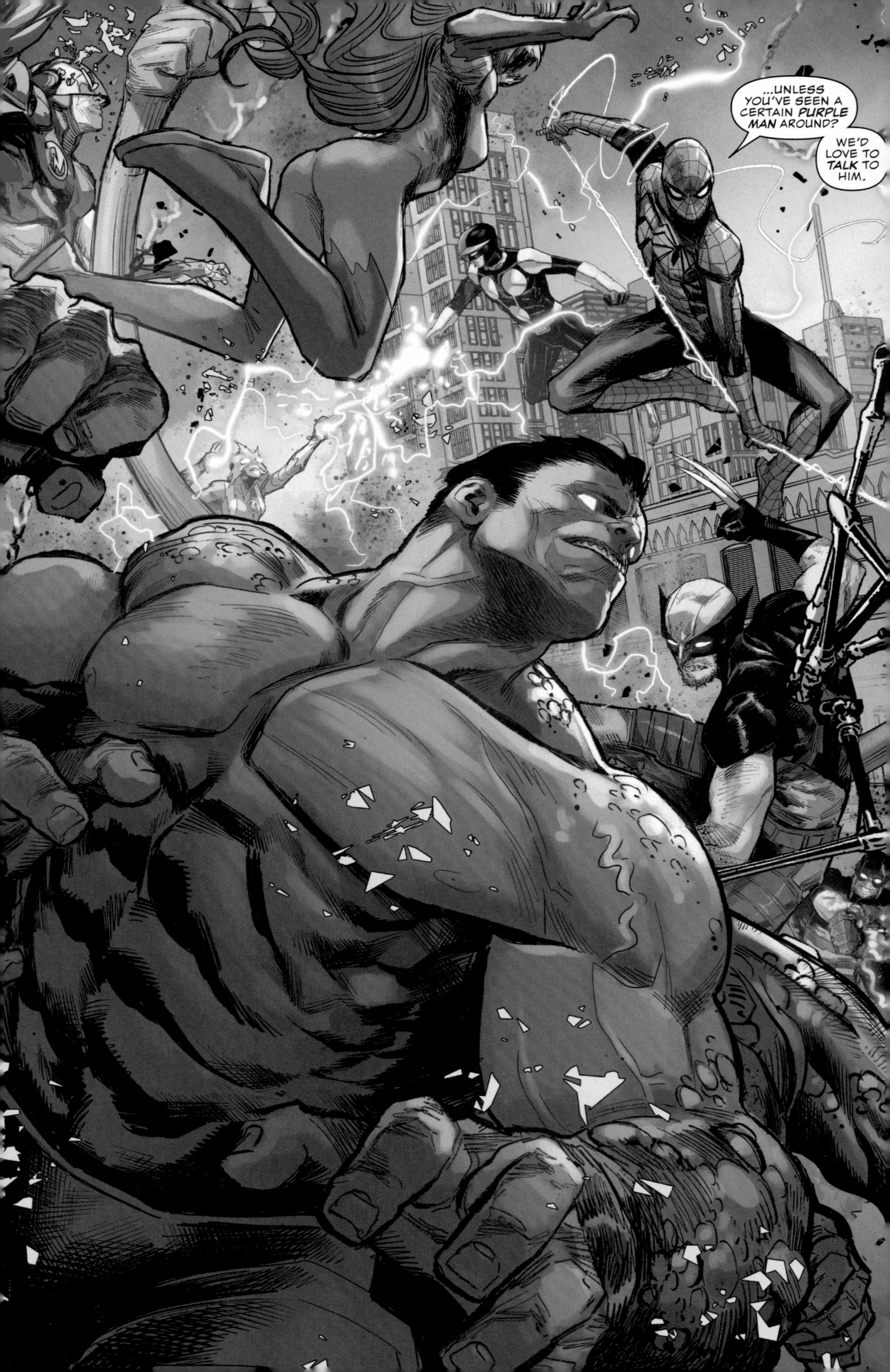
...UNLESS YOU'VE SEEN A CERTAIN PURPLE MAN AROUND?
WE'D LOVE TO TALK TO HIM.

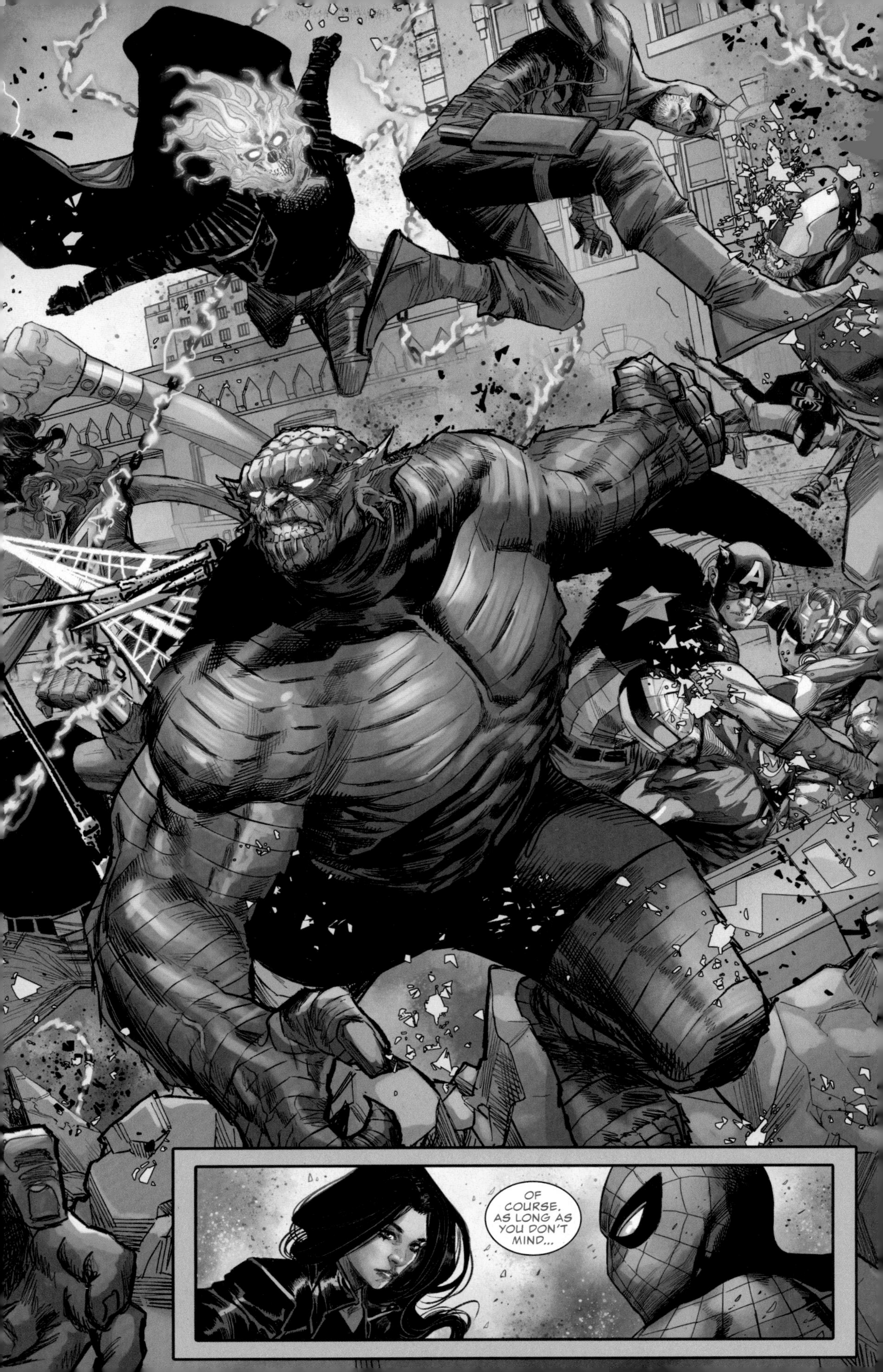
OF COURSE, AS LONG AS YOU DON'T MIND...

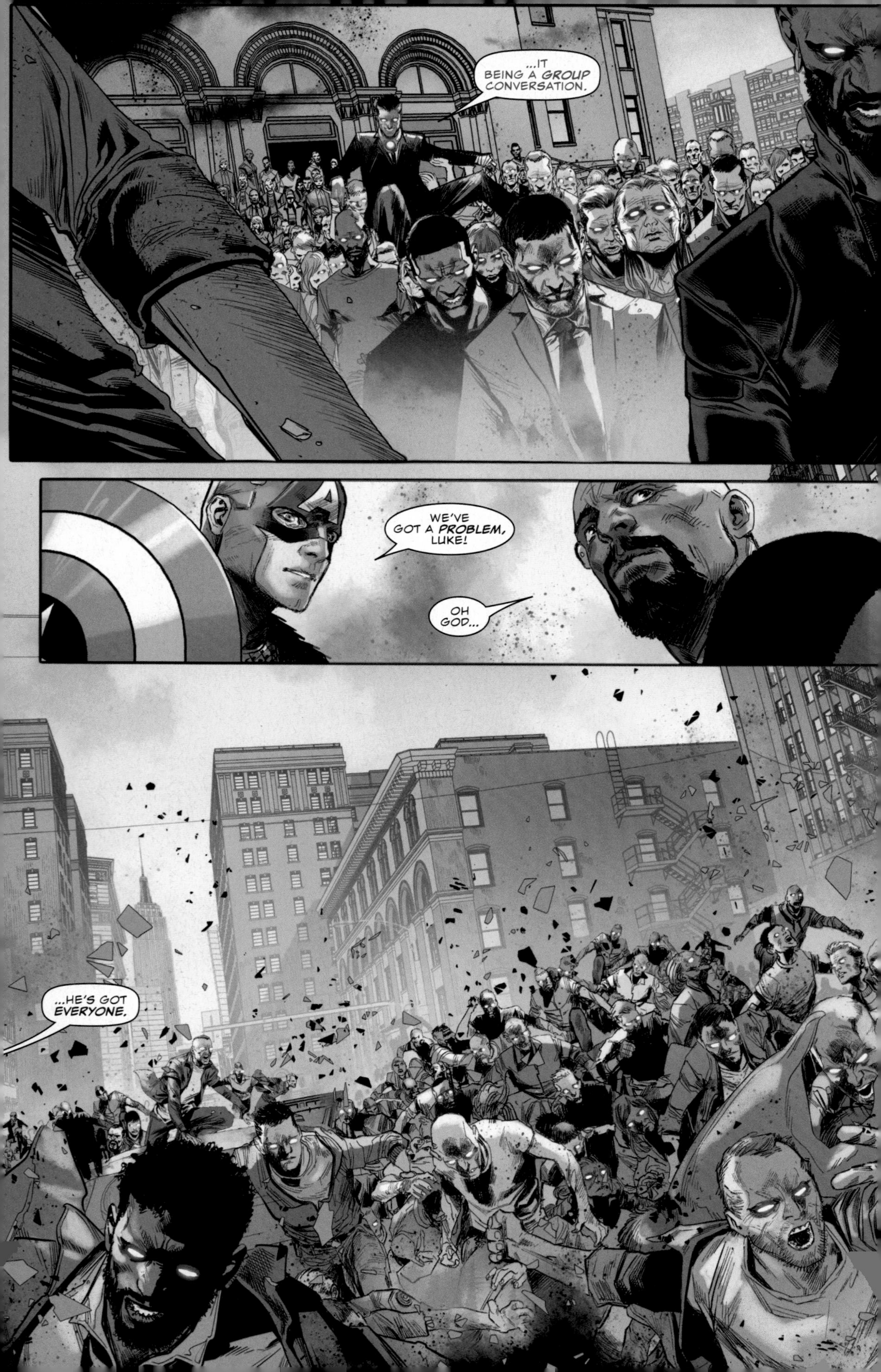
...IT BEING A GROUP CONVERSATION.
WE'VE GOT A PROBLEM, LUKE!
OH GOD...
...HE'S GOT EVERYONE.

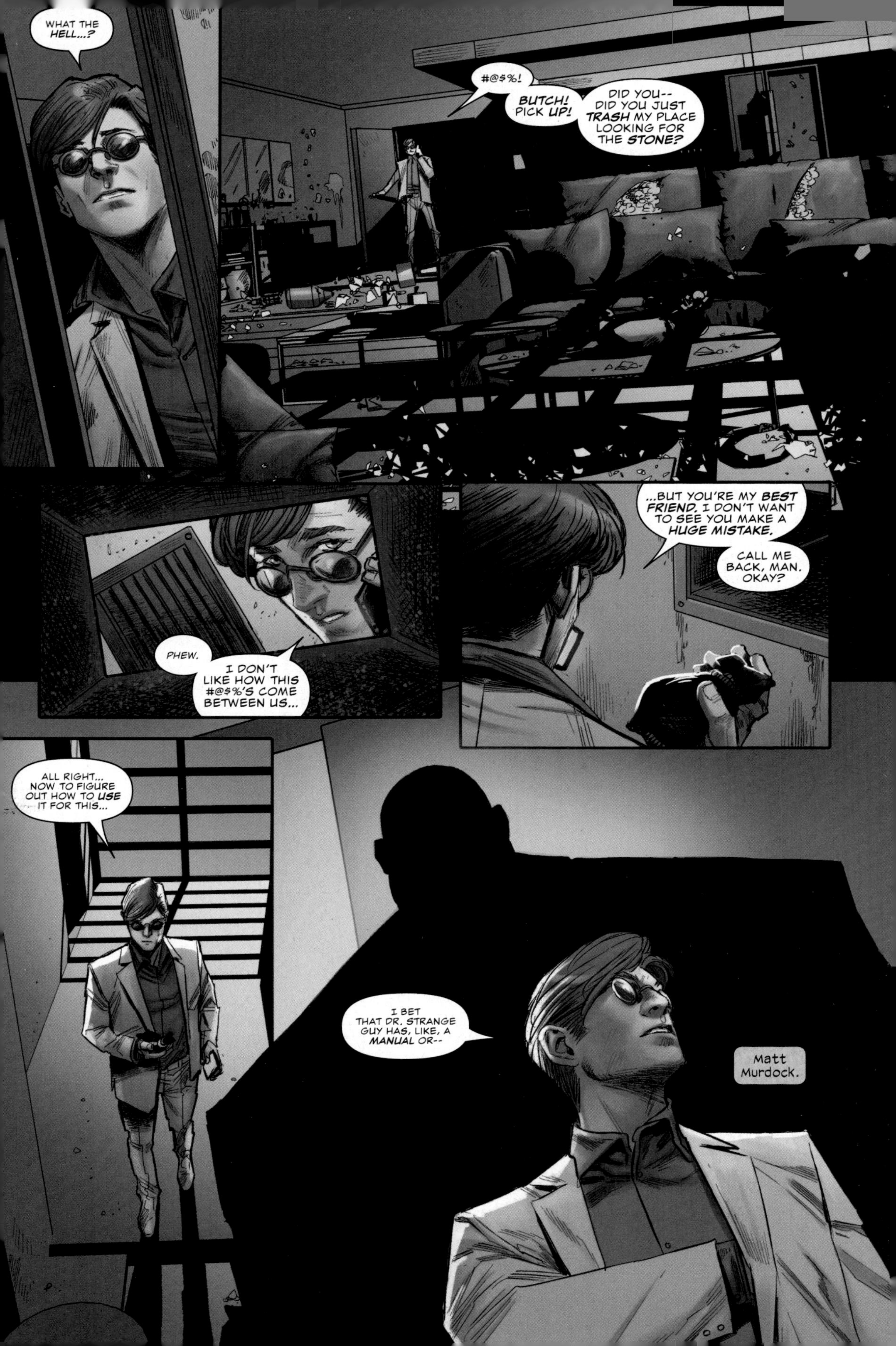
WHAT THE HELL...?
#@$%!
BUTCH! PICK UP!
DID YOU-- DID YOU JUST TRASH MY PLACE LOOKING FOR THE STONE?
PHEW.
I DON'T LIKE HOW THIS #@$%'S COME BETWEEN US...
...BUT YOU'RE MY BEST FRIEND. I DON'T WANT TO SEE YOU MAKE A HUGE MISTAKE.
CALL ME BACK, MAN. OKAY?
ALL RIGHT... NOW TO FIGURE OUT HOW TO USE IT FOR THIS...
I BET THAT DR. STRANGE GUY HAS, LIKE, A MANUAL OR--
Matt Murdock.

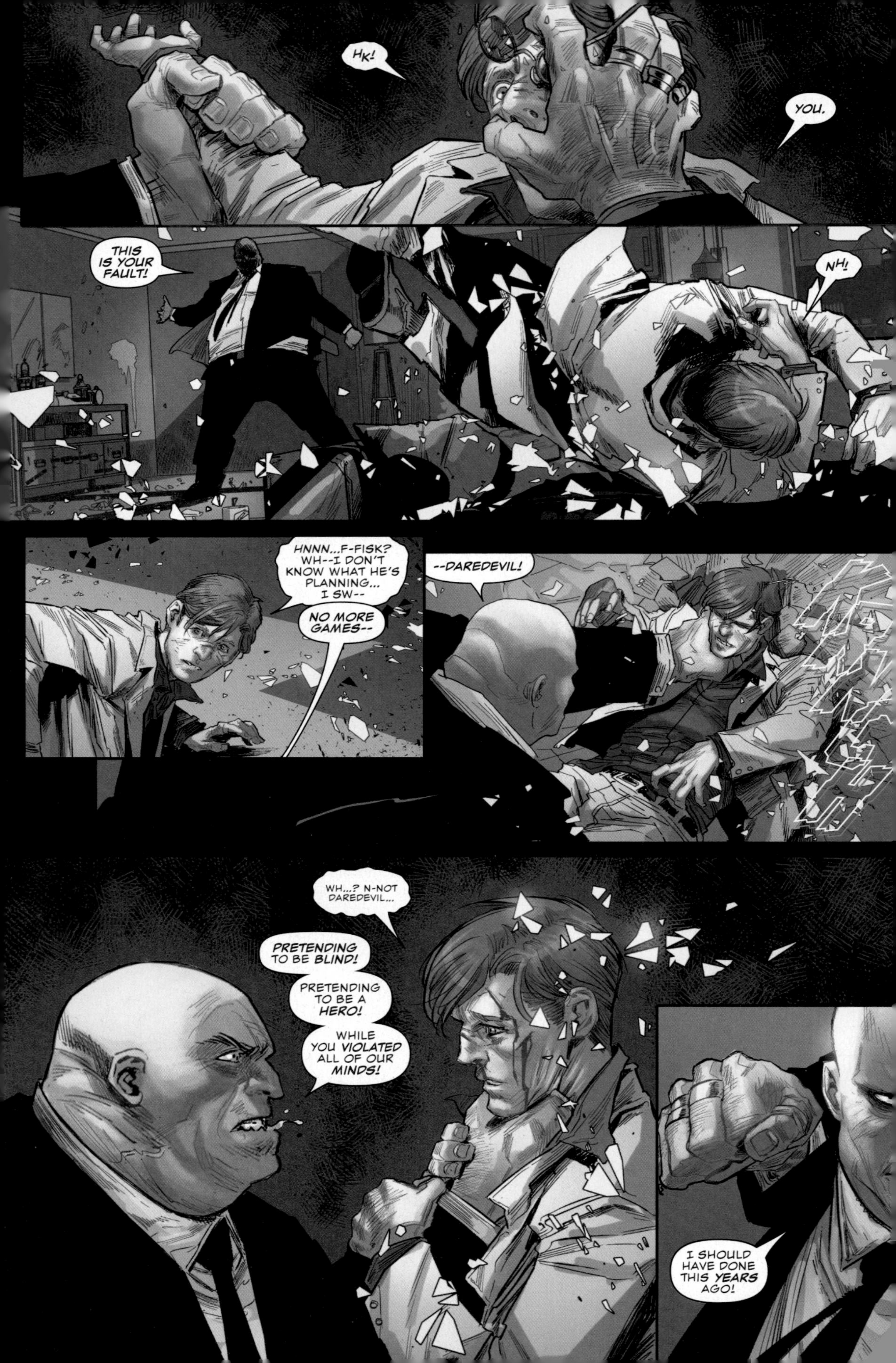
HK!
YOU.
THIS IS YOUR FAULT!
NH!
HNNN...F-FISK? WH--I DON'T KNOW WHAT HE'S PLANNING... I SW--
NO MORE GAMES--
--DAREDEVIL!
WH...? N-NOT DAREDEVIL...
PRETENDING TO BE BLIND!
PRETENDING TO BE A HERO!
WHILE YOU VIOLATED ALL OF OUR MINDS!
I SHOULD HAVE DONE THIS YEARS AGO!

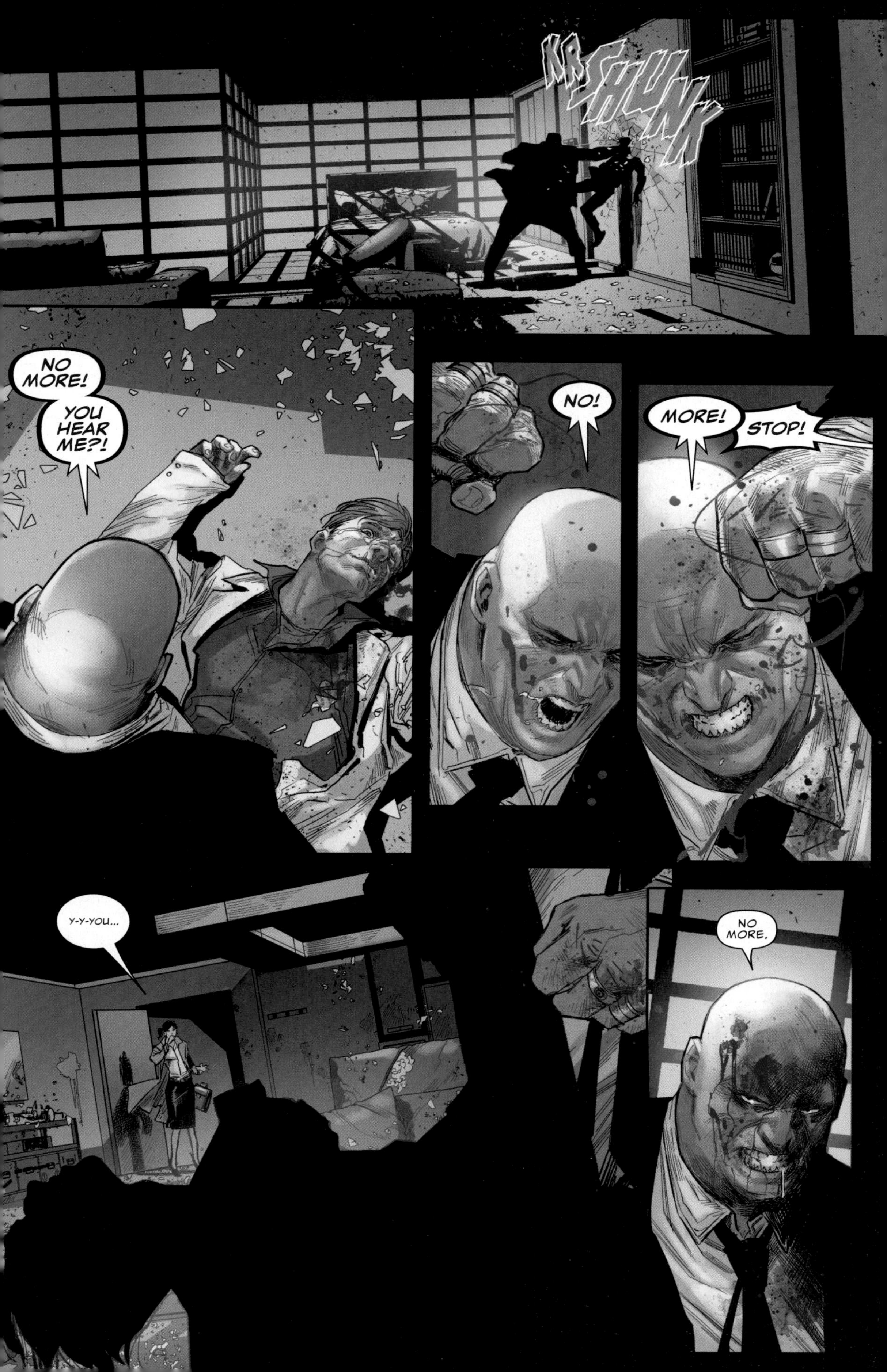

KRSHUNK
NO MORE!
YOU HEAR ME?!
NO!
MORE!
STOP!
Y-Y-YOU...
NO MORE.

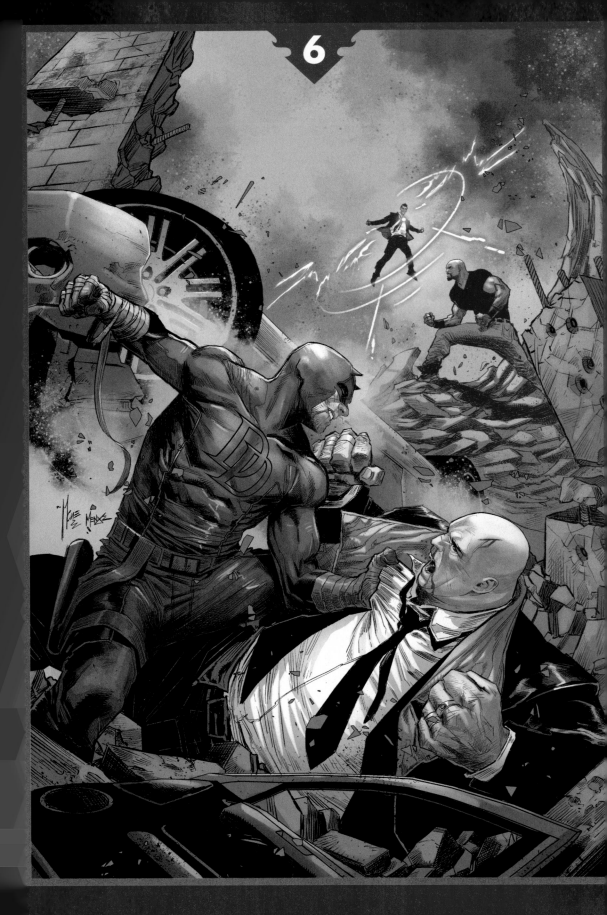

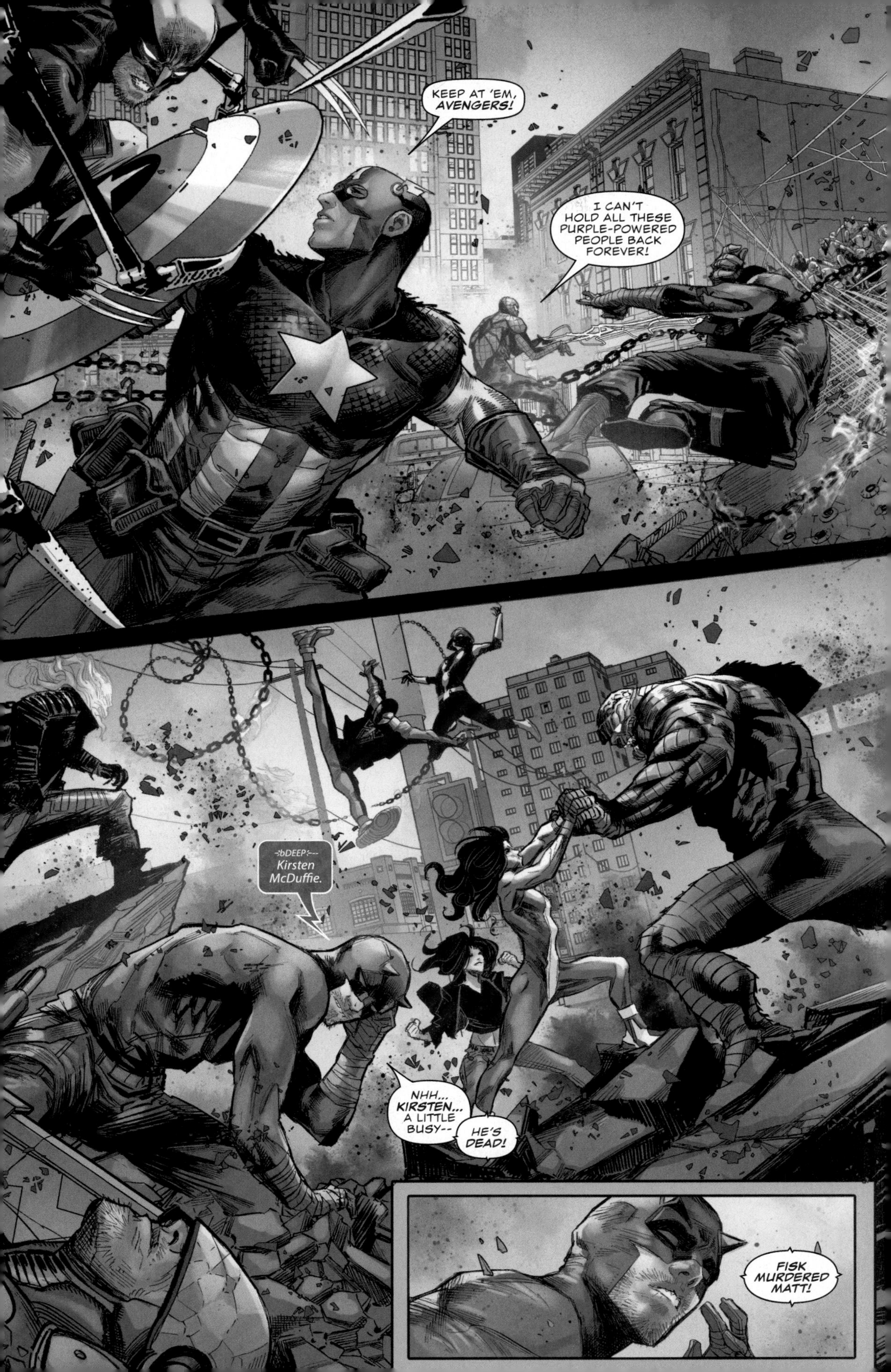
KEEP AT 'EM, AVENGERS!
I CAN'T HOLD ALL THESE PURPLE-POWERED PEOPLE BACK FOREVER!
-bDEEP- Kirsten McDuffie.
NHH... KIRSTEN... A LITTLE BUSY--
HE'S DEAD!
FISK MURDERED MATT!

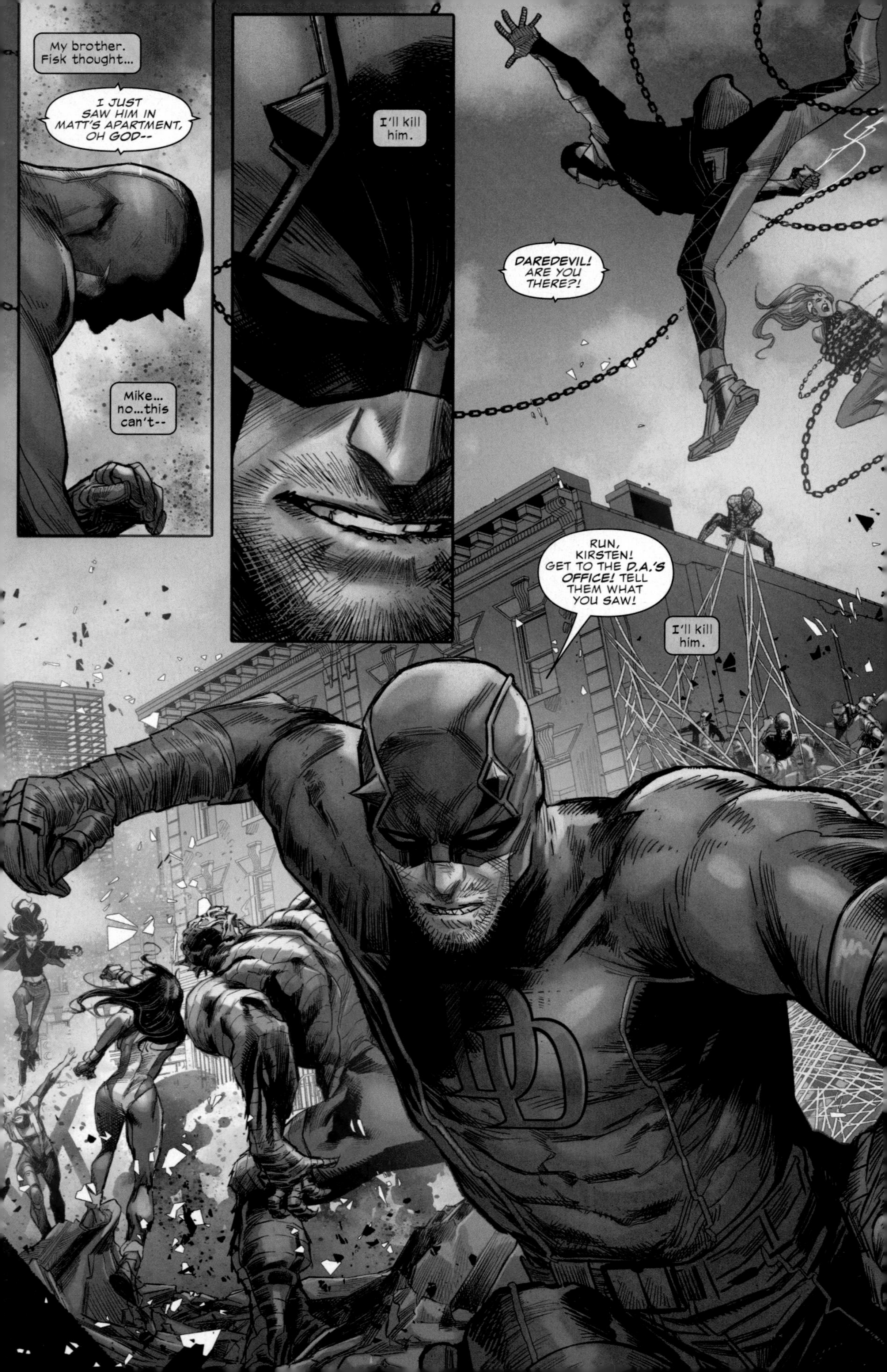
My brother. Fisk thought...
I JUST SAW HIM IN MATT'S APARTMENT, OH GOD--
Mike... no...this can't--
I'll kill him.
DAREDEVIL! ARE YOU THERE?!
RUN, KIRSTEN! GET TO THE D.A.'S OFFICE! TELL THEM WHAT YOU SAW!
I'll kill him.

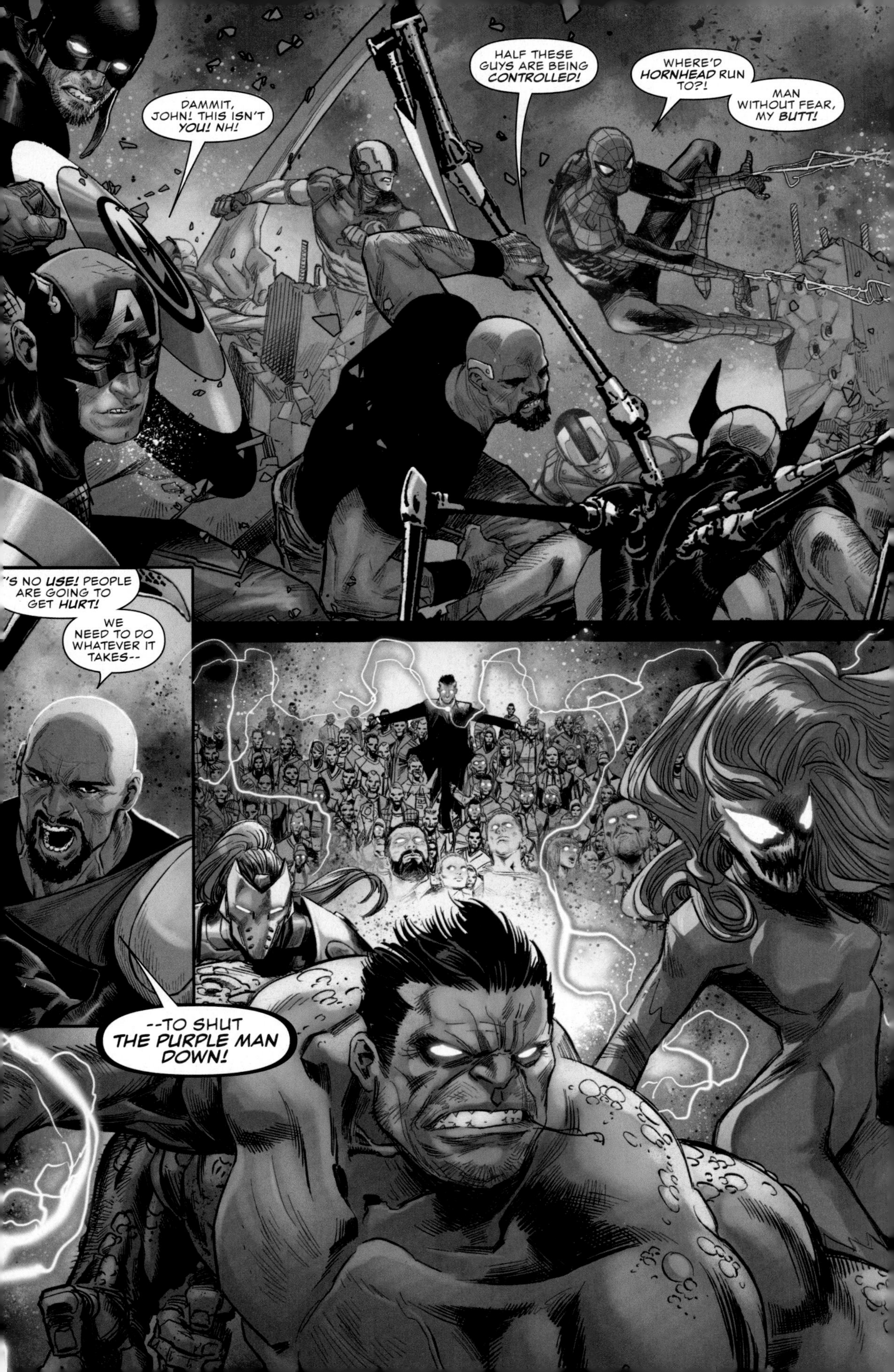
DAMMIT, JOHN! THIS ISN'T YOU! NH!
HALF THESE GUYS ARE BEING CONTROLLED!
WHERE'D HORNHEAD RUN TO?!
MAN WITHOUT FEAR, MY BUTT!
'S NO USE! PEOPLE ARE GOING TO GET HURT!
WE NEED TO DO WHATEVER IT TAKES--
--TO SHUT THE PURPLE MAN DOWN!

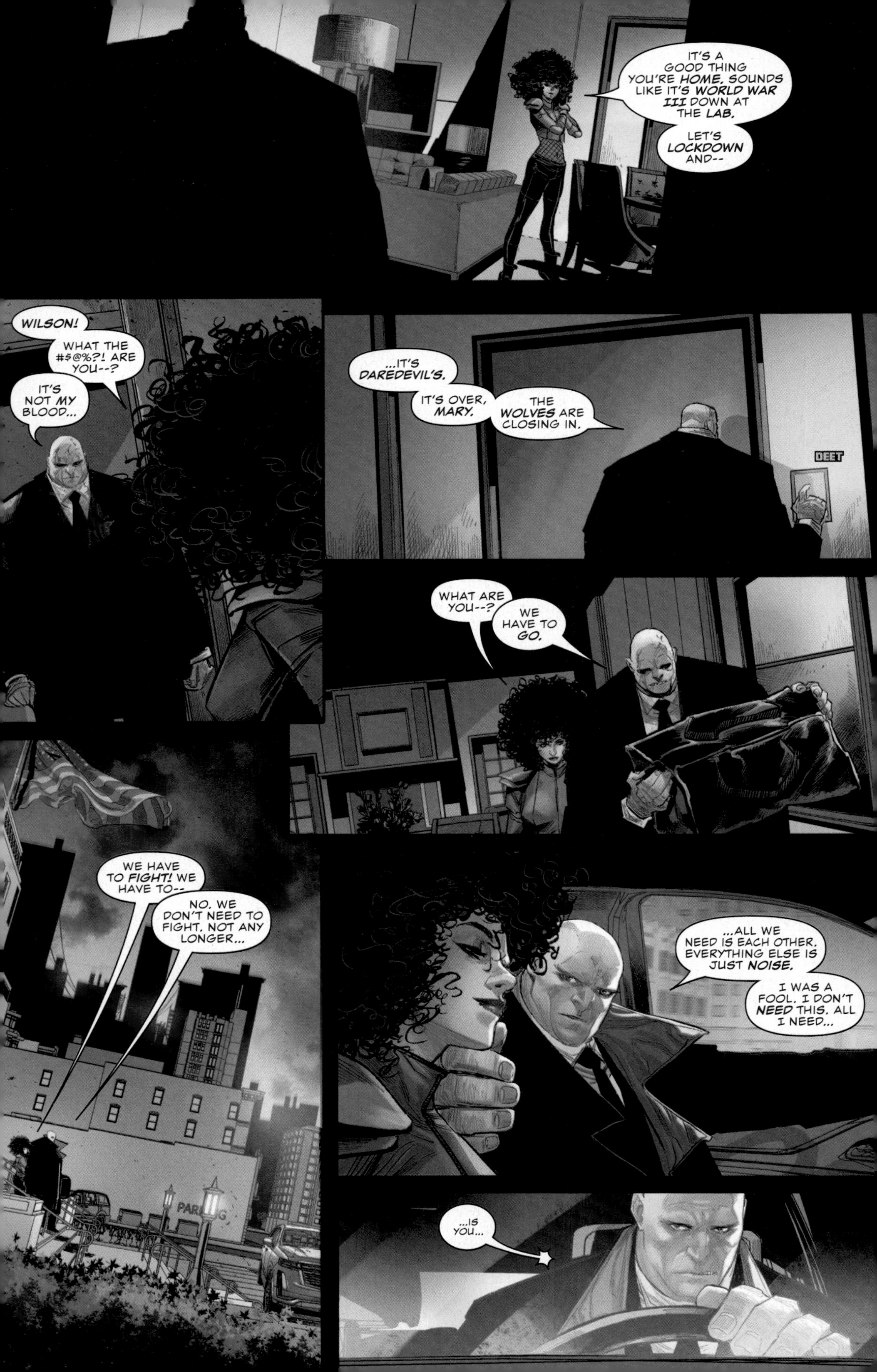

IT'S A GOOD THING YOU'RE HOME. SOUNDS LIKE IT'S WORLD WAR III DOWN AT THE LAB.
LET'S LOCKDOWN AND--
WILSON!
WHAT THE #$@%?! ARE YOU--?
IT'S NOT MY BLOOD...
...IT'S DAREDEVIL'S.
IT'S OVER, MARY.
THE WOLVES ARE CLOSING IN.
DEET
WHAT ARE YOU--?
WE HAVE TO GO.
WE HAVE TO FIGHT! WE HAVE TO--
NO. WE DON'T NEED TO FIGHT. NOT ANY LONGER...
...ALL WE NEED IS EACH OTHER. EVERYTHING ELSE IS JUST NOISE.
I WAS A FOOL. I DON'T NEED THIS. ALL I NEED...
...IS YOU...

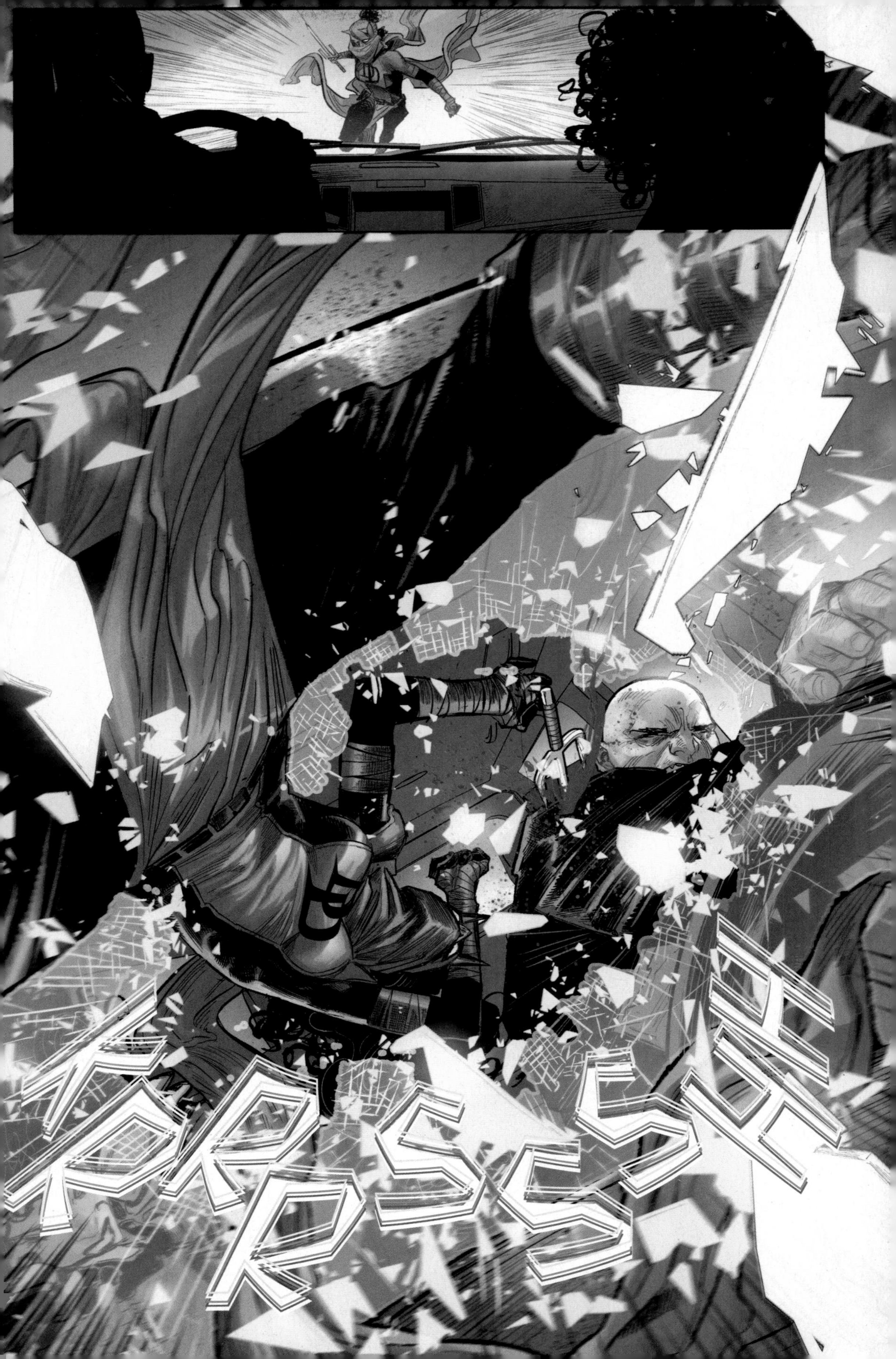
KRSSH

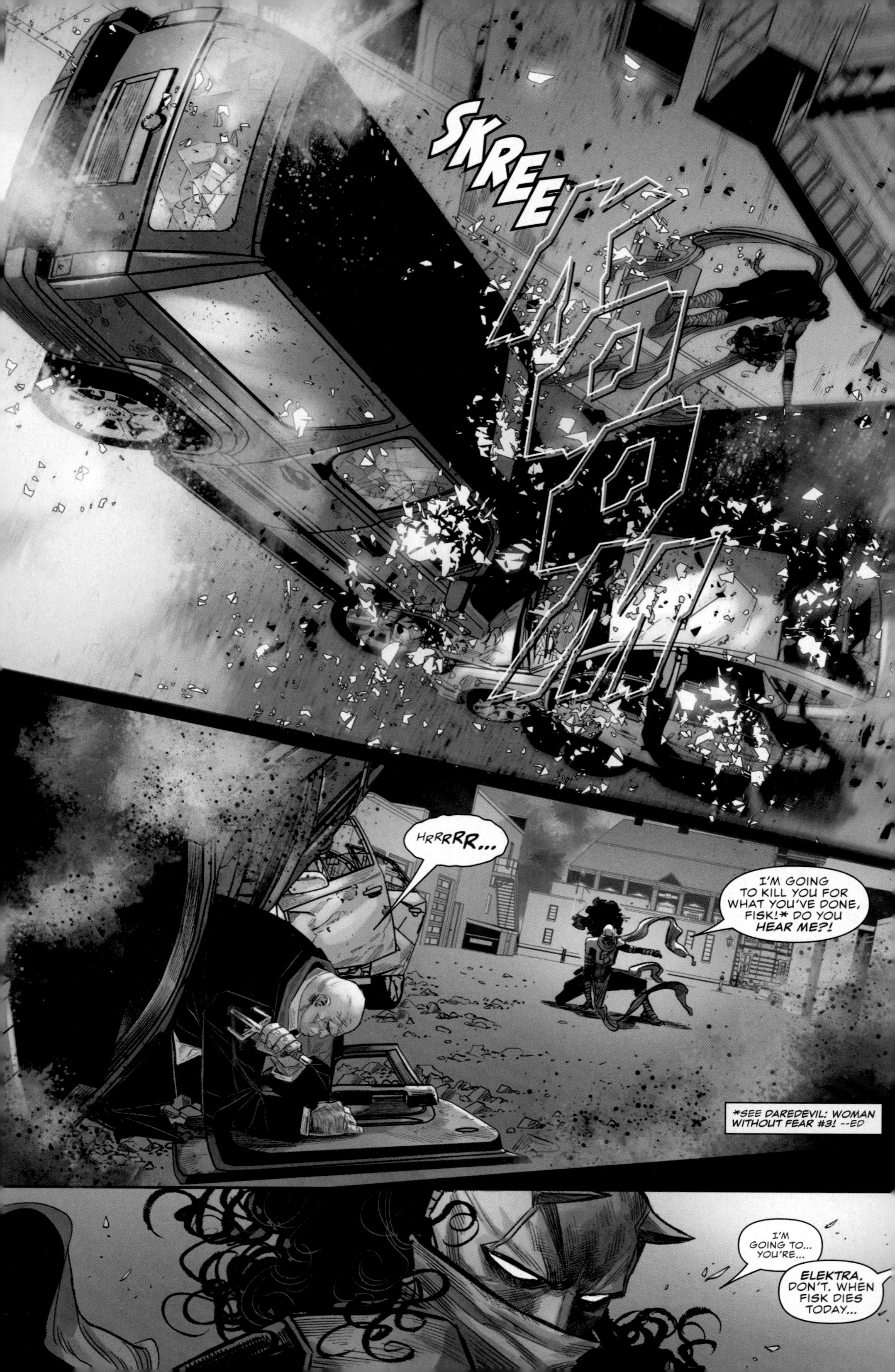
SKREEEEE
HRRRRR...
I'M GOING TO KILL YOU FOR WHAT YOU'VE DONE, FISK!* DO YOU HEAR ME?!
*SEE DAREDEVIL: WOMAN WITHOUT FEAR #3! --ED
I'M GOING TO... YOU'RE...
ELEKTRA. DON'T. WHEN FISK DIES TODAY...

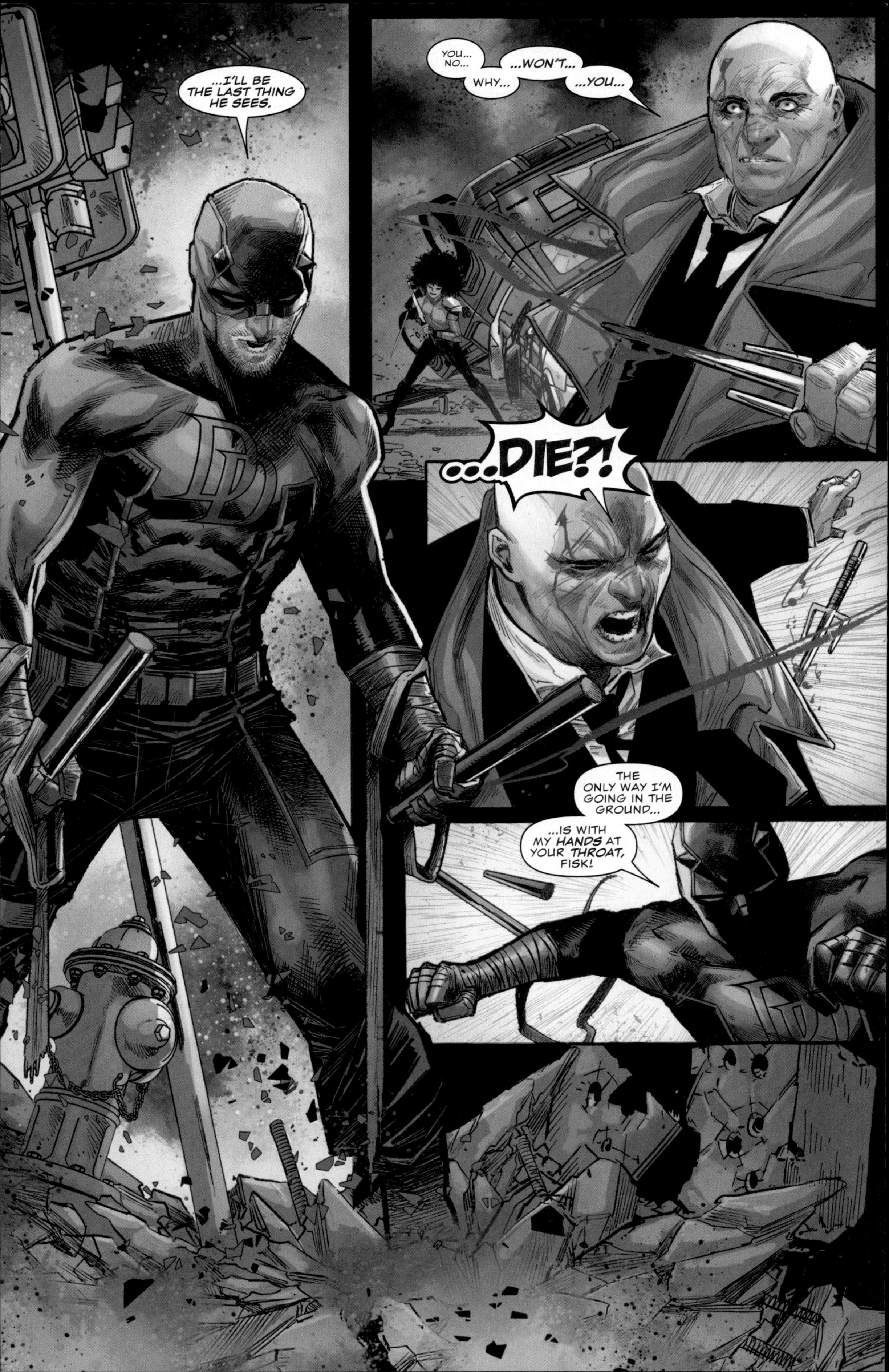

...I'LL BE THE LAST THING HE SEES.
YOU... NO...
WHY...
...WON'T...
...YOU...
...DIE?!
THE ONLY WAY I'M GOING IN THE GROUND...
...IS WITH MY HANDS AT YOUR THROAT, FISK!

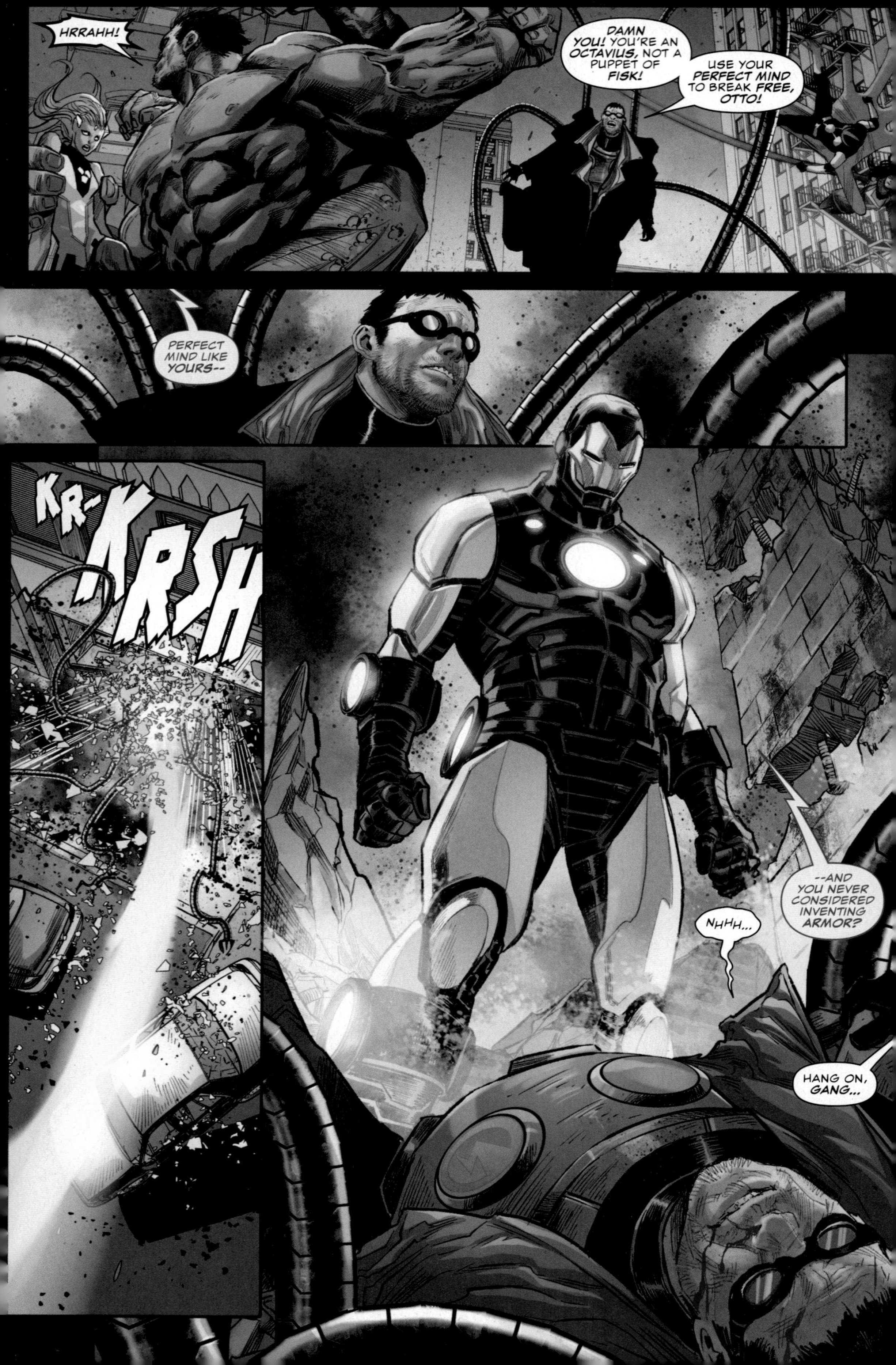
HRRAHH!
DAMN YOU! YOU'RE AN OCTAVIUS, NOT A PUPPET OF FISK!
USE YOUR PERFECT MIND TO BREAK FREE, OTTO!
PERFECT MIND LIKE YOURS--
KR-KRSH
--AND YOU NEVER CONSIDERED INVENTING ARMOR?
NHHH...
HANG ON, GANG...

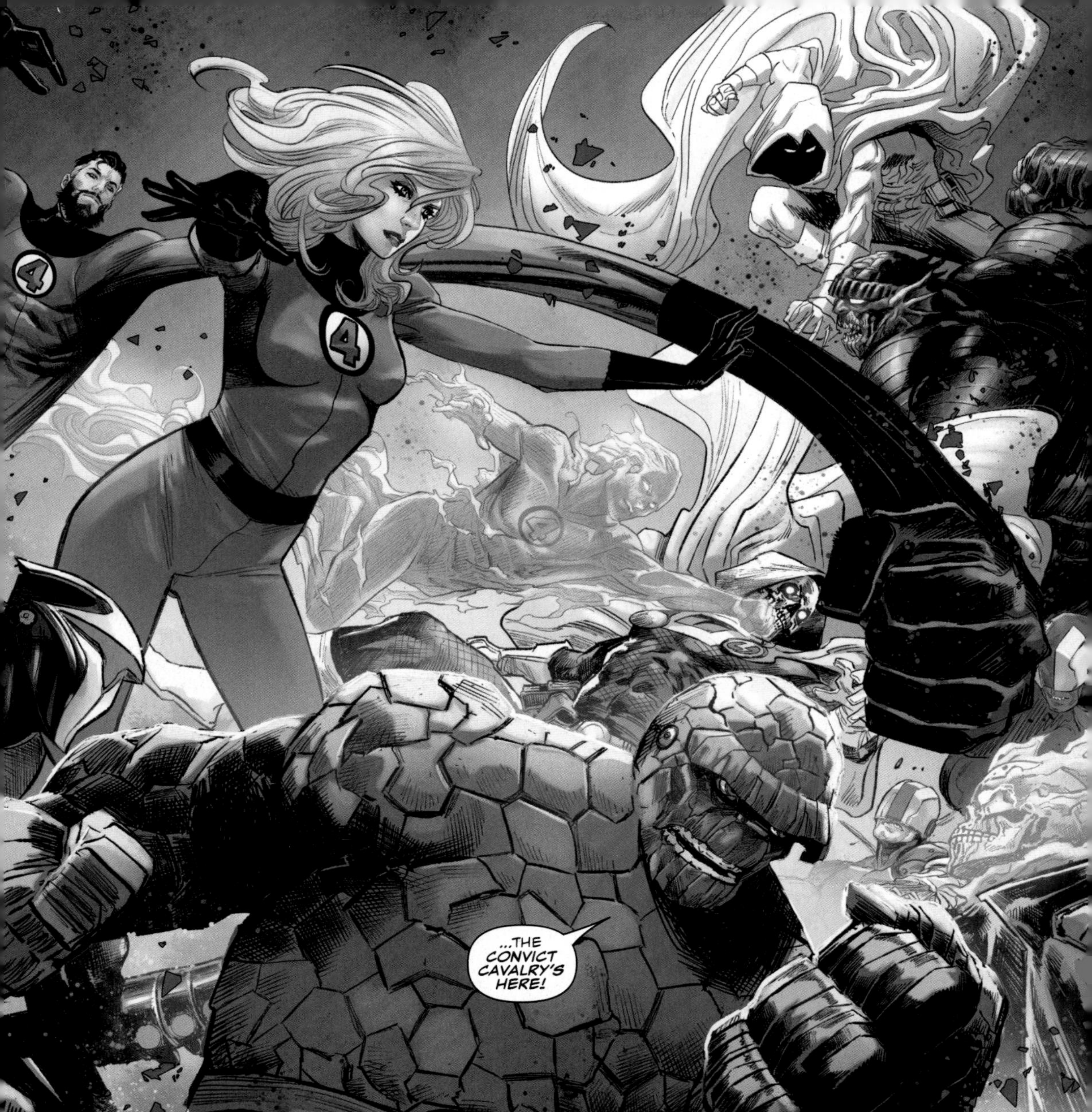
...THE CONVICT CAVALRY'S HERE!

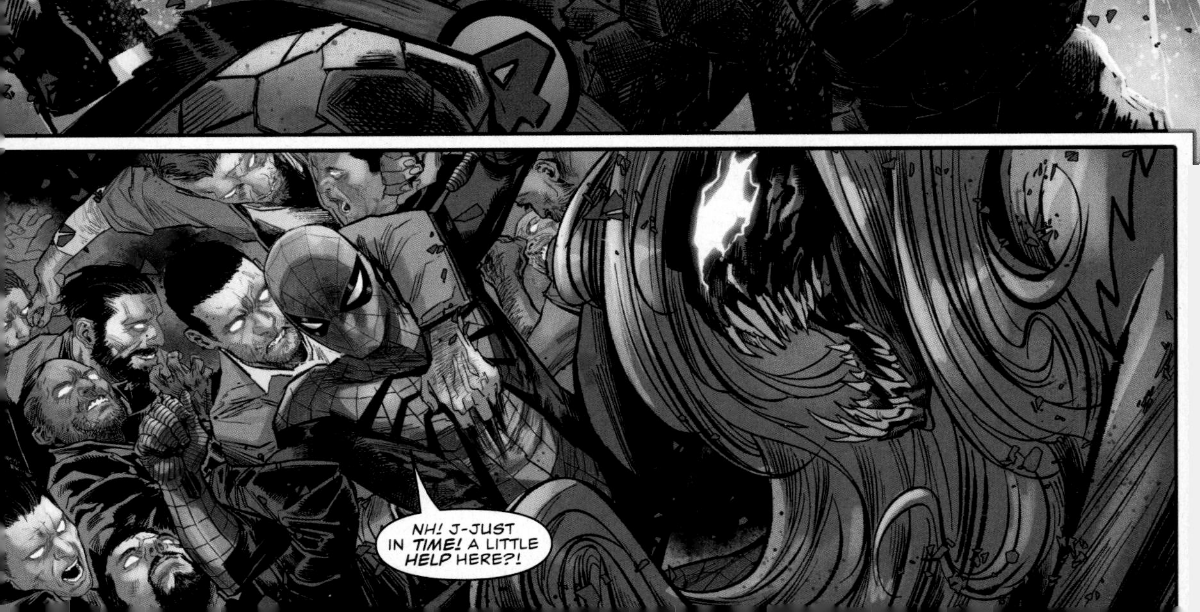
NH! J-JUST IN TIME! A LITTLE HELP HERE?!

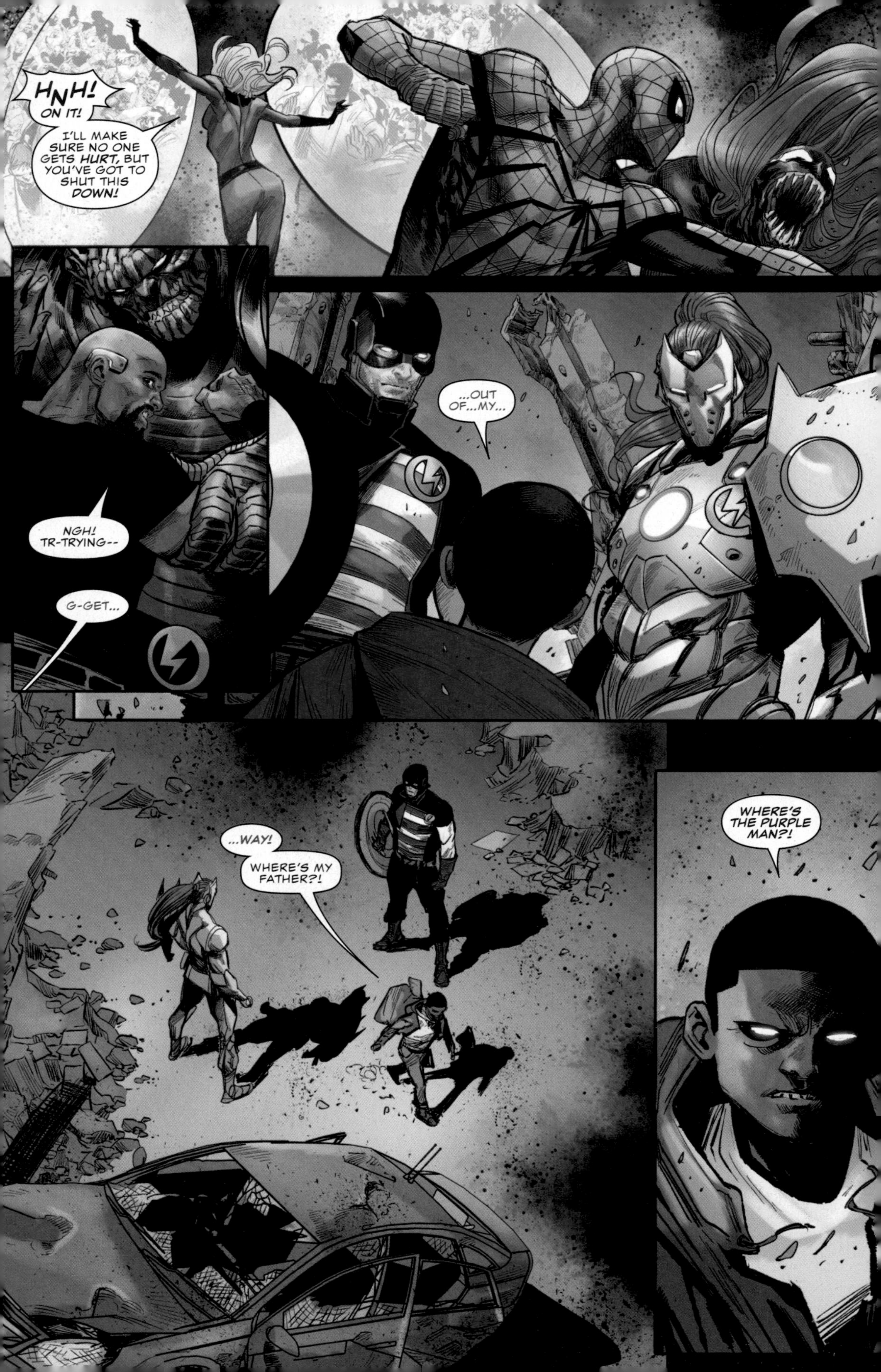
HNH! ON IT!
I'LL MAKE SURE NO ONE GETS HURT, BUT YOU'VE GOT TO SHUT THIS DOWN!
NGH! TR-TRYING--
G-GET...
...OUT OF...MY...
...WAY!
WHERE'S MY FATHER?!
WHERE'S THE PURPLE MAN?!

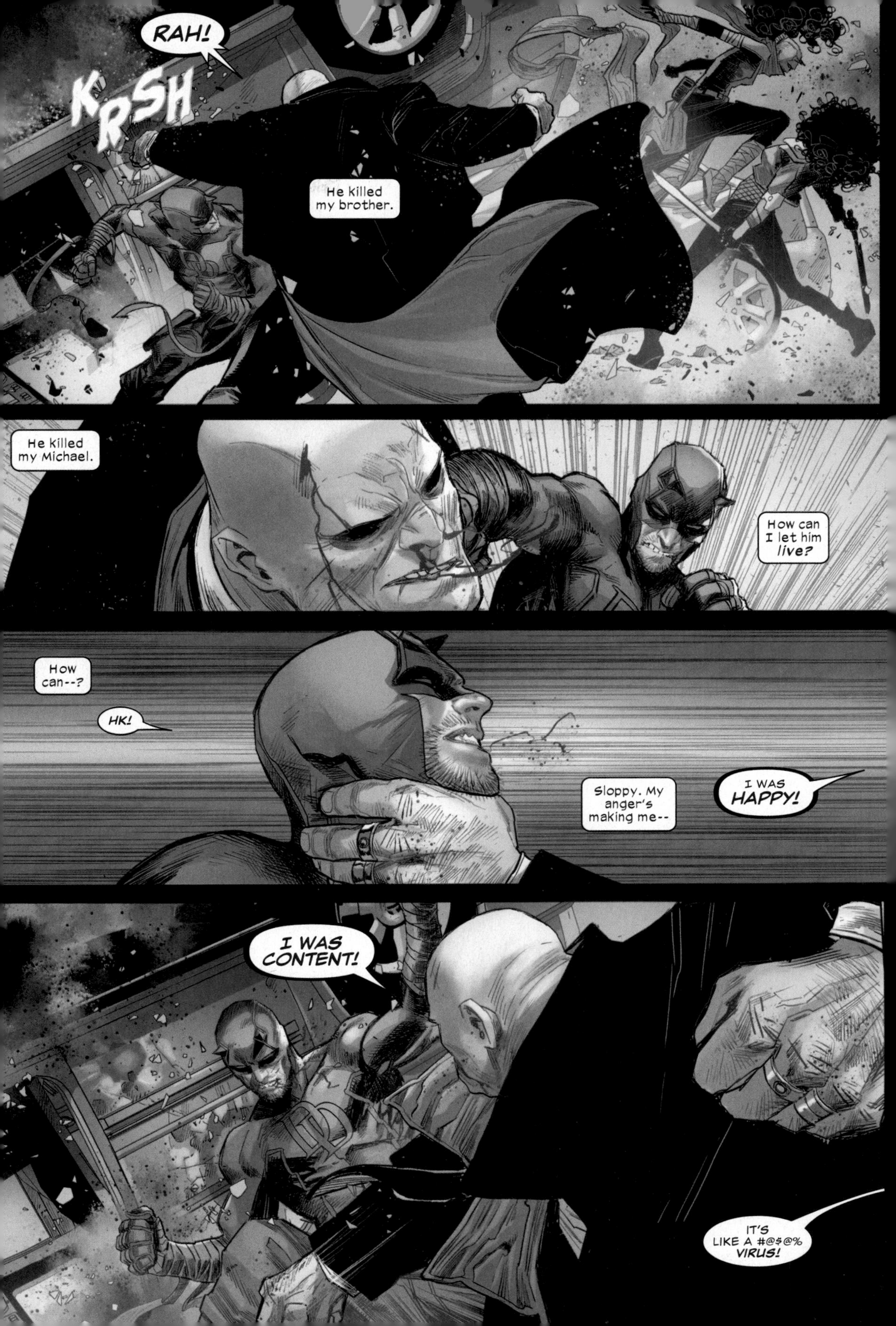
RAH!
KRSH
He killed my brother.
He killed my Michael.
How can I let him *live?*
How can--?
HK!
Sloppy. My anger's making me--
I WAS HAPPY!
I WAS CONTENT!
IT'S LIKE A #@$@% VIRUS!

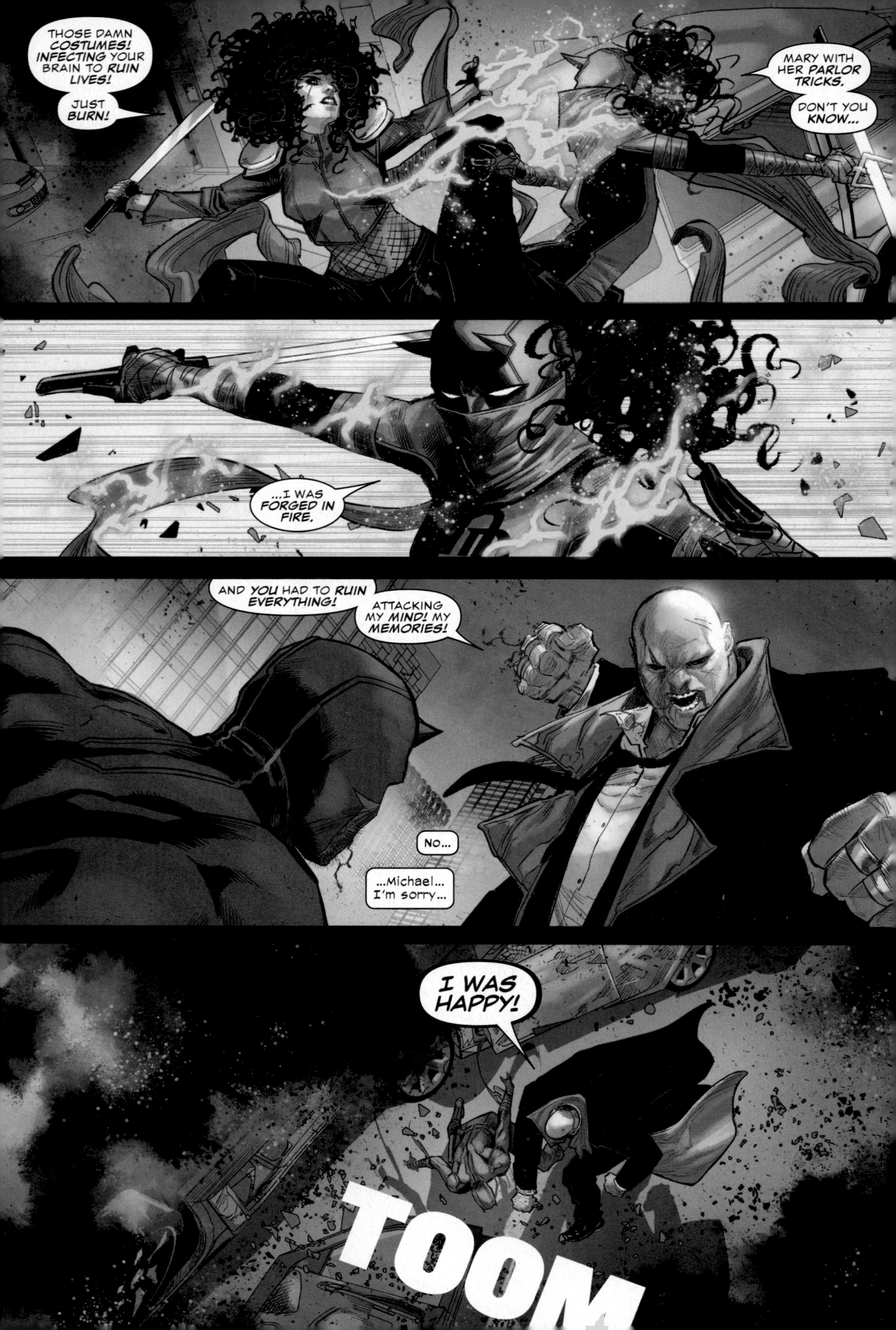
THOSE DAMN COSTUMES! INFECTING YOUR BRAIN TO RUIN LIVES!
JUST BURN!
MARY WITH HER PARLOR TRICKS.
DON'T YOU KNOW...
...I WAS FORGED IN FIRE.
AND YOU HAD TO RUIN EVERYTHING!
ATTACKING MY MIND! MY MEMORIES!
No...
...Michael... I'm sorry...
I WAS HAPPY!
TOOM

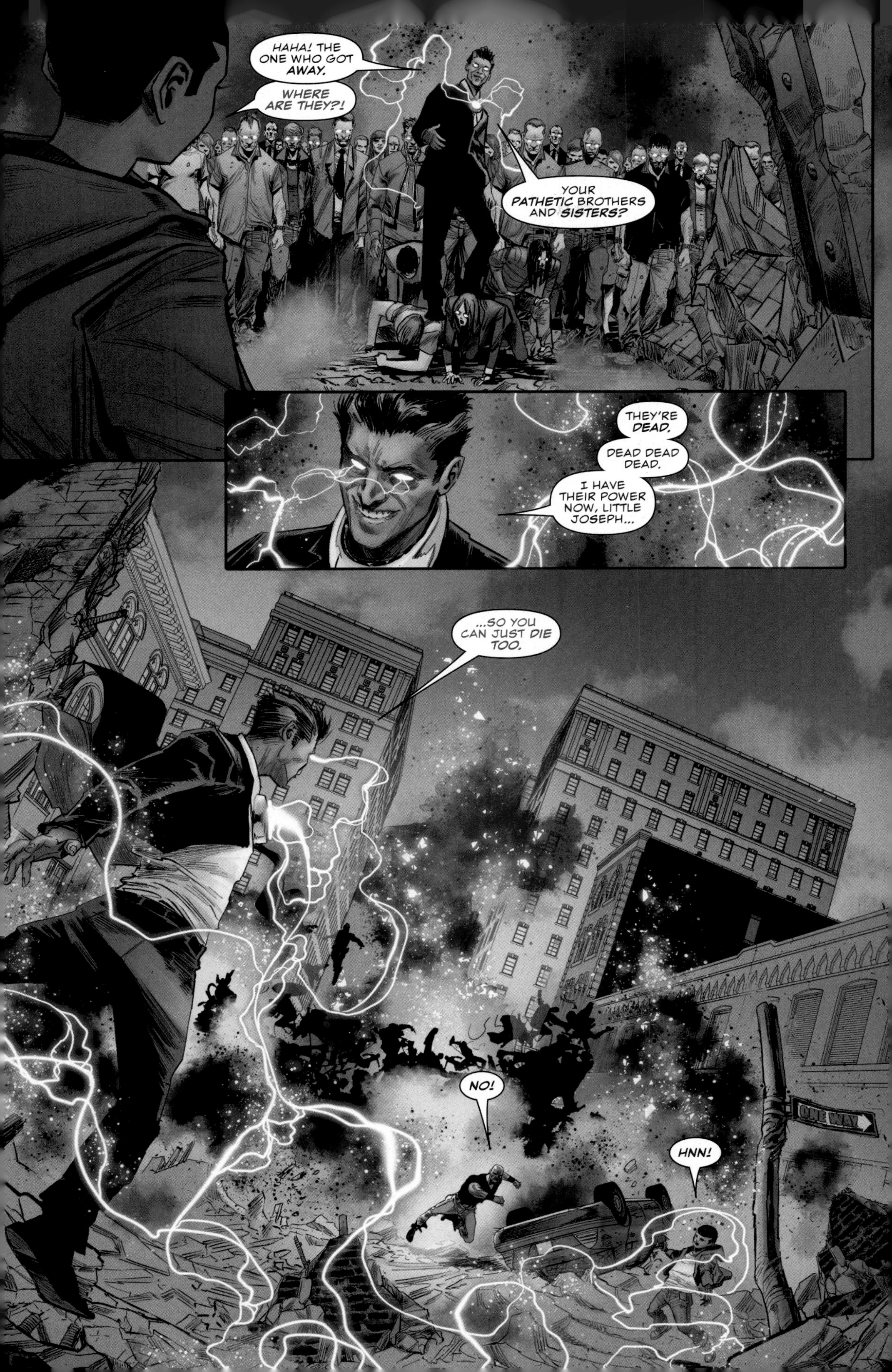
HAHA! THE ONE WHO GOT AWAY.
WHERE ARE THEY?!
YOUR PATHETIC BROTHERS AND SISTERS?
THEY'RE DEAD.
DEAD DEAD DEAD.
I HAVE THEIR POWER NOW, LITTLE JOSEPH...
...SO YOU CAN JUST DIE TOO.
NO!
HNN!
ONE WAY

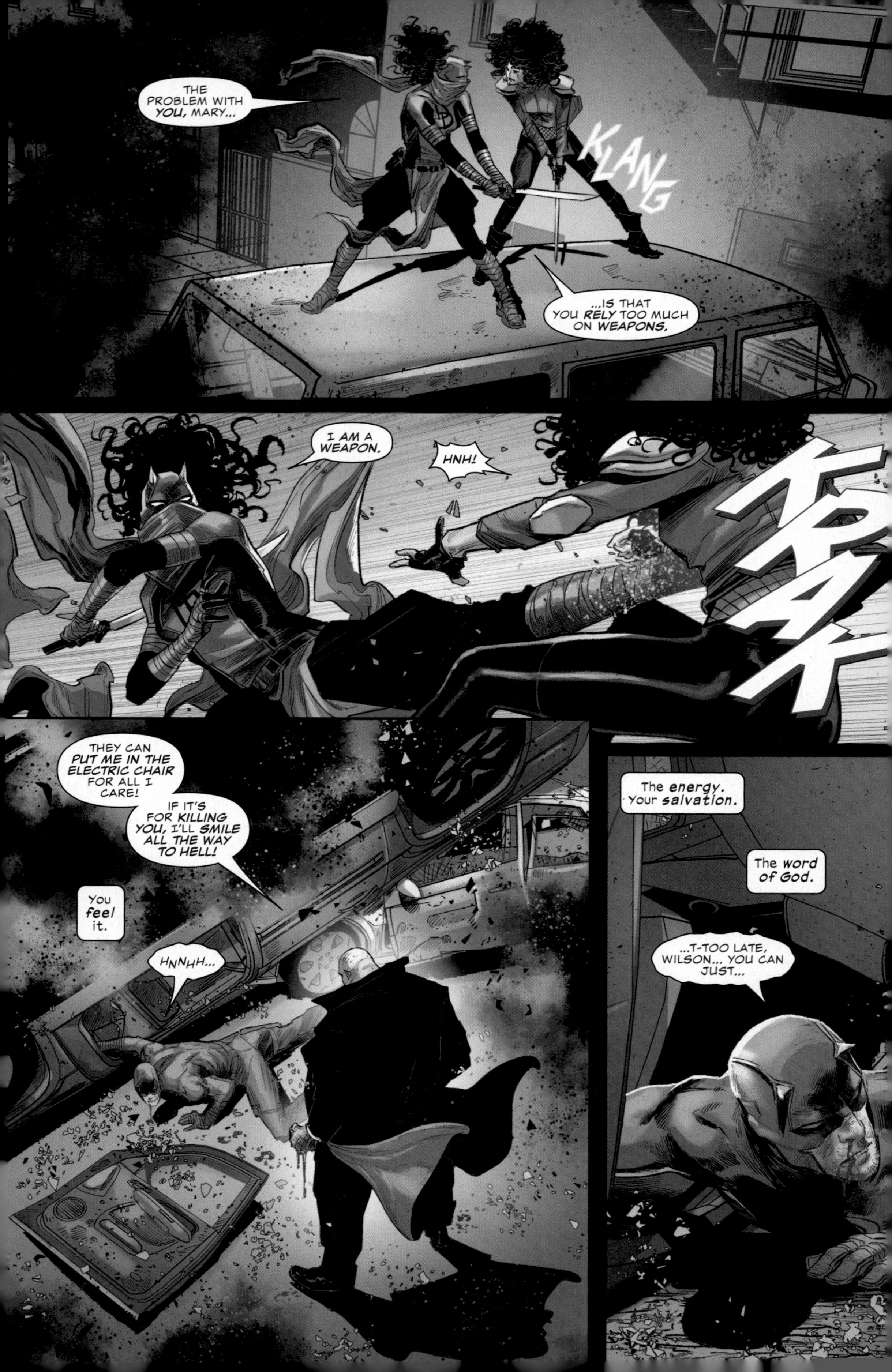
THE PROBLEM WITH YOU, MARY...
KLANG
...IS THAT YOU RELY TOO MUCH ON WEAPONS.
I AM A WEAPON.
HNH!
KRAK
THEY CAN PUT ME IN THE ELECTRIC CHAIR FOR ALL I CARE!
IF IT'S FOR KILLING YOU, I'LL SMILE ALL THE WAY TO HELL!
You feel it.
HNNHH...
The energy. Your salvation.
The word of God.
...T-TOO LATE, WILSON... YOU CAN JUST...

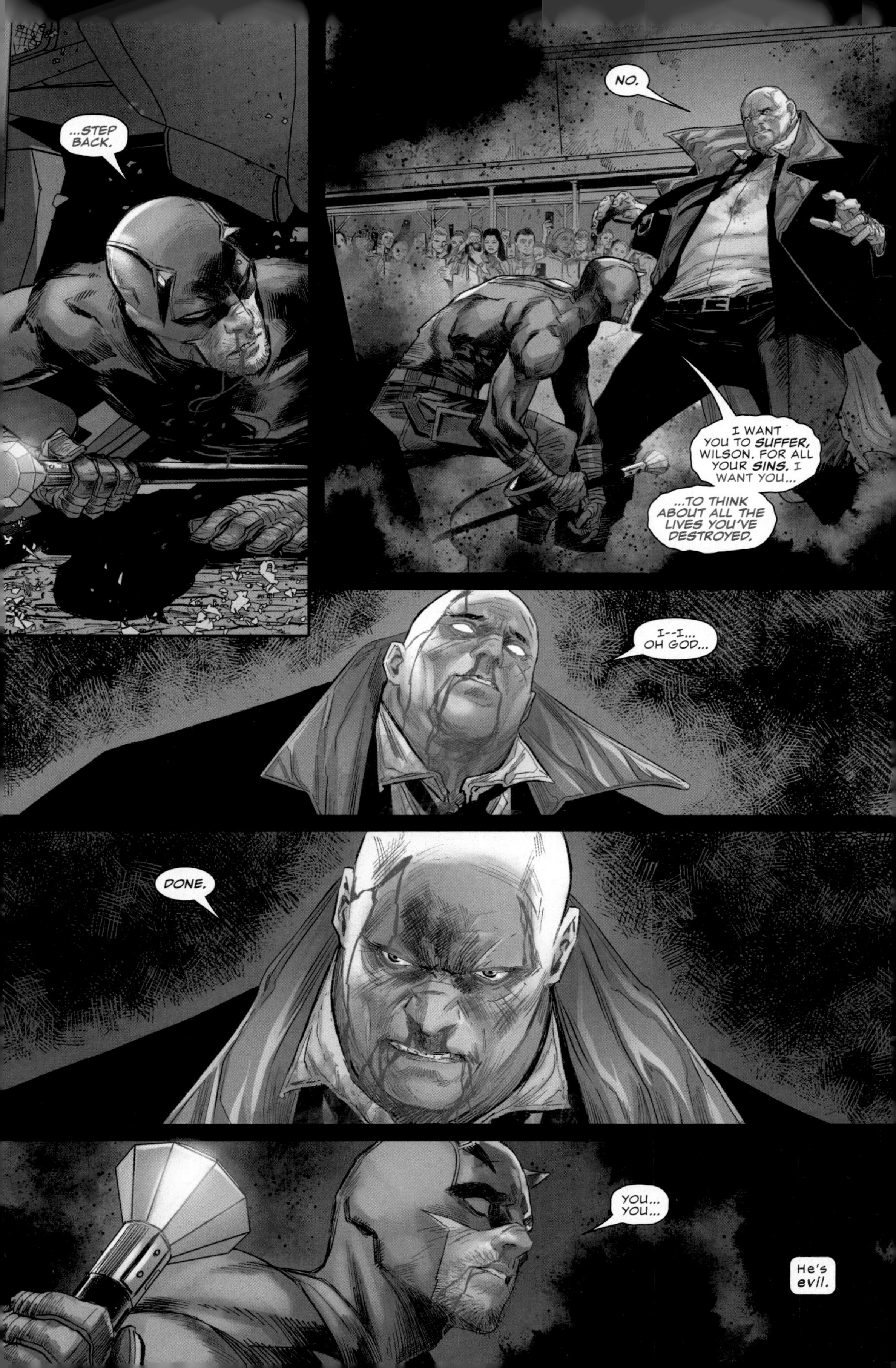
...STEP BACK.
NO.
I WANT YOU TO SUFFER, WILSON. FOR ALL YOUR SINS. I WANT YOU...
...TO THINK ABOUT ALL THE LIVES YOU'VE DESTROYED.
I--I... OH GOD...
DONE.
YOU... YOU...
He's evil.

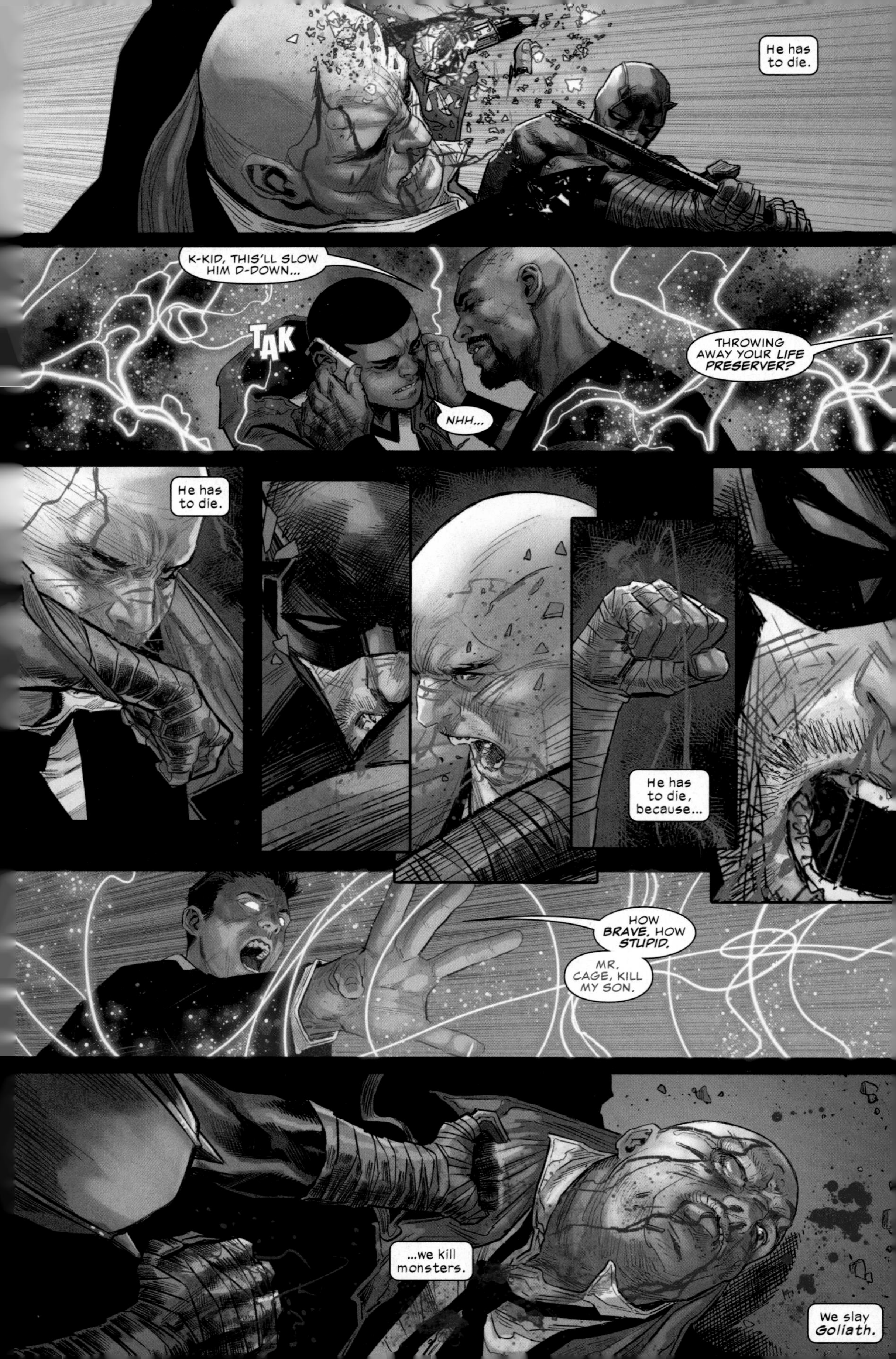
He has to die.
K-KID, THIS'LL SLOW HIM D-DOWN...
TAK
NHH...
THROWING AWAY YOUR LIFE PRESERVER?
He has to die.
He has to die, because...
HOW BRAVE. HOW STUPID.
MR. CAGE, KILL MY SON.
...we kill monsters.
We slay Goliath.

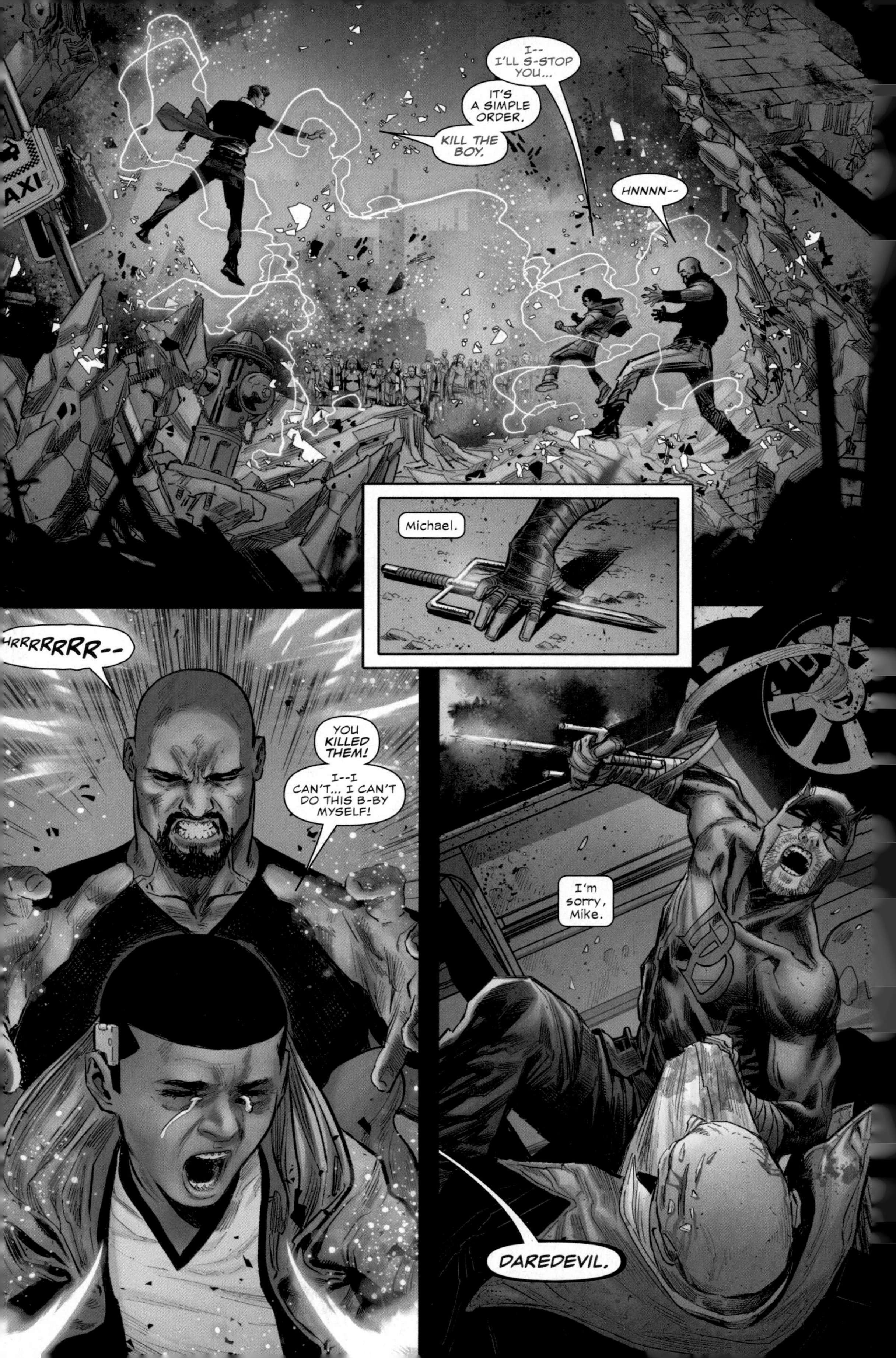
IT'S A SIMPLE ORDER.
KILL THE BOY.
I-- I'LL S-STOP YOU...
HNNNN--
Michael.
HRRRRRRR--
YOU KILLED THEM!
I--I CAN'T... I CAN'T DO THIS B-BY MYSELF!
I'm sorry, Mike.
DAREDEVIL.

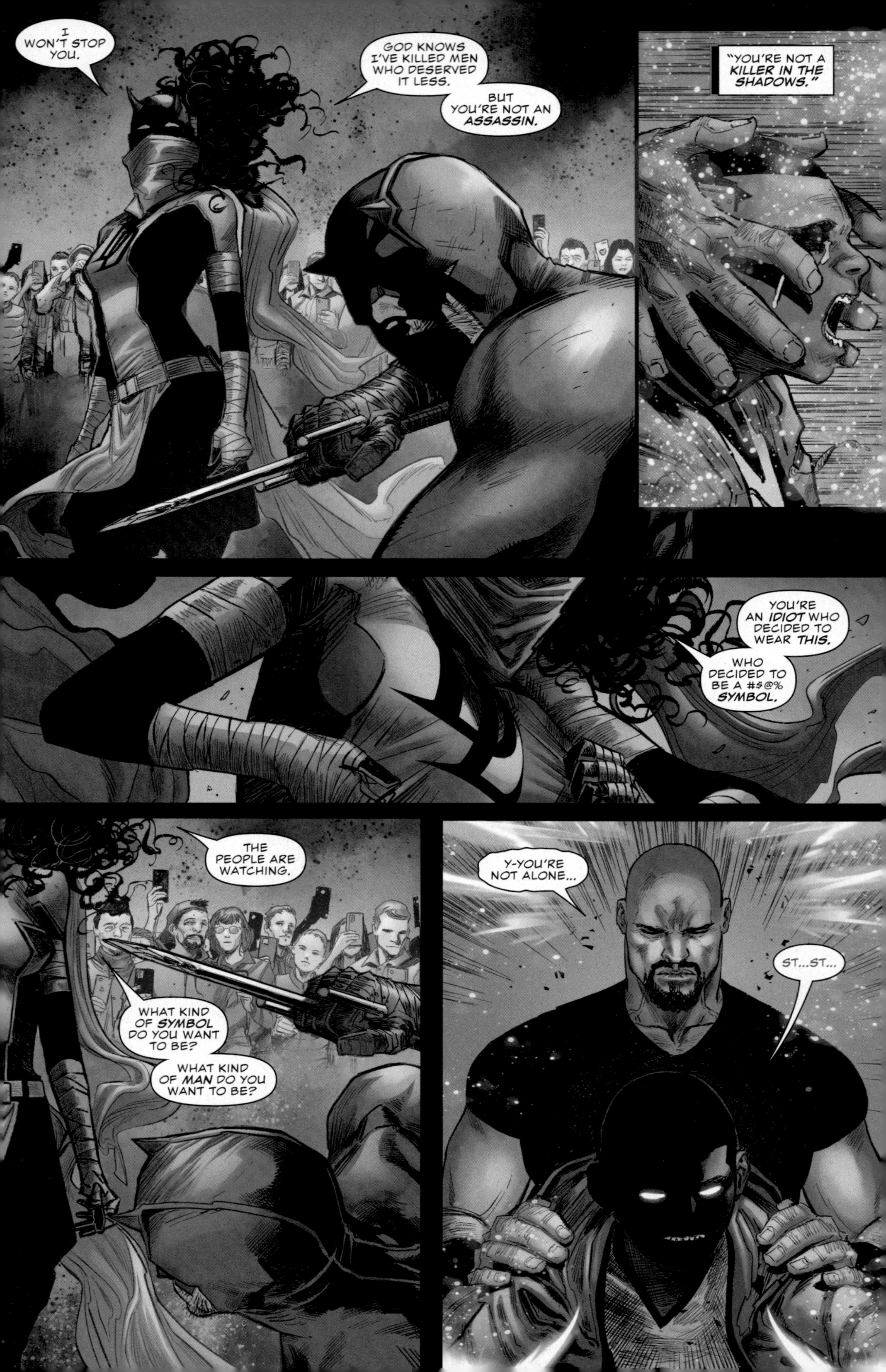
I WON'T STOP YOU.
GOD KNOWS I'VE KILLED MEN WHO DESERVED IT LESS.
BUT YOU'RE NOT AN ASSASSIN.
"YOU'RE NOT A KILLER IN THE SHADOWS."
YOU'RE AN IDIOT WHO DECIDED TO WEAR THIS.
WHO DECIDED TO BE A #$@% SYMBOL.
THE PEOPLE ARE WATCHING.
WHAT KIND OF SYMBOL DO YOU WANT TO BE?
WHAT KIND OF MAN DO YOU WANT TO BE?
Y-YOU'RE NOT ALONE...
ST...ST...

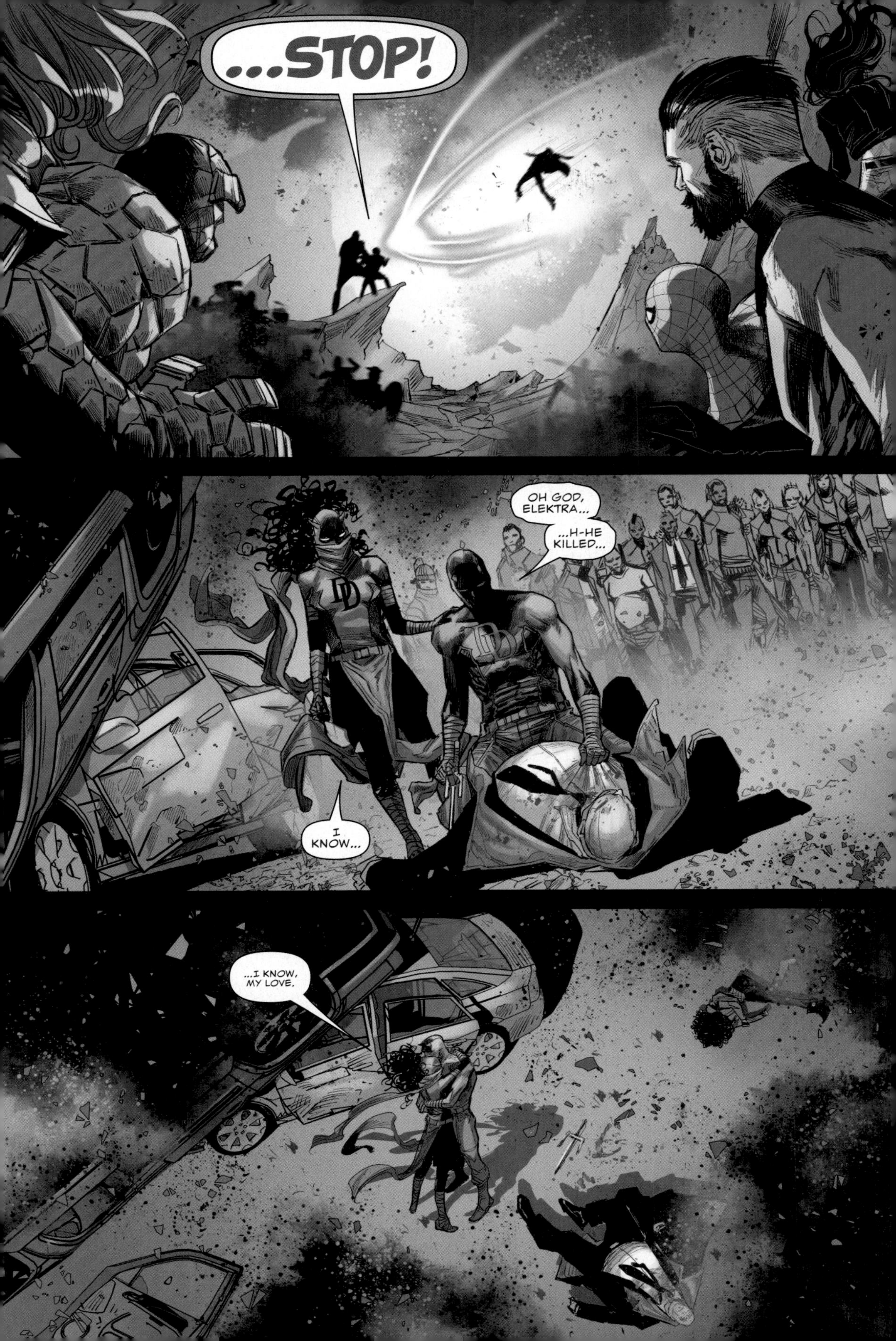
...STOP!
OH GOD, ELEKTRA...
...H-HE KILLED...
I KNOW...
...I KNOW, MY LOVE.

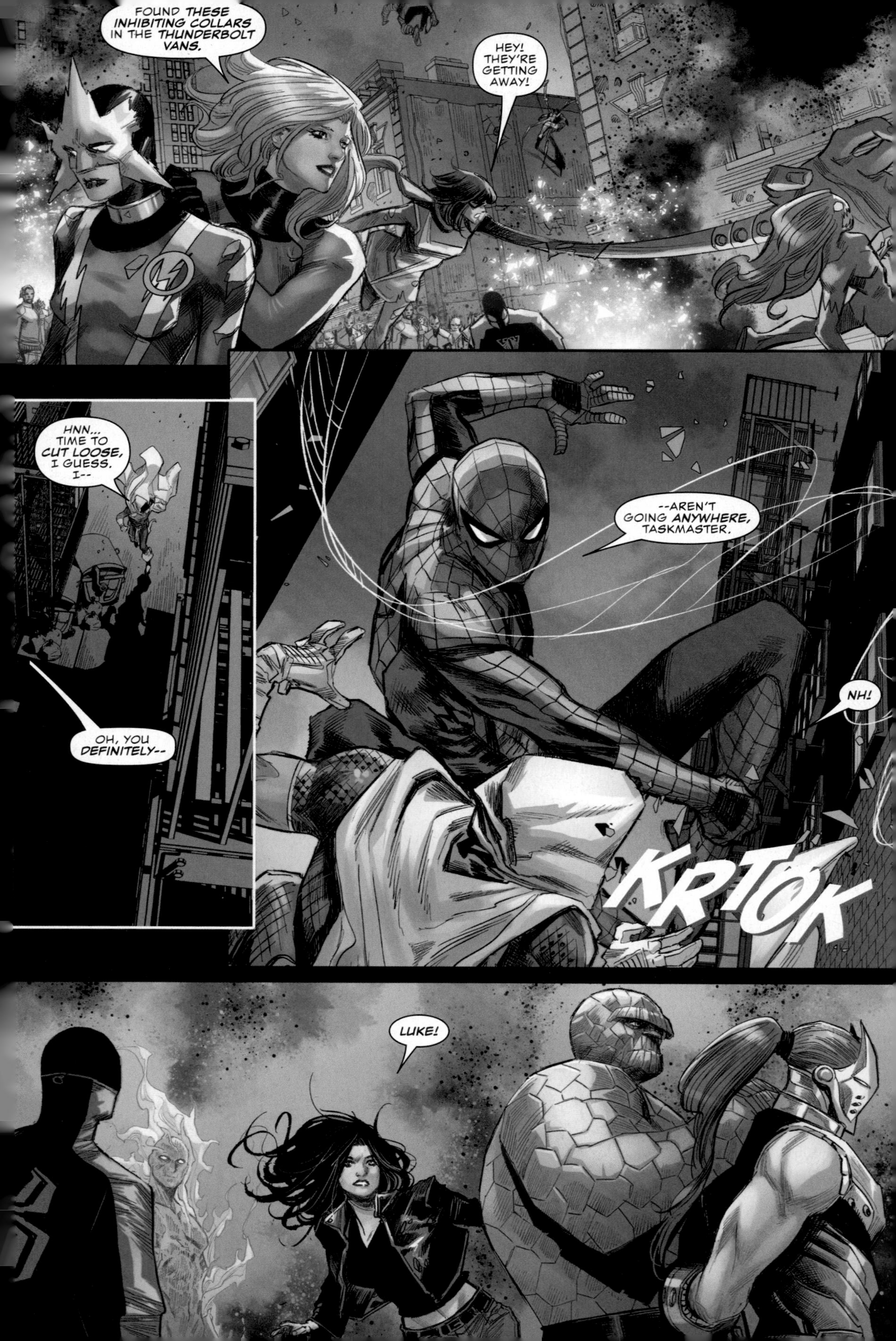
FOUND THESE INHIBITING COLLARS IN THE THUNDERBOLT VANS.
HEY! THEY'RE GETTING AWAY!
HNN... TIME TO CUT LOOSE, I GUESS. I--
OH, YOU DEFINITELY--
--AREN'T GOING ANYWHERE, TASKMASTER.
NH!
KRTOK
LUKE!

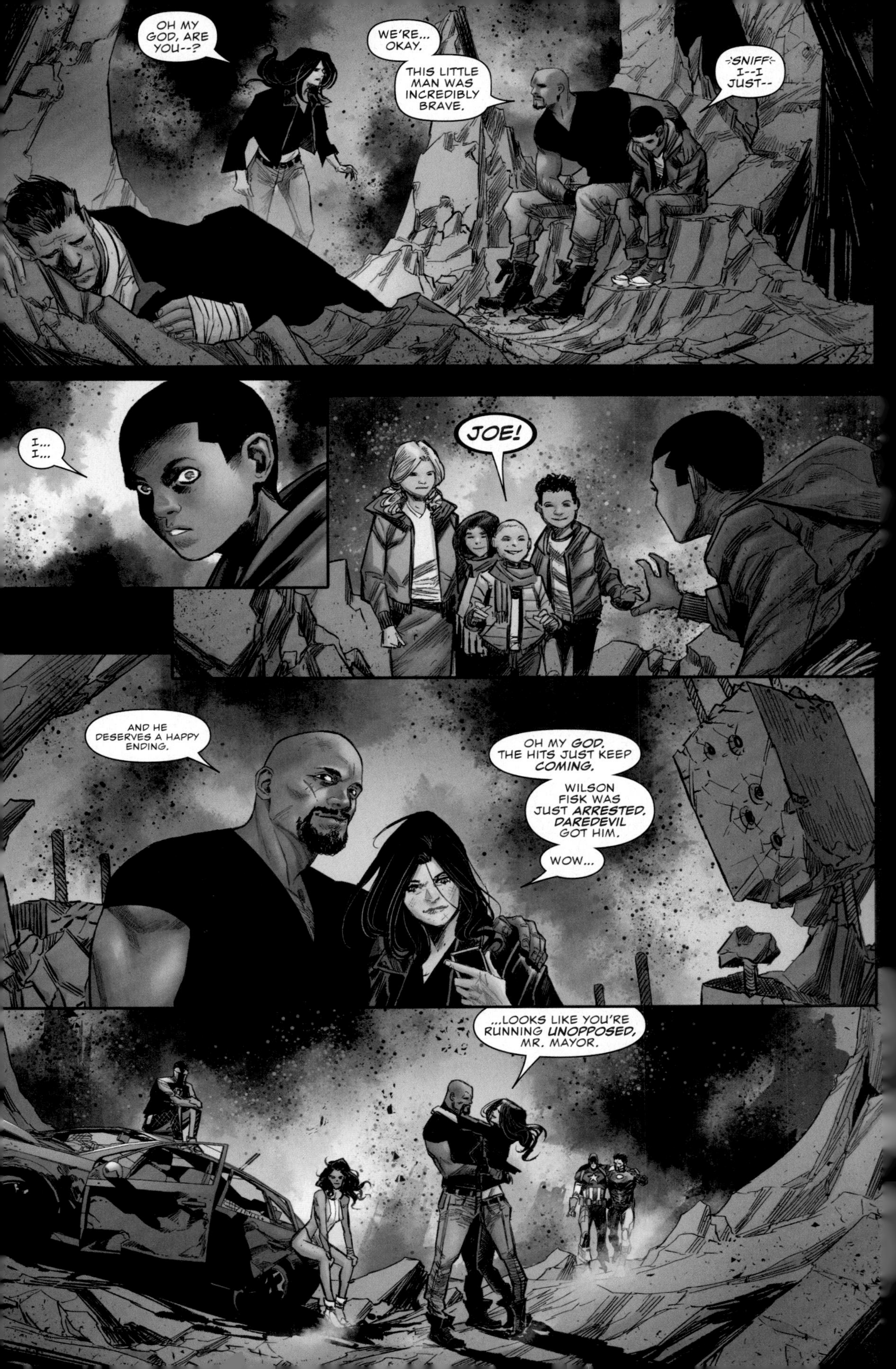
OH MY GOD, ARE YOU--?
WE'RE... OKAY.
THIS LITTLE MAN WAS INCREDIBLY BRAVE.
SNIFF I--I JUST--
I... I...
JOE!
AND HE DESERVES A HAPPY ENDING.
OH MY GOD. THE HITS JUST KEEP COMING.
WILSON FISK WAS JUST ARRESTED. DAREDEVIL GOT HIM.
WOW...
...LOOKS LIKE YOU'RE RUNNING UNOPPOSED, MR. MAYOR.

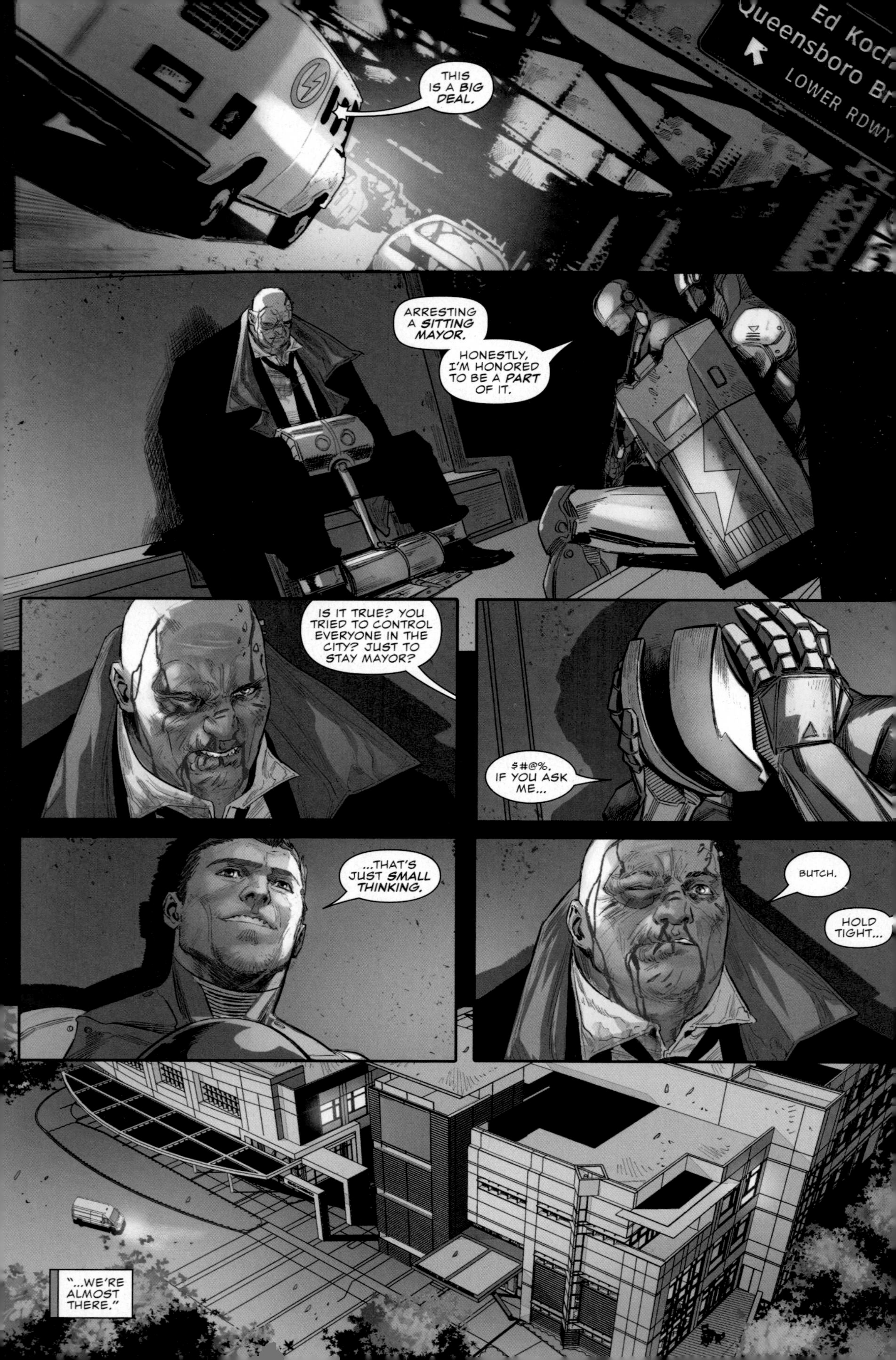
Ed Koch
Queensboro Br
LOWER RDWY
THIS IS A BIG DEAL.
ARRESTING A SITTING MAYOR.
HONESTLY, I'M HONORED TO BE A PART OF IT.
IS IT TRUE? YOU TRIED TO CONTROL EVERYONE IN THE CITY? JUST TO STAY MAYOR?
$#@%. IF YOU ASK ME...
...THAT'S JUST SMALL THINKING.
BUTCH.
HOLD TIGHT...
"...WE'RE ALMOST THERE."

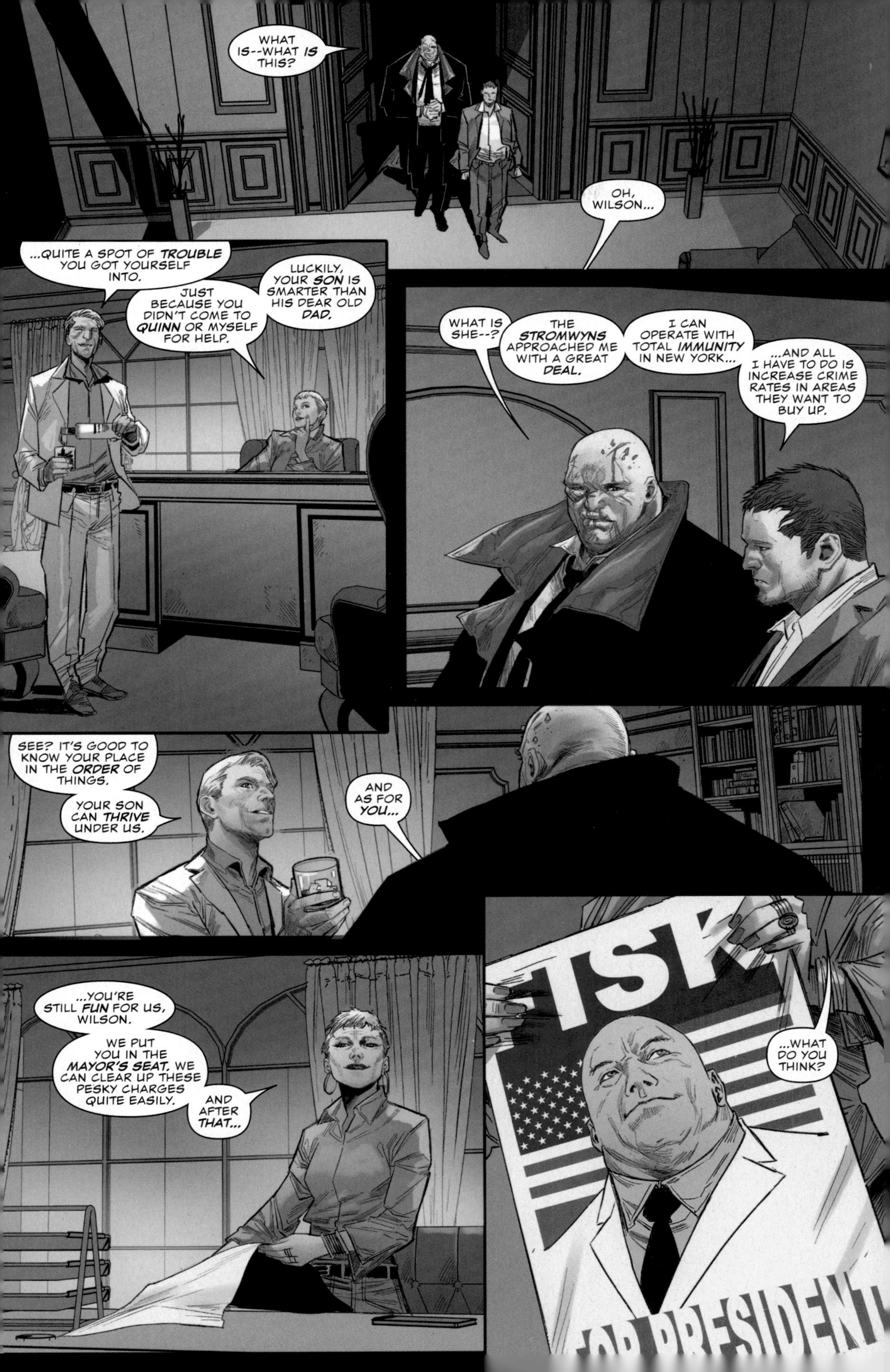
WHAT IS--WHAT IS THIS?
OH, WILSON...
...QUITE A SPOT OF TROUBLE YOU GOT YOURSELF INTO.
JUST BECAUSE YOU DIDN'T COME TO QUINN OR MYSELF FOR HELP.
LUCKILY, YOUR SON IS SMARTER THAN HIS DEAR OLD DAD.
WHAT IS SHE--?
THE STROMWYNS APPROACHED ME WITH A GREAT DEAL.
I CAN OPERATE WITH TOTAL IMMUNITY IN NEW YORK...
...AND ALL I HAVE TO DO IS INCREASE CRIME RATES IN AREAS THEY WANT TO BUY UP.
SEE? IT'S GOOD TO KNOW YOUR PLACE IN THE ORDER OF THINGS.
YOUR SON CAN THRIVE UNDER US.
AND AS FOR YOU...
...YOU'RE STILL FUN FOR US, WILSON.
WE PUT YOU IN THE MAYOR'S SEAT. WE CAN CLEAR UP THESE PESKY CHARGES QUITE EASILY.
AND AFTER THAT...
...WHAT DO YOU THINK?

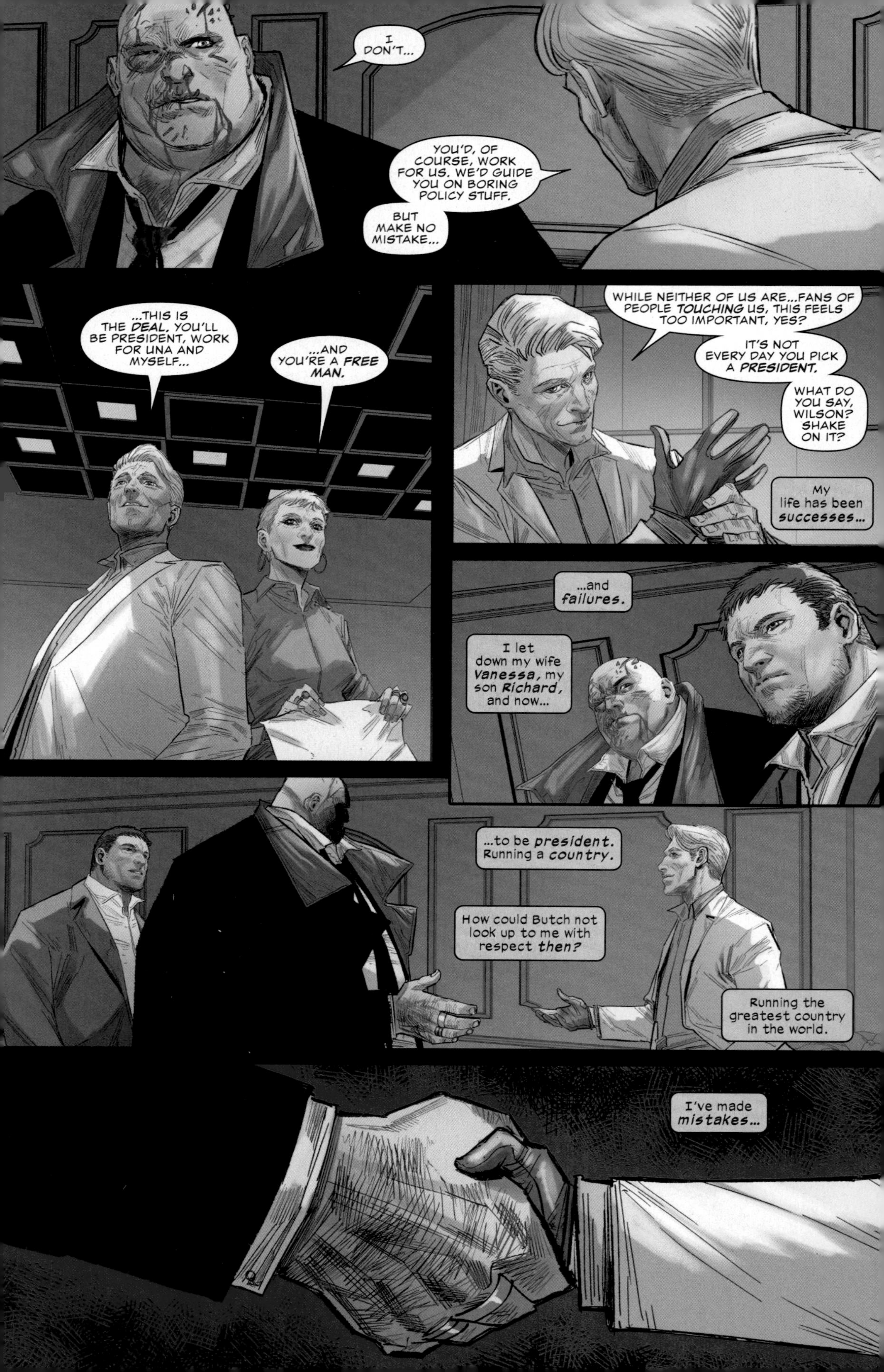
I DON'T...
YOU'D, OF COURSE, WORK FOR US. WE'D GUIDE YOU ON BORING POLICY STUFF.
BUT MAKE NO MISTAKE...
...THIS IS THE DEAL. YOU'LL BE PRESIDENT, WORK FOR UNA AND MYSELF...
...AND YOU'RE A FREE MAN.
WHILE NEITHER OF US ARE...FANS OF PEOPLE TOUCHING US, THIS FEELS TOO IMPORTANT, YES?
IT'S NOT EVERY DAY YOU PICK A PRESIDENT.
WHAT DO YOU SAY, WILSON? SHAKE ON IT?
My life has been successes...
...and failures.
I let down my wife Vanessa, my son Richard, and now...
...to be president. Running a country.
How could Butch not look up to me with respect then?
Running the greatest country in the world.
I've made mistakes...

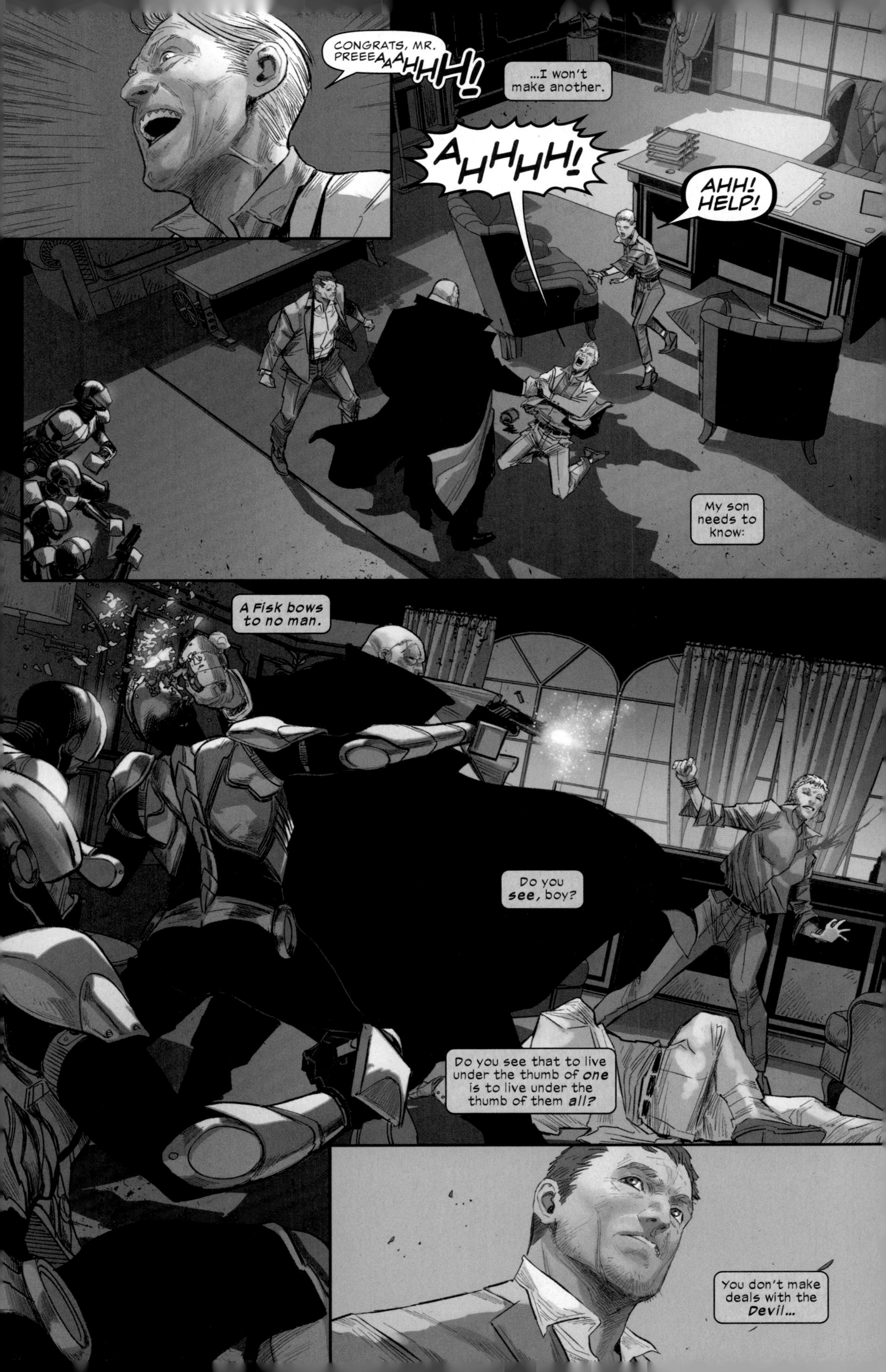
CONGRATS, MR. PREEEAAAHHH!
...I won't make another.
AHHHH!
AHH! HELP!
My son needs to know:
A Fisk bows to no man.
Do you see, boy?
Do you see that to live under the thumb of one is to live under the thumb of them all?
You don't make deals with the Devil...

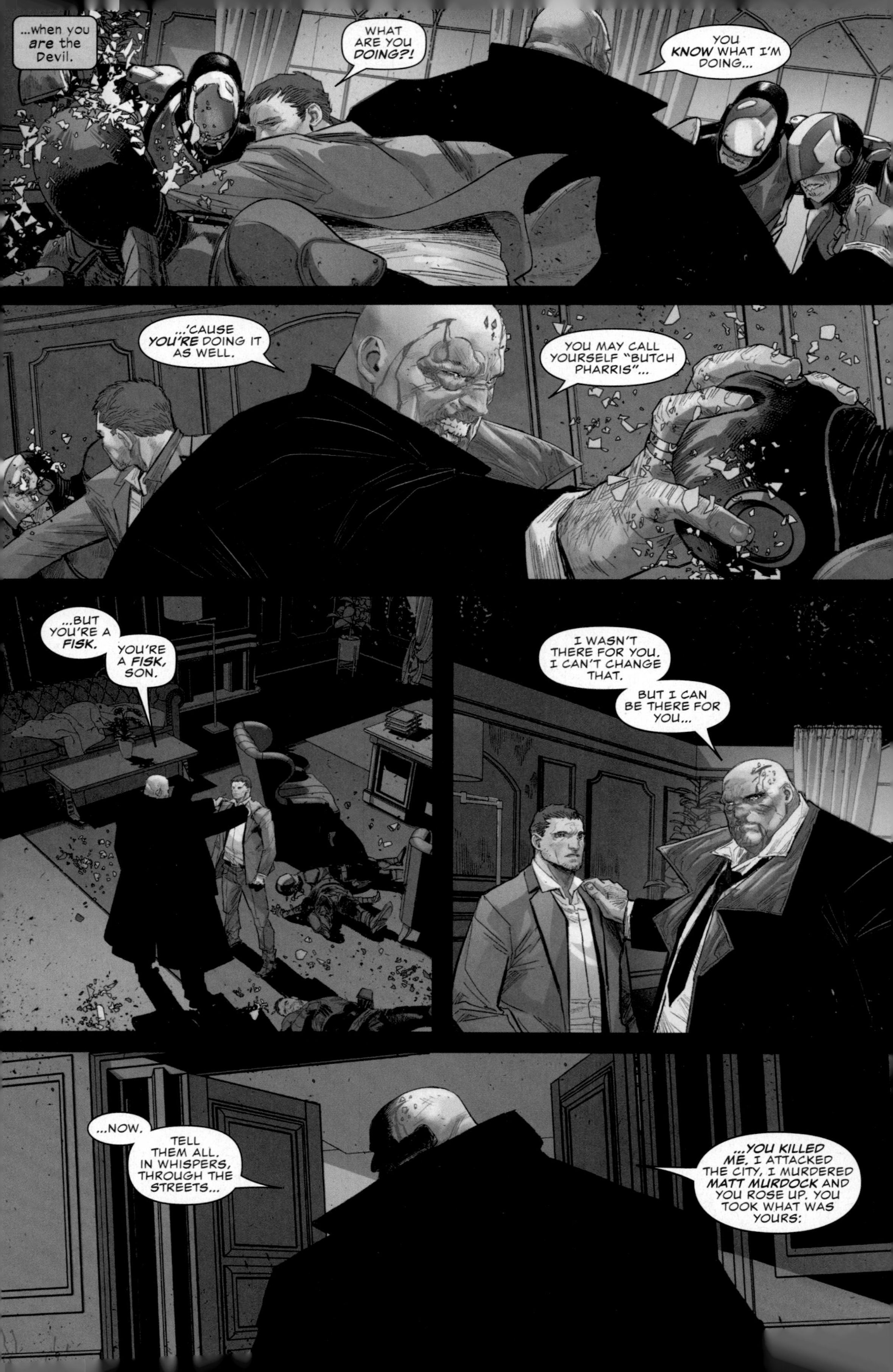
...when you are the Devil.
WHAT ARE YOU DOING?!
YOU KNOW WHAT I'M DOING...
...'CAUSE YOU'RE DOING IT AS WELL.
YOU MAY CALL YOURSELF "BUTCH PHARRIS"...
...BUT YOU'RE A FISK.
YOU'RE A FISK, SON.
I WASN'T THERE FOR YOU. I CAN'T CHANGE THAT.
BUT I CAN BE THERE FOR YOU...
...NOW.
TELL THEM ALL. IN WHISPERS, THROUGH THE STREETS...
...YOU KILLED ME. I ATTACKED THE CITY, I MURDERED MATT MURDOCK AND YOU ROSE UP. YOU TOOK WHAT WAS YOURS:

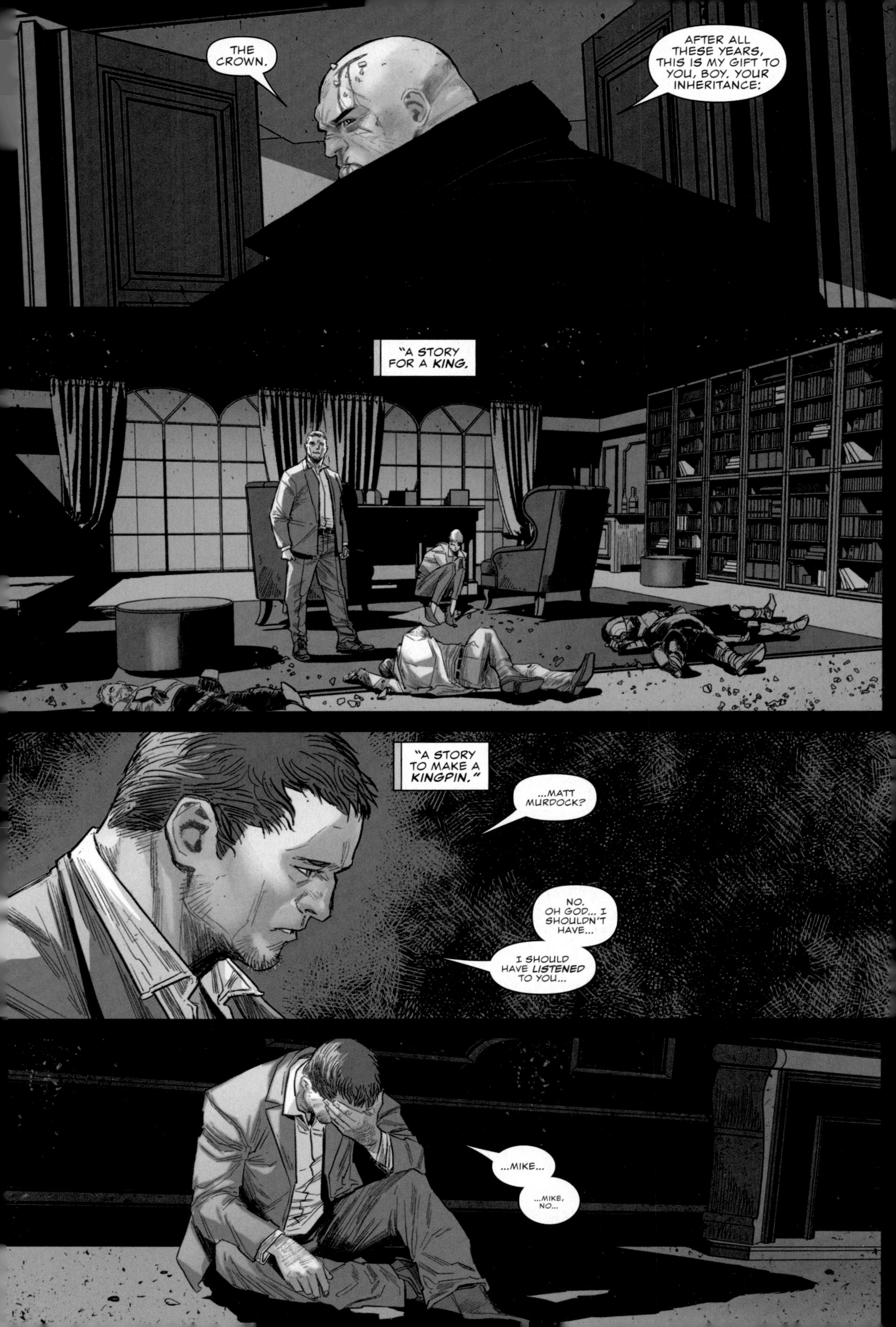
THE CROWN.
AFTER ALL THESE YEARS, THIS IS MY GIFT TO YOU, BOY. YOUR INHERITANCE:
"A STORY FOR A KING.
"A STORY TO MAKE A KINGPIN."
...MATT MURDOCK?
NO, OH GOD... I SHOULDN'T HAVE...
I SHOULD HAVE LISTENED TO YOU...
...MIKE...
...MIKE, NO...

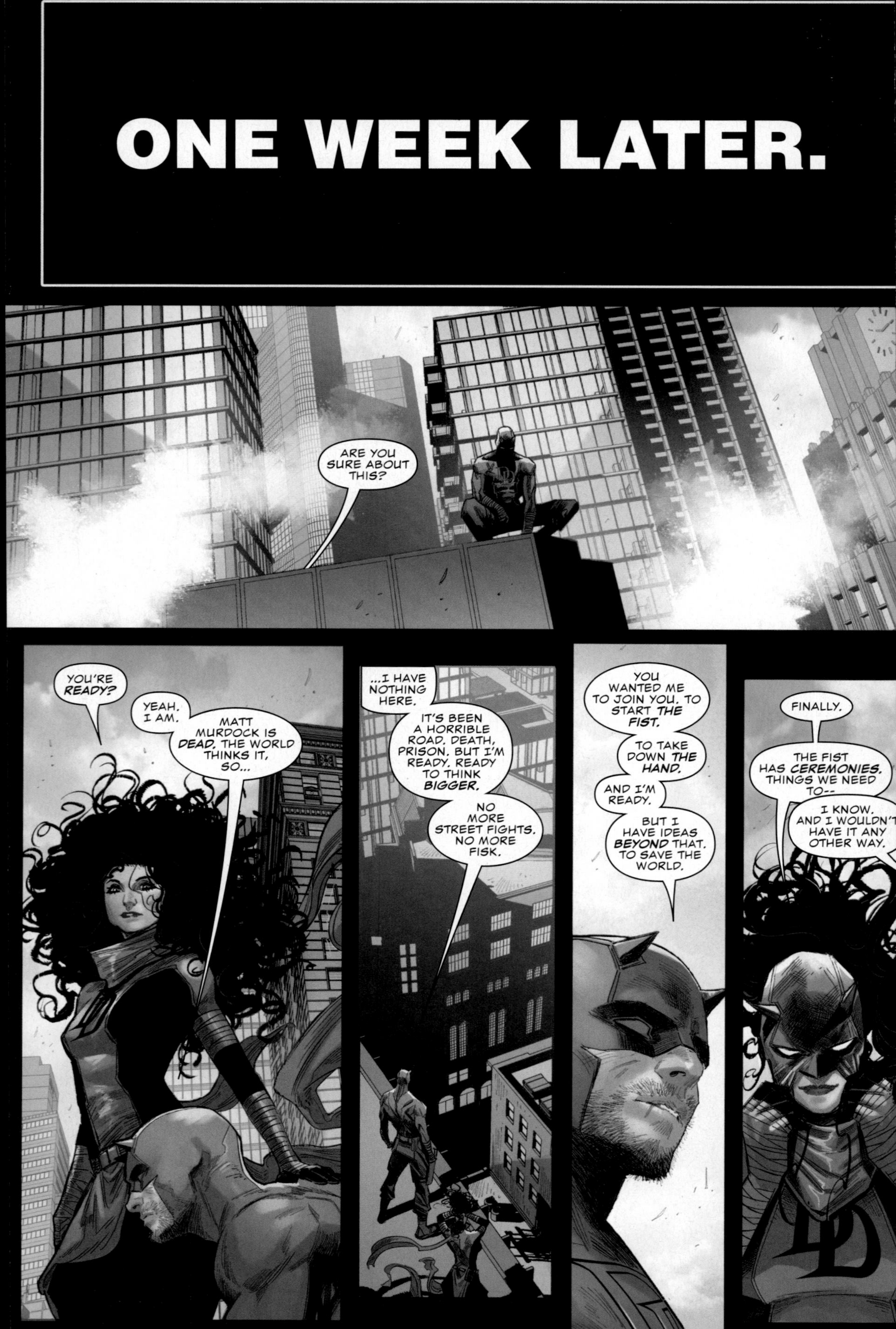
ONE WEEK LATER.
ARE YOU SURE ABOUT THIS?
YOU'RE *READY?*
YEAH. I AM.
MATT MURDOCK IS *DEAD.* THE WORLD THINKS IT, SO...
...I HAVE NOTHING HERE.
IT'S BEEN A HORRIBLE ROAD. DEATH, PRISON. BUT I'M READY. READY TO THINK *BIGGER.*
NO MORE STREET FIGHTS. NO MORE FISK.
YOU WANTED ME TO JOIN YOU. TO START *THE FIST.*
TO TAKE DOWN *THE HAND.*
AND I'M READY.
BUT I HAVE IDEAS *BEYOND* THAT. TO SAVE THE WORLD.
FINALLY.
THE FIST HAS *CEREMONIES.* THINGS WE NEED TO--
I KNOW. AND I WOULDN'T HAVE IT ANY OTHER WAY.

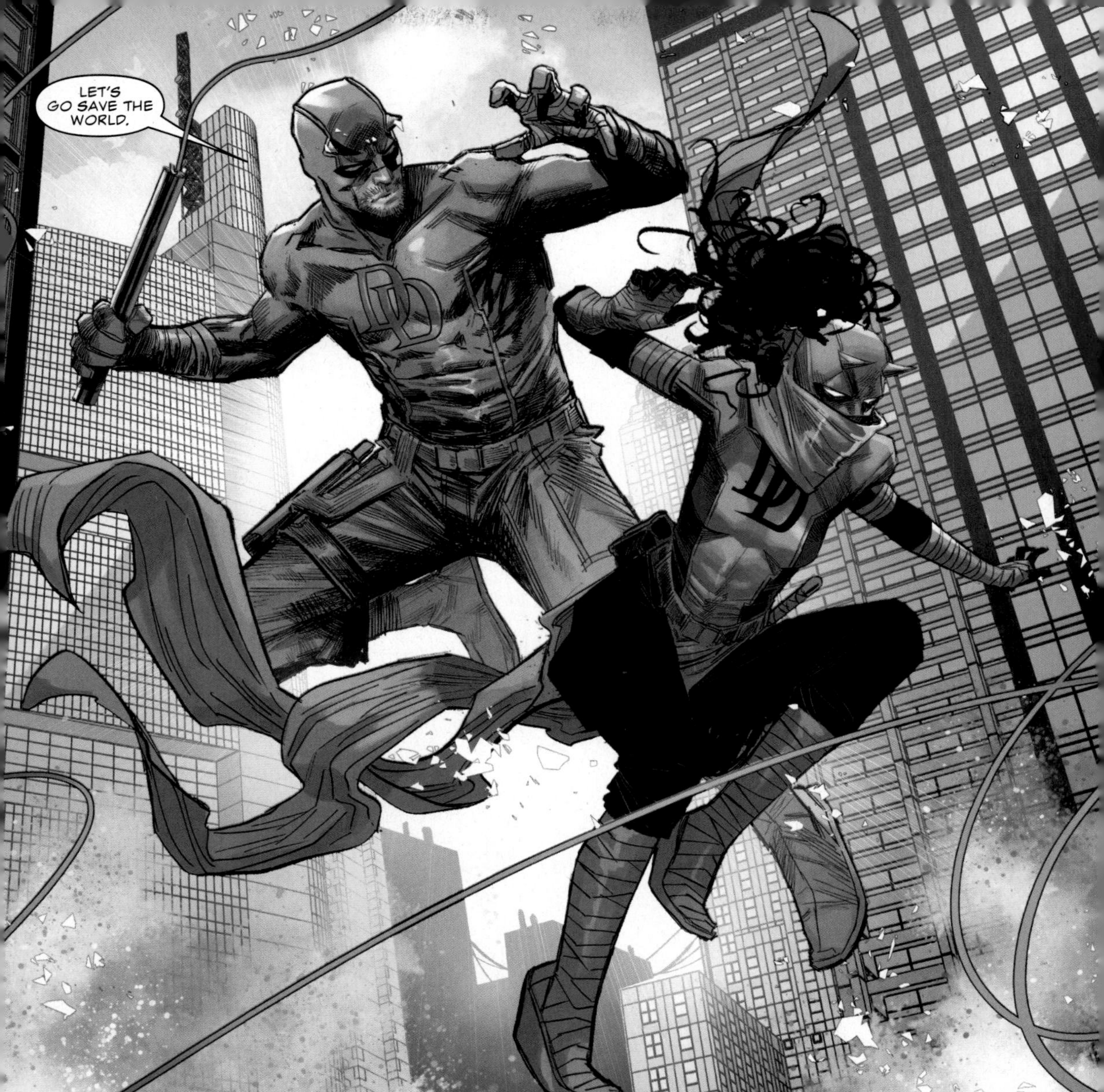
LET'S GO SAVE THE WORLD.

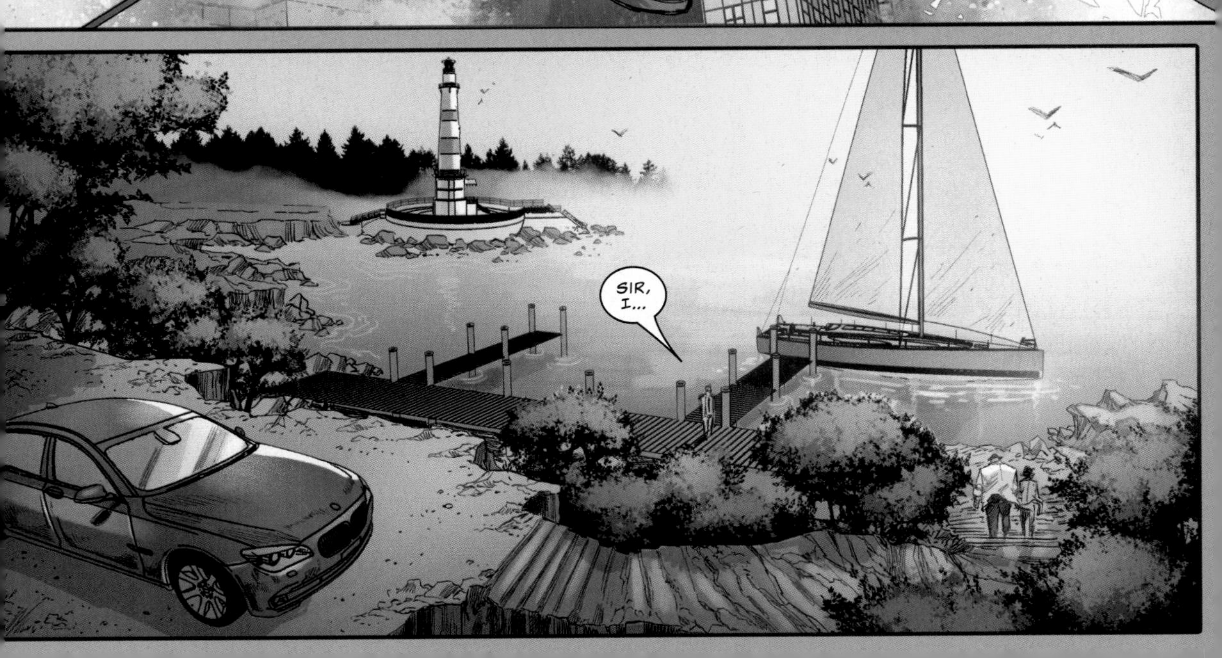
SIR, I...

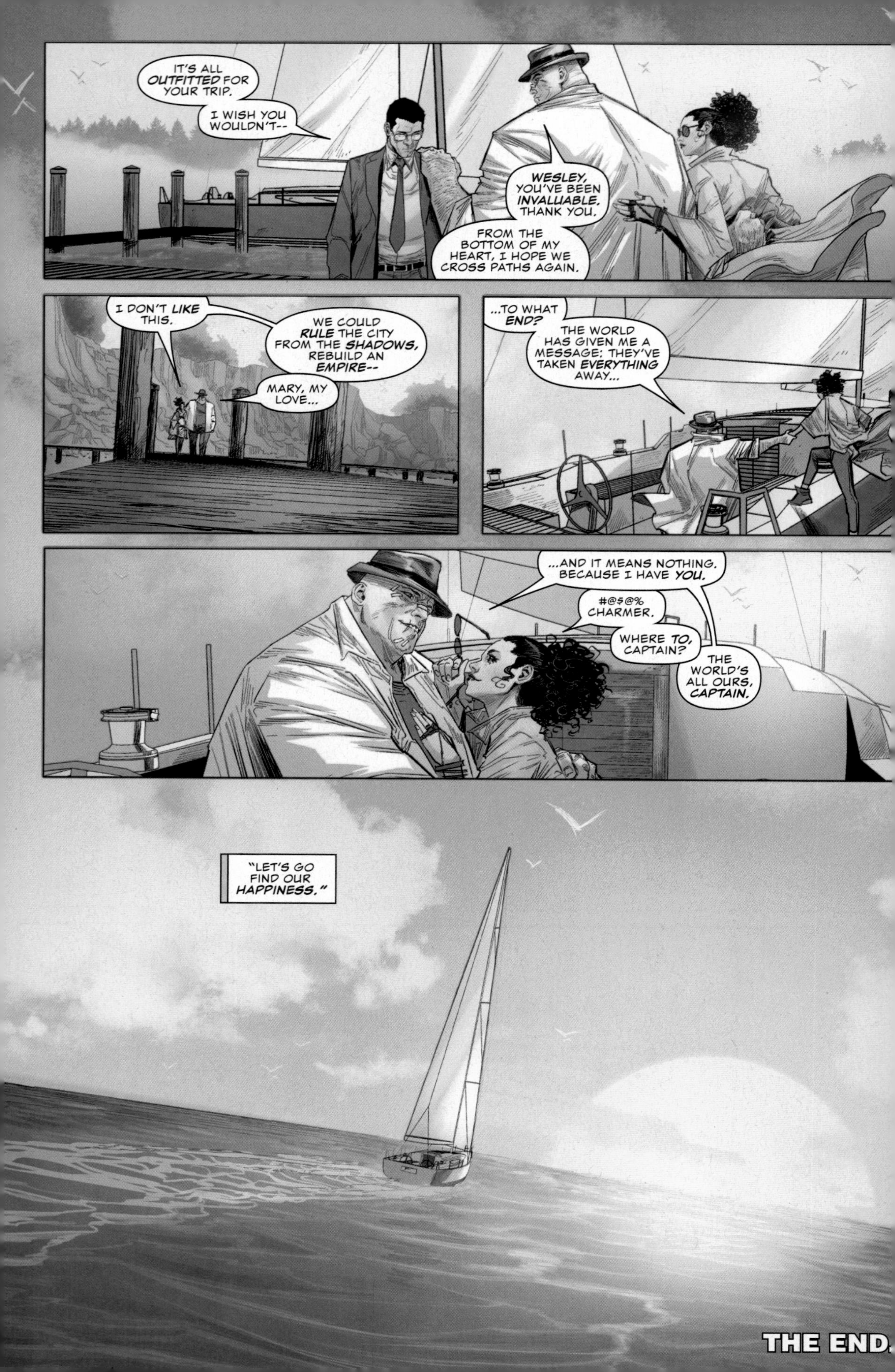
IT'S ALL OUTFITTED FOR YOUR TRIP.
I WISH YOU WOULDN'T--
WESLEY, YOU'VE BEEN INVALUABLE. THANK YOU.
FROM THE BOTTOM OF MY HEART, I HOPE WE CROSS PATHS AGAIN.
I DON'T LIKE THIS.
WE COULD RULE THE CITY FROM THE SHADOWS, REBUILD AN EMPIRE--
MARY, MY LOVE...
...TO WHAT END?
THE WORLD HAS GIVEN ME A MESSAGE: THEY'VE TAKEN EVERYTHING AWAY...
...AND IT MEANS NOTHING. BECAUSE I HAVE YOU.
#@$@% CHARMER.
WHERE TO, CAPTAIN?
THE WORLD'S ALL OURS, CAPTAIN.
"LET'S GO FIND OUR HAPPINESS."
THE END.

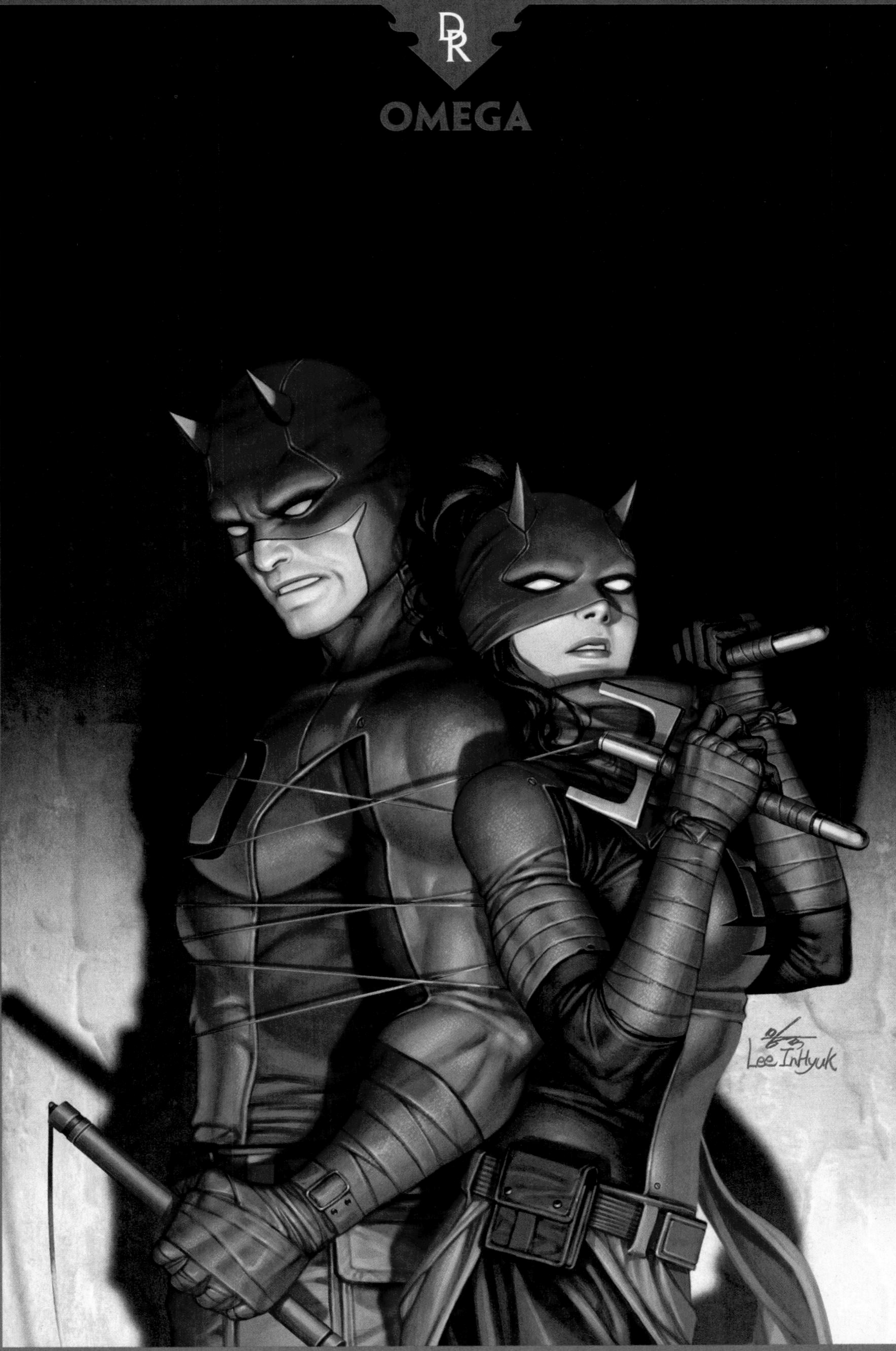
OMEGA
Lee InHyuk

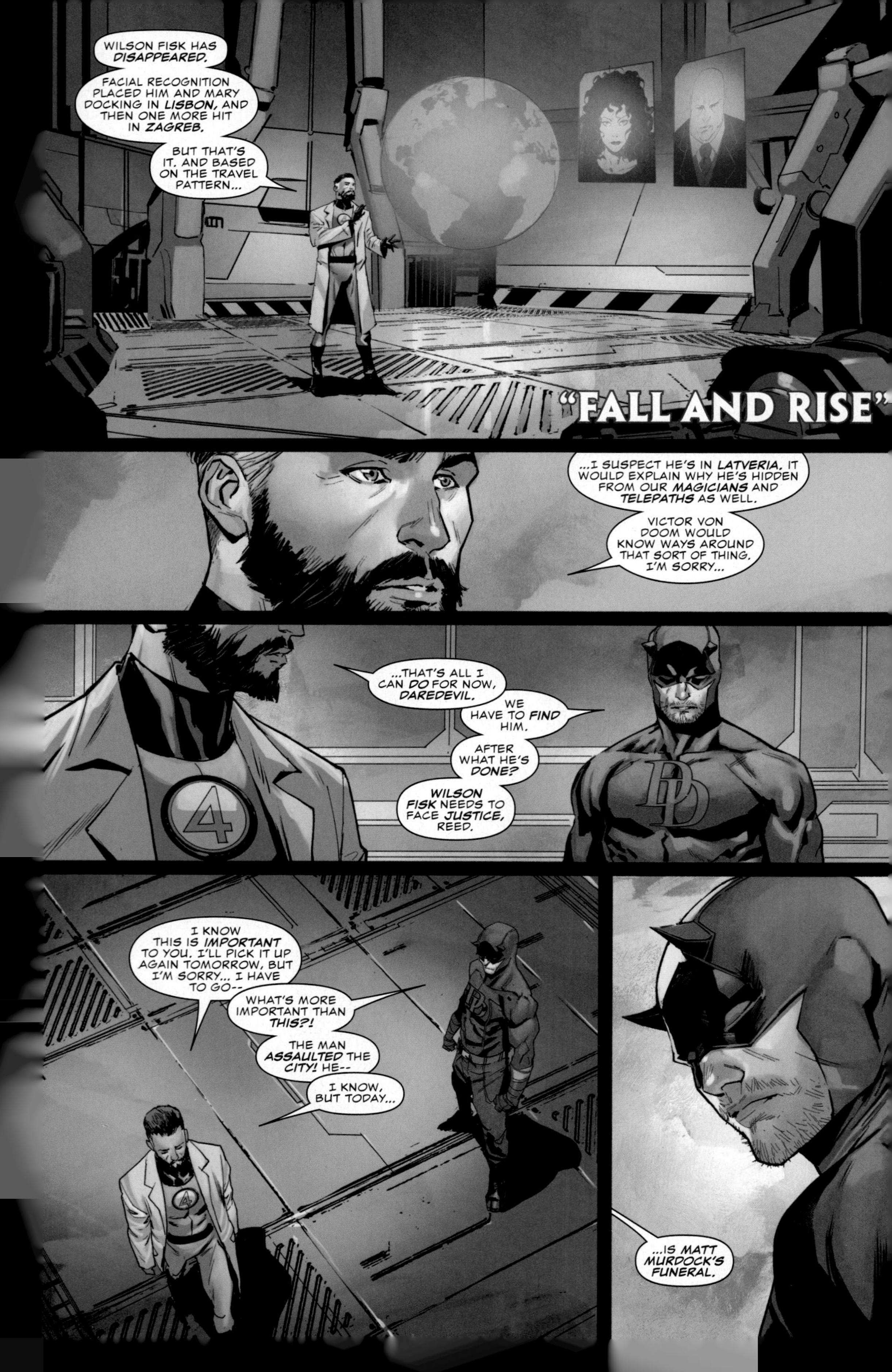
WILSON FISK HAS DISAPPEARED.
FACIAL RECOGNITION PLACED HIM AND MARY DOCKING IN LISBON, AND THEN ONE MORE HIT IN ZAGREB.
BUT THAT'S IT. AND BASED ON THE TRAVEL PATTERN...
"FALL AND RISE"
...I SUSPECT HE'S IN LATVERIA. IT WOULD EXPLAIN WHY HE'S HIDDEN FROM OUR MAGICIANS AND TELEPATHS AS WELL.
VICTOR VON DOOM WOULD KNOW WAYS AROUND THAT SORT OF THING. I'M SORRY...
...THAT'S ALL I CAN DO FOR NOW, DAREDEVIL.
WE HAVE TO FIND HIM.
AFTER WHAT HE'S DONE?
WILSON FISK NEEDS TO FACE JUSTICE, REED.
I KNOW THIS IS IMPORTANT TO YOU. I'LL PICK IT UP AGAIN TOMORROW, BUT I'M SORRY... I HAVE TO GO--
WHAT'S MORE IMPORTANT THAN THIS?!
THE MAN ASSAULTED THE CITY! HE--
I KNOW, BUT TODAY...
...IS MATT MURDOCK'S FUNERAL.

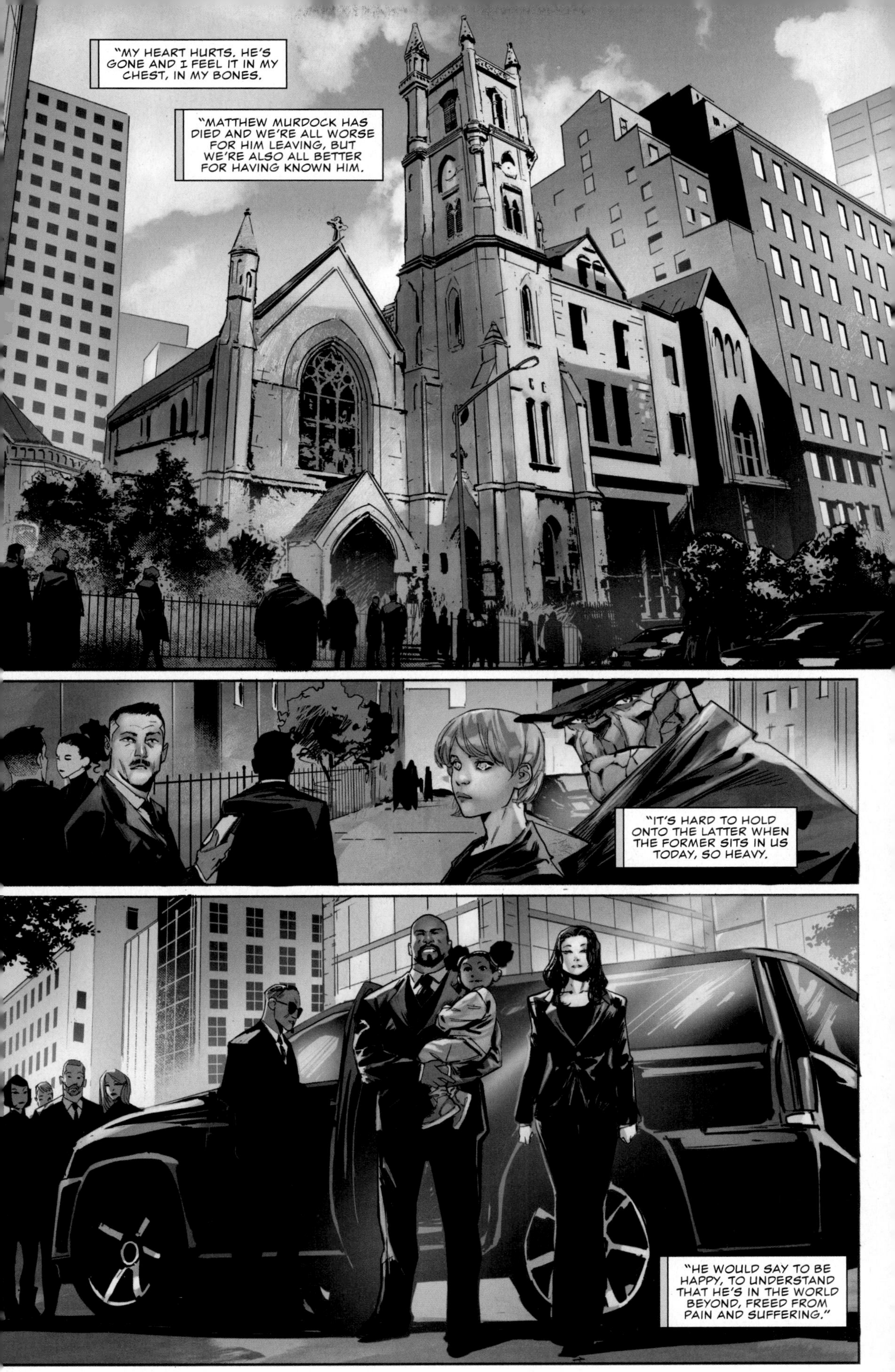
"MY HEART HURTS. HE'S GONE AND I FEEL IT IN MY CHEST, IN MY BONES.
"MATTHEW MURDOCK HAS DIED AND WE'RE ALL WORSE FOR HIM LEAVING, BUT WE'RE ALSO ALL BETTER FOR HAVING KNOWN HIM.
"IT'S HARD TO HOLD ONTO THE LATTER WHEN THE FORMER SITS IN US TODAY, SO HEAVY.
"HE WOULD SAY TO BE HAPPY, TO UNDERSTAND THAT HE'S IN THE WORLD BEYOND, FREED FROM PAIN AND SUFFERING."

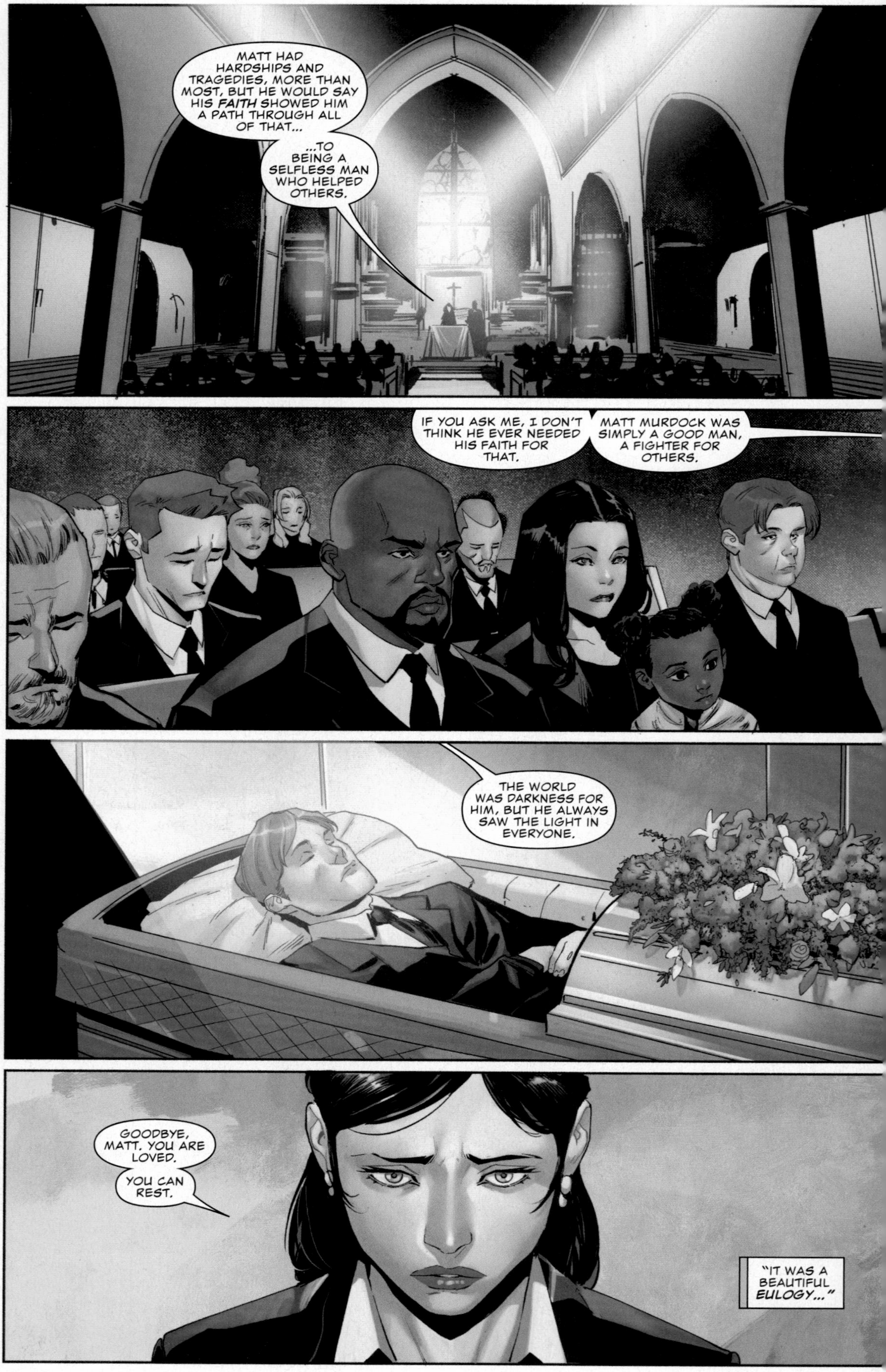
MATT HAD HARDSHIPS AND TRAGEDIES, MORE THAN MOST, BUT HE WOULD SAY HIS FAITH SHOWED HIM A PATH THROUGH ALL OF THAT...
...TO BEING A SELFLESS MAN WHO HELPED OTHERS.
IF YOU ASK ME, I DON'T THINK HE EVER NEEDED HIS FAITH FOR THAT.
MATT MURDOCK WAS SIMPLY A GOOD MAN, A FIGHTER FOR OTHERS.
THE WORLD WAS DARKNESS FOR HIM, BUT HE ALWAYS SAW THE LIGHT IN EVERYONE.
GOODBYE, MATT. YOU ARE LOVED.
YOU CAN REST.
"IT WAS A BEAUTIFUL EULOGY..."

...I WAS SURPRISED *YOU* WEREN'T THE ONE DELIVERING IT, MR. NELSON.

THOUGHT *MURDOCK* WAS YOUR BEST FRIEND.

I... COULDN'T BRING MYSELF TO.

AND I KNEW *KIRSTEN* WOULD DO THE BEST JOB.

THANKS FOR COMING, MR. *JAMESON.* I'M SURE--I'M SURE MATT WOULD HAVE APPRECIATED IT...

YEAH, WELL, EVEN THOUGH IT WAS A *SHORT* STINT-- AN UNELECTED ONE AT THAT--

--FORMER MAYORS HAVE A *BOND.*

BESIDES...

...I RECORDED THE WHOLE THING FOR MY *PODCAST.*

HAVE YOU *SUBSCRIBED?* YOU JUST GO TO W-W-W-DOT--

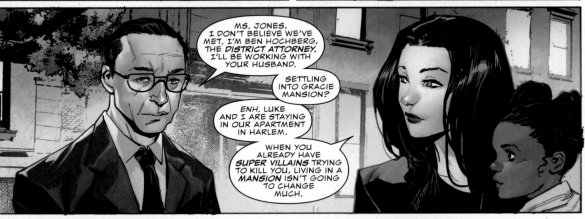

MS. JONES, I DON'T BELIEVE WE'VE MET. I'M BEN HOCHBERG, THE *DISTRICT ATTORNEY.* I'LL BE WORKING WITH YOUR HUSBAND.

SETTLING INTO GRACIE MANSION?

ENH. *LUKE* AND I ARE STAYING IN OUR APARTMENT IN HARLEM.

WHEN YOU ALREADY HAVE *SUPER VILLAINS* TRYING TO KILL YOU, LIVING IN A *MANSION* ISN'T GOING TO CHANGE MUCH.

HEH, I SUPPOSE NOT. I SEE YOU STILL HAVE THE MAYOR'S *SECURITY* THOUGH.

LUKE DIDN'T WANT THEM TO LOSE THEIR *JOBS* JUST BECAUSE HE'S *BULLETPROOF.*

HM. NOT SURE THE *TAXPAYERS* WILL LIKE THAT...

HEY...YOU WERE THERE FOR THE *CLEANUP* AFTER *THE PURPLE MAN'S* ATTACK, YEAH?

WHAT HAPPENED TO HIS *KIDS*? WE KNOW *SOCIAL SERVICES* CAME...

WELL, THE FOUR *DEPOWERED* ONES WERE KEPT TOGETHER. WITH A NICE FOSTER FAMILY IN QUEENS.

JOSEPH THOUGH... HE'S *TRICKIER*. HIS *POWERS* HAVE MADE IT HARD TO--

NOPE. ABSOLUTELY *NOT*.

MR. MAYOR, I'M JUST HERE TO PAY MY *RESPECTS*--

SURE. *BUTCH PHARRIS*, THE NEW *KINGPIN OF CRIME*, WANTS TO "PAY RESPECTS."

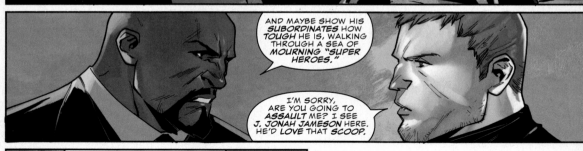

AND MAYBE SHOW HIS *SUBORDINATES* HOW *TOUGH* HE IS, WALKING THROUGH A SEA OF MOURNING "*SUPER HEROES*."

I'M SORRY, ARE YOU GOING TO *ASSAULT* ME? I SEE J. JONAH JAMESON HERE. HE'D *LOVE* THAT *SCOOP*.

LOOK, JUST GET IN YOUR *CAR* AND *GO*. THE *MAYOR* ISN'T GOING TO LET *OPTICS* STOP HIM FROM TURNING THIS INTO *TWO* FUNERALS.

MR. RAND HERE SPEAKS THE *TRUTH*.

I JUST WANTED TO... MY *FATHER* KILLED HIM.

IT WAS A *HORRIBLE* ACT FROM A *HORRIBLE* MAN, AND I JUST WANTED TO...

FORGET IT. I'M SORRY.

WAIT... "*FATHER*"?

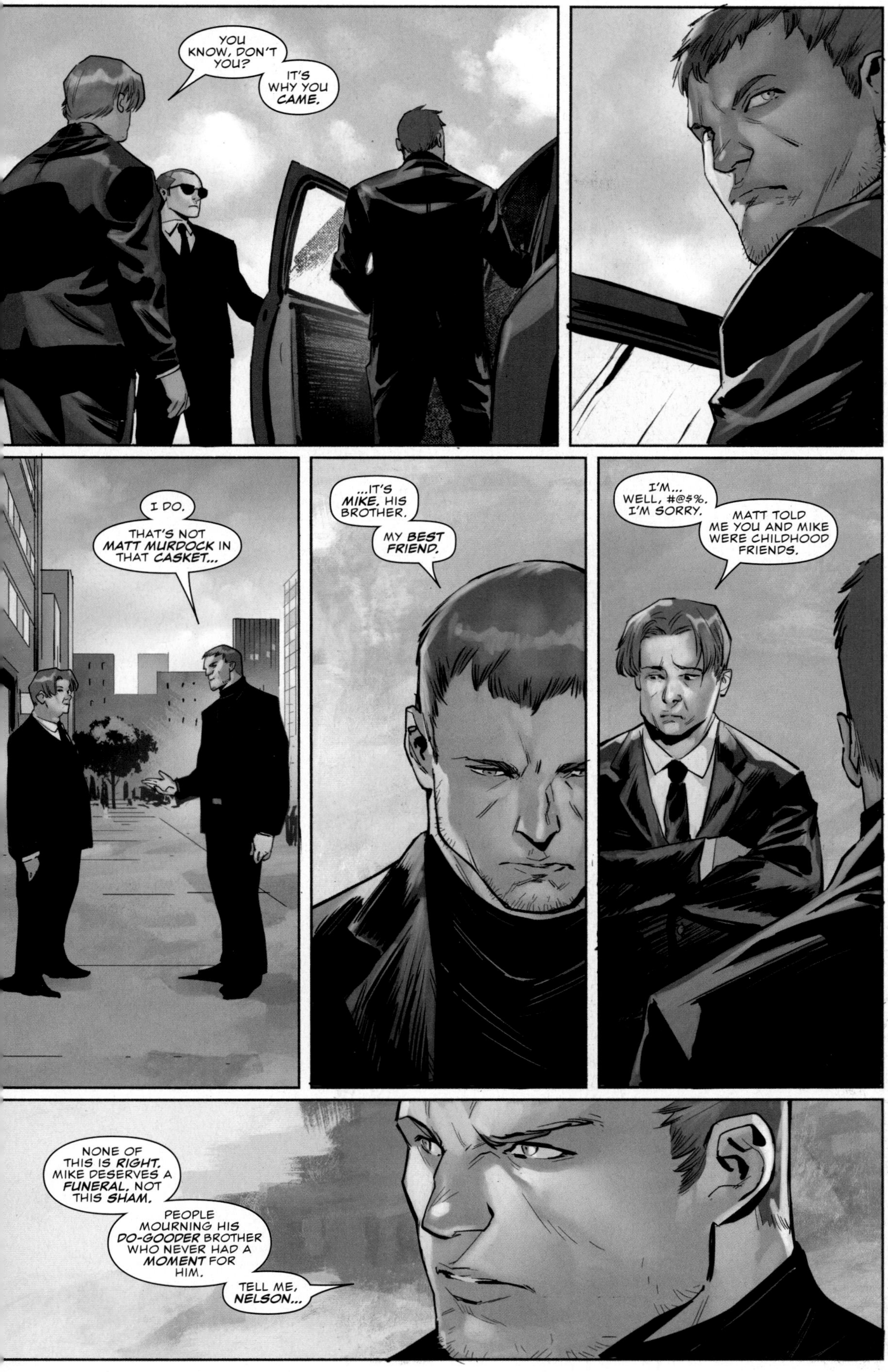

YOU KNOW, DON'T YOU?
IT'S WHY YOU CAME.
I DO.
THAT'S NOT MATT MURDOCK IN THAT CASKET...
...IT'S MIKE. HIS BROTHER.
MY BEST FRIEND.
I'M... WELL, #@$%. I'M SORRY.
MATT TOLD ME YOU AND MIKE WERE CHILDHOOD FRIENDS.
NONE OF THIS IS RIGHT. MIKE DESERVES A FUNERAL, NOT THIS SHAM.
PEOPLE MOURNING HIS DO-GOODER BROTHER WHO NEVER HAD A MOMENT FOR HIM.
TELL ME, NELSON...

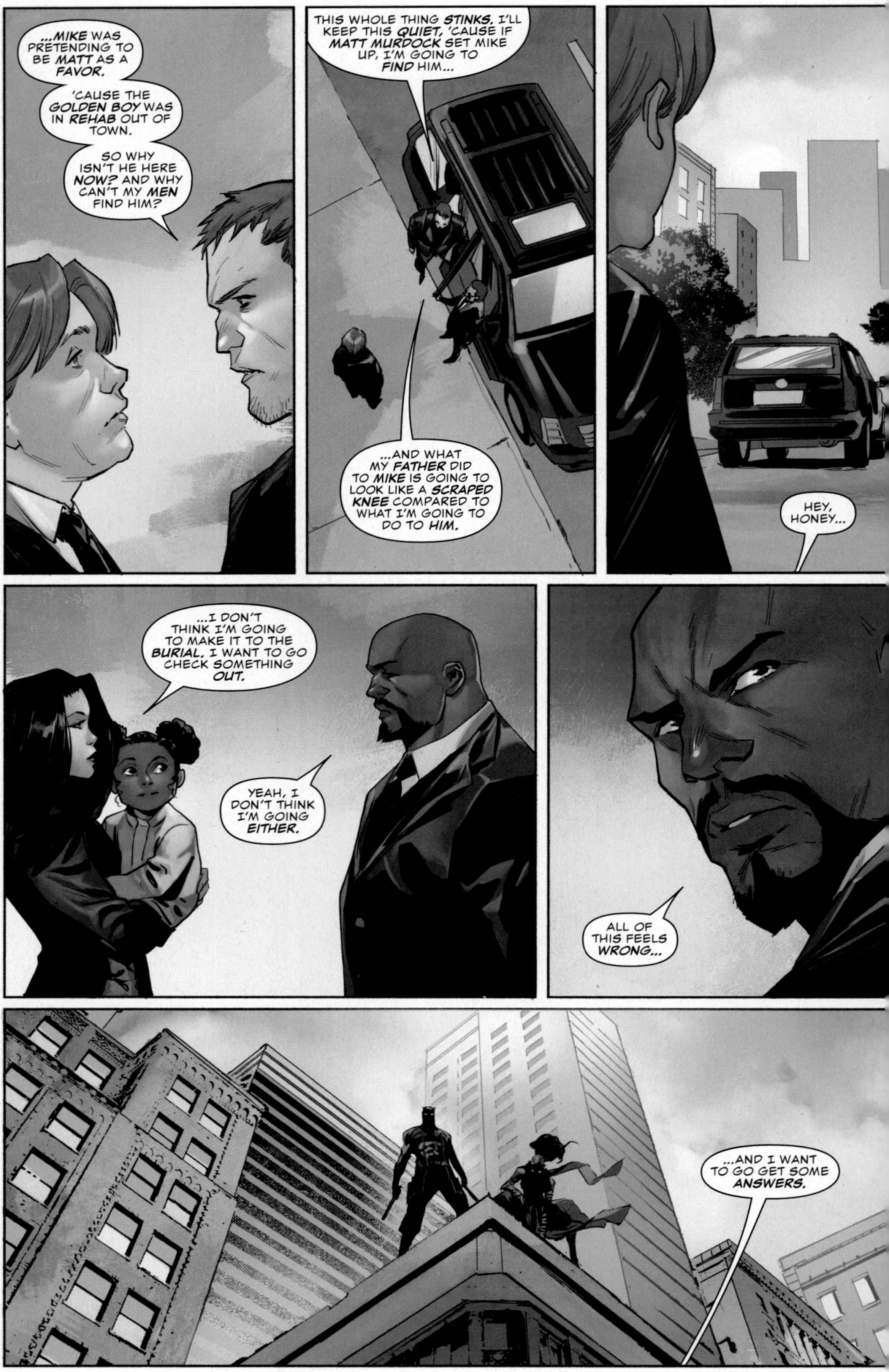
...MIKE WAS PRETENDING TO BE MATT AS A FAVOR.
'CAUSE THE GOLDEN BOY WAS IN REHAB OUT OF TOWN.
SO WHY ISN'T HE HERE NOW? AND WHY CAN'T MY MEN FIND HIM?
THIS WHOLE THING STINKS. I'LL KEEP THIS QUIET, 'CAUSE IF MATT MURDOCK SET MIKE UP, I'M GOING TO FIND HIM...
...AND WHAT MY FATHER DID TO MIKE IS GOING TO LOOK LIKE A SCRAPED KNEE COMPARED TO WHAT I'M GOING TO DO TO HIM.
HEY, HONEY...
...I DON'T THINK I'M GOING TO MAKE IT TO THE BURIAL. I WANT TO GO CHECK SOMETHING OUT.
YEAH, I DON'T THINK I'M GOING EITHER.
ALL OF THIS FEELS WRONG...
...AND I WANT TO GO GET SOME ANSWERS.

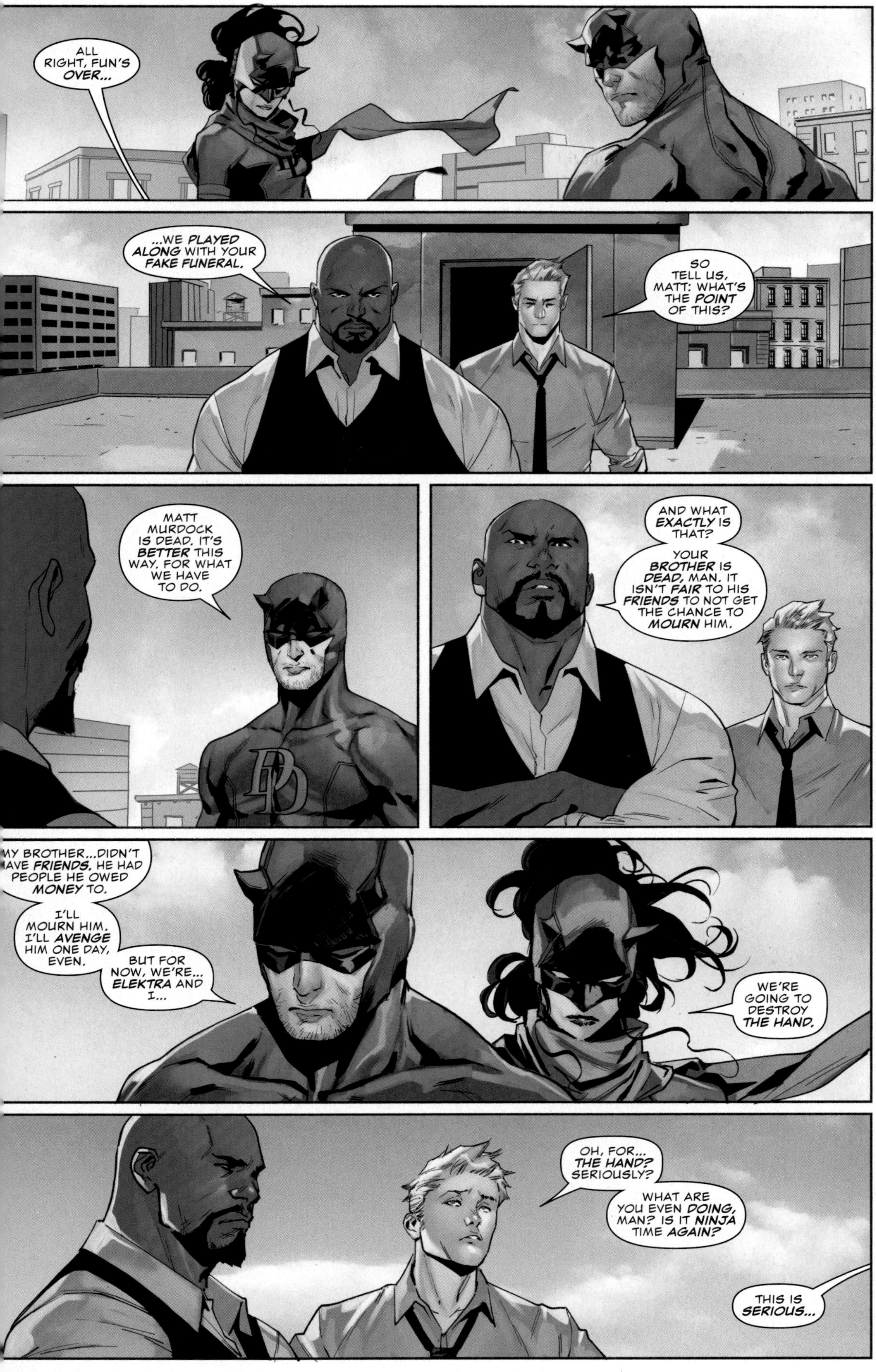
ALL RIGHT, FUN'S OVER...
...WE PLAYED ALONG WITH YOUR FAKE FUNERAL.
SO TELL US, MATT: WHAT'S THE POINT OF THIS?
MATT MURDOCK IS DEAD. IT'S BETTER THIS WAY. FOR WHAT WE HAVE TO DO.
AND WHAT EXACTLY IS THAT?
YOUR BROTHER IS DEAD, MAN. IT ISN'T FAIR TO HIS FRIENDS TO NOT GET THE CHANCE TO MOURN HIM.
MY BROTHER...DIDN'T HAVE FRIENDS. HE HAD PEOPLE HE OWED MONEY TO.
I'LL MOURN HIM. I'LL AVENGE HIM ONE DAY, EVEN.
BUT FOR NOW, WE'RE... ELEKTRA AND I...
WE'RE GOING TO DESTROY THE HAND.
OH, FOR... THE HAND? SERIOUSLY?
WHAT ARE YOU EVEN DOING, MAN? IS IT NINJA TIME AGAIN?
THIS IS SERIOUS...

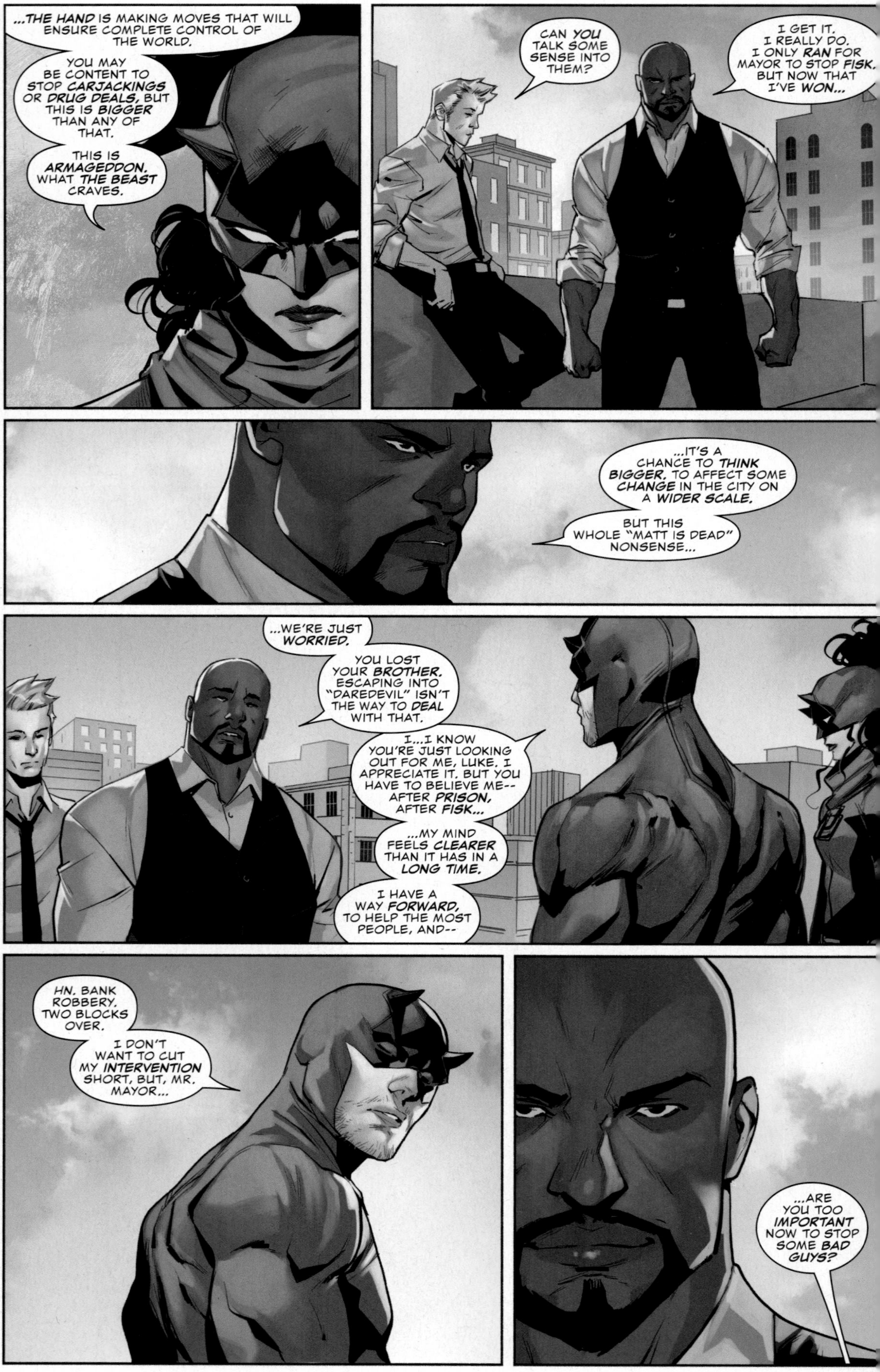
...THE HAND IS MAKING MOVES THAT WILL ENSURE COMPLETE CONTROL OF THE WORLD.
YOU MAY BE CONTENT TO STOP CARJACKINGS OR DRUG DEALS, BUT THIS IS BIGGER THAN ANY OF THAT.
THIS IS ARMAGEDDON. WHAT THE BEAST CRAVES.
CAN YOU TALK SOME SENSE INTO THEM?
I GET IT. I REALLY DO. I ONLY RAN FOR MAYOR TO STOP FISK. BUT NOW THAT I'VE WON...
...IT'S A CHANCE TO THINK BIGGER. TO AFFECT SOME CHANGE IN THE CITY ON A WIDER SCALE.
BUT THIS WHOLE "MATT IS DEAD" NONSENSE...
...WE'RE JUST WORRIED.
YOU LOST YOUR BROTHER. ESCAPING INTO "DAREDEVIL" ISN'T THE WAY TO DEAL WITH THAT.
I...I KNOW YOU'RE JUST LOOKING OUT FOR ME, LUKE. I APPRECIATE IT. BUT YOU HAVE TO BELIEVE ME-- AFTER PRISON, AFTER FISK...
...MY MIND FEELS CLEARER THAN IT HAS IN A LONG TIME.
I HAVE A WAY FORWARD, TO HELP THE MOST PEOPLE, AND--
HN. BANK ROBBERY. TWO BLOCKS OVER.
I DON'T WANT TO CUT MY INTERVENTION SHORT, BUT, MR. MAYOR...
...ARE YOU TOO IMPORTANT NOW TO STOP SOME BAD GUYS?

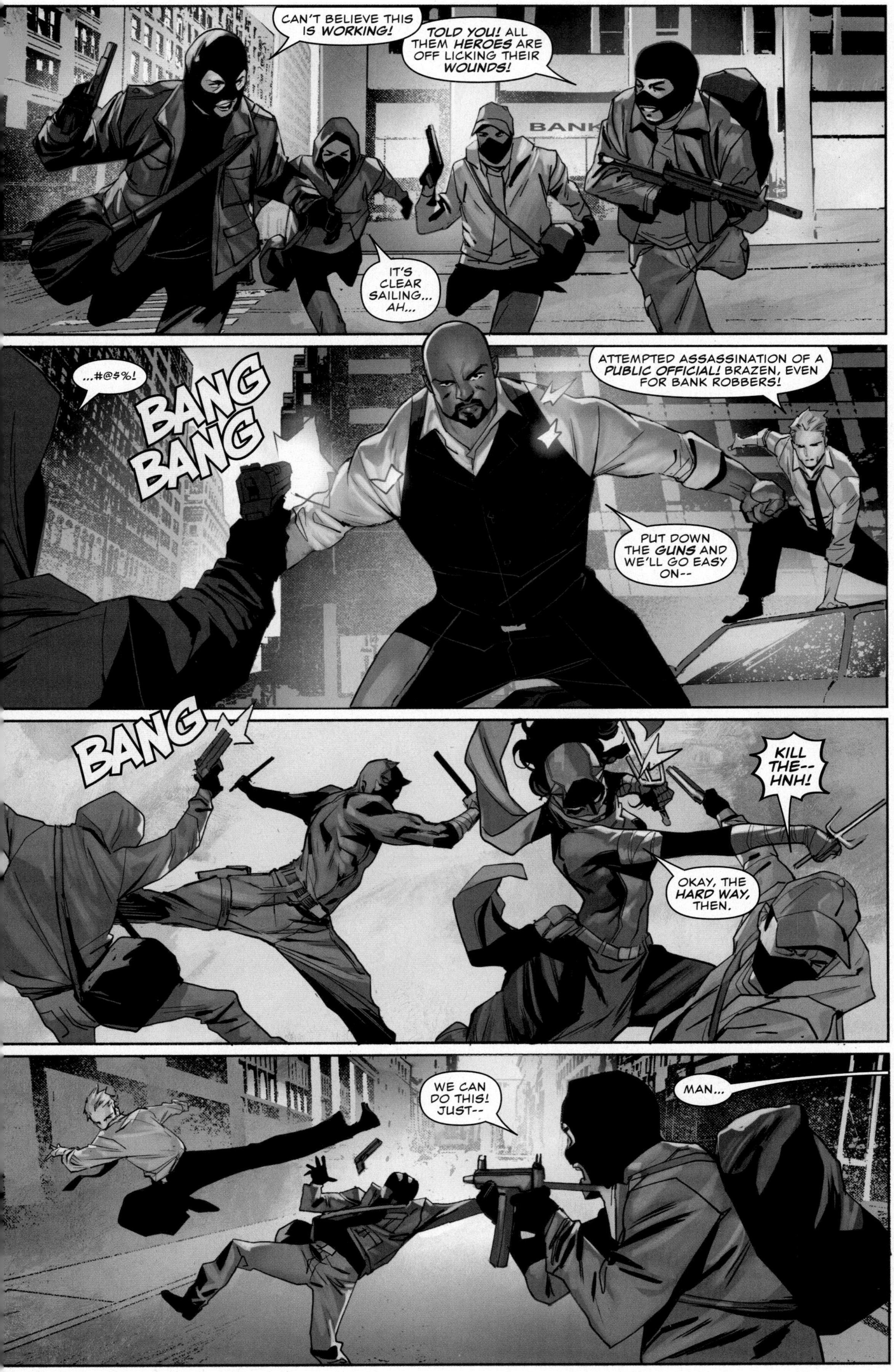
CAN'T BELIEVE THIS IS WORKING!
TOLD YOU! ALL THEM HEROES ARE OFF LICKING THEIR WOUNDS!
IT'S CLEAR SAILING... AH...
...#@$%!
BANG BANG
ATTEMPTED ASSASSINATION OF A PUBLIC OFFICIAL! BRAZEN, EVEN FOR BANK ROBBERS!
PUT DOWN THE GUNS AND WE'LL GO EASY ON--
BANG
KILL THE-- HNH!
OKAY, THE HARD WAY, THEN.
WE CAN DO THIS! JUST--
MAN...

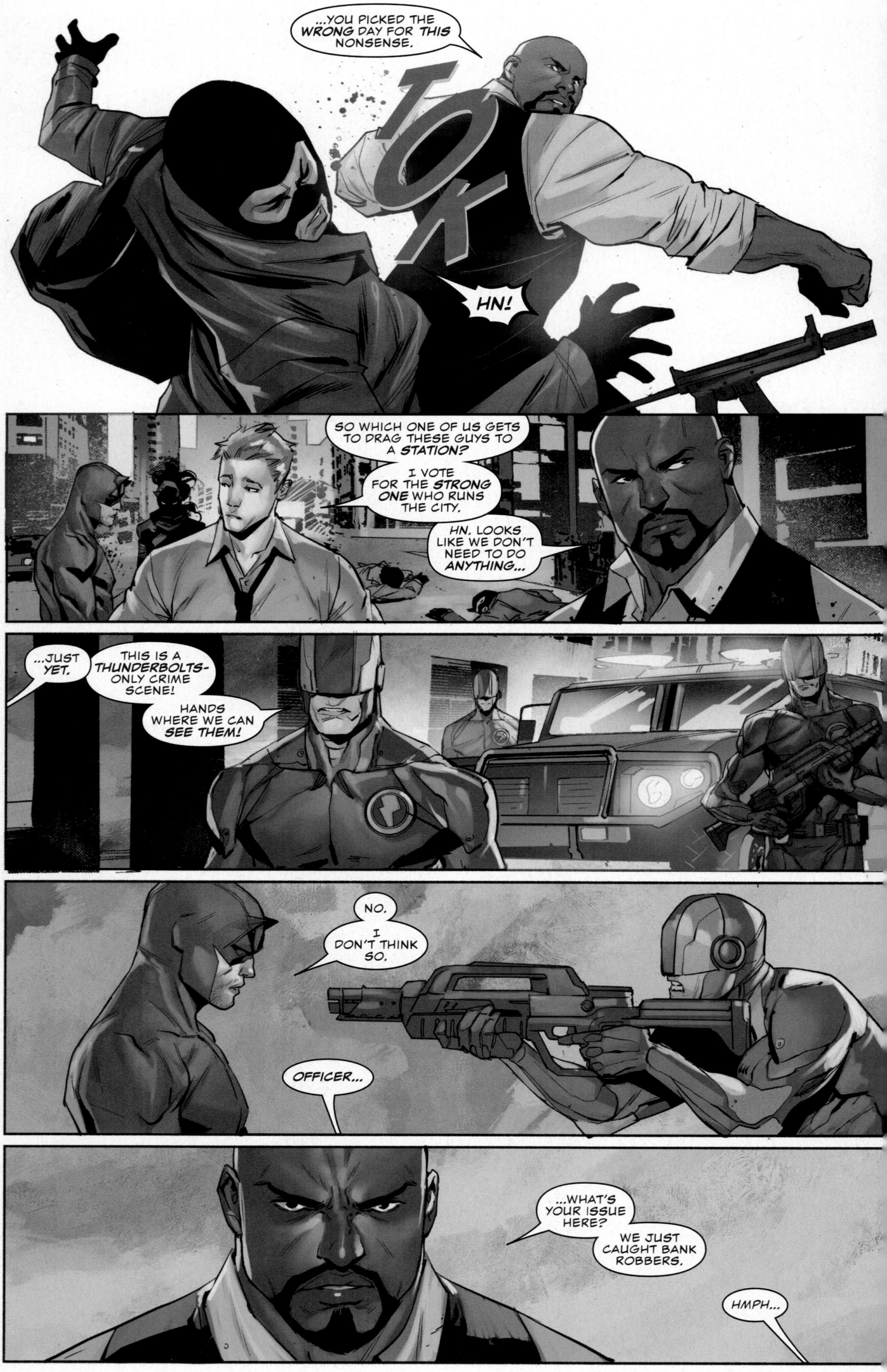
...YOU PICKED THE WRONG DAY FOR THIS NONSENSE.
TOK
HN!
SO WHICH ONE OF US GETS TO DRAG THESE GUYS TO A STATION?
I VOTE FOR THE STRONG ONE WHO RUNS THE CITY.
HN. LOOKS LIKE WE DON'T NEED TO DO ANYTHING...
...JUST YET.
THIS IS A THUNDERBOLTS-ONLY CRIME SCENE!
HANDS WHERE WE CAN SEE THEM!
NO.
I DON'T THINK SO.
OFFICER...
...WHAT'S YOUR ISSUE HERE?
WE JUST CAUGHT BANK ROBBERS.
HMPH...

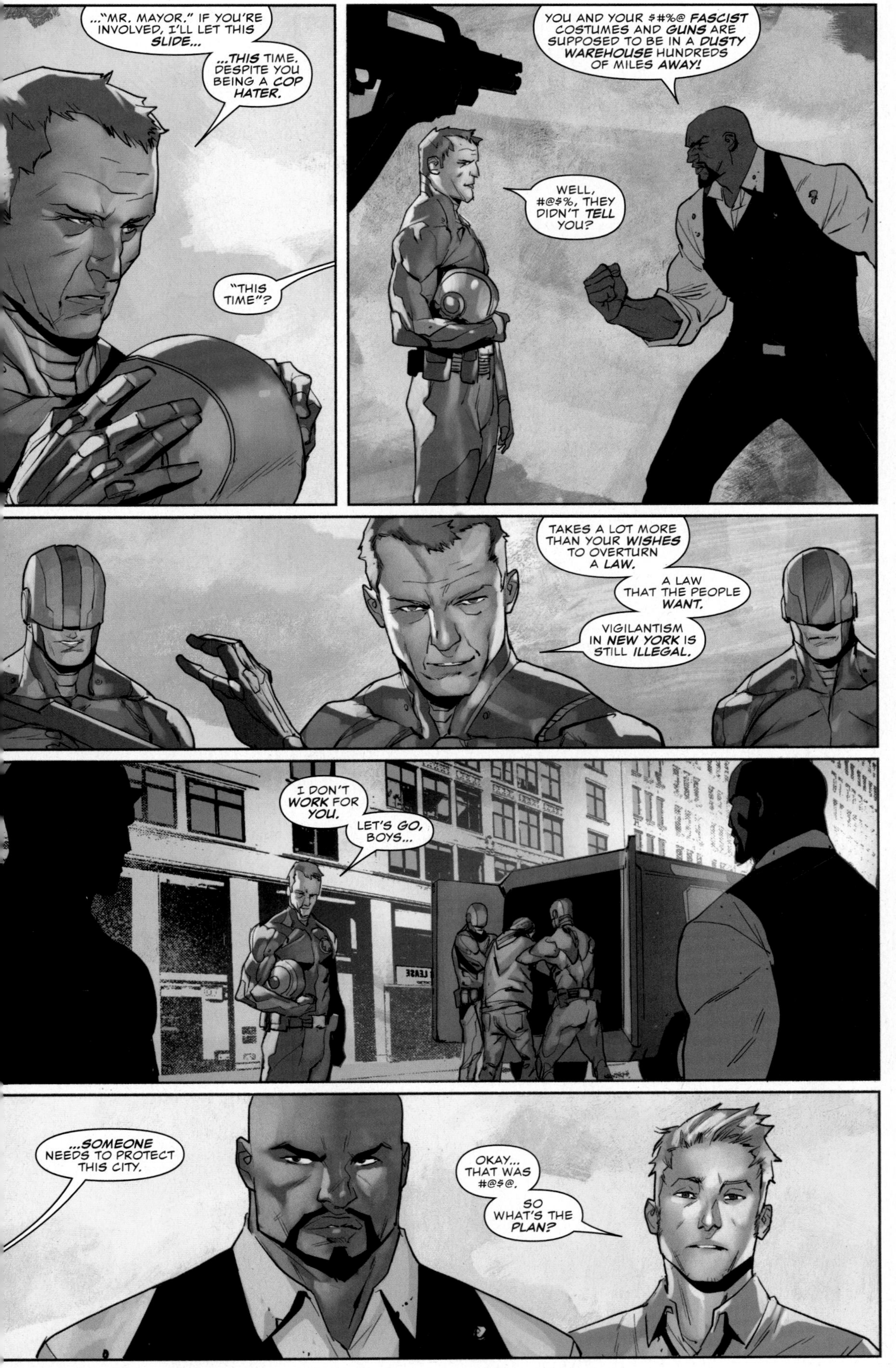
..."MR. MAYOR." IF YOU'RE INVOLVED, I'LL LET THIS SLIDE...
...THIS TIME. DESPITE YOU BEING A COP HATER.
"THIS TIME"?
YOU AND YOUR $#%@ FASCIST COSTUMES AND GUNS ARE SUPPOSED TO BE IN A DUSTY WAREHOUSE HUNDREDS OF MILES AWAY!
WELL, #@$%, THEY DIDN'T TELL YOU?
TAKES A LOT MORE THAN YOUR WISHES TO OVERTURN A LAW.
A LAW THAT THE PEOPLE WANT.
VIGILANTISM IN NEW YORK IS STILL ILLEGAL.
I DON'T WORK FOR YOU.
LET'S GO, BOYS...
LEASE
...SOMEONE NEEDS TO PROTECT THIS CITY.
OKAY... THAT WAS #@$@.
SO WHAT'S THE PLAN?

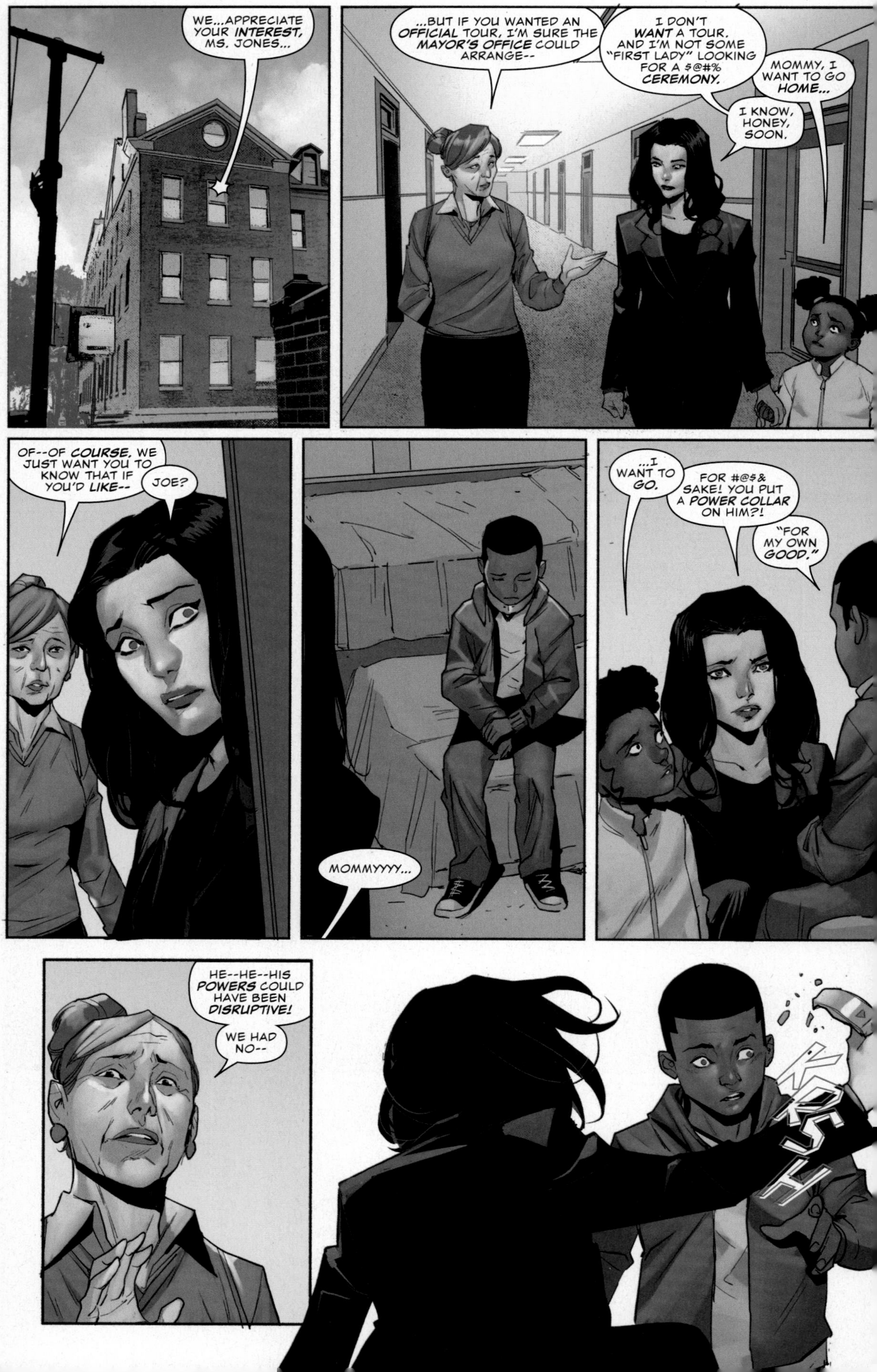
WE...APPRECIATE YOUR INTEREST, MS. JONES...
...BUT IF YOU WANTED AN OFFICIAL TOUR, I'M SURE THE MAYOR'S OFFICE COULD ARRANGE--
I DON'T WANT A TOUR. AND I'M NOT SOME "FIRST LADY" LOOKING FOR A $@#% CEREMONY.
MOMMY, I WANT TO GO HOME...
I KNOW, HONEY, SOON.
OF--OF COURSE. WE JUST WANT YOU TO KNOW THAT IF YOU'D LIKE--
JOE?
MOMMYYYY...
...I WANT TO GO.
FOR #@$& SAKE! YOU PUT A POWER COLLAR ON HIM?!
"FOR MY OWN GOOD."
HE--HE--HIS POWERS COULD HAVE BEEN DISRUPTIVE!
WE HAD NO--
KRSSH

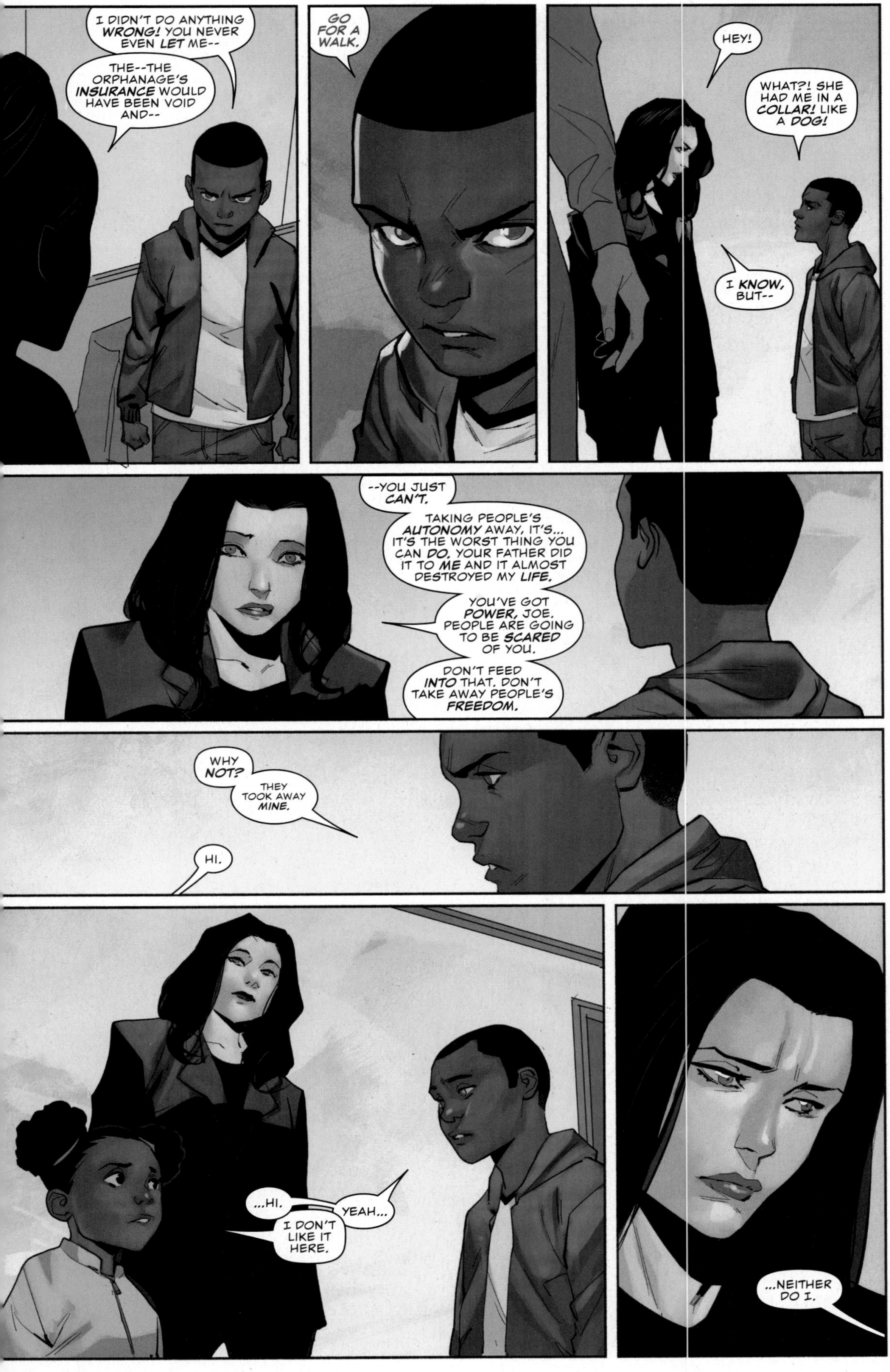
I DIDN'T DO ANYTHING WRONG! YOU NEVER EVEN LET ME--
THE--THE ORPHANAGE'S INSURANCE WOULD HAVE BEEN VOID AND--
GO FOR A WALK.
HEY!
WHAT?! SHE HAD ME IN A COLLAR! LIKE A DOG!
I KNOW, BUT--
--YOU JUST CAN'T.
TAKING PEOPLE'S AUTONOMY AWAY, IT'S... IT'S THE WORST THING YOU CAN DO. YOUR FATHER DID IT TO ME AND IT ALMOST DESTROYED MY LIFE.
YOU'VE GOT POWER, JOE. PEOPLE ARE GOING TO BE SCARED OF YOU.
DON'T FEED INTO THAT. DON'T TAKE AWAY PEOPLE'S FREEDOM.
WHY NOT?
THEY TOOK AWAY MINE.
HI.
...HI.
YEAH...
I DON'T LIKE IT HERE.
...NEITHER DO I.

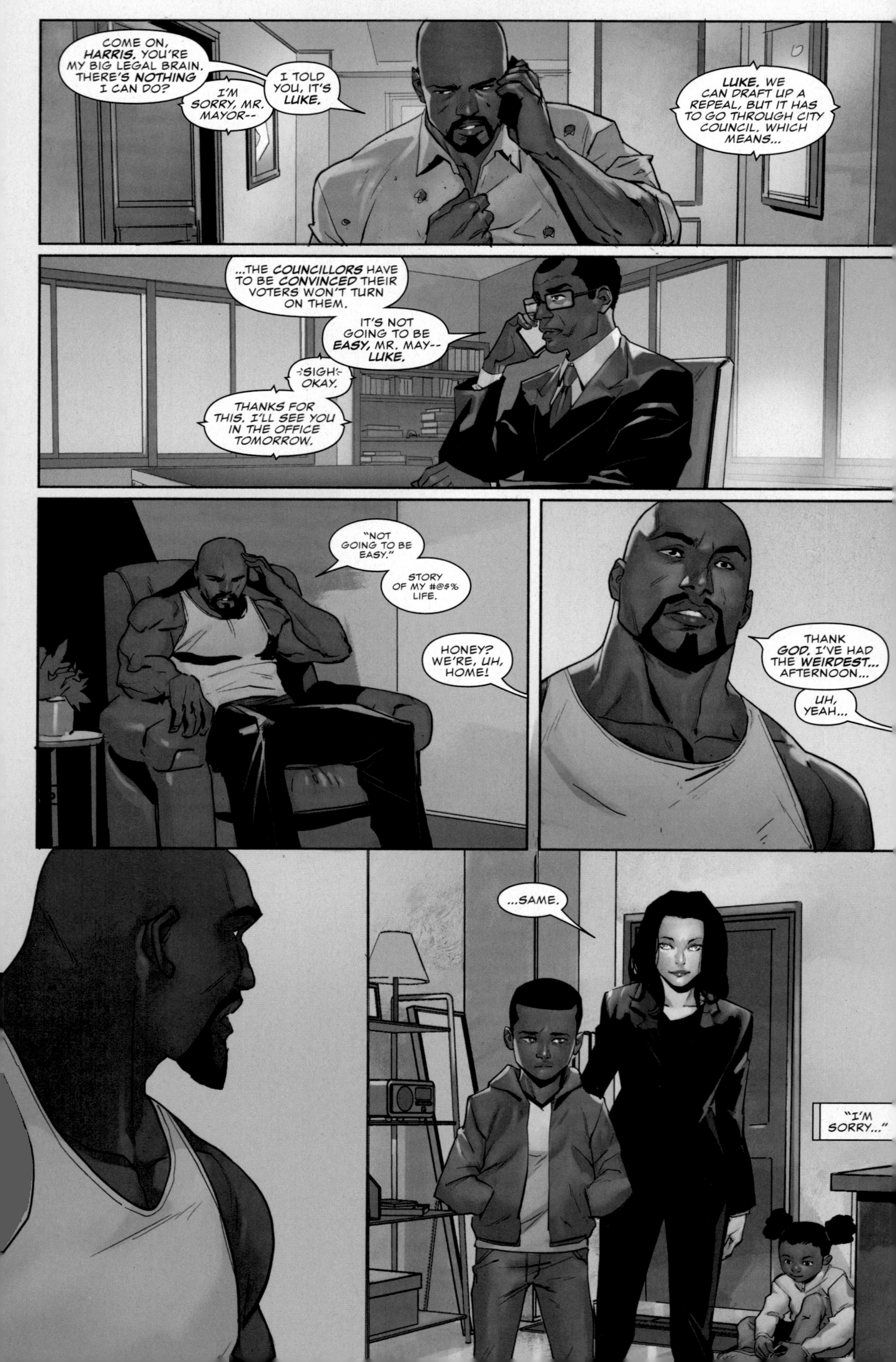

COME ON, HARRIS. YOU'RE MY BIG LEGAL BRAIN. THERE'S NOTHING I CAN DO?
I'M SORRY, MR. MAYOR--
I TOLD YOU, IT'S LUKE.
LUKE. WE CAN DRAFT UP A REPEAL, BUT IT HAS TO GO THROUGH CITY COUNCIL, WHICH MEANS...
...THE COUNCILLORS HAVE TO BE CONVINCED THEIR VOTERS WON'T TURN ON THEM.
IT'S NOT GOING TO BE EASY, MR. MAY-- LUKE.
SIGH OKAY.
THANKS FOR THIS. I'LL SEE YOU IN THE OFFICE TOMORROW.
"NOT GOING TO BE EASY."
STORY OF MY #@$% LIFE.
HONEY? WE'RE, UH, HOME!
THANK GOD, I'VE HAD THE WEIRDEST... AFTERNOON...
UH, YEAH...
...SAME.
"I'M SORRY..."

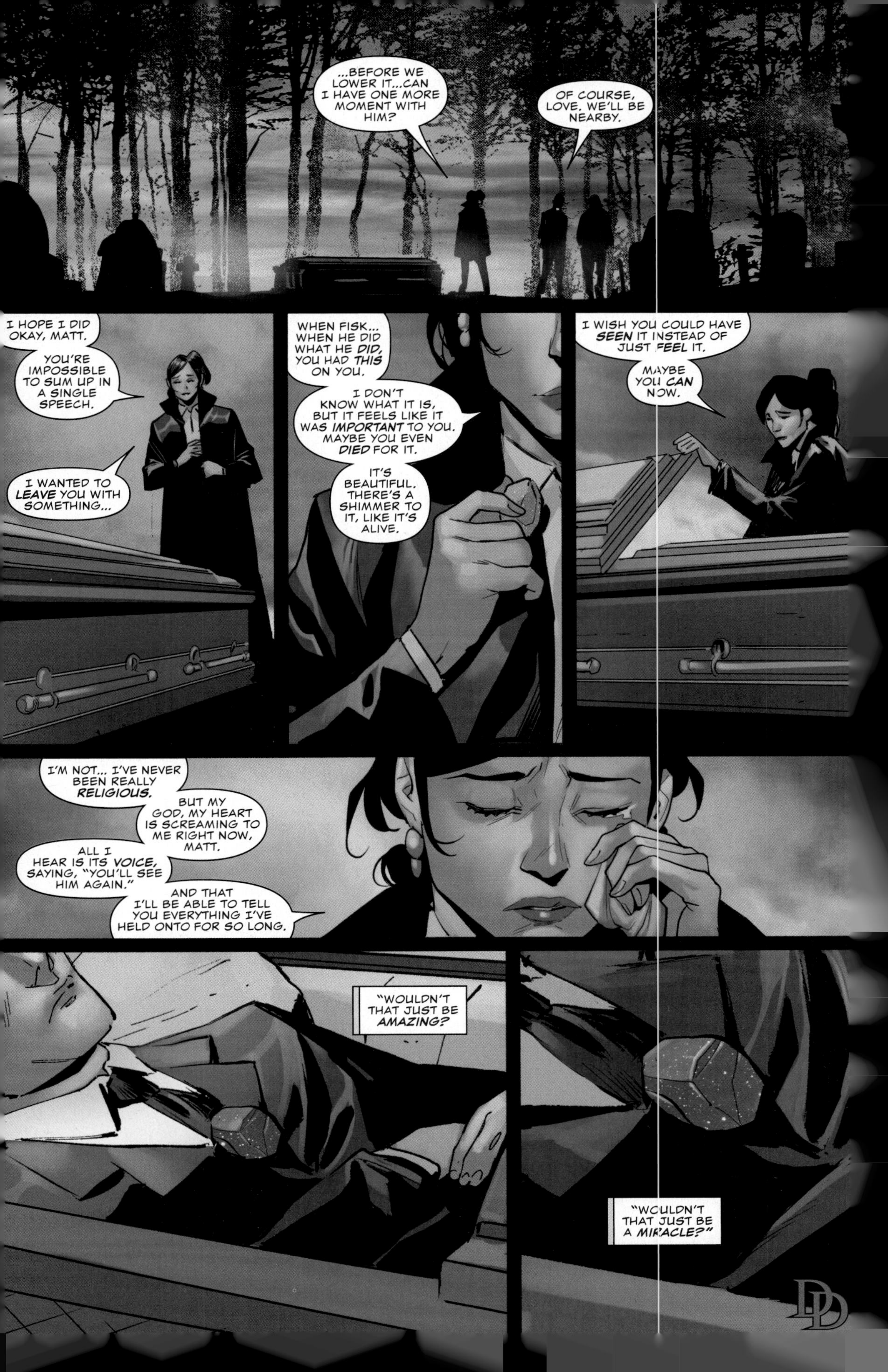
...BEFORE WE LOWER IT...CAN I HAVE ONE MORE MOMENT WITH HIM?
OF COURSE, LOVE. WE'LL BE NEARBY.
I HOPE I DID OKAY, MATT.
YOU'RE IMPOSSIBLE TO SUM UP IN A SINGLE SPEECH.
I WANTED TO LEAVE YOU WITH SOMETHING...
WHEN FISK... WHEN HE DID WHAT HE DID, YOU HAD THIS ON YOU.
I DON'T KNOW WHAT IT IS, BUT IT FEELS LIKE IT WAS IMPORTANT TO YOU. MAYBE YOU EVEN DIED FOR IT.
IT'S BEAUTIFUL. THERE'S A SHIMMER TO IT, LIKE IT'S ALIVE.
I WISH YOU COULD HAVE SEEN IT INSTEAD OF JUST FEEL IT.
MAYBE YOU CAN NOW.
I'M NOT... I'VE NEVER BEEN REALLY RELIGIOUS.
BUT MY GOD, MY HEART IS SCREAMING TO ME RIGHT NOW, MATT.
ALL I HEAR IS ITS VOICE, SAYING, "YOU'LL SEE HIM AGAIN."
AND THAT I'LL BE ABLE TO TELL YOU EVERYTHING I'VE HELD ONTO FOR SO LONG.
"WOULDN'T THAT JUST BE AMAZING?
"WOULDN'T THAT JUST BE A MIRACLE?"

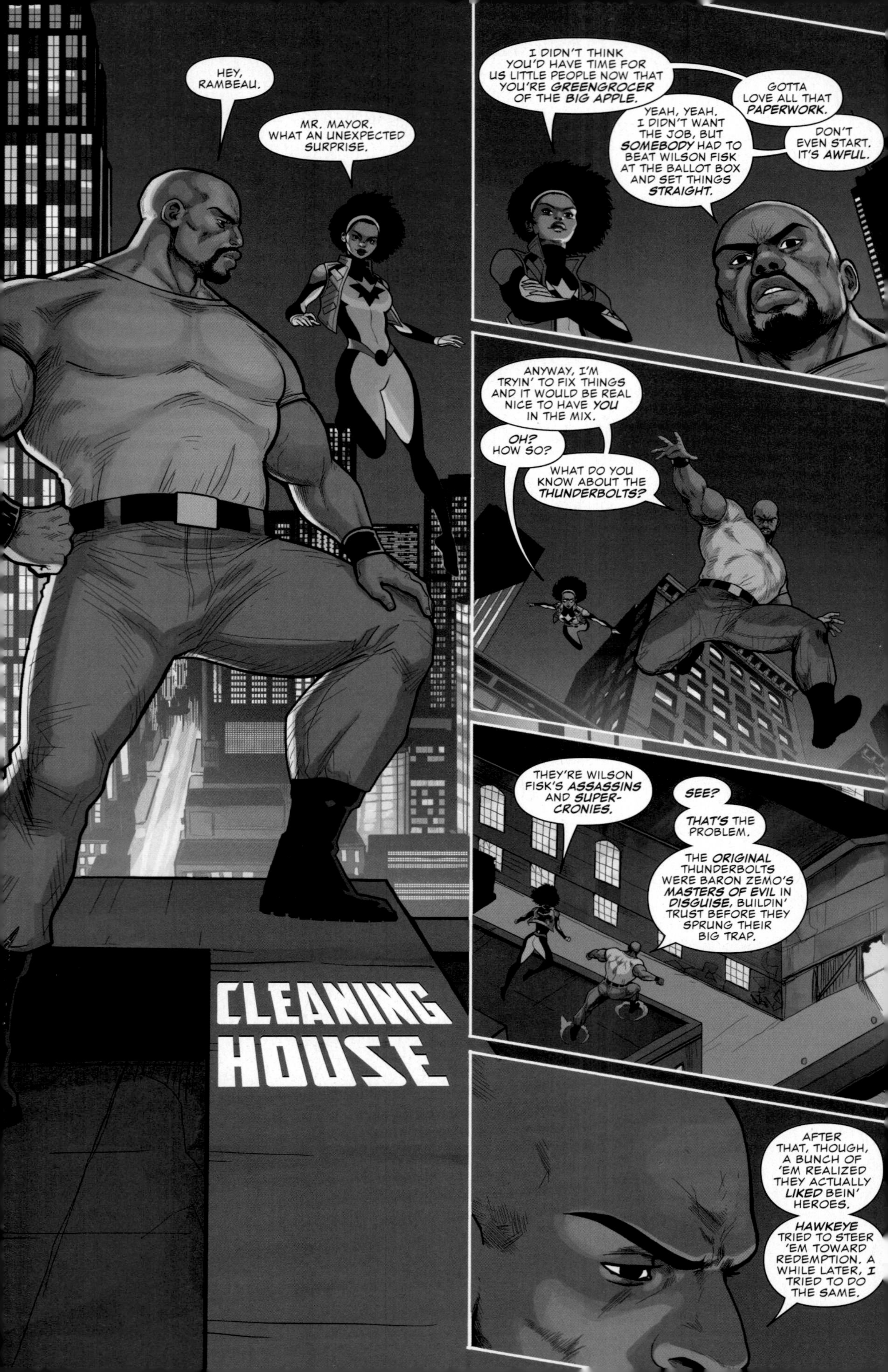
HEY, RAMBEAU.
MR. MAYOR. WHAT AN UNEXPECTED SURPRISE.
CLEANING HOUSE
I DIDN'T THINK YOU'D HAVE TIME FOR US LITTLE PEOPLE NOW THAT YOU'RE GREENGROCER OF THE BIG APPLE.
YEAH, YEAH. I DIDN'T WANT THE JOB, BUT SOMEBODY HAD TO BEAT WILSON FISK AT THE BALLOT BOX AND SET THINGS STRAIGHT.
GOTTA LOVE ALL THAT PAPERWORK.
DON'T EVEN START. IT'S AWFUL.
ANYWAY, I'M TRYIN' TO FIX THINGS AND IT WOULD BE REAL NICE TO HAVE YOU IN THE MIX.
OH? HOW SO?
WHAT DO YOU KNOW ABOUT THE THUNDERBOLTS?
THEY'RE WILSON FISK'S ASSASSINS AND SUPER-CRONIES.
SEE?
THAT'S THE PROBLEM.
THE ORIGINAL THUNDERBOLTS WERE BARON ZEMO'S MASTERS OF EVIL IN DISGUISE, BUILDIN' TRUST BEFORE THEY SPRUNG THEIR BIG TRAP.
AFTER THAT, THOUGH, A BUNCH OF 'EM REALIZED THEY ACTUALLY LIKED BEIN' HEROES.
HAWKEYE TRIED TO STEER 'EM TOWARD REDEMPTION. A WHILE LATER, I TRIED TO DO THE SAME.

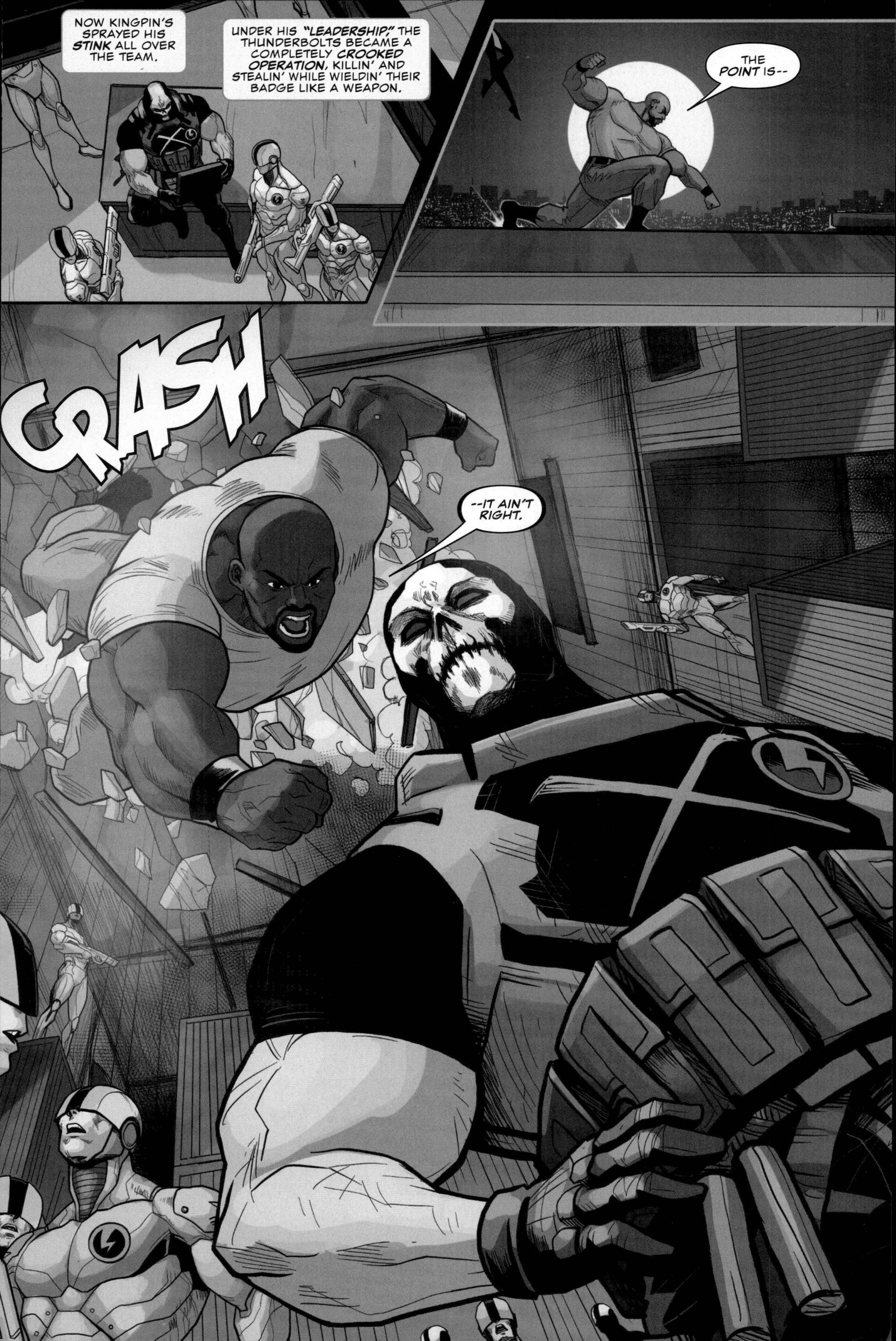
NOW KINGPIN'S SPRAYED HIS STINK ALL OVER THE TEAM.
UNDER HIS "LEADERSHIP," THE THUNDERBOLTS BECAME A COMPLETELY CROOKED OPERATION, KILLIN' AND STEALIN' WHILE WIELDIN' THEIR BADGE LIKE A WEAPON.
THE POINT IS--
CRASH
--IT AIN'T RIGHT.

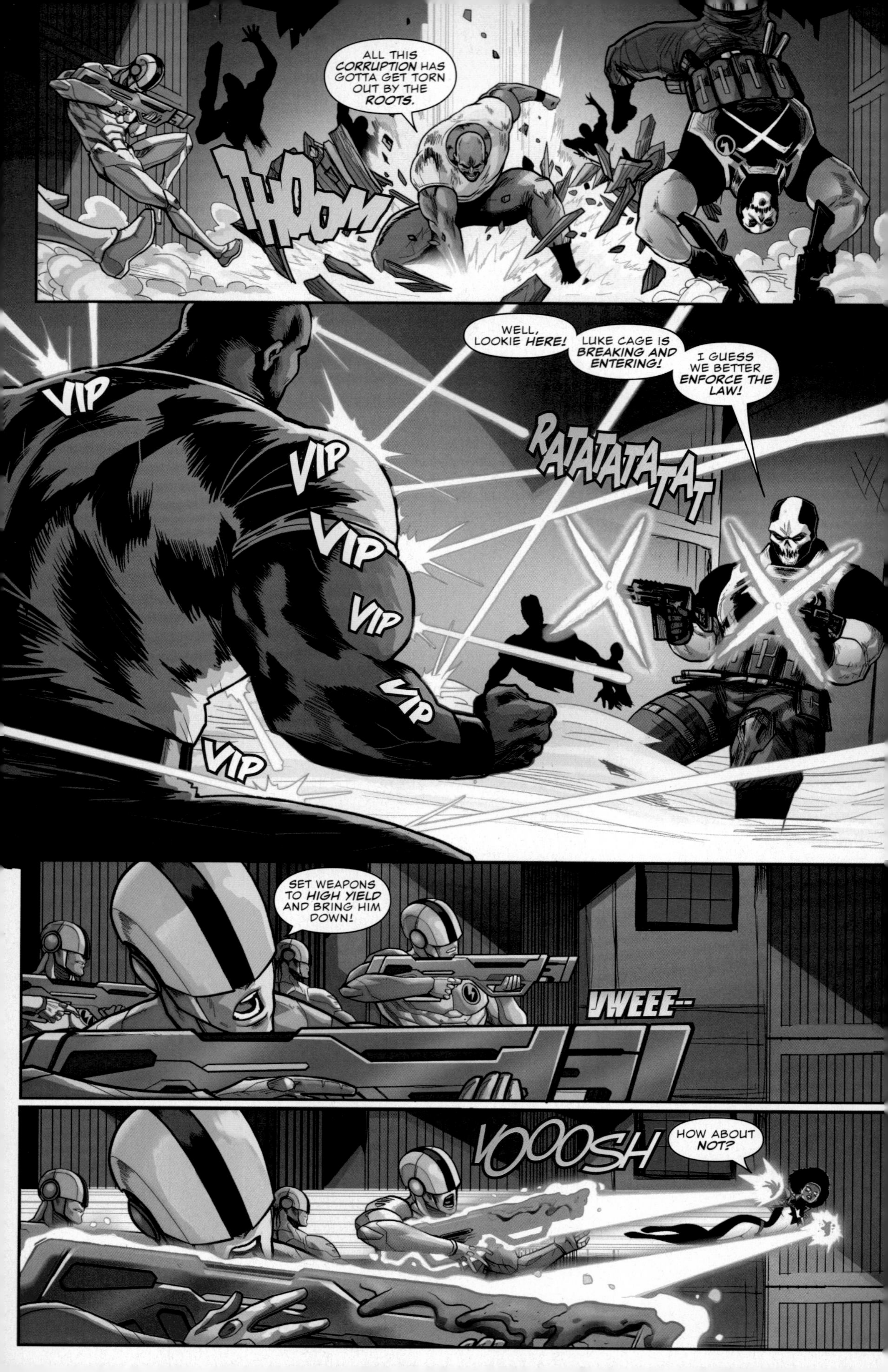
ALL THIS CORRUPTION HAS GOTTA GET TORN OUT BY THE ROOTS.
THOOM
WELL, LOOKIE HERE!
LUKE CAGE IS BREAKING AND ENTERING!
I GUESS WE BETTER ENFORCE THE LAW!
RATATATATATAT
VIP
VIP
VIP
VIP
VIP
VIP
SET WEAPONS TO HIGH YIELD AND BRING HIM DOWN!
VWEEE--
VOOOSH
HOW ABOUT NOT?

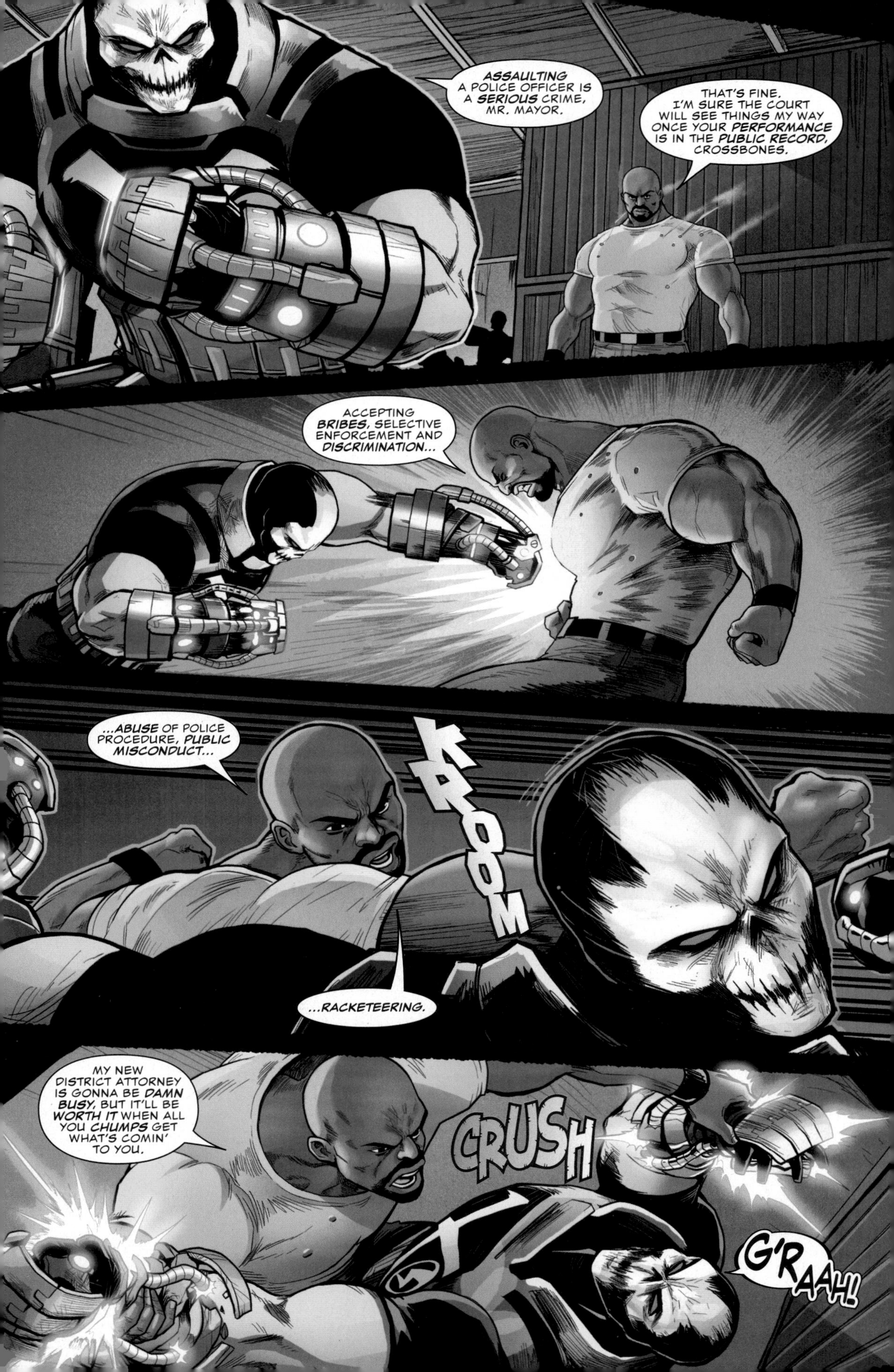
ASSAULTING A POLICE OFFICER IS A SERIOUS CRIME, MR. MAYOR.
THAT'S FINE. I'M SURE THE COURT WILL SEE THINGS MY WAY ONCE YOUR PERFORMANCE IS IN THE PUBLIC RECORD, CROSSBONES.
ACCEPTING BRIBES, SELECTIVE ENFORCEMENT AND DISCRIMINATION...
...ABUSE OF POLICE PROCEDURE, PUBLIC MISCONDUCT...
KROOM
...RACKETEERING.
MY NEW DISTRICT ATTORNEY IS GONNA BE DAMN BUSY, BUT IT'LL BE WORTH IT WHEN ALL YOU CHUMPS GET WHAT'S COMIN' TO YOU.
CRUSH
G'RAAH!

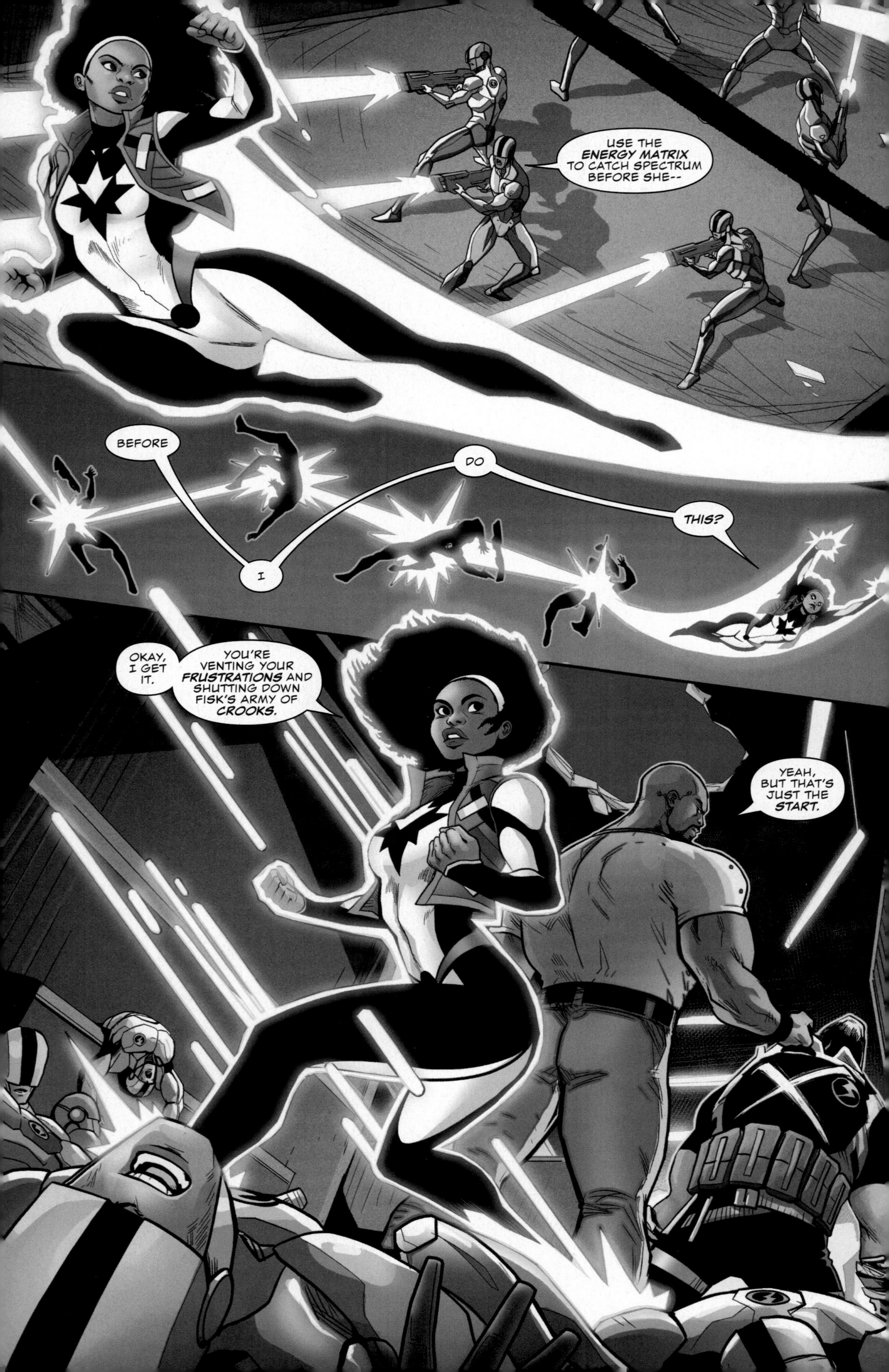
USE THE ENERGY MATRIX TO CATCH SPECTRUM BEFORE SHE--
BEFORE
I
DO
THIS?
OKAY, I GET IT.
YOU'RE VENTING YOUR FRUSTRATIONS AND SHUTTING DOWN FISK'S ARMY OF CROOKS.
YEAH, BUT THAT'S JUST THE START.

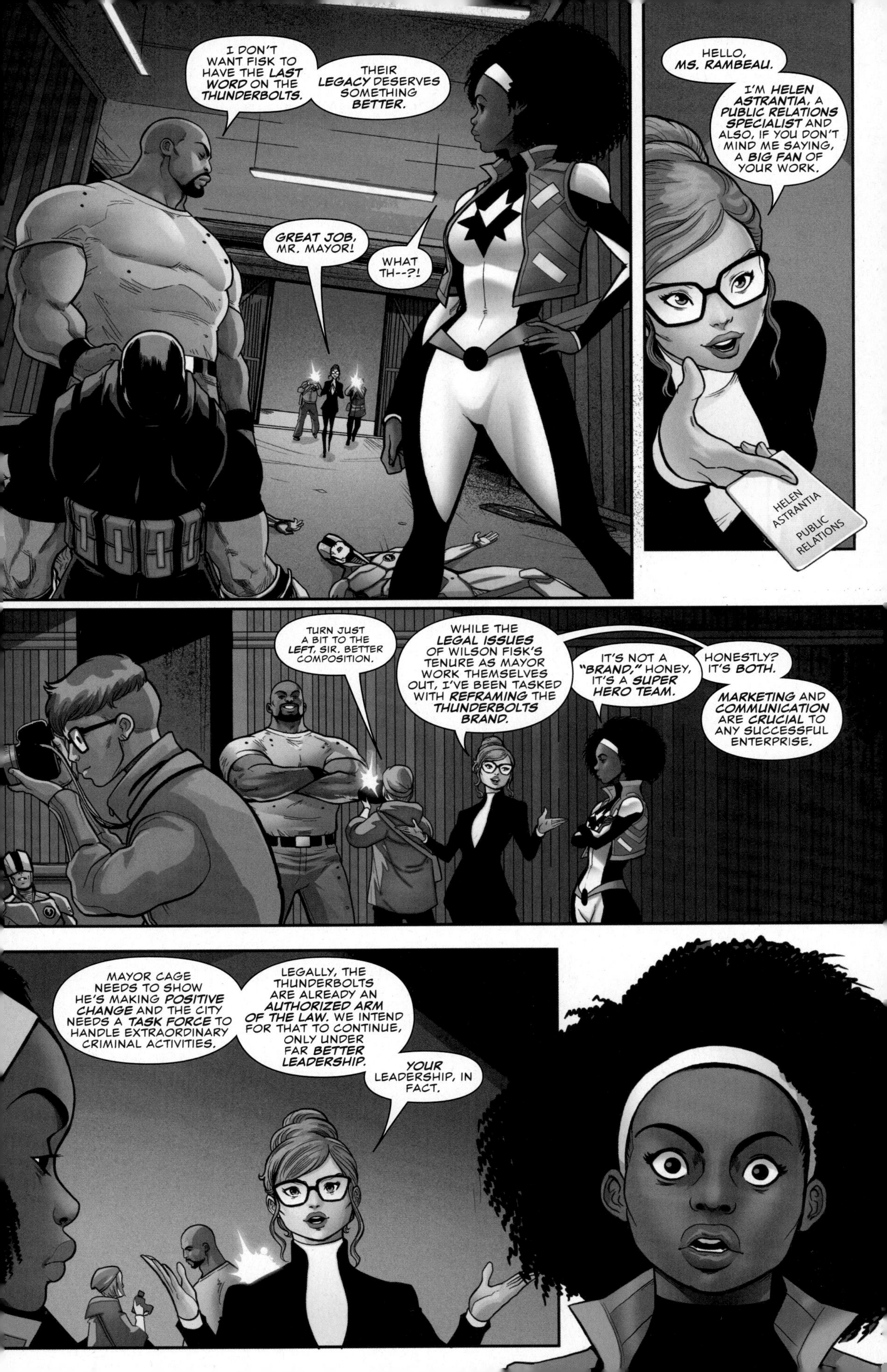
I DON'T WANT FISK TO HAVE THE LAST WORD ON THE THUNDERBOLTS.
THEIR LEGACY DESERVES SOMETHING BETTER.
GREAT JOB, MR. MAYOR!
WHAT TH--?!
HELLO, MS. RAMBEAU.
I'M HELEN ASTRANTIA, A PUBLIC RELATIONS SPECIALIST AND ALSO, IF YOU DON'T MIND ME SAYING, A BIG FAN OF YOUR WORK.
HELEN ASTRANTIA
PUBLIC RELATIONS
TURN JUST A BIT TO THE LEFT, SIR. BETTER COMPOSITION.
WHILE THE LEGAL ISSUES OF WILSON FISK'S TENURE AS MAYOR WORK THEMSELVES OUT, I'VE BEEN TASKED WITH REFRAMING THE THUNDERBOLTS BRAND.
IT'S NOT A "BRAND," HONEY, IT'S A SUPER HERO TEAM.
HONESTLY? IT'S BOTH.
MARKETING AND COMMUNICATION ARE CRUCIAL TO ANY SUCCESSFUL ENTERPRISE.
MAYOR CAGE NEEDS TO SHOW HE'S MAKING POSITIVE CHANGE AND THE CITY NEEDS A TASK FORCE TO HANDLE EXTRAORDINARY CRIMINAL ACTIVITIES.
LEGALLY, THE THUNDERBOLTS ARE ALREADY AN AUTHORIZED ARM OF THE LAW. WE INTEND FOR THAT TO CONTINUE, ONLY UNDER FAR BETTER LEADERSHIP.
YOUR LEADERSHIP, IN FACT.

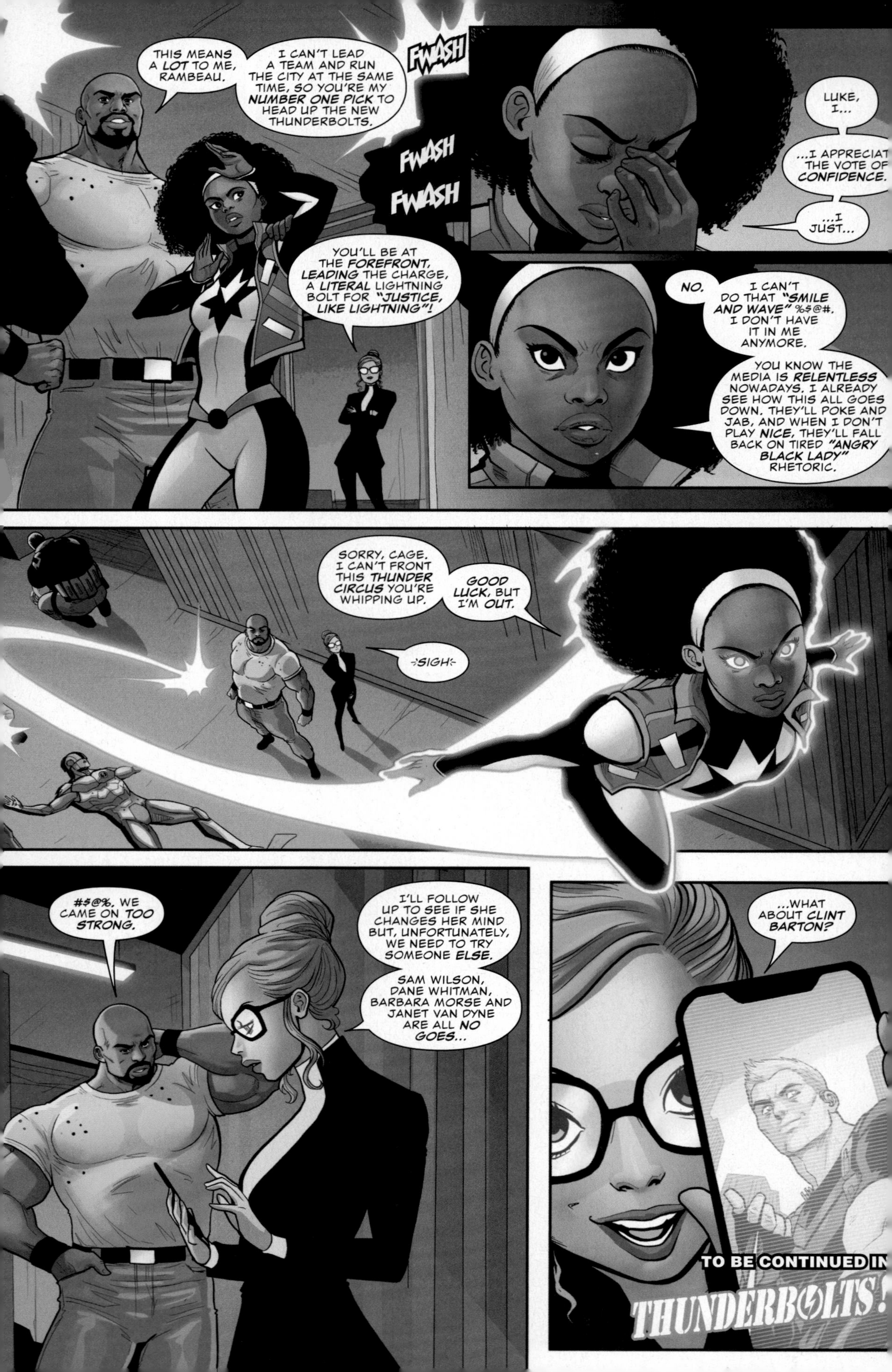
THIS MEANS A LOT TO ME, RAMBEAU.
I CAN'T LEAD A TEAM AND RUN THE CITY AT THE SAME TIME, SO YOU'RE MY NUMBER ONE PICK TO HEAD UP THE NEW THUNDERBOLTS.
FWASH
FWASH
FWASH
YOU'LL BE AT THE FOREFRONT, LEADING THE CHARGE, A LITERAL LIGHTNING BOLT FOR "JUSTICE, LIKE LIGHTNING"!
LUKE, I...
...I APPRECIAT THE VOTE OF CONFIDENCE.
...I JUST...
NO.
I CAN'T DO THAT "SMILE AND WAVE" %$@#. I DON'T HAVE IT IN ME ANYMORE.
YOU KNOW THE MEDIA IS RELENTLESS NOWADAYS. I ALREADY SEE HOW THIS ALL GOES DOWN. THEY'LL POKE AND JAB, AND WHEN I DON'T PLAY NICE, THEY'LL FALL BACK ON TIRED "ANGRY BLACK LADY" RHETORIC.
SORRY, CAGE. I CAN'T FRONT THIS THUNDER CIRCUS YOU'RE WHIPPING UP.
GOOD LUCK, BUT I'M OUT.
SIGH
#$@%. WE CAME ON TOO STRONG.
I'LL FOLLOW UP TO SEE IF SHE CHANGES HER MIND BUT, UNFORTUNATELY, WE NEED TO TRY SOMEONE ELSE.
SAM WILSON, DANE WHITMAN, BARBARA MORSE AND JANET VAN DYNE ARE ALL NO GOES...
...WHAT ABOUT CLINT BARTON?
TO BE CONTINUED IN
THUNDERBOLTS!

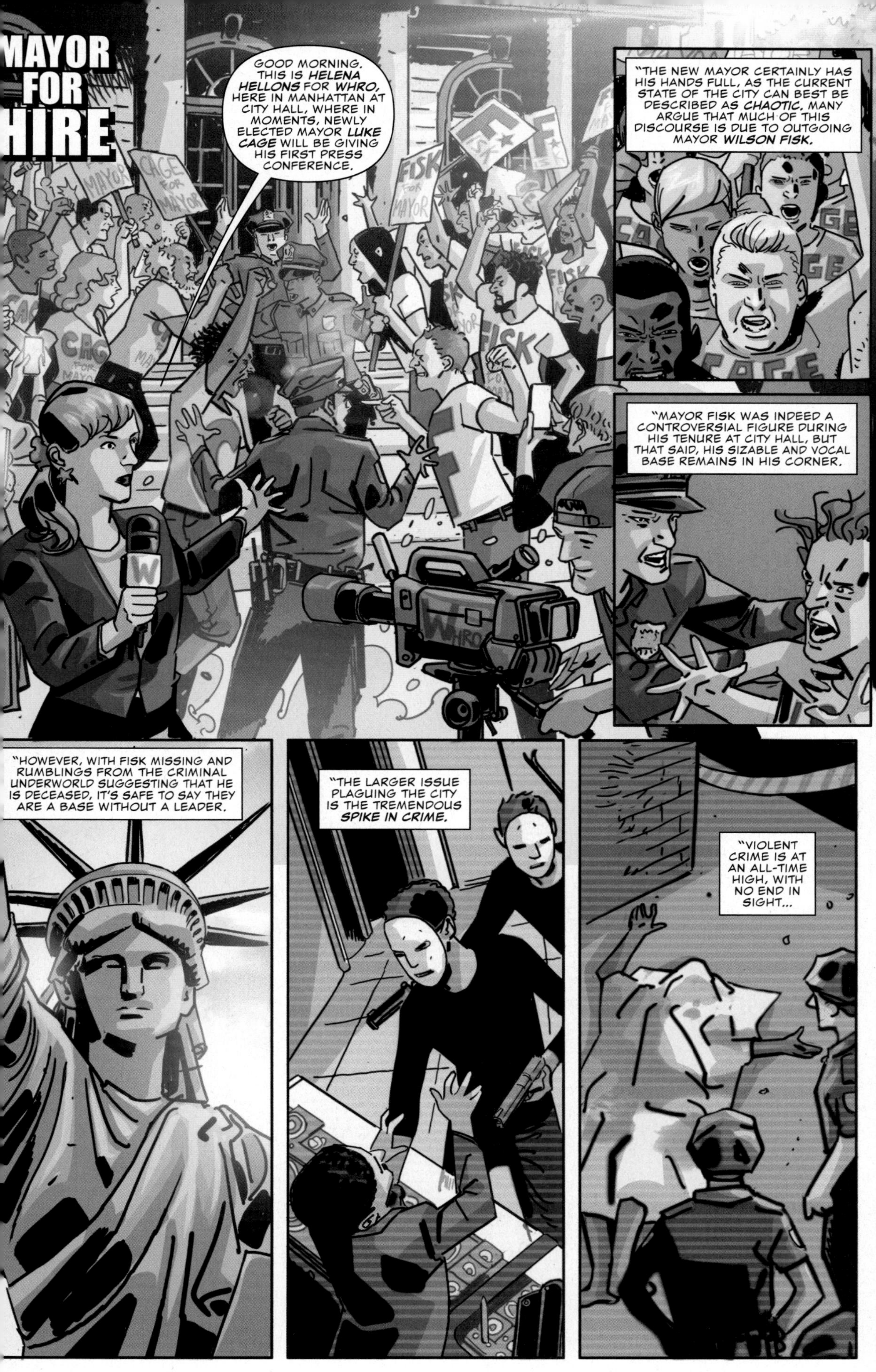
MAYOR FOR HIRE
GOOD MORNING. THIS IS HELENA HELLONS FOR WHRO, HERE IN MANHATTAN AT CITY HALL, WHERE IN MOMENTS, NEWLY ELECTED MAYOR LUKE CAGE WILL BE GIVING HIS FIRST PRESS CONFERENCE.
CAGE FOR MAYOR
FISK FOR MAYOR
"THE NEW MAYOR CERTAINLY HAS HIS HANDS FULL, AS THE CURRENT STATE OF THE CITY CAN BEST BE DESCRIBED AS CHAOTIC. MANY ARGUE THAT MUCH OF THIS DISCOURSE IS DUE TO OUTGOING MAYOR WILSON FISK.
"MAYOR FISK WAS INDEED A CONTROVERSIAL FIGURE DURING HIS TENURE AT CITY HALL, BUT THAT SAID, HIS SIZABLE AND VOCAL BASE REMAINS IN HIS CORNER.
"HOWEVER, WITH FISK MISSING AND RUMBLINGS FROM THE CRIMINAL UNDERWORLD SUGGESTING THAT HE IS DECEASED, IT'S SAFE TO SAY THEY ARE A BASE WITHOUT A LEADER.
"THE LARGER ISSUE PLAGUING THE CITY IS THE TREMENDOUS SPIKE IN CRIME.
"VIOLENT CRIME IS AT AN ALL-TIME HIGH, WITH NO END IN SIGHT...

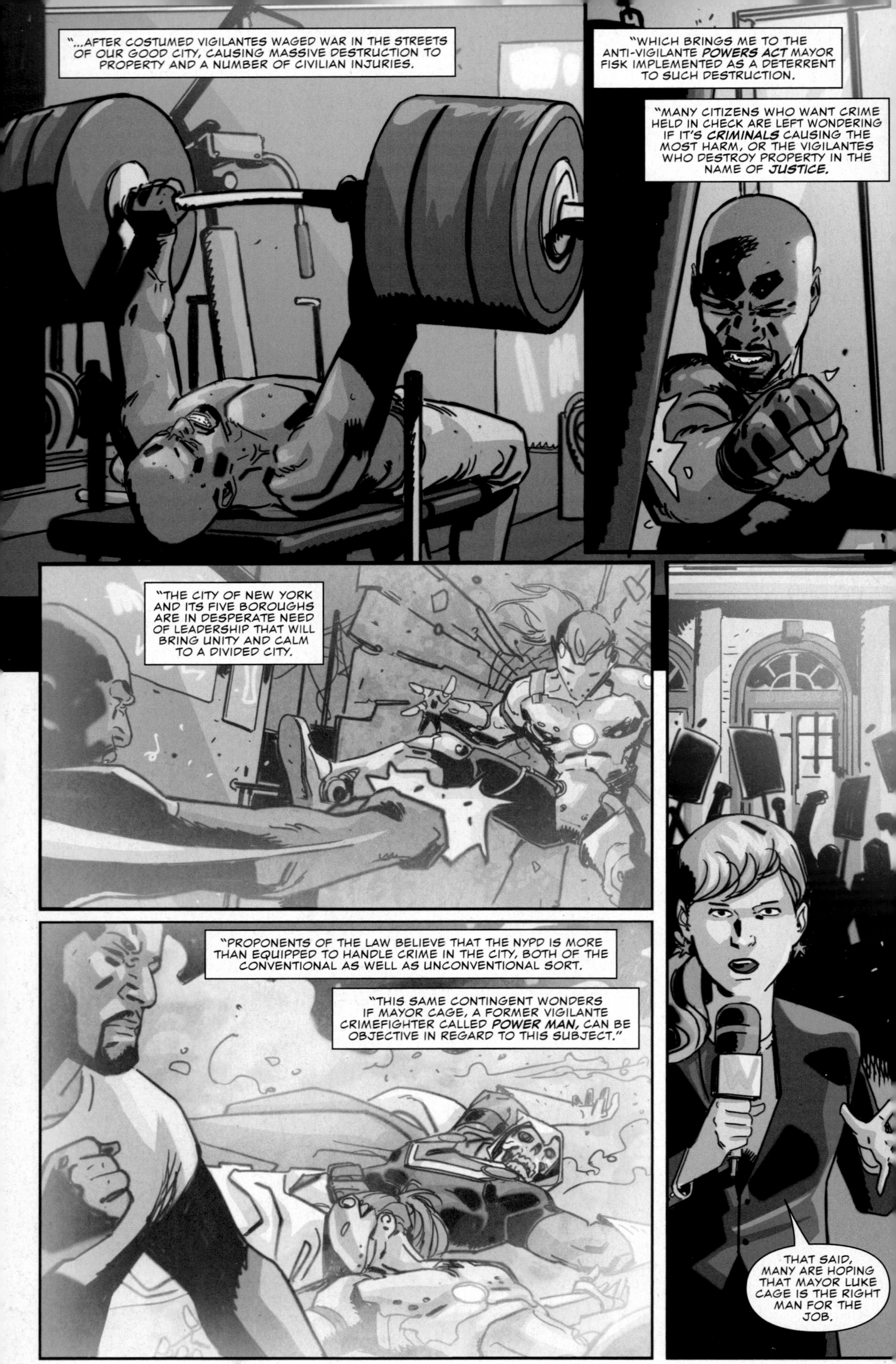
"...AFTER COSTUMED VIGILANTES WAGED WAR IN THE STREETS OF OUR GOOD CITY, CAUSING MASSIVE DESTRUCTION TO PROPERTY AND A NUMBER OF CIVILIAN INJURIES.
"WHICH BRINGS ME TO THE ANTI-VIGILANTE POWERS ACT MAYOR FISK IMPLEMENTED AS A DETERRENT TO SUCH DESTRUCTION.
"MANY CITIZENS WHO WANT CRIME HELD IN CHECK ARE LEFT WONDERING IF IT'S CRIMINALS CAUSING THE MOST HARM, OR THE VIGILANTES WHO DESTROY PROPERTY IN THE NAME OF JUSTICE.
"THE CITY OF NEW YORK AND ITS FIVE BOROUGHS ARE IN DESPERATE NEED OF LEADERSHIP THAT WILL BRING UNITY AND CALM TO A DIVIDED CITY.
"PROPONENTS OF THE LAW BELIEVE THAT THE NYPD IS MORE THAN EQUIPPED TO HANDLE CRIME IN THE CITY, BOTH OF THE CONVENTIONAL AS WELL AS UNCONVENTIONAL SORT.
"THIS SAME CONTINGENT WONDERS IF MAYOR CAGE, A FORMER VIGILANTE CRIMEFIGHTER CALLED POWER MAN, CAN BE OBJECTIVE IN REGARD TO THIS SUBJECT."
THAT SAID, MANY ARE HOPING THAT MAYOR LUKE CAGE IS THE RIGHT MAN FOR THE JOB.

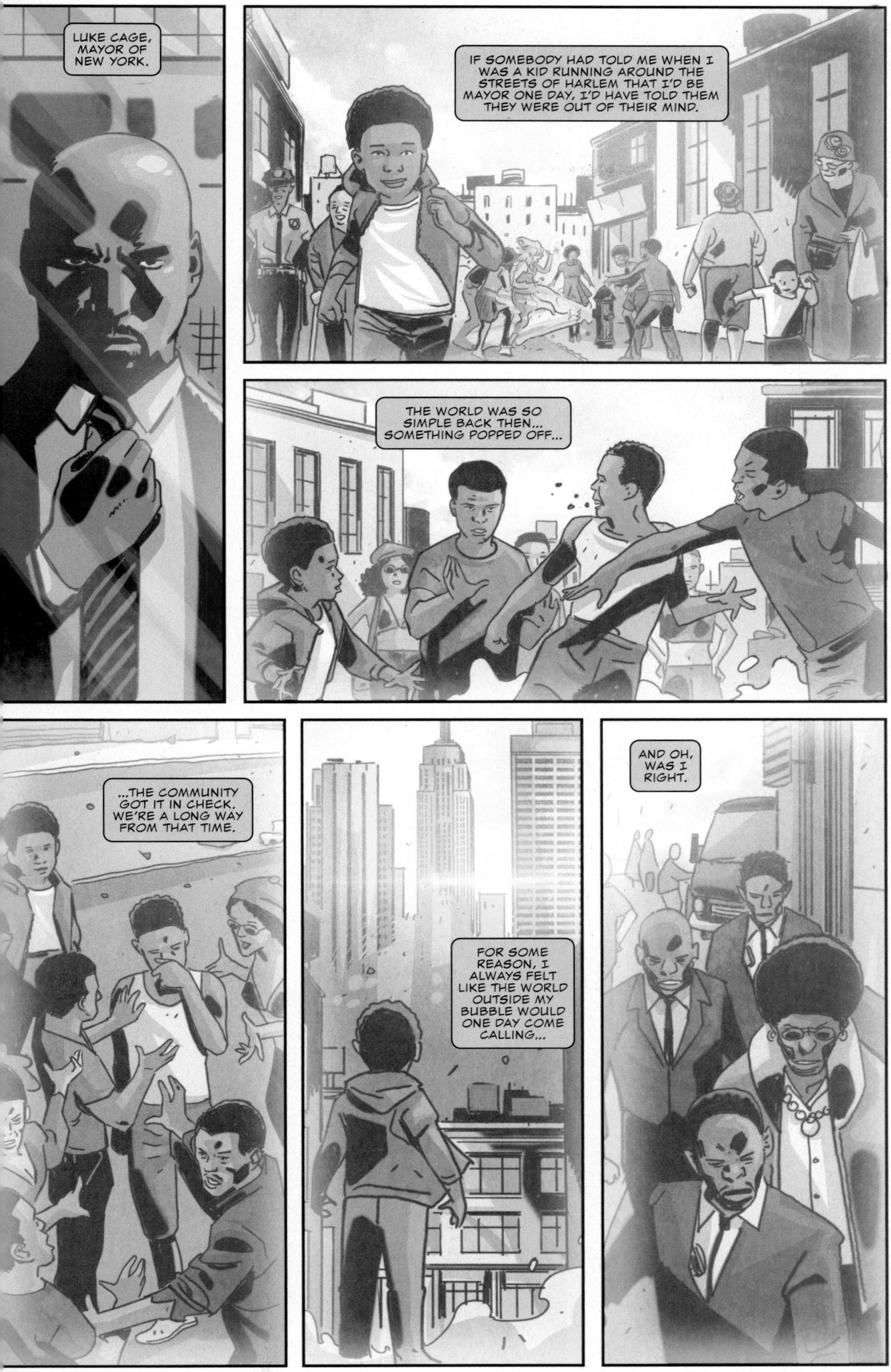
LUKE CAGE, MAYOR OF NEW YORK.
IF SOMEBODY HAD TOLD ME WHEN I WAS A KID RUNNING AROUND THE STREETS OF HARLEM THAT I'D BE MAYOR ONE DAY, I'D HAVE TOLD THEM THEY WERE OUT OF THEIR MIND.
THE WORLD WAS SO SIMPLE BACK THEN... SOMETHING POPPED OFF...
...THE COMMUNITY GOT IT IN CHECK. WE'RE A LONG WAY FROM THAT TIME.
FOR SOME REASON, I ALWAYS FELT LIKE THE WORLD OUTSIDE MY BUBBLE WOULD ONE DAY COME CALLING...
AND OH, WAS I RIGHT.

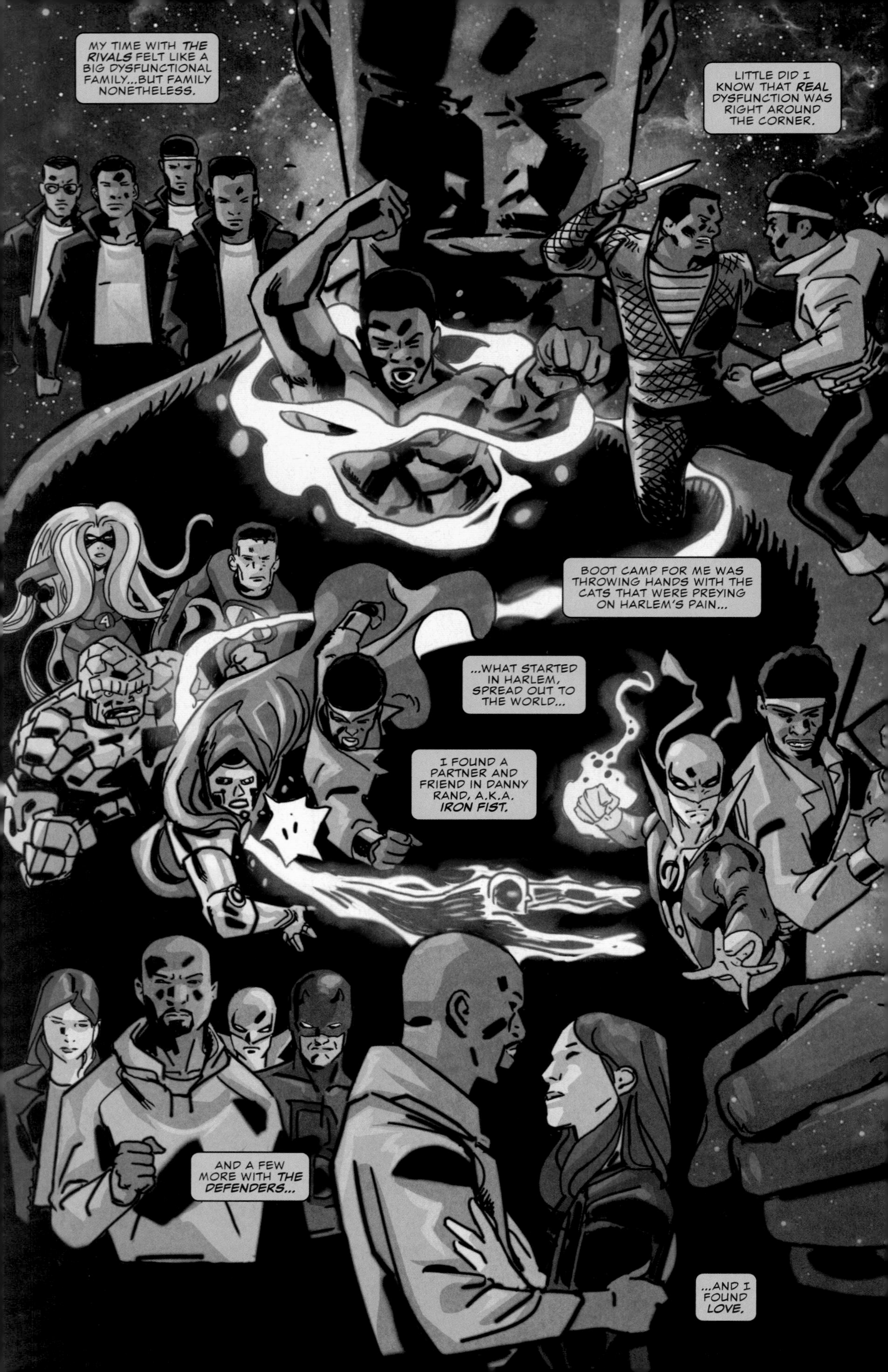
MY TIME WITH THE RIVALS FELT LIKE A BIG DYSFUNCTIONAL FAMILY...BUT FAMILY NONETHELESS.
LITTLE DID I KNOW THAT REAL DYSFUNCTION WAS RIGHT AROUND THE CORNER.
BOOT CAMP FOR ME WAS THROWING HANDS WITH THE CATS THAT WERE PREYING ON HARLEM'S PAIN...
...WHAT STARTED IN HARLEM, SPREAD OUT TO THE WORLD...
I FOUND A PARTNER AND FRIEND IN DANNY RAND, A.K.A. IRON FIST.
AND A FEW MORE WITH THE DEFENDERS...
...AND I FOUND LOVE.

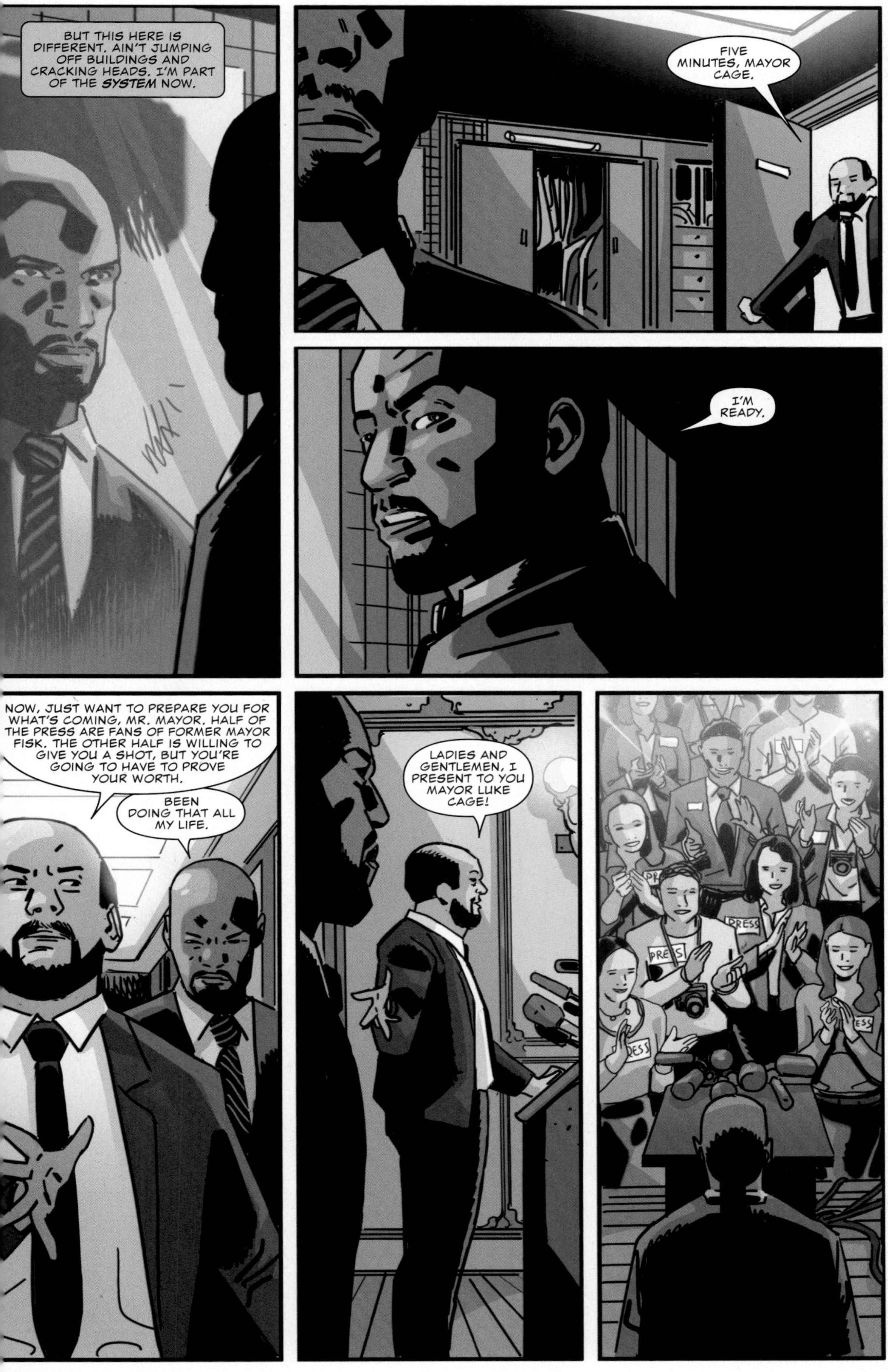

BUT THIS HERE IS DIFFERENT. AIN'T JUMPING OFF BUILDINGS AND CRACKING HEADS. I'M PART OF THE ***SYSTEM*** NOW.
FIVE MINUTES, MAYOR CAGE.
I'M READY.
NOW, JUST WANT TO PREPARE YOU FOR WHAT'S COMING, MR. MAYOR. HALF OF THE PRESS ARE FANS OF FORMER MAYOR FISK. THE OTHER HALF IS WILLING TO GIVE YOU A SHOT, BUT YOU'RE GOING TO HAVE TO PROVE YOUR WORTH.
BEEN DOING THAT ALL MY LIFE.
LADIES AND GENTLEMEN, I PRESENT TO YOU MAYOR LUKE CAGE!
PRESS
PRESS
PRESS

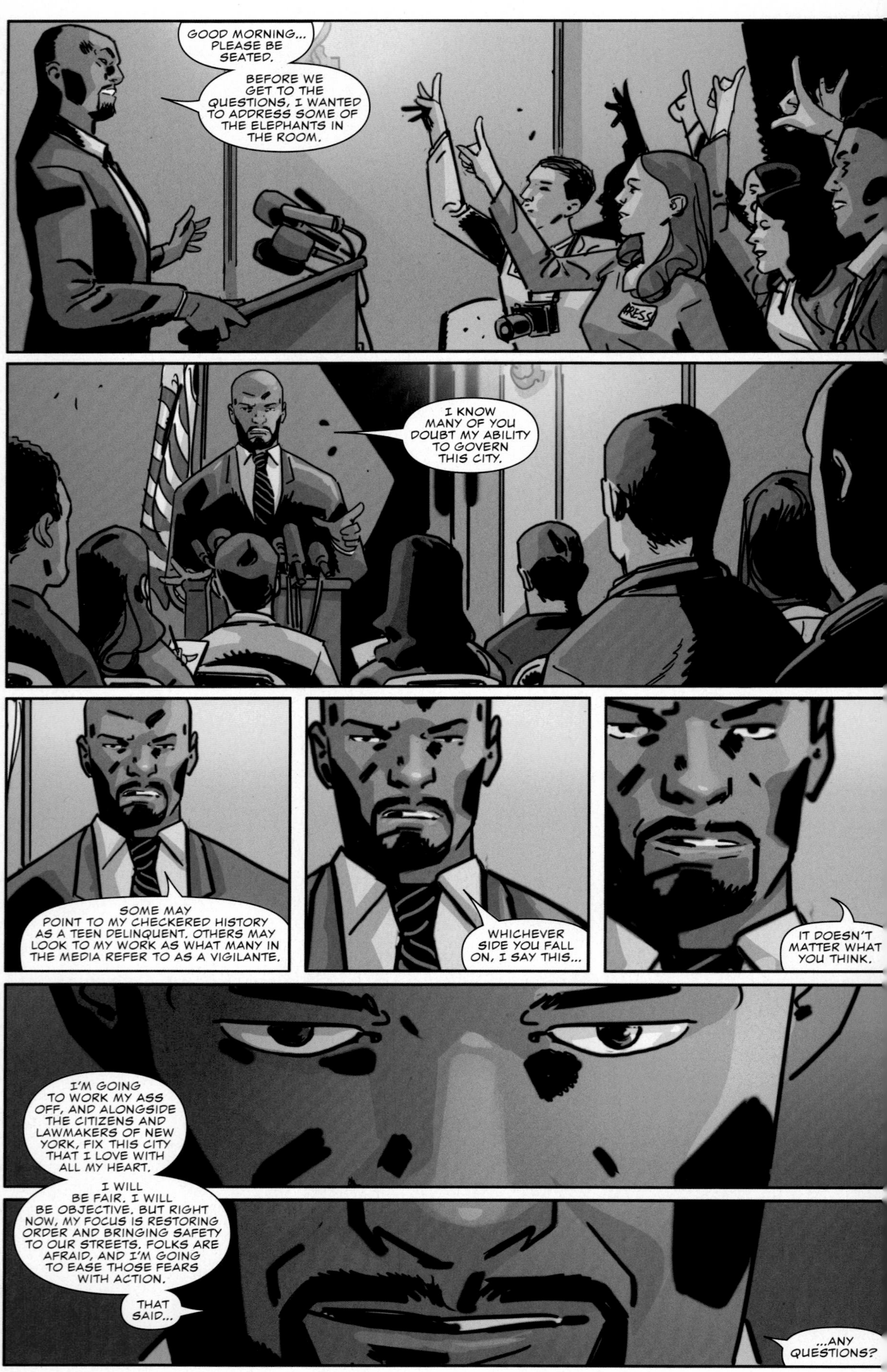
GOOD MORNING... PLEASE BE SEATED.
BEFORE WE GET TO THE QUESTIONS, I WANTED TO ADDRESS SOME OF THE ELEPHANTS IN THE ROOM.
PRESS
I KNOW MANY OF YOU DOUBT MY ABILITY TO GOVERN THIS CITY.
SOME MAY POINT TO MY CHECKERED HISTORY AS A TEEN DELINQUENT. OTHERS MAY LOOK TO MY WORK AS WHAT MANY IN THE MEDIA REFER TO AS A VIGILANTE.
WHICHEVER SIDE YOU FALL ON, I SAY THIS...
IT DOESN'T MATTER WHAT YOU THINK.
I'M GOING TO WORK MY ASS OFF, AND ALONGSIDE THE CITIZENS AND LAWMAKERS OF NEW YORK, FIX THIS CITY THAT I LOVE WITH ALL MY HEART.
I WILL BE FAIR. I WILL BE OBJECTIVE. BUT RIGHT NOW, MY FOCUS IS RESTORING ORDER AND BRINGING SAFETY TO OUR STREETS. FOLKS ARE AFRAID, AND I'M GOING TO EASE THOSE FEARS WITH ACTION.
THAT SAID...
...ANY QUESTIONS?

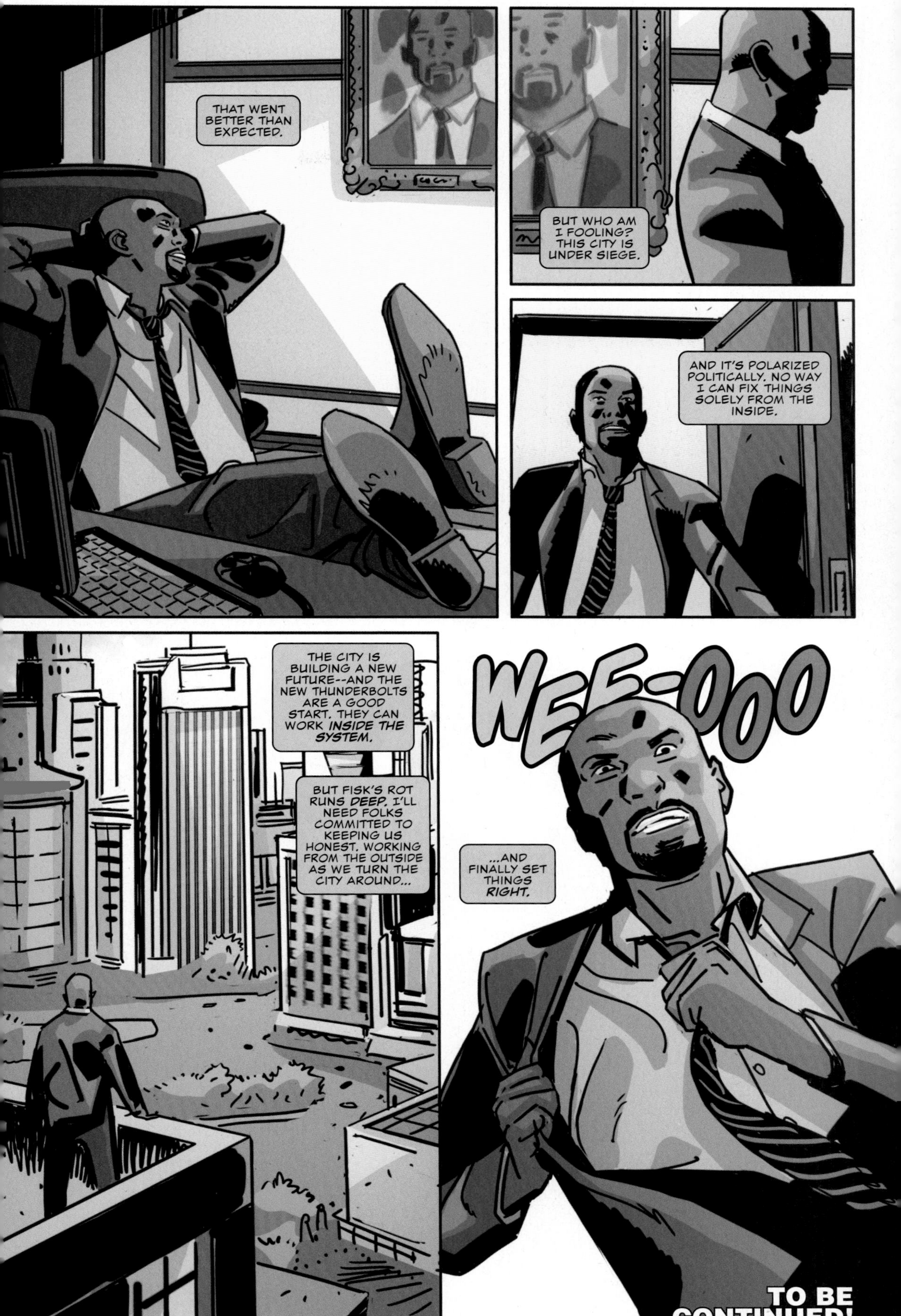
THAT WENT BETTER THAN EXPECTED.
BUT WHO AM I FOOLING? THIS CITY IS UNDER SIEGE.
AND IT'S POLARIZED POLITICALLY. NO WAY I CAN FIX THINGS SOLELY FROM THE INSIDE.
THE CITY IS BUILDING A NEW FUTURE--AND THE NEW THUNDERBOLTS ARE A GOOD START. THEY CAN WORK INSIDE THE SYSTEM.
BUT FISK'S ROT RUNS DEEP. I'LL NEED FOLKS COMMITTED TO KEEPING US HONEST. WORKING FROM THE OUTSIDE AS WE TURN THE CITY AROUND...
WEE-OOO
...AND FINALLY SET THINGS RIGHT.
TO BE CONTINUED!

#1-6 CONNECTING VARIANT BY **MARK BAGLEY**, **ANDREW HENNESSY** & **EDGAR DELGADO**

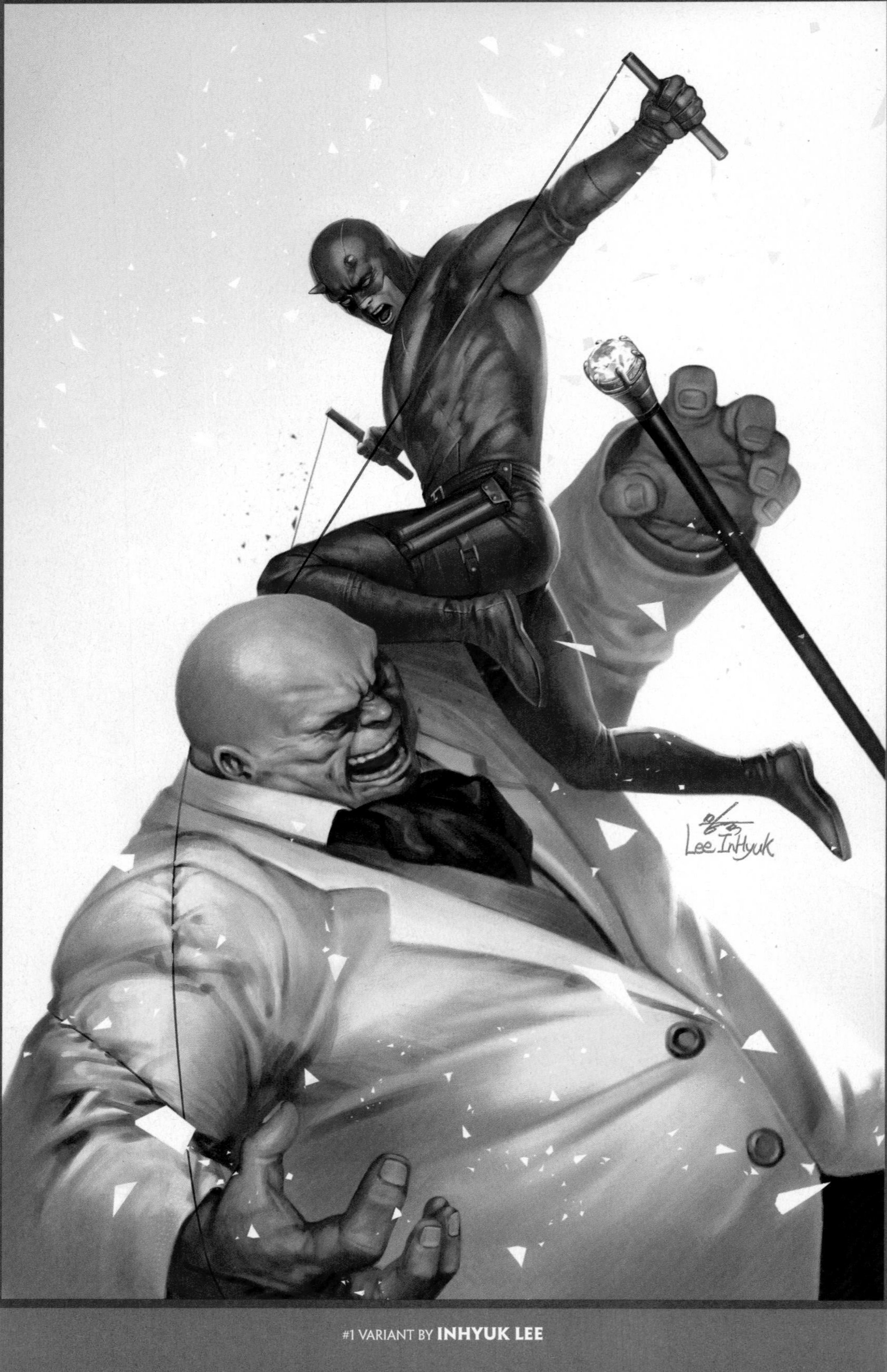
Lee InHyuk

#1 VARIANT BY **INHYUK LEE**

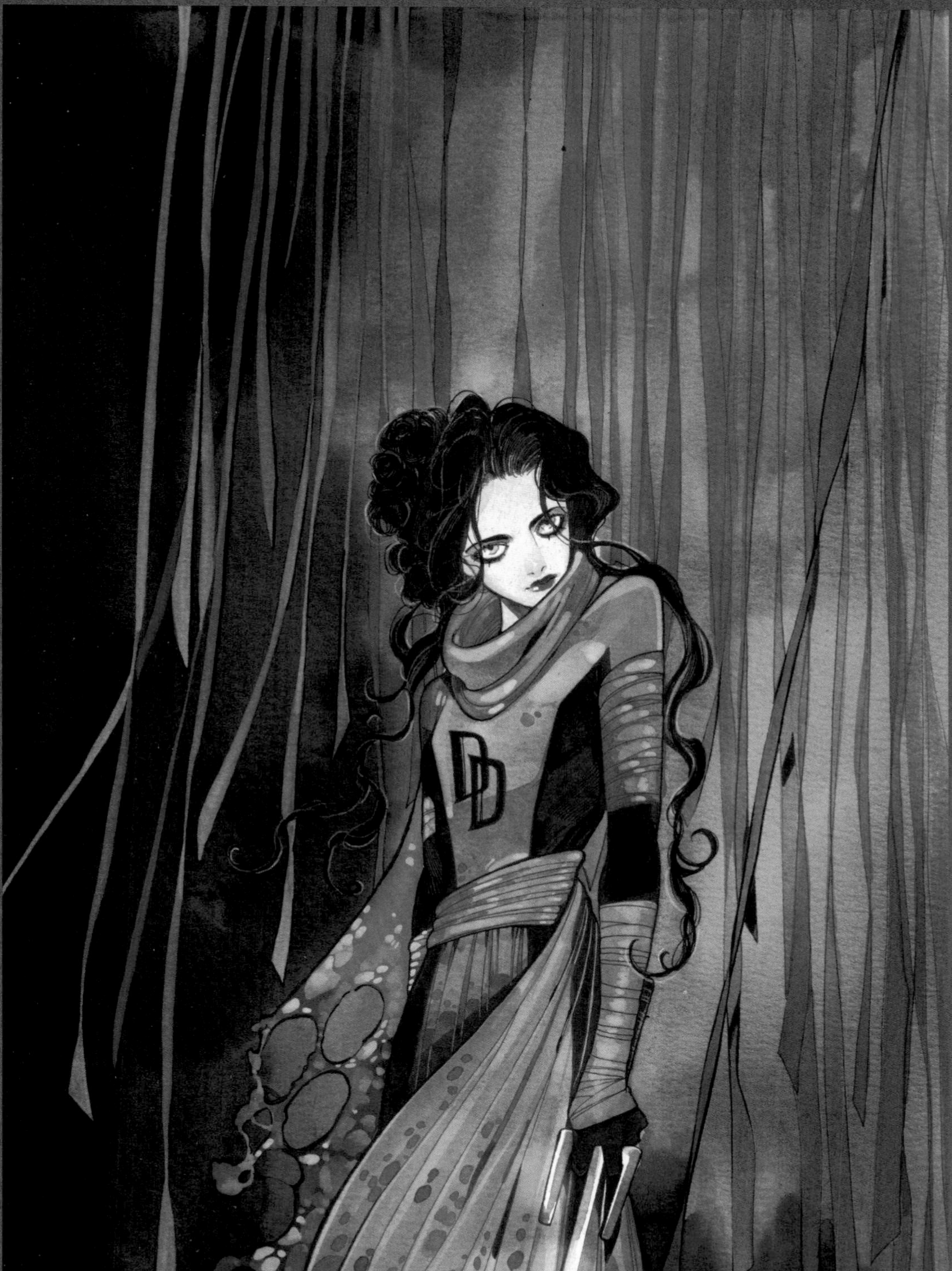

#1 VARIANT BY **PEACH MOMOKO**

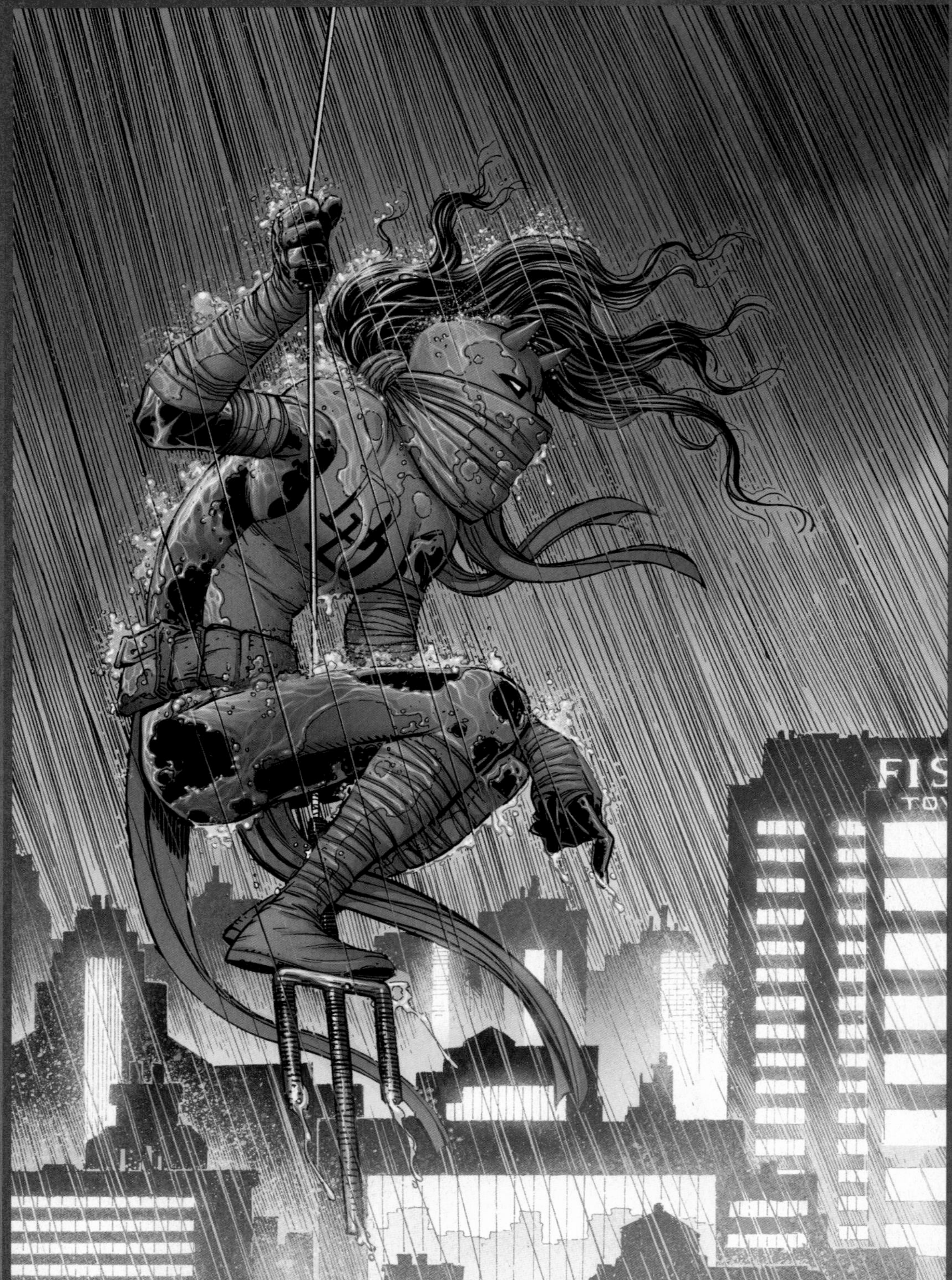
FIS
TOV

#1 VARIANT BY **JOHN ROMITA JR., JOHN DELL & RICHARD ISANOVE**

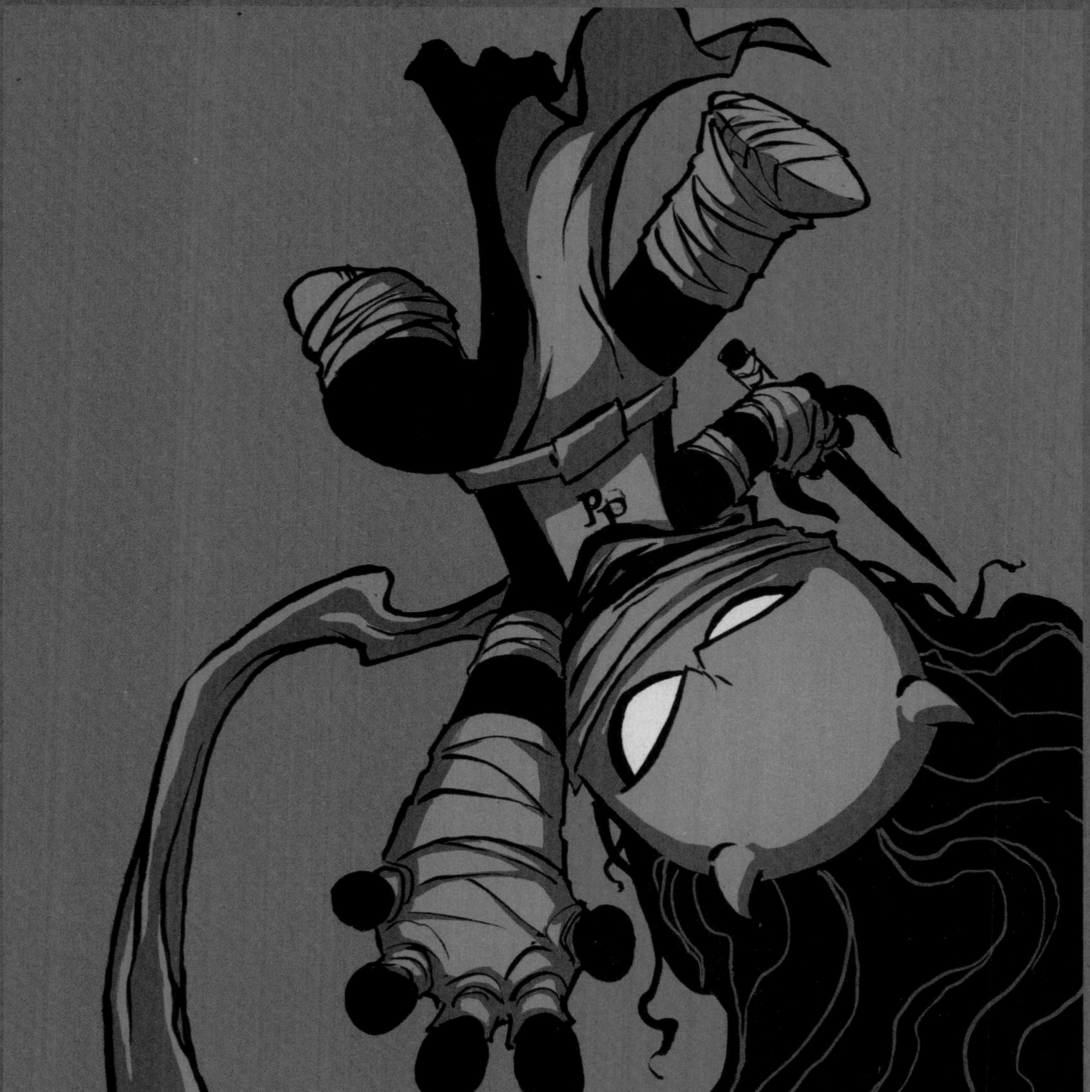
SKOTTIE YOUNG 2021

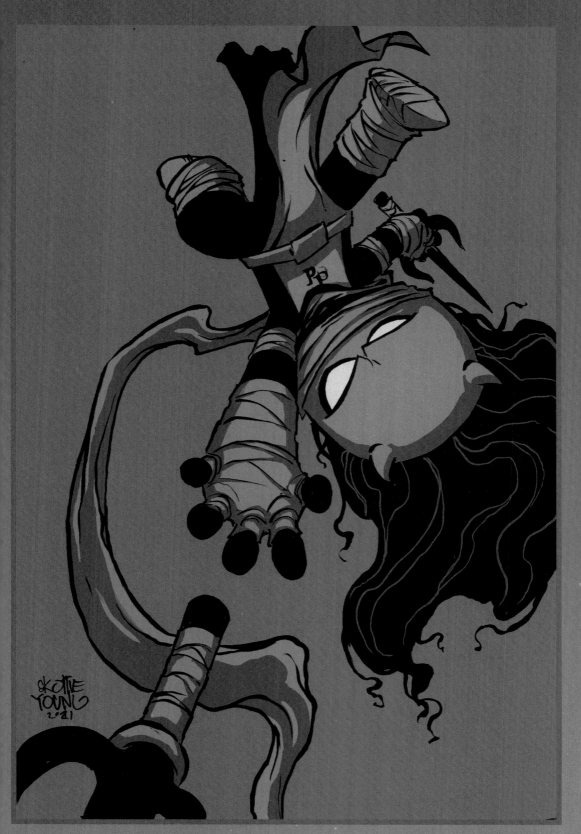

#1 VARIANT BY **SKOTTIE YOUNG**

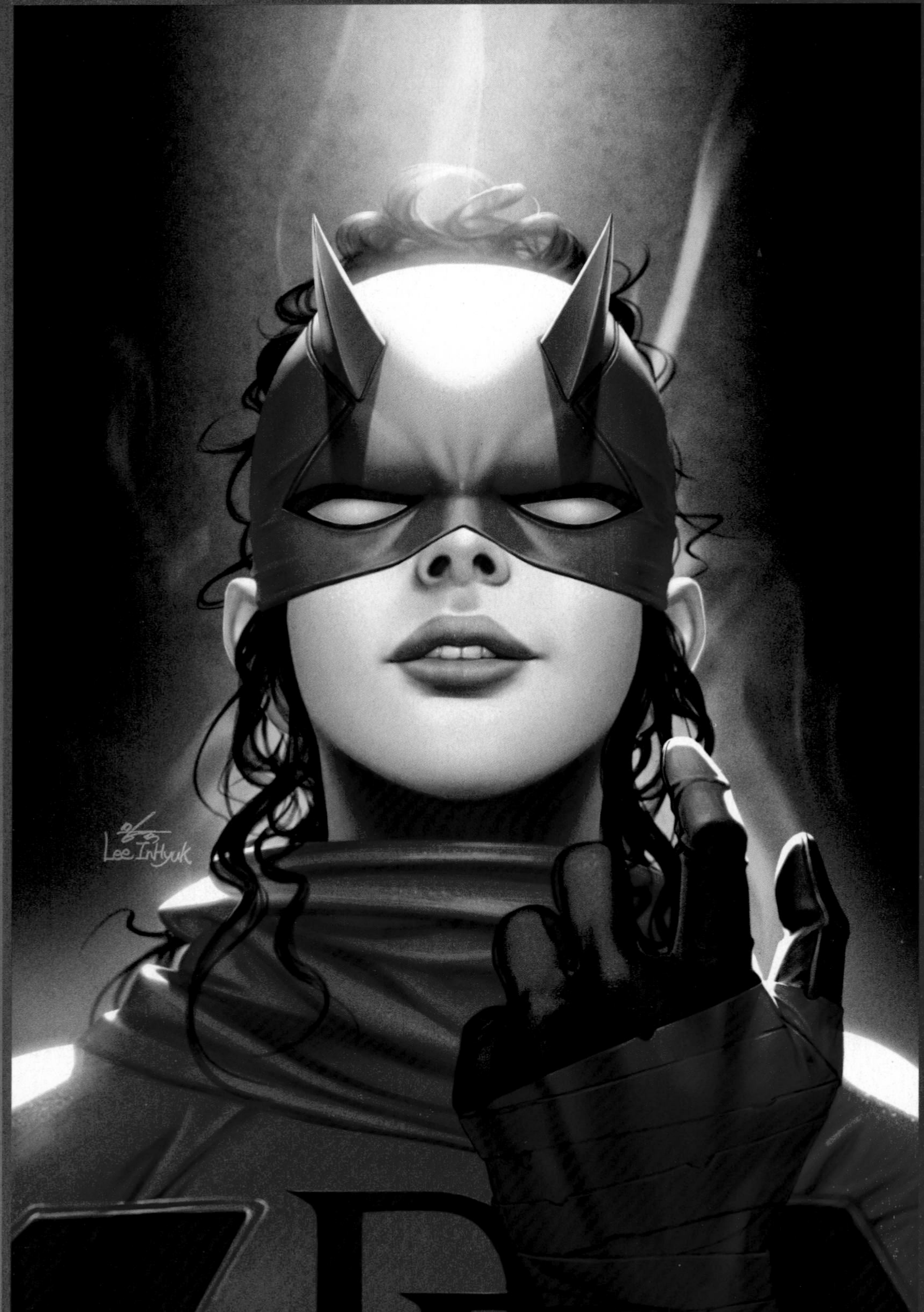
Lee InHyuk

#2 VARIANT BY **INHYUK LEE**

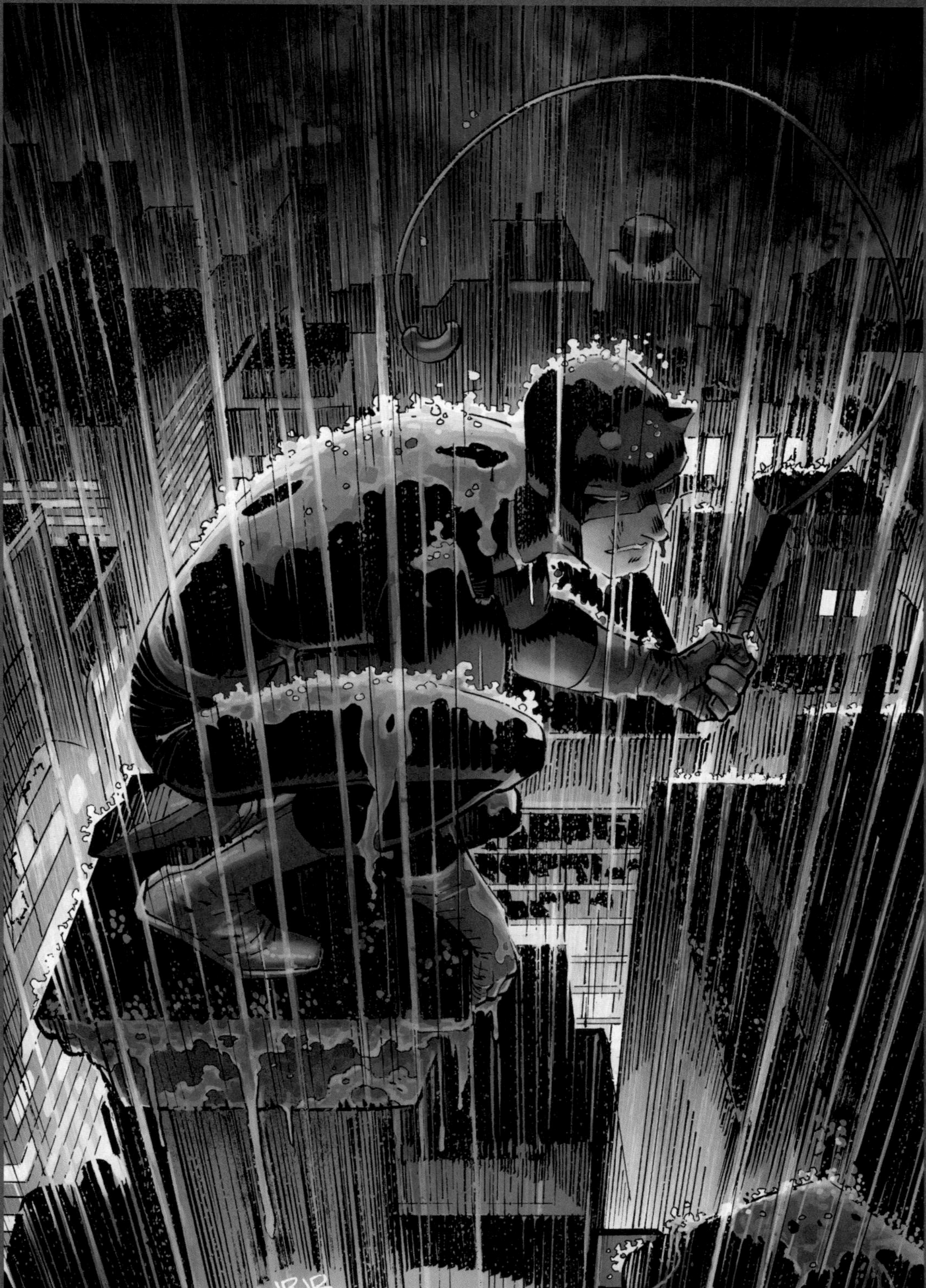
JRJR
JANSON

#2 VARIANT BY **JOHN ROMITA JR.**, **KLAUS JANSON** & **PETER STEIGERWALD**

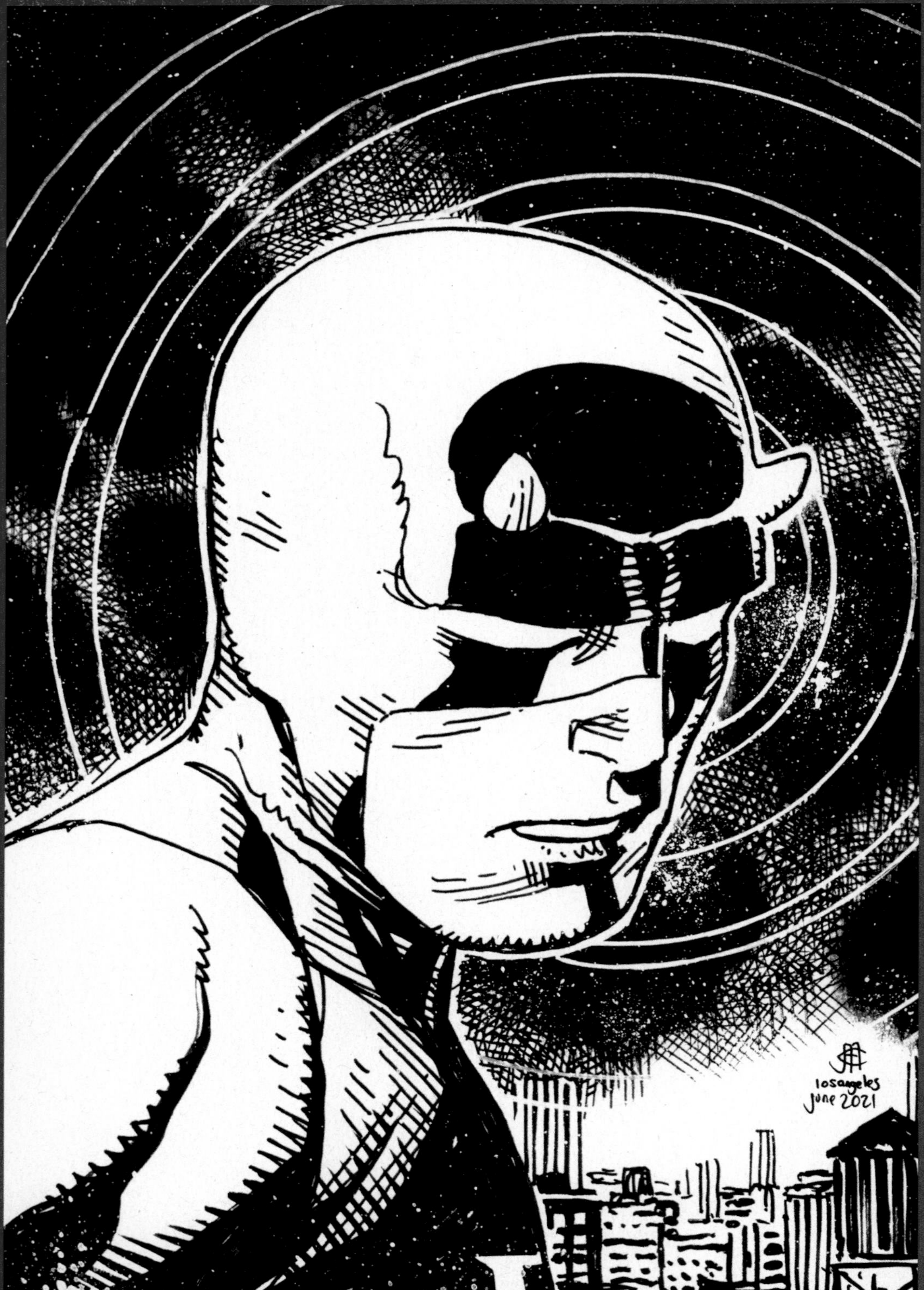
losangeles
june 2021

#3 HEADSHOT SKETCH VARIANT BY **JIM CHEUNG**

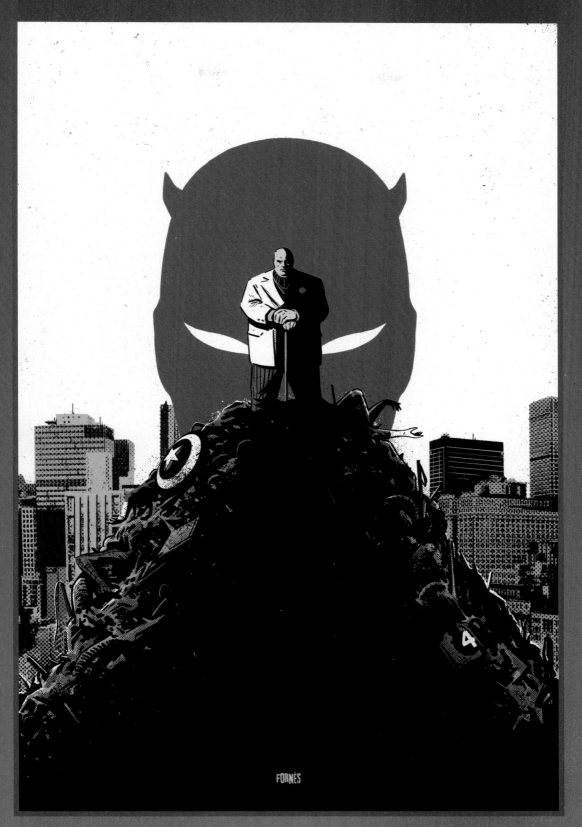

#3 VARIANT BY **JORGE FORNES**

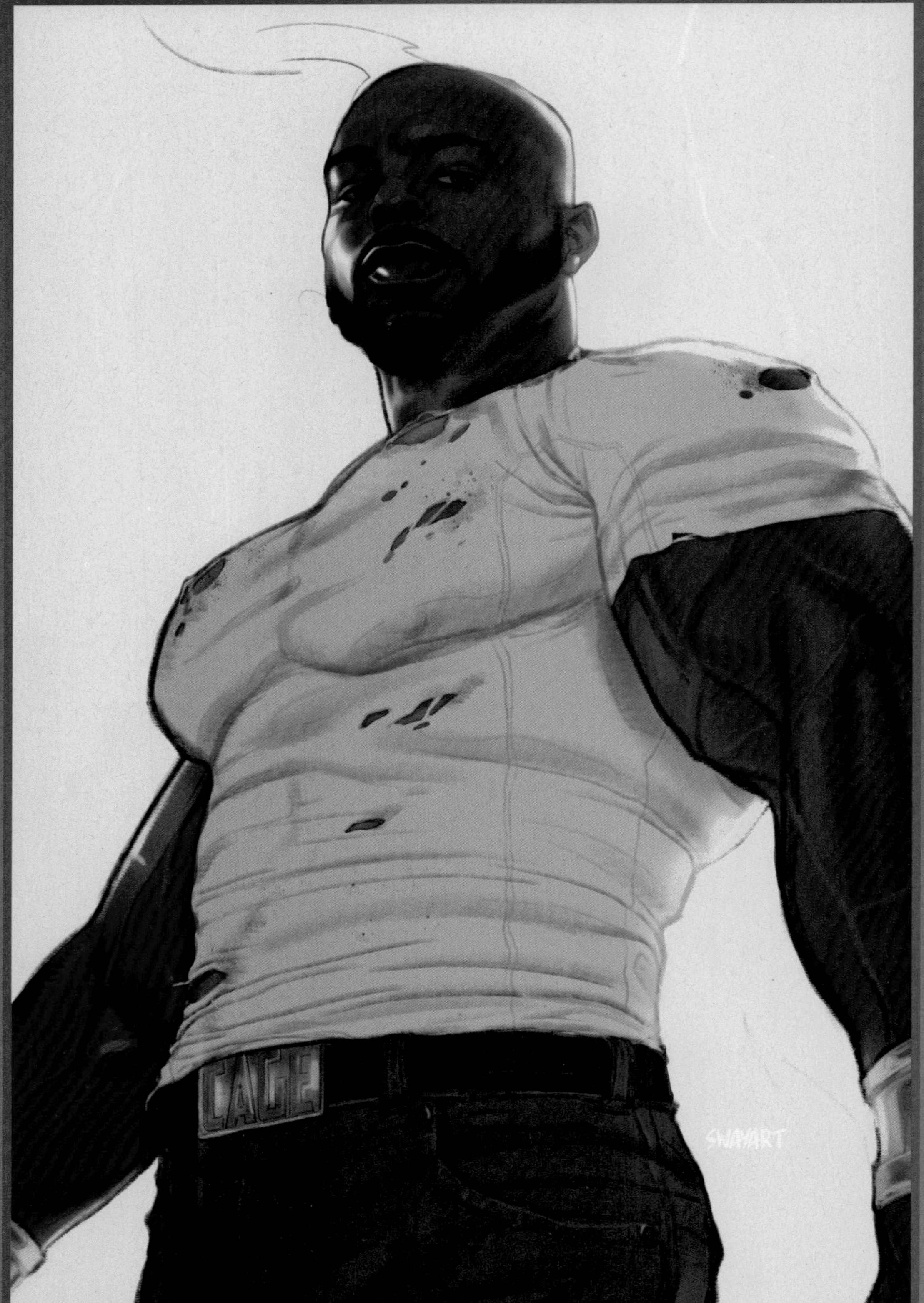
CAGE
SWAYART

#4 VARIANT BY **JOSHUA "SWAY" SWABY**

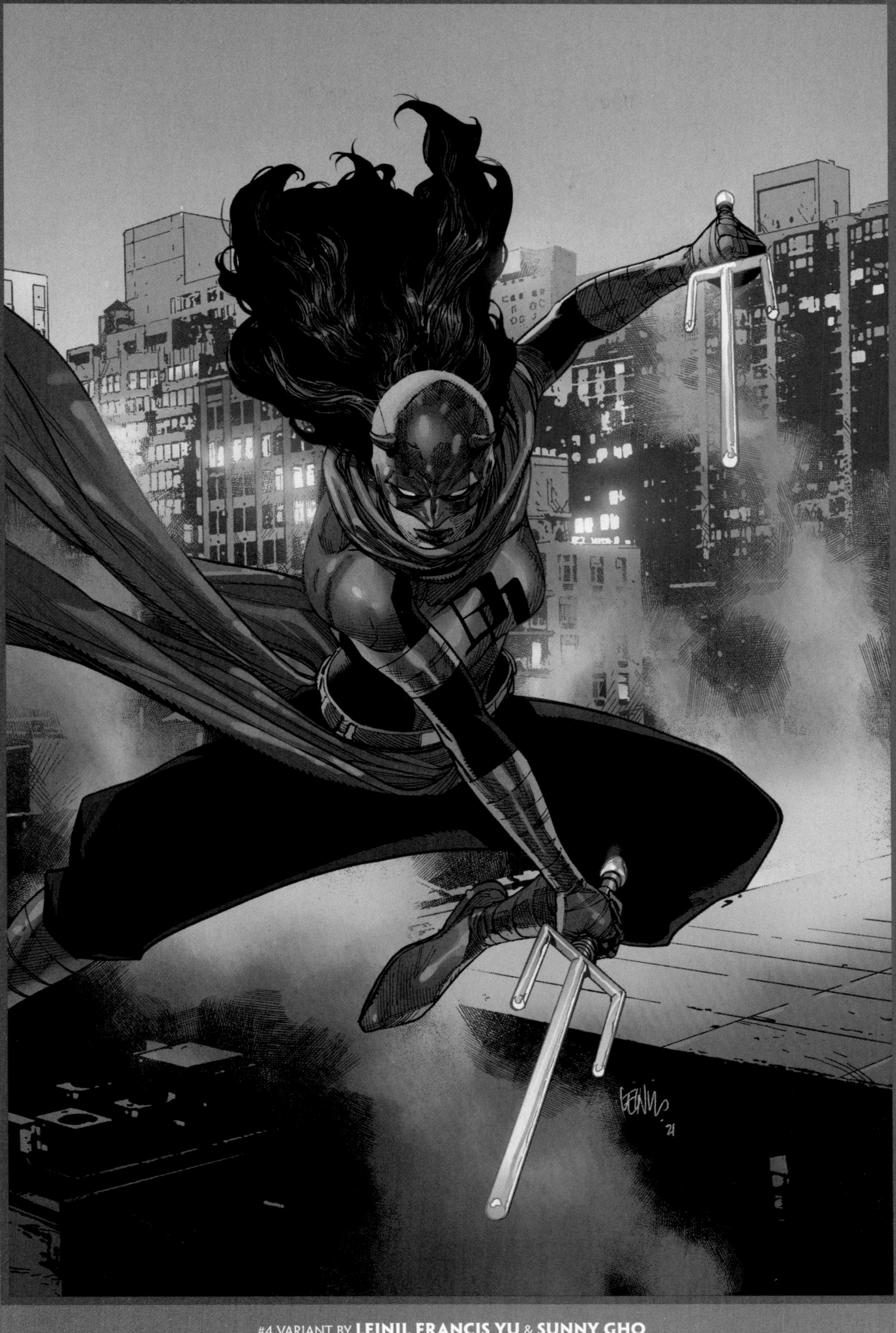

#4 VARIANT BY **LEINIL FRANCIS YU** & **SUNNY GHO**

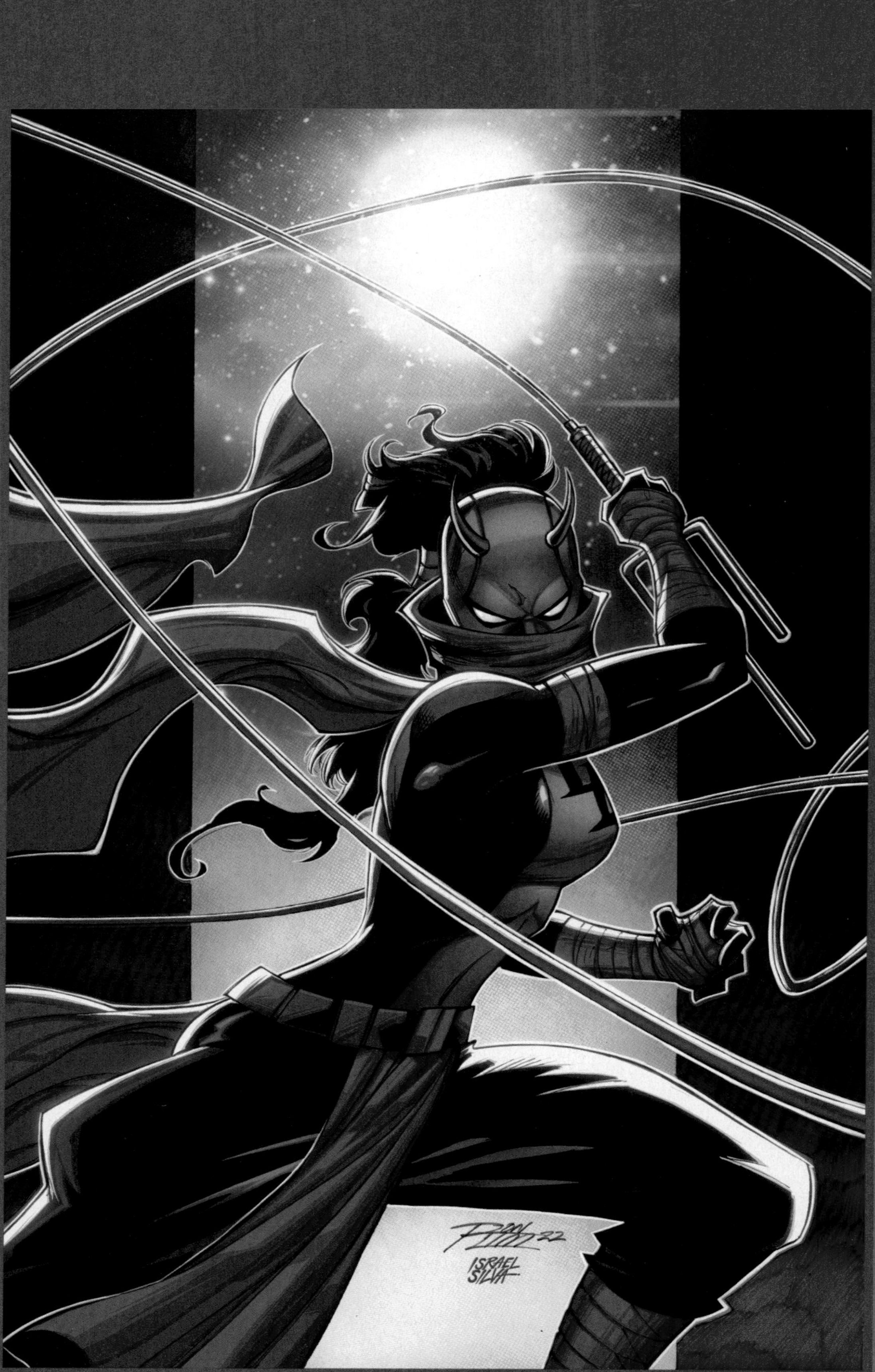

#5 VARIANT BY **RON LIM** & **ISRAEL SILVA**

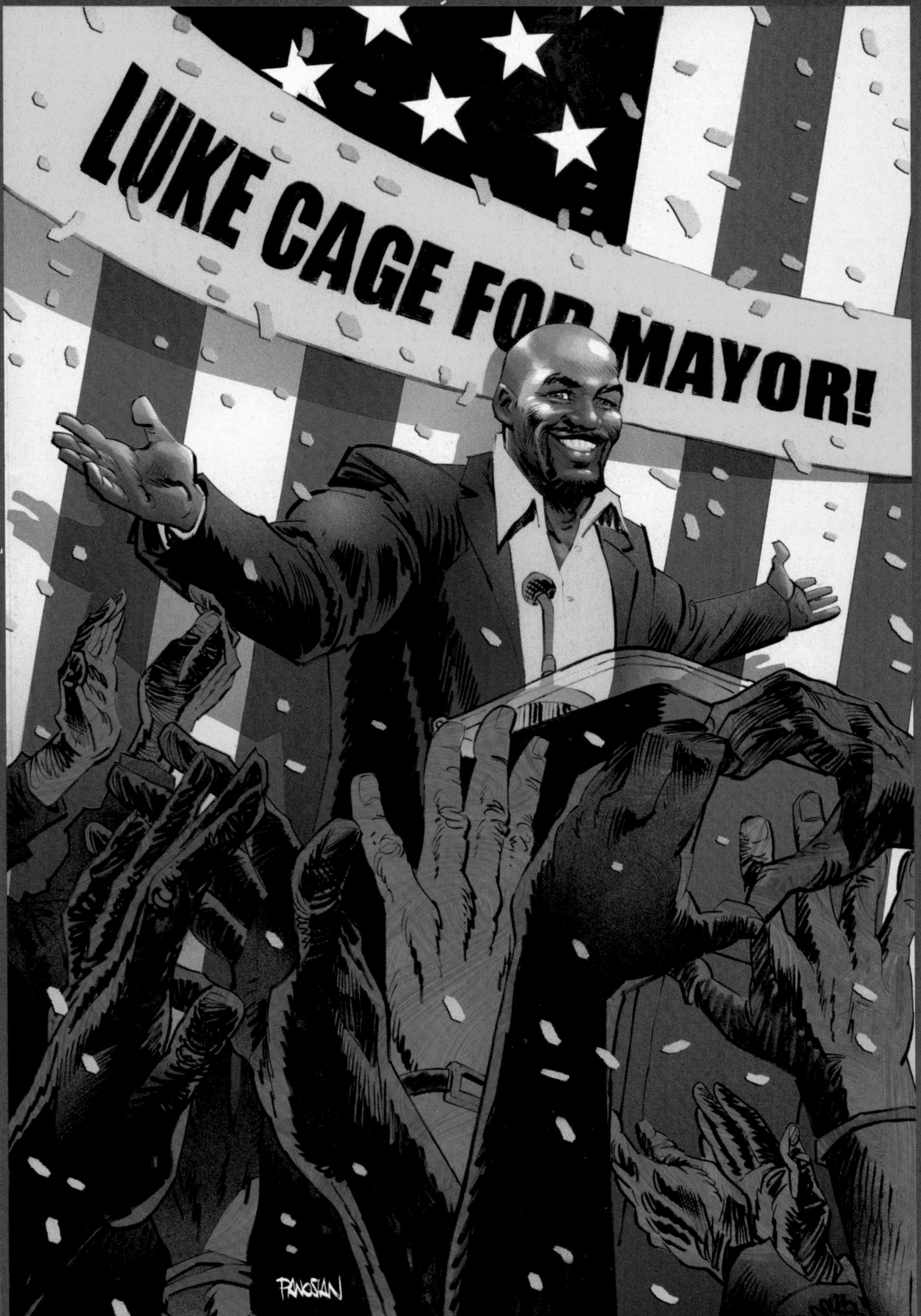
LUKE CAGE FOR MAYOR!
PANOSIAN

#6 SPOILER VARIANT BY **DAN PANOSIAN**

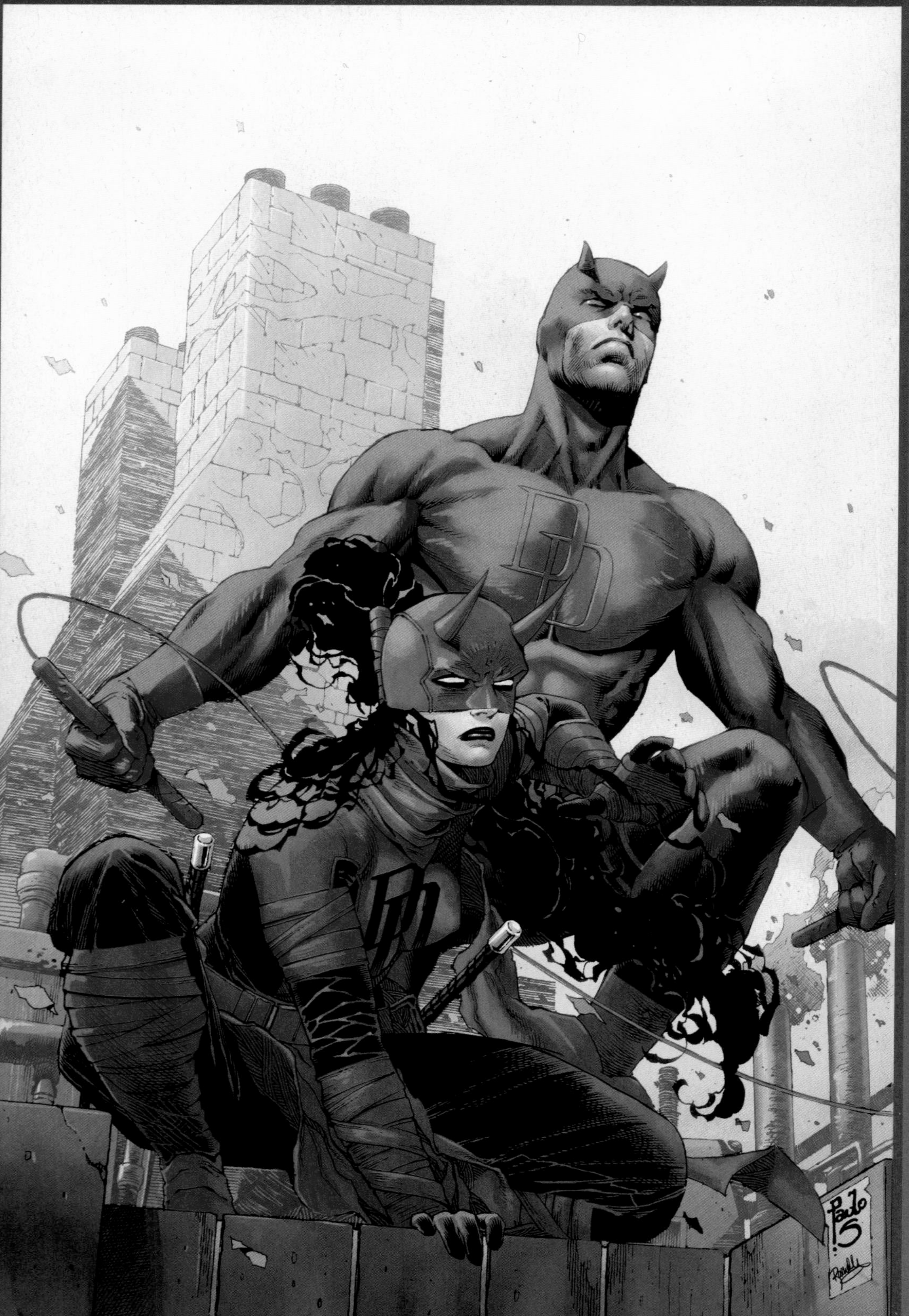

#6 VARIANT BY **PAULO SIQUEIRA** & **RACHELLE ROSENBERG**

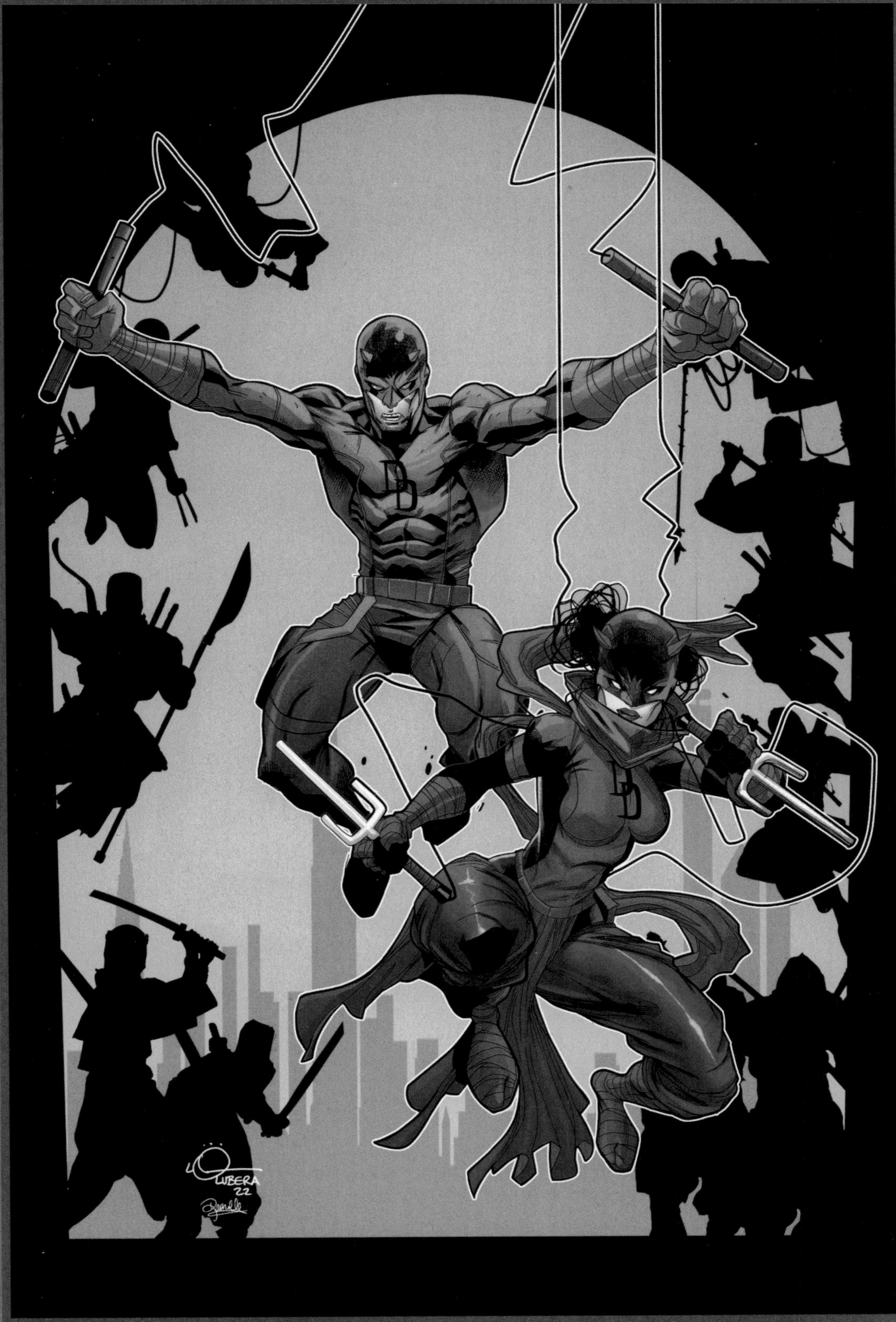
LUBERA
22

DEVIL'S REIGN: OMEGA VARIANT BY **LOGAN LUBERA** & **RACHELLE ROSENBERG**

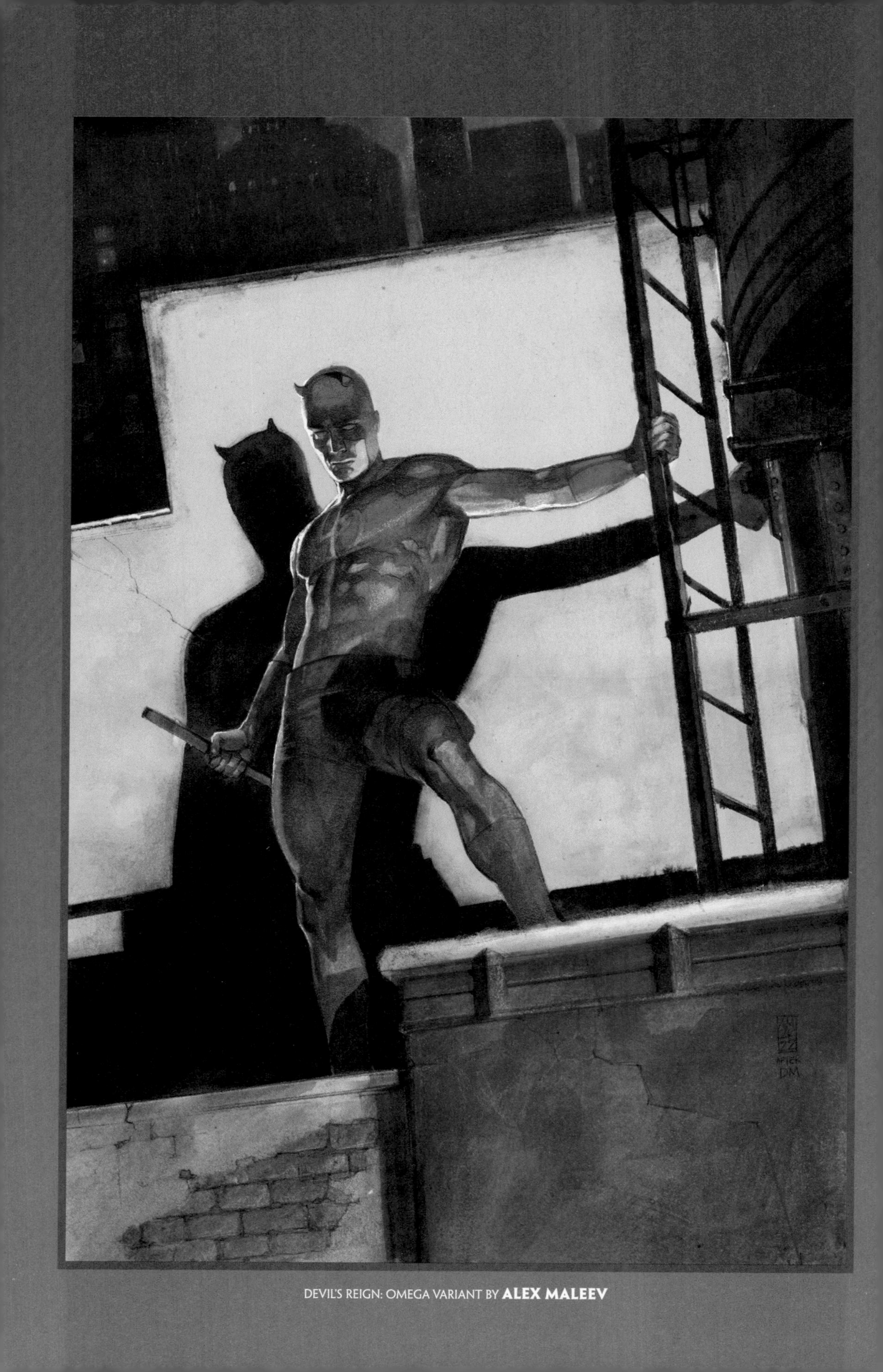

DEVIL'S REIGN: OMEGA VARIANT BY **ALEX MALEEV**

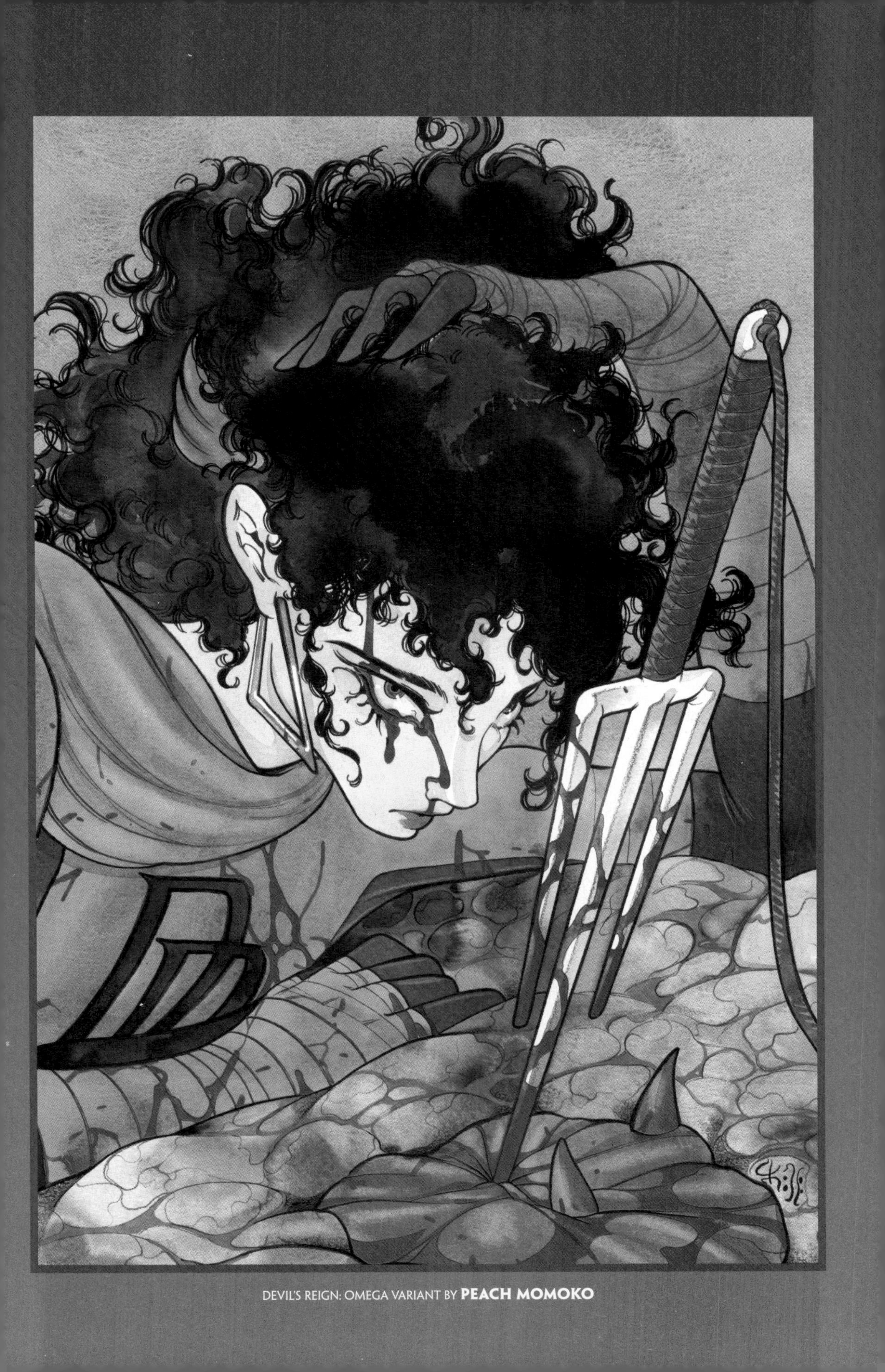

DEVIL'S REIGN: OMEGA VARIANT BY **PEACH MOMOKO**

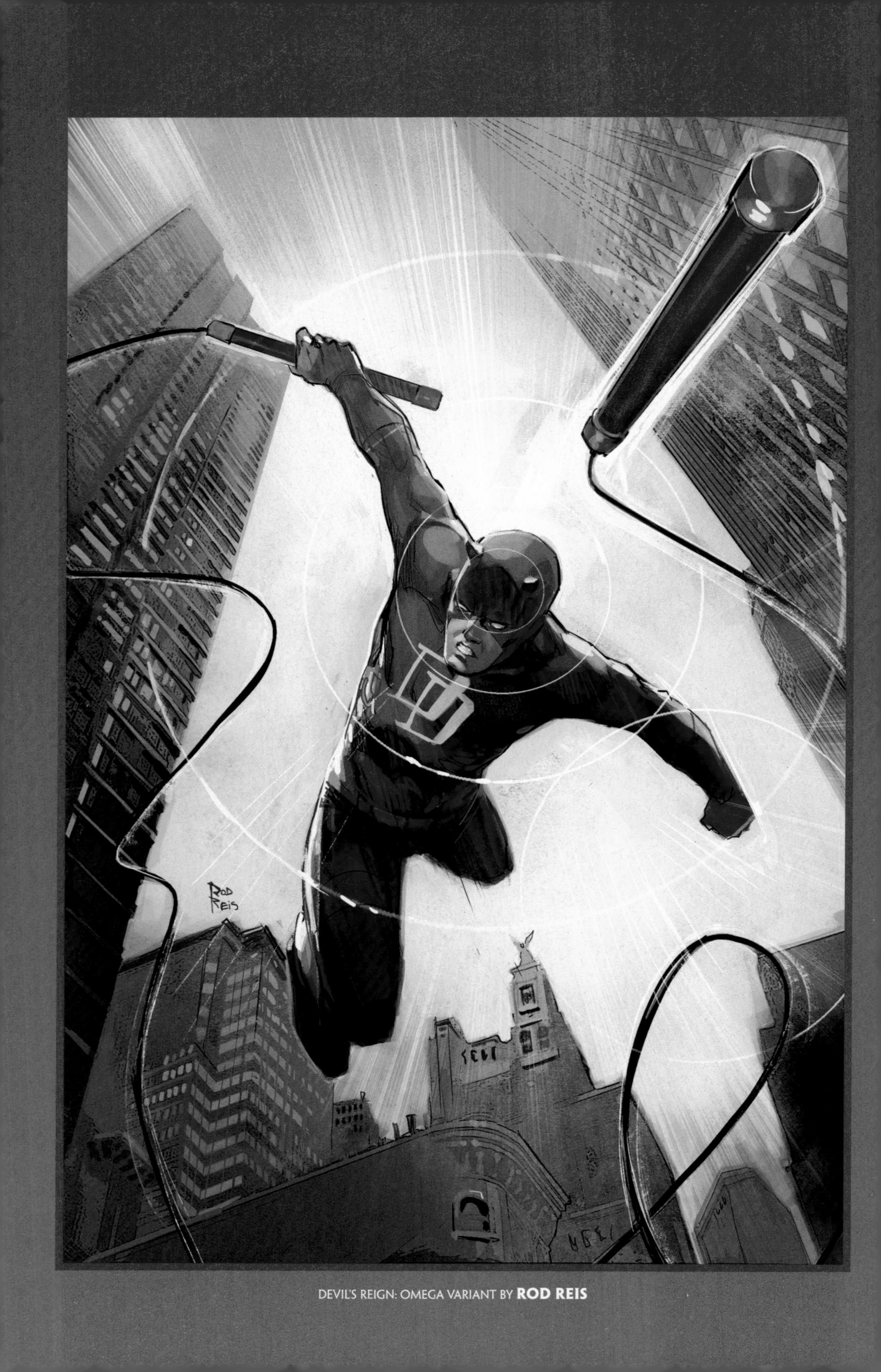
ROD REIS

DEVIL'S REIGN: OMEGA VARIANT BY **ROD REIS**

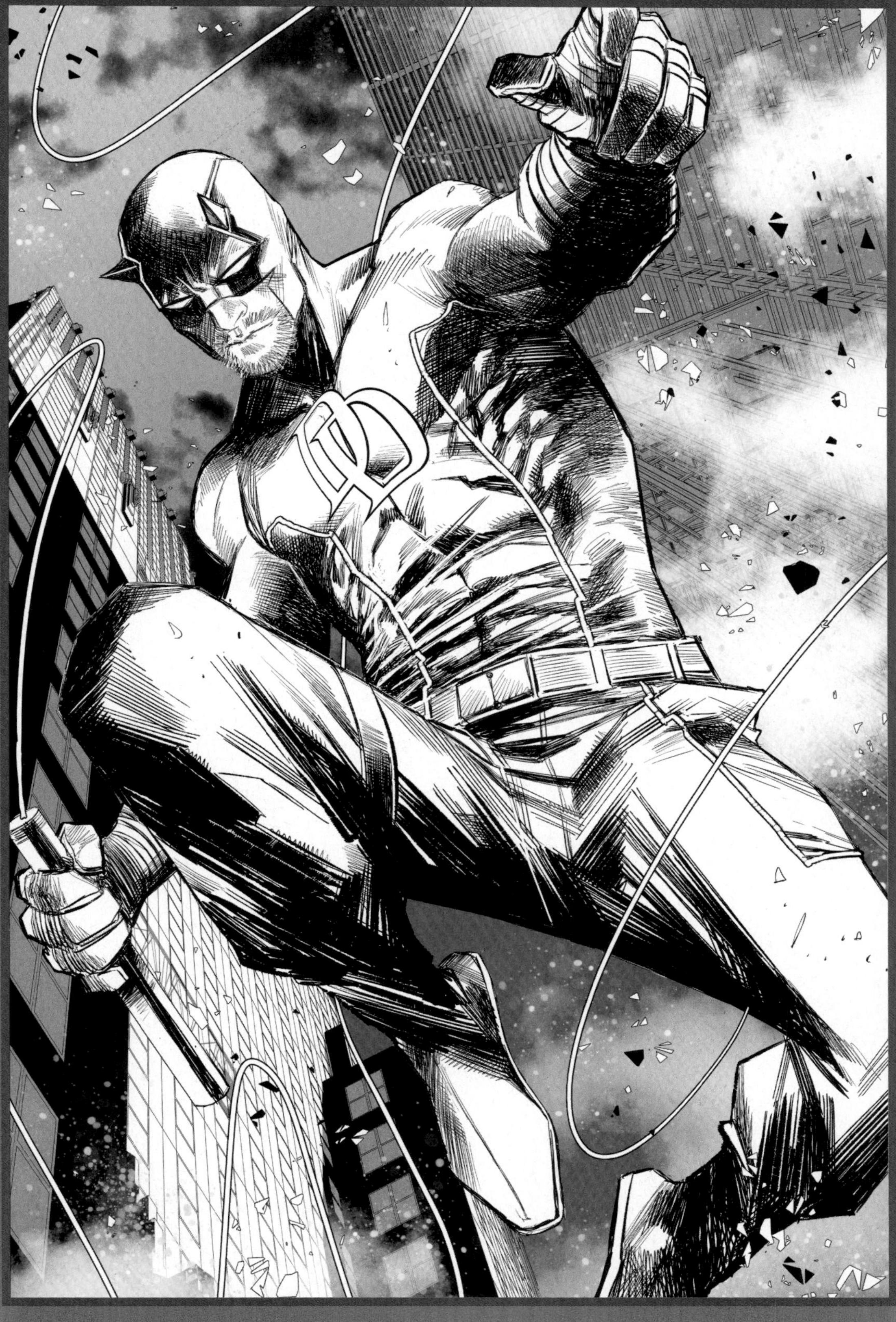

#1 PAGE 2 INKS BY **MARCO CHECCHETTO**

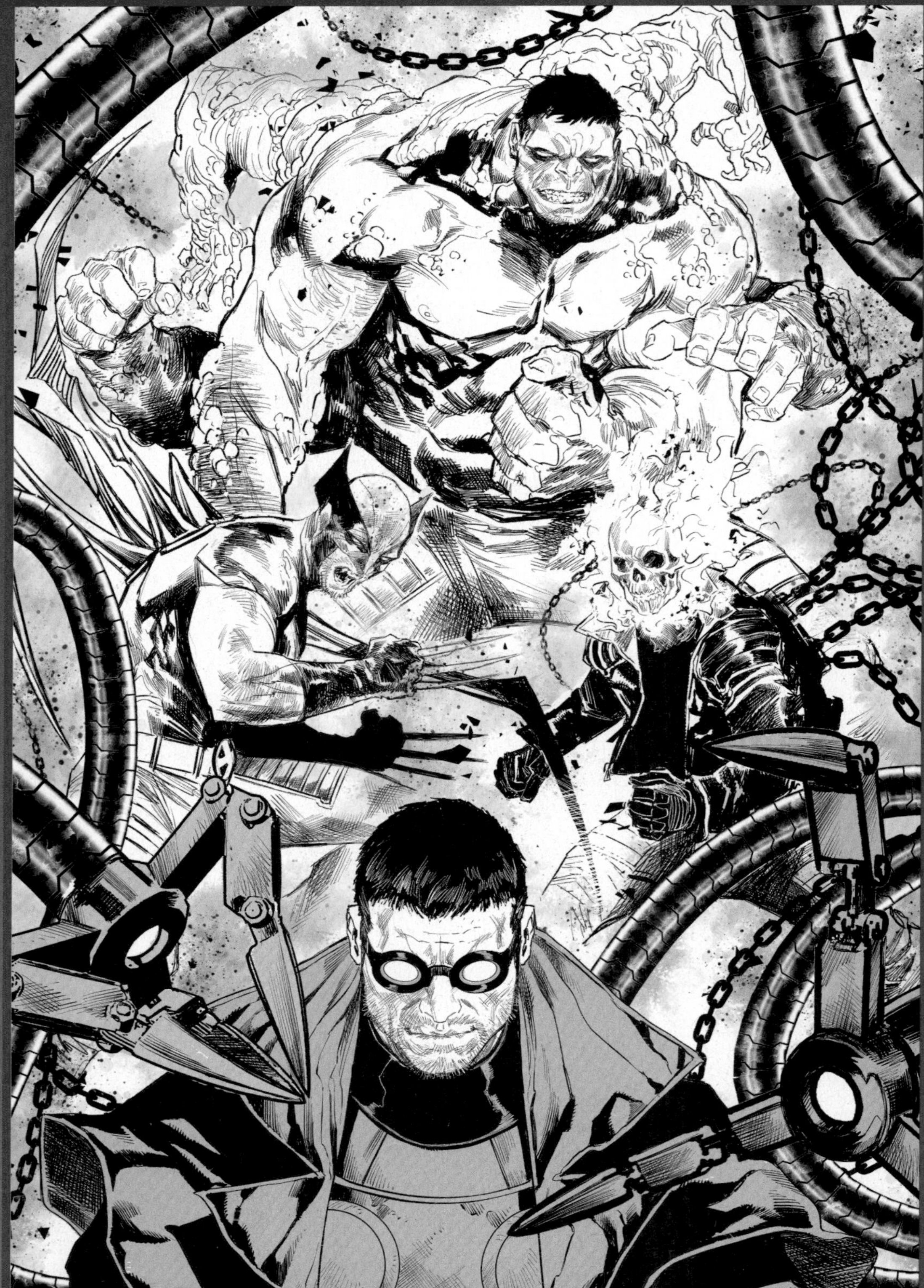

#2 PAGE 21 INKS BY **MARCO CHECCHETTO**

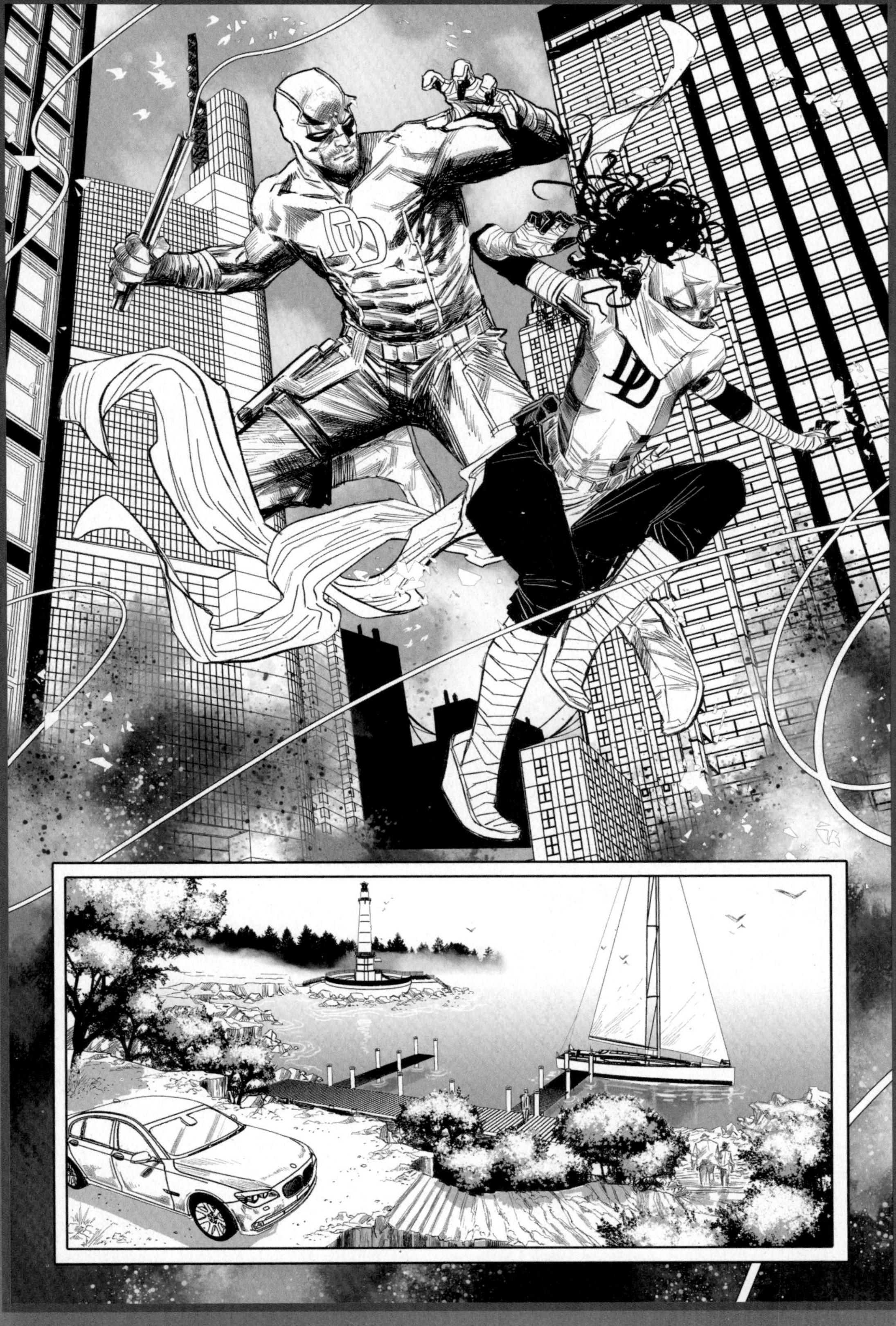

#6 PAGE 29 INKS BY **MARCO CHECCHETTO**

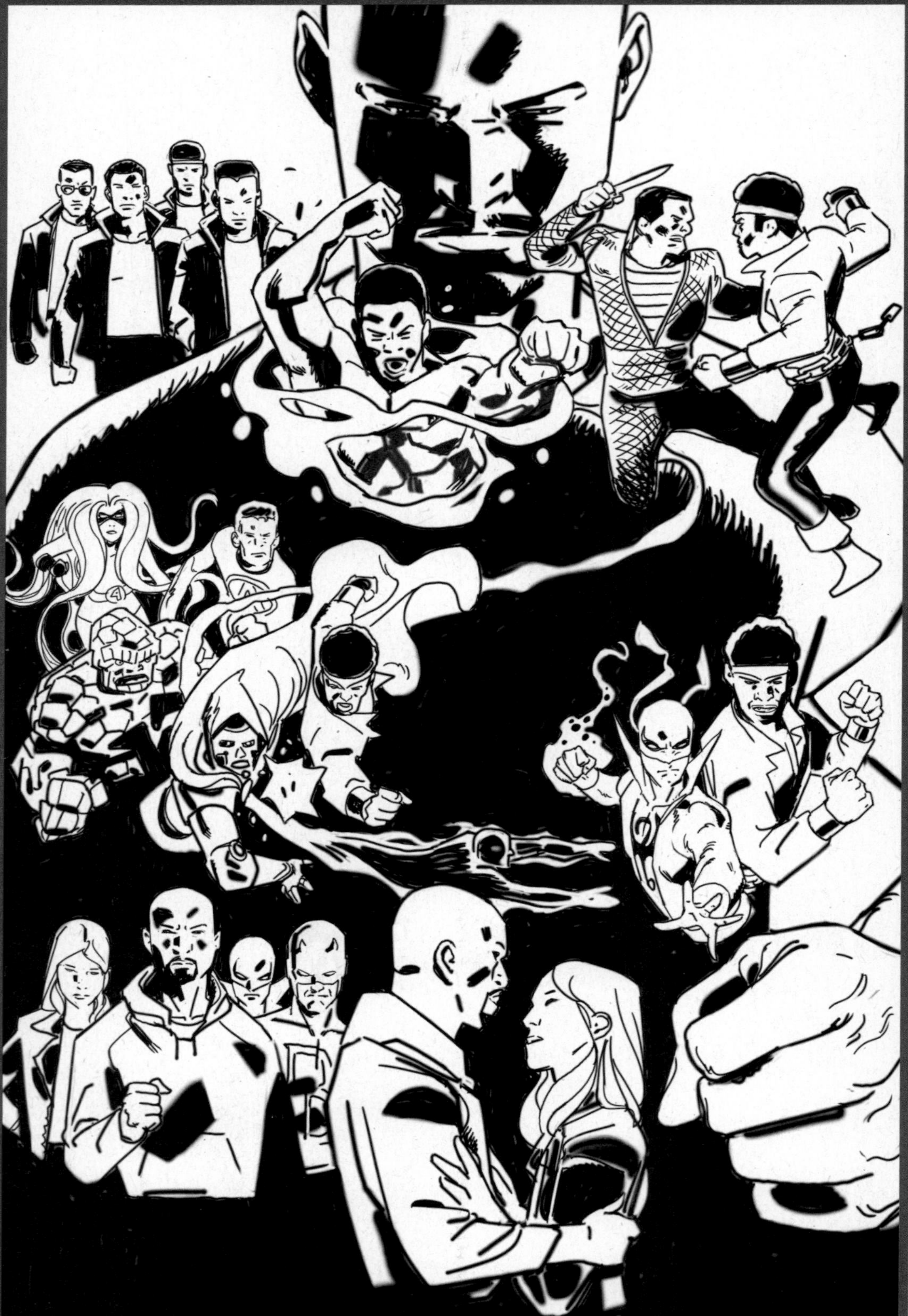

DEVIL'S REIGN: OMEGA PAGE 27 INKS BY **LUCIANO VECCHIO**